DATE			

PLOTS AND CHARACTERS
IN CLASSIC FRENCH FICTION

THE PLOTS AND CHARACTERS SERIES

Robert L. Gale
General Editor

PLOTS AND CHARACTERS
IN CLASSIC FRENCH FICTION

Benjamin E. Hicks

1981

Archon Books

© 1981 Benjamin E. Hicks

First published in 1981

Archon Books, The Shoe String Press, Inc.
995 Sherman Avenue, Hamden, Connecticut 06514

Printed in the United States of America

Library of Congress Cataloging in Publication Data

Hicks, Benjamin E.
    Plots and characters in classic French fiction.

    (The Plots and characters series)
    1. French fiction—Stories, plots, etc.
2. Characters and characteristics in literature.
I. Title.   II. Series: Plots and characters series.
PQ631.H5   843'.009'24   81-1709
ISBN 0-208-01703-8   AACR2

To Carol

CONTENTS

PREFACE

The purpose of this volume is to provide plot summaries and character identifications for a select group of significant French prose works. These works cover a span of slightly more than two centuries, from Mme. de Lafayette's *La Princesse de Clèves* (1678), commonly regarded as the first essentially psychological novel in French literature, to Zola's *Germinal* (1885), a work which, while still typifying its author's "naturalism" in subject and tone, represents at the same time a departure for Zola in its socialistic optimism. On the other hand, Huysman's *A Rebours*, written one year before *Germinal*, represents a rejection of the naturalist school and, in its probing of the darker recesses of the human psyche, illustrates—along with many earlier works summarized in this volume—the extent to which the psychological novel has remained a constant in French literature. At the same time, *A Rebours* may be considered a precursor of much that follows in French fiction in our own century.

Some comment should be made concerning the criteria employed for selecting these thirty-two prose works. To some extent, the selection is arbitrary. Many other works could justifiably have been chosen, but considerations of space do not make it possible to enlarge the present scope. However, a conscientious attempt has been made to include those works which have passed the test of time and which are traditionally regarded as major prose works by French authors. One may question the inclusion of such works as *Corinne* by Mme. de Staël and George Sand's *Indiana*, since these two novels may not seem to meet the criteria just stated for inclusion. However, in large part because of the feminist movement, there has been a renewed interest in female writers of the past. Therefore, it seems both timely and appropriate to include two works which, along with *La Princesse de Clèves*, not only deal with problems of women but also are written by women. Certain nineteenth-century authors are represented by more than one work, largely because of the high esteem in which these novels have been held over the decades. Plots of three novels each by Balzac, Flaubert, and Zola have been summarized, because these authors were prolific in the writing of fictional "masterpieces."

In listing characters, I have attempted to be as detailed as possible. For example, I have included unnamed characters who appear only once and who do not influence the action at all. The only characters whose names have not been included are historical characters who do not play a role in the action, i.e., John Law in *Les Lettres persanes* or Charles X in *Le Rouge et le noir*. On the other hand, a historical character such as King Louis XI plays a minor role in the action of *Notre-Dame de Paris;* so I have included him, as well as a few others like him, in the character index. Also, the very nature of the exposition of *La Princesse de Clèves* makes it necessary to list historical characters who are of virtually no importance at all; these characters form such an overwhelming majority that there would be very few left, if they were excluded.

A few words of clarification are needed concerning my system of alphabetizing. Characters with only a last name are listed before those with both a first name and a last name. (For example, in Balzac's *Eugénie Grandet,* Des Grassins, who has no first name, comes before his son, Adolphe des Grassins.) If a character has a title and a last name but no first name, the title is treated as a first name. If there is both a title and a first name, the first name takes precedence over the title. (For example, in Flaubert's *L'Education sentimentale,* Arnoux comes before Jacques Arnoux, who precedes Mme. Marie Angèle Arnoux.) Characters who function with more than one name are cross-listed in the index; in the listing after the individual plot summary, their aliases are indicated in parentheses. Characters of the nobility whose names begin with *d', de, de la, del,* etc., are listed under the word that follows (de Clèves is under Clèves, del Dongo is under Dongo). The same thing is true with *des* unless the letter "d" is capitalized in French because it is part of the last name. Three exceptions have been made: Des Grieux *(Manon Lescaut),* Des Grassins *(Eugénie Grandet),* and Des Esseintes *(A Rebours)* are listed or cross-listed under *Des* because they are referred to, throughout the three novels, as Des Grieux, Des Grassins, and Des Esseintes. With regard to punctuation, it is consistent in listing all characters from all the works, with two exceptions: Many of the nobility in *La Princesse de Clèves* and a lesser number in *Gil Blas* have so many titles, separated by commas, that I deemed it necessary to use a semicolon in separating character listings after the plot summaries, whereas, in the other thirty works, character listings are separated by commas.

Finally, I would like to affirm what I perceive to be the value of a volume such as this one. For reference purposes, names and facts are readily obtainable by consulting the pages which follow. In addition, scholars working in fields other than French literature can refresh their memories by reading the plot summaries. However, I do not believe that such a volume should be limited to the world of scholarship, for an equally important audience is to be found among those who have yet to discover literature and, especially, a foreign literature. I would take great personal satisfaction if, after reading certain plot summaries, curious people had their appetites whetted to the point where they proceeded to read the original, undistorted work, preferably in the language in which it was written. Then I and others who have written volumes in this series would escape the reproach of the late American novelist, James T. Farrell, that academic people write books only for each other.

CHRONOLOGY

1678   Madame de Lafayette, *La Princesse de Clèves*
1715–35   Lesage, *Gil Blas de Santillane*
1721   Montesquieu, *Les Lettres persanes*
1731   Prévost, *Manon Lescaut*
1731–41   Marivaux, *La Vie de Marianne*
1747   Voltaire, "Zadig"
1752   Voltaire, "Micromégas"
1759   Voltaire, "Candide"
1761   Rousseau, *La Nouvelle Héloïse*
1773   Diderot, *Jacques le fataliste*
1782   Laclos, *Les Liaisons dangereuses*
1787   Bernardin de Saint-Pierre, *Paul et Virginie*
1801   Chateaubriand, "Atala"
1802   Chateaubriand, "René"
1807   Madame de Staël, *Corinne*
1816   Constant, *Adolphe*
1831   Hugo, *Notre-Dame de Paris*
1831   Sand, *Indiana*
1831   Stendhal, *Le Rouge et le noir*
1833   Balzac, *Eugénie Grandet*
1834   Balzac, *Le Père Goriot*
1839   Stendhal, *La Chartreuse de Parme*
1846   Balzac, *La Cousine Bette*
1849   Sand, *La Petite Fadette*
1857   Flaubert, *Madame Bovary*
1862   Flaubert, *Salammbô*
1862   Hugo, *Les Misérables*
1869   Flaubert, *L'Education sentimentale*
1877   Zola, *L'Assommoir*
1880   Zola, *Nana*
1884   Huysmans, *A Rebours*
1885   Zola, *Germinal*

PLOTS

A Rebours, Huysmans, 1884.

Jean des Esseintes is the last descendant of a rich and noble family which has become progressively more decadent from one generation to the next. Until he reaches the age of thirty, he leads a dissipated life of pleasure. Then, having long sought in vain for human contact which is meaningful to him, he finds himself totally oppressed, filled with boredom and disgust. Suddenly, one day, feeling that his body and his nerves are rapidly deteriorating, he withdraws from society, without telling anyone where he is going.

Des Esseintes purchases a house which, although not far from Paris, is nevertheless quite isolated from the capital. In decorating it, he revels in the unusual in every detail. Two domestics from the old Des Esseintes estate, accustomed to living a cloistered existence, adjust easily to his eccentricities, one of which is arising at dusk for breakfast, dining at eleven at night, and supping at five in the morning before retiring to his bed at dawn.

Movement seems futile to Des Esseintes; he believes that imagination can easily replace the vulgar reality of facts. Therefore, he sees to it that the artificial replaces the natural in his surroundings. To Des Esseintes, the essential is to know how to make one's mind concentrate on a single point, to know how to separate oneself sufficiently in order to bring about hallucination and to be able to substitute the illusion of reality for reality itself. Artifice is the true mark of the refined genius. The sight of other human beings plunges Des Esseintes into a state of hypertension, so despicable does he find them all.

To satisfy one of his fancies, Des Esseintes purchases a tortoise in an attempt to establish a striking contrast between the color of its shell and the color scheme in his oriental rug. To ensure this contrast, he glazes the tortoise's shell with gold, then incrusts it with designs made of precious stones, both real and artificial. However, the poor tortoise, unable to bear the dazzling luxury imposed upon it, soon dies.

Des Esseintes also revels in his huge, elegant collection of art and literature. His books are all preciously bound. Among the many Latin authors whose work he possesses, the only one he truly likes is Petronius, who, in his opinion, admirably depicts and analyzes in detail, in his *Satyricon,* the depraved morals of his period. Among the paintings and engravings with which Des Esseintes surrounds himself, his preference is for those which bring into relief the ferocious and the lugubrious. The paintings of Gustave Moreau, particularly his *Salomé* and *The Apparition,* appeal because Moreau creates an unknown world, unrestricted by time. Des Esseintes admires the hallucinatory quality of Jan Luyken's engravings, whereas the sinister work of Odilon Redon seems to Des Esseintes a transposition into another art form of the mirages of hallucination and the effects of fear which he admires so much in the work of Edgar Allan Poe. As for Des Esseintes's bedroom, it is fashioned after a monastic cell with modifications to accommodate his taste in art.

Many evenings are spent dreaming and reminiscing by the fire. Two memories stand out: the unhappy marriage of an old friend of whom Des Esseintes is contemptuous, and Des Esseintes's perverse attempt to corrupt a sixteen-year-old youth of the working class by taking the boy to an elegant house of prostitution. For a time, solitude is like a narcotic to Des Esseintes; hypertension is replaced by torpor. He plunges himself into his Latin studies, as he did as a child. In spite of himself, he struggles with religion, reminding himself, for example, that the church alone preserved art through the Middle Ages and that the appeal of the extraterrestrial has never left him. But the memory of the pessimistic Schopenhauer counterbalances his admiration of the church and leads him once again to despair.

To relieve his anxiety, he determines to realize a concrete project, that of growing precious hothouse flowers. But this choice is modified by the influence of his general ideas: instead of artificial flowers imitating natural flowers, his flowers will be natural flowers, such as the caladium, which look like false flowers. Upon gazing at this sea of hideous plants assembled, Des Esseintes declares that they are collectively a huge syphilis. Feeling his strength fail him, he retires to his room and has a horrendous nightmare in which a woman, syphilis incarnate, attacks him.

These nightmares become so frequent that Des Esseintes is afraid to sleep. His neuroses resurface more strongly than ever. Then he becomes interested in those malicious acts and sins condemned by the church. Under the influence of a drug, he conjures up visions of two of his former mistresses and also that of a young male lover he once had. Hallucinations of odor then begin to plague him; the fragrance of frangipani follows him wherever he goes. Determined to get rid of this odor, Des Esseintes becomes an expert in creating flower smells, savoring each one he is able to produce. Finally, when he feels the need to retreat into his study to escape these odors, the overwhelming smell of frangipani comes in through the open window, stronger than ever. His nostrils exhausted, his helpless nerves shattered, Des Esseintes falls unconscious on the windowsill.

One day, after recuperating somewhat, Des Esseintes suddenly announces that he is going to travel. This solitude which he so ardently craved now greatly distresses him. Influenced by his reading of Dickens, whom he once loathed, he now is determined to visit England. A few hours before his departure, he buys a Baedeker guide at a British bookstore and dines at a British restaurant in Paris. As the time of his departure draws near, he remembers how disillusioned he once was upon visiting Holland and cannot bring himself to get on his feet to catch the train for London. Deciding that he has sufficiently saturated himself with British life, Des Esseintes returns home with his trunks, his suitcases, his umbrellas, and his canes, experiencing the physical exhaustion and moral fatigue of one who has just completed a long and perilous voyage. He takes refuge once again in his collection of books. The few more modern authors whom he admires are Baudelaire, Poe, Pascal, the cleric Hallo, and Barbey d' Aurevilly, all of whose preoccupations with the darker side of human nature stimulate his own neuroses.

Suddenly the weather changes drastically from squalls and mist to a torrid heat. So overcome is Des Esseintes that he begins to lose his equilibrium. He goes outside and finds shelter in the shade and grass; this is the first time in years that he spends a significant amount of time in the open air. The sight of youngsters fighting nearby causes him to reflect on the cruel law of the survival of the fittest. His hypochondria increases and he wonders if he must take to his bed for good.

Although his physical malady comes temporarily under control, his ennui does not. He has so refined himself through reading that his enjoyment of it has been sterilized. No longer can he discover any writing to content his secret, undefinable longings. His hatred of the contemporary world has now greatly affected his literary and artistic tastes; he will have nothing to do with works whose limited subjects deal with modern life. He admires Mallarmé, who lived his solitary and literary life far from society, delighting in the surprises of the intellect. Des Esseintes awaits the moment, soon to come, when an erudite scholar will prepare for the French language a glossary similar to that a scholar once completed for the Latin language, noting its last spasms and sounding its death rattle.

Suddenly Des Esseintes's nervous disorders become so heightened that a physician is summoned. Upon discovering that his emaciated body is responding to the medicine prescribed, Des Esseintes conceives of the notion of substituting this nourishment for food. His penchant for the artificial will thus reach the supreme goal, he hopes. However, this plan is thwarted by the physician, who declares that a cure, which will take years, will be possible only if Des Esseintes abandons his solitude and returns to Paris to live an ordinary mode of existence. It is a matter of life and death.

With great reluctance, Des Esseintes follows the physician's orders, all the while despairing of ever meeting a man whose soul is delicate and exquisite enough to undersand Mallarmé. His attempt to resign himself to his fate is soon swept aside by rage. He finally utters a prayer in which he begs for pity for "the Christian who doubts, the sceptic who would believe, the convict of life embarking alone in the night, under a sky no longer illumined by the consoling beacons of ancient faith."

d'Aligurande, Coachman (unnamed), Doctor (unnamed), Domestics (two, unnamed), Jean des Esseintes, M. des Esseintes, Mme. des Esseintes, Gatonax, Homosexual (unnamed), Auguste Langlois, Lapidary (unnamed), Mme. Laure, Montchevrel, Physician (unnamed), Dom Prosper, Miss Urania, Vanda, Ventriloquist (unnamed), Woman (unnamed).

Adolphe, Constant, 1816.

Adolphe, a young man of twenty-two, has just finished his studies at the University of Gottingue, where he managed to distinguish himself scholastically while leading a dissipated life. His father wishes him to travel before preparing for a brilliant career. Unfortunately, Adolphe and his father have difficulty communicating. The son mistakes the father's timidity for coldness and irony, believing himself judged unfavorably when the fact is that the father feels unloved. Adolphe retreats into his own inner world, forming only solitary plans. His unfulfilled need for understanding causes him to become indifferent to everything. The notion of death fortifies his indifference as he abandons himself to vague reveries and concludes that no goal is worth the effort. Upon travelling to another town, Adolphe is welcomed by society; but ha quickly becomes bored by the mediocrity which surrounds him, and is consequently thought of as aloof, disdainful, and even immoral. However, he is so distracted and inattentive to others that he is unaware of the impression he has made.

This state of mind ceases when Adolphe suddenly becomes interested in having a liaison with a woman in order to flatter his self-esteem. Adolphe chooses as a conquest worthy of him a Polish woman renowned for her beauty who is ten years his senior and who, for the past ten years, has been the devoted mistress of the Count de P.... Ellénore is a woman of such character and background that her situation seems ill suited to her. For her part, she lives in almost constant inner turmoil. Initially, Ellénore responds favorably to Adolphe. They read English poets and take long walks together. However, Adolphe's self-esteem and the goal he has set hinder his spontaneous appreciation of Ellénore. He invents many means of conquest, but his timidity prevents him from executing them. Finally, Adolphe manages to write a letter confessing his love to Ellénore. Ellénore, believing his transport to be the passing fancy of a young man impassioned for the first time, responds politely but refuses to see him until the Count de P... returns from a trip. When Adolphe finally does see Ellénore, he observes that she is paler than usual and also visibly moved upon seeing him. He threatens to leave immediately if she will not see him the following day. She yields. Adolphe's entreaties are so impassioned that it is not long before Ellénore's resistance has been totally worn down. She gives herself to him entirely, confessing that she has never felt so much in love. Adolphe believes at this moment that his love for Ellénore will be eternal.

With M. de P... away for six weeks, Adolphe sees Ellénore constantly. She becomes so attached to him that he begins to feel a loss of personal freedom; she insists upon knowing exactly when Adolphe will return and what he does when he is away from her. Now Ellénore is no longer a goal but a tie. She refuses to be reassured and to heed his advice that she be more prudent. At the same time, he cannot bear to hurt her. The pain Adolphe feels he is causing Ellénore makes him feel guilty. At the same time, Adolphe resents these feelings. He consoles himself by acknowledging that his liaison with Ellénore cannot last.

Time passes and Adolphe is never able to summon up the courage to speak honestly with Ellénore and to terminate their relationship. He allows himself to prolong his stay, in spite of both his father's objections and his own reluctance to remain with Ellénore. Ellénore, meanwhile, breaks off her relationship with the Count de P..., causing herself to be condemned by society. When Adolphe finally returns to his father, Ellénore soon follows him there. They have a violent quarrel and make accusations which hurt them both. However, that night, Adolphe learns that his father plans to order Ellénore to leave. Feeling both indignation on one hand and pity for Ellénore on the other, Adolphe decides to play the role of protector and flees with his mistress. Ellénore is fully aware of Adolphe's true feelings toward her but cannot bear to live without him.

When Ellénore receives word from Poland that her father has died and that she is his sole heiress, she refuses to go there without Adolphe. Adolphe accompanies her to Poland, having persuaded himself that once she is established in her native land, he will be able to leave her. In Poland, Adolphe meets his father's old friend, the Baron de T..., who immediately understands Adolphe's situation. The Baron urges Adolphe to overcome the one obstacle that stands between him and success in life: Ellénore. Even while verbally defending Ellénore, Adolphe acknowledges to himself the truth of the Baron's words. Furthermore, his terror of causing Ellénore pain and sorrow has not helped her and has only resulted in a lack of self-esteem on his part.

As Adolphe's personal situation with Ellénore deteriorates even further, he begins to spend more time with the Baron de T.... One day, Adolphe is shown letters from his father to the Baron which reveal deep sorrow over Adolphe's wasted life. Adolphe vows that he will now leave Ellénore but, as usual, procrastinates rather than take immediate action.

One morning, Adolphe discovers that Ellénore has become delirious with fever during the night. Adolphe is quick to discover two letters which Ellénore has read, one which he wrote to the Baron de T... announcing his intention of leaving Ellénore, and the other written to Ellénore by the Baron himself.

Before dying, Ellénore tells Adolphe not to blame himself; she is at fault for expecting his life to be consumed by love as hers has been. Adolphe immediately becomes morbid and senses that he will never be loved again with the intensity that Ellénore loved him. Ellénore begs Adolphe not to read but to burn a letter which she has written to him. Shortly thereafter, she dies in his arms. Adolphe cannot refrain from reading the letter. In it, Ellénore reproaches Adolphe for staying with her out of pity since he seriously harmed himself as well as her. If he had left she could at least have been able to believe him to be generous. She lacked the strength to leave him because of the extent of her love; since he did not love her, it was up to him to act.

Weeks, then months, go by. Adolphe is barely able to function without Ellénore. The freedom which he craved so much when Ellénore was alive now weighs heavily upon him. He greatly misses that dependance which had so often revolted him. All of Adolphe's brilliant potential has gone to waste. He seeks no useful occupation but merely wanders aimlessly throughout Europe, indifferent to all that surrounds him.

It is while travelling in Italy that the narrator meets Adolphe in such a state. Later, after inadvertently coming into possession of Adolphe's correspondence, the narrator decides that no harm will be done anyone if he publishes Adolphe's story, the one which has just been summarized.

Adolphe, Ellénore, Father (unnamed) of Adolphe, Friend (unnamed) of Adolphe, Friend (unnamed) of Ellénore, Count de P..., Baron de T..., Woman (unnamed).

L'Assommoir, Zola, 1877.

In the early 1850s, Gervaise Macquart, a young woman of twenty-two, arrives in Paris from Provence with her longtime lover, Auguste Lantier, and their two illegitimate children, Claude, eight, and Etienne, four. The extravagant Lantier thinks only of amusing himself and, in several months, squanders all the money they have left. The family is now obliged to live in a squalid hotel, while pawning nearly all their possessions. One night, Lantier fails to come home. The next day, while doing washing, the grief-stricken Gervaise discovers that he has deserted her for another woman. When taunted by this woman's sister, Virginie, Gervaise turns on the vicious creature and nearly kills her. Then, filled with covert terror, she returns to the hotel room with her two little ones.

Three weeks later, Gervaise, who has found employment as a laundress, finds herself being courted by Coupeau, an attractive and earnest zinc worker of modest means. Initially, Gervaise does not allow herself to take him seriously because of her experience with Lantier. Eventually, however, she concludes that since she might never have been able to raise her children had Lantier stayed with her, all is for the best. For more than a month, Gervaise and Coupeau continue to be the best of friends. Then he asks her to marry him. Convinced that he is not a drinker and that he will help provide for her children, Gervaise accepts his proposal. Coupeau insists that they visit his sister and brother-in-law, the Lorilleux, to ask for their approval. The miserly makers of gold chains, disappointed at losing the money Coupeau pays them for his board, receive the couple coldly in their leprous-looking attic apartment. Furious, Coupeau vows that the wedding will take place anyway.

Gervaise does not want to have any wedding festivities but is overruled by Coupeau, even though he must borrow money. A small reception for fifteen people is held at a fairly cheap wineshop. The wedding day itself is marred by delays at the mayor's office and a thunderstorm which puts everyone in a bad mood. One guest proposes a visit to the Louvre. Most of what the guests see there is incomprehensible to them and bores them. Gervaise senses that Coupeau behaves like a coward in the presence of his domineering sister, Mme. Lorilleux, who constantly insults Gervaise. The dinner at the wineshop ends in a heated dispute with the manager over the bill. In addition, several of the men get quite drunk. The final straw for Gervaise comes when an old drunk stumbles against her as they return to their hotel. His drunken utterings seem like a curse to her and make her feel anxious about the future.

Four years of hard toil follow, but they are happy years, during which Gervaise and Coupeau lead a steady life. Claude is sent off to school in Provence, where he will be looked after by a kindly benefactor. Gervaise and Coupeau are able to save money from their joint earnings and move into a better place, which has a large room with a small closet and kitchen. Their daughter, Anna (Nana), is born shortly thereafter. Three years later, enough money has been saved for Gervaise to realize her ambition, to have a laundry shop of her own. Just as she is about to rent a place, tragedy strikes. Coupeau, while trying to fix the last sheets of zinc to a roof, trips and falls into the street. Although he is critically injured, Gervaise refuses to have him hospitalized; she insists upon caring for him herself. Because of his very slow recovery, their savings are depleted. Finally, after four months, Coupeau regains full use of his legs but he does not return to work. A drastic change of attitude has taken place within this once industrious man. Slowly but surely, laziness has invaded both his body and his mind. Gervaise is obliged to work overtime to support the family. Coupeau also becomes quarrelsome and begins to drink. In addition, he abuses Etienne, whose presence he resents. A kind young neighbor, Goujet, who has befriended the couple and who secretly loves Gervaise, begs her to accept a loan from him so that she may have the laundry shop she wants so badly.

At first Gervaise continues to work hard, keeping long hours to make her shop a success. Business is so good that she is able to hire two assistants and an apprentice. Coupeau, however, does not make life any easier for her. He continues to idle away the days, spending the money his wife gives him at the local wineshop, "L'Assommoir" ("The Bludgeon"). Slowly but surely he increases the amount of wine he drinks and sometimes appears at the laundry shop in an inebriated state. Gervaise continues to be tolerant of her husband, as their life takes a slow, downward course. Coupeau's relatives, the Lorilleux couple, jealous of Gervaise's success, declare an all-out war on her. Nana begins to become a discipline problem. Coupeau's aged mother, no longer able to support herself, comes to live with them in their small quarters. Three difficult years pass.

In spite of her thriving business, Gervaise manages to save no money at all and repays very little of her debt to Goujet. She becomes aware that Coupeau, who initially imbibed only wine, has begun drinking hard liquor, which makes him even more hostile and abusive whenever he gets drunk. Now she despairs of ever finding happiness. Instead, Gervaise herself becomes a spendthrift and spares nothing in order to eat and drink well. She grows stouter and stouter by the month. On her saint day, she prepares a lavish, multi-course dinner to which she invites a dozen guests. In order to buy the enormous quantity of wine she desires to serve, she pawns her wedding ring. The feast is a huge success; all the guests eat and drink gluttonously. Although Coupeau has to be retrieved from a wineshop in order to participate, he does not spoil the event. There is a close call, however, because he becomes furious upon spotting Lantier eating and drinking in a nearby tavern. Although eight years have gone by since Lantier abandoned Gervaise and Coupeau has no reason to be jealous, alcohol has begun to damage his brain. On this festive night, however, Coupeau surprises his fearful wife by inviting her ex-lover to join the party, which finally comes to an end just before dawn, by which time all the benumbed participants collapse in a stupor.

Several days later, Lantier reappears with Coupeau, who encourages him to visit them regularly. Gervaise feels uncomfortable but says nothing. The two men become regular drinking companions. Lantier's activities when he is not with them remain a mystery; but he dazzles everyone in the family, including the Lorilleux, by his well-groomed appearance and flattering remarks. After a short time, his visits seem quite natural; he insinuates himself into the good graces of everyone except Goujet, who realizes the threat Lantier poses to Gervaise's well-being. Within a year, Lantier has moved in as a member of the family, at the insistence of Coupeau, who seems pleased that the local gossips think of theirs as a ménage à trois. This event causes much distress to Gervaise and the children. At the suggestion of Goujet, always Etienne's protector, the unhappy lad, now twelve, is sent to Lille to become an apprentice for Goujet's former employer, an engine builder.

Another year passes. Gervaise sinks deeper into debt and gradually loses her will to get ahead. Although the two men in her life continue to drink heavily together, Lantier is able to control his drinking and slips away when the former zinc worker becomes drunk. Coupeau has degenerated to the point where he can no longer drink without putting himself into a hideous state. Finally, he goes on a spree and fails to return home for three days. Gervaise loses all respect for him when he is finally found, lying across their bed, snoring and covered with filth, like a pig wallowing in mire. Lantier invites her to sleep in his bed. She struggles to resist but finally succumbs to the wiles of the tempter. Little Nana gazes at them with dilated, wondering eyes.

That winter, Coupeau's elderly mother becomes quite ill. Gervaise, whose business has nearly gone to the dogs, can hardly tolerate the ill-tempered old woman. Sloth has destroyed Gervaise's energy, and she finds every pretext to justify her inaction. She becomes indifferent to everything as the house sinks a little deeper into the mire each week. Finally, everything they own of any value has been absorbed by the pawnshop. Mother Coupeau finally dies. On the day of her burial, Gervaise finally yields to the pressure of Coupeau and Lantier by selling the laundry shop to her old enemy Virginie, before the landlord evicts them. As for Lantier, he asks to keep his room there with Virginie and her unsuspecting husband, a policeman. The Coupeaus move into a wretched little lodging on the sixth floor of the same building.

Their new quarters are scarcely larger than one's hand. Gervaise, Coupeau, and Nana, now thirteen years old, are constantly at each other's throats. Gervaise is rehired by her old employer, but the quality of her work has now deteriorated and she works so infrequently that she brings in very little. Coupeau squanders what little he makes by drinking his daily pint of "vitriol." By now, Gervaise is so sick of Coupeau that she frequently wishes he were dead. Two years pass. The couple nearly starves and freezes to death during the severe winter months. Coupeau is suddenly hospitalized with inflammation of the lungs and must be transferred to an asylum because his seizures of delirium tremens disturb the other patients. After his release from the asylum, he quickly resumes consumption of his daily pint. One night, Gervaise, whose will has never been strong, seeks out Coupeau at "L'Assommoir" and, after failing to persuade him to leave, gets drunk with him.

Meanwhile, Nana is becoming a wayward child. At age fifteen, she has become quite coquettish. For two years, she has worked at the artificial flower factory where her other aunt, the tolerant Mme. Lerat, is forewoman. Despite the latter's efforts to control her niece, Nana, badly inclined already because of child neglect, revels in the company of her coarse coworkers, many of them girls already worn out with misery and vice. One day, a well-dressed gentleman of about fifty is observed following Nana. She tries to avoid him at first, but the persistent button manufacturer pursues her day after day. When Coupeau hears of this, he beats his daughter harder than ever. This is not surprising since there has always been more of a badgering propensity than any impulse of rectitude in the manner by which Coupeau seeks to cow and rule Nana. Up to now, she has displayed the cunning but rancorous submission of a hunted animal. But, as another unbearable winter approaches, Nana vows that this cursed life will not continue for her. One night, upon returning home, she finds her father and mother in a drunken stupor. Her father has long since ceased to count for her, but now her mother is also going downhill in her esteem. She quickly goes out the door and does not return.

Six months pass. One night, Coupeau and Gervaise discover Nana dancing wildly at a public music hall. They drag her home and beat her, but this hardly stops the determined girl. For over a year, she comes and goes as she pleases, lodging off and on with her parents; she has long since become immune to their insults and beatings. Then, one day, Nana leaves for good. Lantier reports, sometime later, that he has seen her in a carriage with a viscount.

Meanwhile, because of the terrible effects of alcohol upon him, Coupeau has become one of the living dead. His body has shrunk and become so bent and unsteady that he looks twice his forty years. His hands shake so violently that he has difficulty holding a glass. Six months after Nana's final departure, Gervaise finds herself alone, shivering from cold and starving to death; Coupeau has been missing for several days. She has deteriorated so much that no one will hire her. At this point, she has fallen into a state of bestial indifference; she prefers to die rather than move her fingers. All of their relatives and old friends, filled with contempt, have abandoned both Gervaise and Coupeau. Gervaise's only concern while she is still alive is to find something to eat. Reduced to begging in the street, she accidentally encounters her old friend Goujet, who has suffered in silence while observing the steady decline of the woman he loves. She falls on her knees before him, devours the stew he offers her, allows him to kiss her, and then flees in shame, feeling that meeting the one person she still cares for under such abominable circumstances is her final degradation. She wishes to die; twenty years of this life in Paris is too much to bear. Misery, however, is reluctant to kill her so quickly.

Several more days go by. Etienne, now an engineer on a railway line, sends his mother a few francs, enabling her to eat. Then she is informed that her pig of a husband is in critical condition at the Sainte-Anne asylum. When Gervaise visits Coupeau, he does not recognize her. He makes senseless grimaces and animal noises, and dances wildly, seriously wounding himself in the process. For four entire days, he yells and dances continuously. Then, even when he finally succumbs to sleep, his feet continue to move for a long time. Only death stops them, at long last.

Gervaise lingers for several more months, falling lower and lower, submitting to the grossest outrages, dying of starvation a little more every day. Evicted from her sixth-floor quarters, she finishes out her wretched life in a hole under a staircase in the building. One morning, upon detecting a smell in the passage, someone discovers her already decaying body.

Adèle, Amanda, Auguste, Augustine (two), Badinguet, Mère Baquet, Baudequin, Bazouge, "Bec-Salé," M. Bénard, Mme. Bénard, "Bibi-la-Grillade," Bijard, Eulalie Bijard, Henriette Bijard, Jules Bijard, Mme. Bijard, Boche, Mme. Boche, Pauline Boche, Bourguignon, Bru, Caroline, Champion, Charles (two), Mlle. Clemens, Clock Maker (unnamed), Colombe, Coquet Family, Linguerlot Coquet, Coudeloup, Coupeau, Anna (Nana) Coupeau, Mme. Coupeau, Mmes. Cudorge (two), Doctor (unnamed), Doorkeeper (unnamed), Eulalie, Mme. Fauconnier, Victor Fauconnier, François, Gaudron, Gaudron (Jr.), Mme. Gaudron, Gentlemen (two, unnamed), Goujet, Mme. Goujet, Mlle. Josse, Lace Mender (unnamed), Auguste Lantier, Claude Lantier, Etienne Lantier, Lehongre, Mme. Lehongre, Léonie, Mme. Lerat, Lorilleux, Anna Lorilleux, Mère Louis, Gervaise Macquart, Madinier, Man (unnamed), Marescot, Marsoullier, Mayor (unnamed), "Mes-Bottes," Meyer, Midwife (unnamed), Mistress of Washhouse (unnamed), Péquignot, "Pied-de-Céleri," Poisson, Priest (unnamed), Mme. Putois, Mlle. Remanjou, Sophie, Surgeon (unnamed), Thérèse, Thomas, Mme. Titreville, Mme. Vigouroux, Virginie, Women (two, unnamed), Zidore.

"Atala," Chateaubriand, 1801.

Chactas, a blind, elderly Natchez Indian, tells René, a self-exiled Frenchman, of his love as a youth for a Muskogee Indian maiden named Atala. Chactas's love for Atala has endured all these years.

After Chactas's father is killed in a war with the Muskogees, young Chactas is transported to St. Augustine, where an old Castilian named Lopez cares for him for several years. However, since Chactas is unhappy away from the solitary forest, Lopez reluctantly gives him permission to leave the civilized world. Chactas is soon captured by the Muskogees and sentenced to be burned at the stake. He is set free by Atala, a beautiful Indian maiden who has been converted to Christianity. Chactas refuses to flee unless the reluctant Atala will follow him. They fall in love, but Atala's fervent prayers help her resist the temptation to succumb to her passion. For days, the two live alone, surrounded by the beauties of nature. Atala confesses to Chactas that, in spite of her great love for him, she will never be able to marry but refuses to explain why.

One day, after Chactas and Atala have found shelter from a violent storm, Atala confesses that her real father is not Simaghan, a Muskogee chief, but a white man, the very same Lopez who had raised Chactas. The young lovers are beside themselves with joy. Only the arrival of an old man prevents them from attaining the supreme moment of happiness. The intruder is Father Aubry, who directs a mission of Indians who have converted to Christianity. When Father Aubry leads Atala and Chactas to his cave in the mountains, Atala declares that Heaven has sent him in order to save her.

Father Aubry offers to instruct Chactas in the Christian religion and then marry the young couple. Chactas sheds tears of joy but Atala becomes deathly pale. The next morning, Atala is found to be critically ill. Before dying, she makes a full confession to Chactas and Father Aubry. Conceived out of wedlock, she was born on the verge of death. To save the infant's life, her Christian mother made a vow to the Holy Virgin that Atala would always remain a virgin. Sixteen years later, Atala promised her dying mother to carry out her vow. She now tells Chactas of all the torment she has suffered because of her passion for him. Not knowing that the church has the necessary powers to release her from her vow, she has taken fatal poison. Atala dies, begging to be forgiven.

Father Aubry's words of consolation and the example of his Christian resignation finally calm Chactas. Atala is buried simply and with dignity under the arch of a natural bridge, at the entrance to the Indian Groves of Death. All of nature witnesses her burial. Urged by Father Aubry to return to the Natchez tribe, Chactas departs after visiting his beloved Atala's grave one last time.

Atala, Father Aubry, Céluta, Chactas, Philippe Lopez, Outalissi, René, Simaghan.

"Candide," Voltaire, 1759.

This particular *conte philosophique* ("philosophical tale") provides perhaps the best example of Voltaire's favorite weapon, irony. In "Candide," which has as its subtitle "Optimism," he attacks this particular philosophy and has as its mouthpiece a ludicrous character, the pedagogue Pangloss. In a brief summary, it is virtually impossible to capture the humor which results from Voltaire's use of irony and I shall rarely attempt to do so. Let it suffice to say that the irony stems primarily from the contrast between the optimism ("all is well") expressed by Pangloss and his brainwashed disciple, Candide, and the series of atrocities which befall Candide and his acquaintances. In addition, by having supposedly dead characters reappear, Voltaire pokes fun at many novels of the seventeenth and eighteenth centuries, in which so many such romanesque elements are prevalent.

***

In the province of Westphalia, in the chateau of M. le baron de Thunder-ten-tronckh, lives a simpleminded young man named Candide. He is the pupil of Master Pangloss, who has taught him that there is no effect without a cause and that all is for the best in this best of all possible worlds.

One fine day, Candide is kicked out of the chateau because the Baron finds him behind a screen with Cunégonde, the Baron's plump, lascivious daughter. After wandering aimlessly for a time, Candide is approached by two recruitment officers who force him to join the army of the Bulgares, where he is harshly treated and is even obliged to run the gauntlet. At the time of his recovery from this punishment, the Bulgares declare war on the Abares. Candide witnesses massive slaughter and devastation but is finally able to escape to Holland, where he is given food by a charitable Anabaptist.

The following day, Candide meets a beggar whose body has been devoured by syphilis. This hideous creature turns out to be Pangloss. Pangloss informs Candide of the massacre of the entire Thunder-ten-tronckh family, including Cunégonde, who was violated many times and disemboweled. Pangloss also describes to Candide how such a great cause as love has produced such an abominable effect (syphilis) on him. Nevertheless, he remains steadfast in his optimism. Candide's friend Jacques, the Anabaptist, pays for Pangloss's medical care and the latter loses only an eye and an ear.

Pangloss and Candide accompany Jacques on a voyage to Lisbon. Just as they are in sight of the port of Lisbon, a monumental earthquake kills nearly everyone on board, including the good Anabaptist. Candide and Pangloss struggle to shore.

The following day, the Inquisition holds an auto-da-fé in order to ward off the earthquake. Pangloss is hanged for having hedged on the questions of liberty and original sin. Candide escapes with another thrashing and is led away by an old woman as the earth trembles anew.

The Old Woman nurses Candide back to health and then takes him to a lovely country house where he is reunited with his beloved Cunégonde, who has miraculaously survived all the atrocities that have come her way. She is currently the shared mistress of two men: don Issachar, a wealthy Jewish banker in whose house she is living, and the Grand Inquisitor. Candide, Cunégonde, and the Old Woman are soon forced to flee, however, because Candide inadvertently murders both don Issachar and the Grand Inquisitor.

The fugitives are able to book passage on a ship to South America. During the crossing, Candide expresses his belief that it is undoubtedly in the New World that the best of all possible worlds is to be found. Cunégonde expresses pessimism and complains of her lot. The Old Woman relates in graphic detail the innumerable vicissitudes of her life, including the loss of one buttock to a troop of hungry soldiers. She concludes her tale of horrors by declaring that every passenger on board has often cursed his life and thought himself to be the most wretched of human beings. The impressionable Candide begins to question the wisdom of Pangloss's optimistic outlook.

Upon their arrival in South America, Cunégonde captivates the governor of Buenos Aires, who offers to marry her. At the same time, a ship arrives in pursuit of the murderer of the Grand Inquisitor. The practical, worldly-wise Old Woman urges Cunégonde to remain with the governor for his money and urges Candide to flee.

Candide reluctantly leaves with his faithful valet Cacambo, in search of the Jesuit fathers who have their own powerful kingdom in Paraguay. The Jesuit leader turns out to be none other than the brother of Cunégonde! Their joyous reunion comes to an abrupt halt when Candide announces that he intends to marry Cunégonde. He and the offended Baron come to blows, and the Baron is killed. Candide, disguised as the Jesuit father, flees with Cacambo.

Days later, they are mysteriously transported by boat to a beautiful and luxurious land where gold lies in the streets. When they attempt to pay for a meal with some of it, Candide and Cacambo are laughed at since all is paid for by the government. Candide believes that this must be the best of all possible worlds which Pangloss talked about. Candide and Cacambo spend one month in this ideal country, Eldorado.

However, Candide becomes restless because of his desire to find Cunégonde and asks the king for permission to leave. The king reluctantly consents and, amused, grants his request to take along precious sheep loaded with provisions, including the gold stones of the country. Candide and Cacambo take their leave, feeling hopeful about the future since they are now wealthy.

Within three months, all but two of their sheep have perished. It is decided that Cacambo will go to Buenos Aires to find Cunégonde and will rejoin Candide in Venice. A greedy sea captain tricks the still naive Candide by taking his money and setting sail without him, after having put the two sheep on the ship. A corrupt judge refuses to help. The despairing Candide is now overwhelmed by the wickedness of men and skeptical of the teachings of his master Pangloss. He books passage on a French ship for himself and his newly chosen companion, Martin, who in Candide's mind is the individual most disgusted with his lot.

Their crossing completed, Candide and Martin head for Paris. Their numerous adventures in the French capital convince Candide that Martin's pessimism is well founded. Upon their escape from France, robbed and duped once too often, he believes that they have been set free from hell. Off the English coast, they witness the ceremonious execution of an English admiral because he fought a French admiral at too distant a range. Candide is so appalled that he refuses to set foot on English soil. Their ship finally reaches Venice, and Candide's optimism resurfaces momentarily.

He soon becomes bitterly disillusioned once again when Cacambo fails to appear with Cunégonde. Finally, Cacambo arrives with news that Cunégonde is in Constantinople. They set sail immediately. On the way, Cacambo tells Candide that Cunégonde has completely lost her beauty. Candide vows to love her dutifully, nonetheless. On the galley ship, Candide recognizes two convicts in the slave gang. Another miracle! They are the hanged Pangloss and the murdered Jesuit priest, brother of Cunégonde. In spite of all the horrors to which he has been subjected, Pangloss stubbornly insists that all is for the best because it is unsuitable for a philosopher to recant.

Candide, the Baron, Pangloss, Martin, and Cacambo are finally reunited with Cunégonde and the Old Woman. Needless to say, they do not live happily ever after. Candide's supply of money is depleted with the purchase of a small farm where they all live in a sort of commune. Cunégonde, the Old Woman, Cacambo, and Pangloss all complain constantly about their unhappy lot. Martin, firmly convinced that one is equally miserable everywhere, suffers patiently. The Old Woman wonders which is worse: to suffer all the horrors they have survived or to be bored doing nothing, as they are at present.

They go to consult a famous Dervish. Pangloss asks him why such a strange animal as man was ever born. He is told to mind his own business. Candide receives a similar response when he asks about the enormous amount of evil in the world. The Dervish finally slams the door in Pangloss's face.

On their way back to the farm, they meet an old man who is taking a rest from his farm work. He tells them that he knows nothing of events in Constantinople but merely contents himself with sending there the fruit which he cultivates in his garden. Hard work, he says, removes three great evils from our lives: boredom, vice, and need.

This encounter proves to be a crucial one in the lives of Candide and his friends. The farm begins to reap an abundant harvest. The hopeless Pangloss continues to philosophize incessantly that all events are linked in this best of all possible worlds. A now wiser Candide's final reply, rejecting absurd philosophizing, is that all that is well said but that one must cultivate one's garden.

Abbé (unnamed), Achmet III, Bulgarian Captain (unnamed), Cacambo, Candide, Charles-Edouard, Mlle. Clairon, Cunégonde, Dervish (unnamed), Brother Giroflée, Don Fernando d'Ibaraa y Figuerora y Mascarenes y Lampurdos y Souza, Grand Inquisitor, Don Issachar, Ivan, Jacques, King (unnamed) of Eldorado, Kings of Polaques (two, unnamed), Martin, Mlle. Monime, Old Men (two, unnamed), Old Woman ("la Vieille"), Orator (unnamed), Oreillons, Prince (unnamed) de Massa-Carrara, Princess de Palestrine, Pangloss, Paquette, Marquise de Parolignac, Pococurante, Police Officer (unnamed), Ragotski, Sailor (unnamed), Théodore, Baron de Thunder-ten-tronckh, Baron de Thunder-ten-tronckh (Jr.), Baronness de Thunder-ten-tronchkh, Urbain X, Vanderdendur.

La Chartreuse de Parme, Stendhal, 1839.

The entrance of Bonaparte and his young army into Milan arouses a slumbering, oppressed people. A new way of life springs up; to risk one's life becomes the fashion. Two years after this event Fabrice Valserra del Dongo is born. Fabrice is the son of the Marquis del Dongo, a vicious, liberal-hating nobleman, and the Marquise del Dongo, a timid, long-suffering woman whose fortune is largely controlled by her husband. Fabrice's youth is spent largely in ignorance at the ancestral castle of Grianta. It is here that the Marquis, a voluntary exile, confines his entire family.

Fabrice later spends time at the Jesuit College of Milan, where, because of the influence of his aunt, Countess Gina Pietranera, he is awarded prizes he does not deserve. At the age of twelve, when his father orders him back to Grianta, Fabrice knows nothing of the world other than how to drill and how to sit on a horse. Unfortunately, he has also taken seriously all the religious teachings of the Jesuits. Fabrice's incompetent Latin teacher at Grianta, the nonetheless lovable Abbé Blanès, quickly initiates his tutee into astrology.

In the meantime, Fabrice's aunt, the impassioned Gina Pietranera, now an impoverished young widow, is forced to return to Grianta to live with her brother, for whom she, as well as her nephew, feels contempt. Being beautiful and gay, Gina Pietranera succeeds in bringing joy into the lives of Fabrice, his two sisters, and the children's melancholy mother. Like Fabrice and the servants, Gina Pietranera detests the Austrian conservatives and laughs at the powdered wigs of the Marquis and his older son Ascagne, who is in every way worthy of his father.

When, on 8 March 1815, Fabrice secretly announces to his aunt that he is leaving to join the Emperor Napoleon in battle, she weeps for joy and grief. Nevertheless, she and his frantic mother give him all their worldly possessions. Fabrice immediately sets out for Paris, where disillusionment quickly sets in. He is unable to get near the Emperor and discovers that the Frenchmen he encounters do not share his unbridled enthusiasm. Fabrice's decision to join the army proves to be most unfortunate; his bad French and his exuberance are so suspect that he is arrested as a spy and spends over a month in prison. He is finally set free by a jailer's wife who finds him attractive and gives him the uniform of a hussar who has just died in prison. Fabrice sets out for the army on the day before the battle of Waterloo.

Even though he knows nothing about fighting, Fabrice insists upon joining the soldiers. A sympathetic canteen keeper tries in vain to dissuade him. Fabrice perseveres and by accident finds himself, as bullets start flying, in a company with the famous Marshal Ney. To ingratiate himself, he buys brandy for the entire escort and proceeds to drink so much of it that he fails to catch sight of his hero Napoleon, who passes close by. Finally, the few surviving members of the escort force Fabrice off his horse and steal it for a general. They gallop off, leaving him behind. Disconsolate, he abandons his beautiful vision of war as a noble and universal uplifting of souls thirsting for glory. He miraculously happens upon the same canteen keeper he talked to that morning. She helps him into her cart, where our hero, totally worn out, falls fast asleep.

Shortly thereafter, Fabrice is obliged by circumstances to take flight as best he can. He kills a Prussian soldier, is wounded by military runaways, and ends up being nursed by a kind innkeeper and her two daughters, who then help him to escape from the Prussian authorities. Upon reaching Amiens, he discovers that his wound has formed an abscess. During the two weeks he spends there convalescing, Fabrice has many profound reflections concerning the things which have happened to him. He remains totally uncertain about one point only: was what he saw a battle; and, if so, was that battle Waterloo? Finally, he is able to return to his old hotel in Paris. A letter from his aunt convinces him that he must return home to Grianta. After taking certain necessary precautions because of the treachery of his wicked brother Ascagne, who has accused him to the Milan police of being a liberal traitor, he reaches home safely. However, in order to avoid being arrested, he is obliged to live in exile on one of his mother's properties in the Piedmont region.

Unknown to Fabrice, his aunt, the Countess Pietranera, has begun to feel a very strong attraction toward him. Shortly after Fabrice's departure for France, she falls into a profound melancholy. In this frame of mind, she makes an expedition to Milan, in the hope of finding some news of Napoleon and, indirectly, of Fabrice. She also is anxious to flee for a time from the monotonous life at Grianta. In Milan, she regularly attends the opera at La Scala, where she becomes attracted to Count Mosca, an amiable, intelligent, and liberal-minded individual in spite of his position in the government of the tyrannical Prince of Parma, Ernesto IV. Mosca falls madly in love with the Countess Pietranera. But he must return to Parma and she to Grianta.

A few months later, after much correspondence between the two, Mosca and the Countess are reunited in Milan. Mosca brings with him the wealthy but not terribly noble Duke Sanseverina-Taxis, who, in exchange for an ambassadorship and the Grand Cordon will engage in a marriage of convenience with the Countess and will agree, after the marriage, to leave Parma forever. This will enable Mosca, who is already unhappily married, to support the Countess as his mistress in Parma. The Countess, always eager for adventure and also foreseeing advantages for Fabrice in this arrangement, is easily persuaded to accept Mosca's offer.

The new Duchess Sanseverina-Taxis is given a magnificent welcome by Prince Ernesto IV and the unhappy Princess, his wife. She is quick to make her influence felt and succeeds so well in diminishing the enmities of which Count Mosca is the object that, two months after her arrival at the Court of Parma, Mosca obtains the prestigious post of Prime Minister. The Duchess not only thrives on court life, where danger is always to be feared, but is amused by it. She even succeeds in exerting an influence over the Prince of Parma in his domestic life.

The Count, ever aware of the Duchess Sanseverina's great affection for Fabrice, becomes interested in the exiled young man. He tells the Duchess that Fabrice cannot be an officer (the time of military glory has passed) but that he can one day, under Mosca's protection, become Archbishop of Parma, as three of his ancestors previously did. Fabrice, who would prefer to be a soldier, is initially distressed at the plans made for his future career but finally accepts them. He spends four years at the Ecclesiastical Academy in Naples, where he commits a few acts of folly and never is without mistresses. On the whole, however, Fabrice follows soberly enough the line of conduct laid down for him—that of a great nobleman who is studying theology but who does not rely entirely on theology to bring him advancement.

Fabrice arrives in Parma in 1821 wearing the violet stockings of a novice destined for holy orders and capable of finding in any circumstance the wherewithal to succeed. His aunt is astonished at how polished a diamond he has become. The Count also has an excellent impression of him, although the much older Mosca experiences jealousy in spite of himself when he becomes aware of the intimacy which exists between the Duchess and Fabrice. Two hours after his arrival, Fabrice has an impromptu audience with the Prince; this favor puts him beyond all court rivalry from the outset.

A reckless, irresponsible affair with a young actress named Marietta obliges Mosca to send Fabrice away from the court for a time. In spite of the danger of returning to the area, Fabrice determines to go back to Grianta and seek advice from his old mentor, the Abbé Blanès. En route, he proves how superstitious he has become because of his old teacher's influence. During the course of his tearful reunion with the Abbé, Fabrice discovers that the elderly priest has already made certain predictions concerning both their futures. Fabrice spends the entire next day hidden in the belfry, watching the holy day ceremony below. The view from above causes all the memories of his childhood to surface, making this day of nostalgia one of the happiest of his life.

Upon his return to Parma, Fabrice, thanks to the protection of Count Mosca and the kindness of Archbishop Landriani, is well on his way to being appointed First Vicar General of the Archbishop and, eventually, his Coadjutor with eventual succession to the Archbishopric. However, one day, Fabrice happens to see Marietta, the young actress he once loved, now accompanied by a fellow performer, the insanely jealous Giletti. Giletti attacks Fabrice, who ends up killing Giletti in self-defense. This would seem to be a relatively unimportant incident. However, Count Mosca's political enemies immediately exploit the event, hoping to topple Mosca from power and replace him with General Fabio Conti, governor of the Farnese prison.

Fabrice flees, first to Ferrara, then to Bologna, served and protected all the while by Ludovic, a former coachman of the Duchess Sanseverina. Then the two head for a village just outside of Parma, where Fabrice follows a young singer-actress named Fausta. He believes that he is incapable of genuine, lasting love; vulgar pleasure seems to be all that can attract him. In pursuit of such pleasure with Fausta, he engages in several reckless, daring escapades.

In spite of the valiant efforts of the Duchess Sanseverina and Count Mosca, Fabrice does not remain a free man for long. He is tricked into returning to Parma, at which time Mosca's enemies succeed in having him sentenced to a long imprisonment for having killed Giletti. He is taken to the Farnese tower, which is governed by General Fabio Conti. On his way into the prison, Fabrice sees Clélia Conti, daughter of the governor, whom he met briefly once before. She is too shy to speak to him but worries about his reaction to her. From that point on, the bored Clélia becomes an animated person. She is eager to help Fabrice in any way she can but feels helpless because of her father's position as governor of the prison.

Duchess Sanseverina, beside herself with grief and furious with the Prince for having betrayed her, vows to stop at nothing to save Fabrice, who she fears will be poisoned in prison. She even threatens to end her five-year relationship with Mosca if the Count cannot help Fabrice. However, in spite of their complete devotion to Fabrice's cause, the two are able to do very little.

Fabrice, meanwhile, is oblivious to the fact that his life is in great danger. From his cell high in the prison tower, he is busy watching and trying to attract the attention of Clélia, who has an aviary in another wing of the tower, close to Fabrice's window. Fabrice, truly in love for the first time, is in turn loved by Clélia, who tries to stifle her feelings because she believes Fabrice and the Duchess Sanseverina to be lovers and also because he is destined for holy orders. Months pass. Fabrice and Clélia begin to exchange letters. He is happier than he has ever been, spending entire days thinking about Clélia and seeing her for a few moments each day when she comes to the aviary. When the Duchess, after painstaking effort, outlines to Fabrice elaborate plans she has made for his escape, he is initially reluctant to take action because of his passion for Clélia. However, when she threatens to retire to a convent unless Fabrice promises to try to execute the Duchess Sanseverina's escape plan, he agrees to go ahead. Clélia will even transport into the prison the cords necessary for his escape; the Duchess will slip them to her during a large party. Time is of the essence since it is now a certainty that the Prince, infuriated by the Duchess, will attempt to have Fabrice poisoned. The escape plan is actually that of Ferrante Palla, a doctor and poet as well as a liberal condemned to death who has been hiding in the woods near the Duchess Sanseverina's country estate, stealing and begging in order to support his family. Although Ferrante Palla is slightly mad, he is in love with the Duchess and completely devoted to her.

The Duchess succeeds in handing over the cords to Clélia but nearly ruins everything by having too strong a narcotic given to General Fabio Conti. Clélia becomes terribly frightened. After much effort, she finally bolsters her courage and resolves to execute the plan, but only after making a vow to the Madonna never to see Fabrice again. After nine months of imprisonment, Fabrice barely succeeds in his attempt at escape. He is reunited with the Duchess, who spares no effort to insure his arrival in Piedmont territory, where he is out of danger. The Duchess Sanseverina soon discovers to her chagrin that the spirited, energetic Fabrice she once knew is now lethargic and listless: his thoughts are only of Clélia. Although not a single word about mutual love has ever passed between them, the Duchess cannot help reflecting that she is now second to Clélia Conti in Fabrice's heart. Her unhappiness is as great as his. She is determined that Clélia will marry the Marquis Crescenzi, a handsome young nobleman at the court who has long desired such a union.

After several months, news is received of the death of the Prince of Parma, who has been assassinated by Ferrante Palla at the command of Duchess Sanseverina. The people of Parma, whom Count Mosca is attempting to control, riot; but the revolt is suppressed, and the Prince's son is established at court with the name Ernesto V. The Duchess is recalled to court, and many honors are heaped upon her. She becomes Grand Mistress to the Princess Dowager, who has always had great affection for her, and makes requests to the Princess Dowager regarding Fabrice's safety. The vile Minister of Justice Rassi soon discovers that the Duchess was behind the assassination of the Prince. He attempts to expose and disgrace her, but the Duchess shows herself to be the more powerful of the two. She manages to convince the Prince, smitten with her, to burn the police dossiers which would incriminate her. In addition, after much plotting and anguish, caused largely by Fabrice's rash act of presenting himself for readmission to the Farnese tower before his pardon is official (Fabrice wishes to be near Clélia!), the Duchess not only obtains his acquittal but has him named Coadjutor with the promise that he will succeed Archibishop Landriani as Archbishop of Parma. Fabrice, even though he is in the Prince's favor and is leading a luxurious life, remains deeply unhappy because he is separated from Clélia.

Clélia, having previously promised the Madonna that she will marry the Marquis Crescenzi if Fabrice's life can be saved, has vowed that she will not see Fabrice again. When Clélia's marriage festivities occur, Fabrice takes solitary refuge in the Archbishop's palace to hide his grief. The citizenry venerates him like a saint. Whenever he appears in public, he looks grim, pale, and extremely thin, wearing only a simple black habit, frayed at the collar.

One day, Clélia and Fabrice meet unexpectedly at a party given by the Prince, which Fabrice is obliged to attend. Both realize the extent of their love; and Clélia, in spite of her vow, gives Fabrice her fan as a token of their love. Fabrice immediately becomes a different man. He ends his retreat and returns to occupy his magnificent apartment in the *palazzo* Sanseverina. The Archbishop is convinced that Fabrice has been so motivated because he has been honored by the Prince; the unhappy Duchess understands all too well that it is because he has had a happy encounter with Clélia.

A few days later, the Duchess Sanseverina refuses the Prince's offer to be his Prime Minister and bride, and leaves Parma. Count Mosca resigns shortly thereafter and joins her, at which point they are married, Mosca's estranged wife having recently died. Fabrice remains at court and, taking the Duchess Sanseverina's advice, begins to do a great deal of public preaching in order to retain the favor of the populace. Soon, people are literally crushing each other in order to enter the church, so full of passion and poignancy are the words he utters. After fourteen months, Clélia comes to hear Fabrice and can no longer resist his charms. The lovers see each other at night, Clélia still insisting upon keeping her vow not to see Fabrice in the light of day.

Three years of happiness pass for both Clélia and Fabrice, who, meanwhile, has become the Archbishop of Parma. Then, a caprice of affection changes everything for him and those closest to him. He has a child by Clélia and, after two years, he can no longer bear being separated from Sandrino, his son. With Clélia's reluctant consent, Fabrice has him abducted from the Crescenzi household in order to have Sandrino all to himself. However, the child dies. Clélia, convinced that she has been punished for not carrying out her vow, dies of despair in Fabrice's arms. Fabrice distributes all his wealth, resigns his archbishopric and retires to the Charterhouse of Parma, where he dies one year later. The Duchess Sanseverina survives for only a short time after the death of Fabrice, whom she has never ceased to adore.

Count d'A... (Robert), Duchess d'A..., Adjutant (unnamed), Countess Alvizi, Aniken, Corporal Aubry, General B..., Marquise Balbi, Count Baldi, Barbone, Father Bari, Barone, Bentivoglio, Bettina, Baron Binder, Baroness Binder, Abbé Blanès, Bona, Canon Borda, Bruno, General Bubna, Bulot, Burati, Doctor C..., Signora C..., Carlone, Catena, Cecchina, Abbe de Condillac, Constable (unnamed), Countess Contarini, Don Cesare Conti, Clélia Conti, General Fabio Conti, Crescentini, Giulia Crescenzi, Marquis Crescenzi, Ascagne del Dongo, Fabrice Valserra del Dongo (Giuseppe Bossi, Cavi), Gina del Dongo, Mlle. del Dongo, Marquis del Dongo, Marquise del Dongo, Dugnani, Durati, (Ranuccio-) Ernesto IV, (Ranuccio-) Ernesto V, Fausta F..., Marquis di Felino, Fontana, Footman (unnamed), Fulgenzio, Galeazzo, General (unnamed), General of the Friars Minor, Genevan (unnamed), Marquise Ghisleri, Ghisolfi, Ghita, Giletti, Gonzo, Grillo, Gros, Hayez, Captain Henriot, Princess Isotta, Jacopo, Jailer's Wife (unnamed), Jesuit Superior (unnamed), Count L..., Landlady (unnamed), Father Landriani, Colonel Lange, La Rose, Colonel Le Baron, Limercati, Ludovico, Count M..., Mammaccia, Margot, Marietta, Annetta Marini, Giacomo Marini, Count Mosca (della Rovere Sorezana), Countess Mosca, Marquise N..., Count Nani, Officer (unnamed), Official (unnamed), Orderly (unnamed), General P..., Mme. P..., Count Palanza, Ferrante Palla (Poncet), Clara Paolina (Princess of Parma), Duchess di Partana, Peasant (unnamed), Peppe, Pernice, Pietro-Antonio, Count Pietranera, Postillion, Prina, Rambo, Rassi, Giacomo Rassi, Marquise Raversi, Riscara, Count Rusca, Sandrino, Duke Sanseverina-Taxia, Duchess Sanseverina-Taxis (Gina del Dongo, Countess Pietranera), Sarasine, Mme. Sarasine, Colonel Scotti, Sergeant (unnamed), Servant (two, unnamed), Soldier (unnamed), Teodolinda, Tombone, Toto, Duchess V..., Vasi, Vetturino, Woman (unnamed), Count Zurla-Contarini.

Corinne, Madame de Staël, 1807.
Oswald Lord Nelvil, a young Scottish peer, dejected and guilt-ridden by the death of his father, decides to follow his doctor's advice and vacation in Italy.

En route, he makes the acquaintance of Count d'Erfeuil, a French nobleman, who accompanies Oswald to Rome. Oswald soon discovers that Erfeuil is a curious mixture: he is a snob and a gossip, but a courageous young man as well. Erfeuil's frivolity inspires timidity in the serious Oswald. Erfeuil, in turn, becomes impatient with the melancholy Oswald but also very attached to him. His respect for Oswald increases when the latter, almost single-handedly, saves the entire town of Ancona from being destroyed by a fire. Oswald's melancholy, however, goes unrelieved, except momentarily. His arrival in Rome makes him feel completely isolated and depressed.

The following morning, Oswald's curiosity is aroused by great public excitement over the coronation of the most famous woman of Italy, Corinne, who is a creative genius. Upon seeing her, Oswald becomes deeply moved and desires to be her protector. Corinne also notices Oswald and improvises a poem with him in mind. A completely new sensation overcomes Oswald. After he retrieves Corinne's crown, she thanks him in English, to the delight of the chauvinistic Lord Nelvil.

Erfeuil arranges for Oswald to meet Corinne at her home, which is a marvelous mixture of everything that is agreeable in France, England, and Italy. She graciously receives the two men but will not answer Erfeuil's indirect questions concerning her past. Corinne is eager to please Oswald but uncertain of success because of his calm exterior. He, in turn, is both dazzled and troubled by the extraordinary qualities of this woman, and wonders what his father would have thought of her. Two days later, Oswald learns that Corinne is in love with him. Once they meet, they are ill at ease when alone but she sparkles in conversation as soon as other guests arrive. Later, Oswald is offended by Erfeuil's negative reaction to the possibility that a man such as Oswald might marry Corinne.

Oswald and Corinne see each other constantly. Corinne feels a respect for Oswald that she has not experienced for a long time. Each seems to understand the other's feelings quite well, even though they are of different countries and temperaments. Corinne, eager to prolong Oswald's stay in Rome, spends a great deal of time showing him the splendors of the city, which speak to the soul because of their grandeur. She secretly flatters herself that she has captured Oswald's heart but that his reserve inhibits her from discussing her feelings as her natural abandon would incline her to do. Suddenly, Oswald does not see Corinne for four days. The tormented Lord Nelvil is aware that her charms have captivated him but is also aware that his father would never have approved of his marrying Corinne. During these four days, Corinne's suffering is almost unbearable. She begs Oswald to spare her such grief in the future. Within her soul is an abyss of despair which she can avoid only by preserving herself from love. However, during a visit to the tombs of Rome, Oswald and Corinne are moved to declare their love for each other. And yet Corinne urges Oswald not to plan for the future but to live in the present, enjoying each moment.

Oswald becomes upset when Corinne, who has renounced society for him, decides to attend a ball. With great reluctance, he accompanies her. Corinne pours all her imagination and spontaneity into dancing while the jealous Oswald fears that she is rejecting him. At the ball, he is also annoyed by the manners of the Italians, so unlike those of the British. Corinne is offended and hurt when Oswald verbalizes his opinion, and she refuses to see him for a while. Oswald, feeling remorse for his harsh words to Corinne, is about to attempt to see her when he is visited by Mr. Edgermond, a relative of Lucile Edgermond, whom Oswald's father chose several years before to be his son's bride. When Oswald mentions to Corinne that Edgermond would like to see her perform, she becomes visibly upset but refuses to tell Oswald why. She does agree to do so, however, and captivates Edgermond even though, for the first time in her life, she has difficulty improvising.

The next day, with Edgermond in attendance, Oswald induces Corinne to discuss Italian literature. Corinne responds to Erfeuil's attacks against the Italian theatre and consents to perform in a tragedy, her translation of Shakespeare's *Romeo and Juliet*. Oswald realizes that he is more intoxicated than happy when he is with Corinne, and that her love for him inspires admiration without making him feel secure. He wishes that she would perform for him alone, as an Englishwoman would do. When Corinne performs Juliet and addresses her most moving lines to Oswald, he experiences difficulty distinguishing between truth and fiction.

The exalted Oswald is on the verge of asking Corinne to marry him without seeking information about her secret past, but the memory of his father comes to the foreground once again. Edgermond expresses the opinion to Oswald that Corinne could never be happy in England as an English wife because she belongs in Italy. On the contrary, Oswald should marry a woman like his mother, for example, Lucile, Edgermond's cousin. Oswald's agitation becomes so great that he is soon seriously ill. Corinne rushes to his side and nurses him constantly for six days. She is aware of the conflict raging within Oswald. All that she cares about at the moment is that Oswald not leave her suddenly. Oswald vows that he will not leave her without telling her in person.

To delay the crucial moment when her relationship with him will be determined, Corinne is eager to show the convalescing Oswald the paintings and statues of Rome. Oswald and Corinne have differences of opinion concerning the nature of the subjects the Italian artists chose; these differences reflect the diversity of nations, climates, and religions which the two represent. The following day, they go to see Corinne's paintings at her country estate in Tivoli, where Oswald pleads with Corinne not to hide her past from him any longer. Corinne agrees to discuss it but begs Oswald to wait until the end of Holy Week. Their return to Rome is marked by melancholy.

Corinne announces that she is leaving Oswald for a week. Each year, at the approach of Holy Week, she withdraws to a convent to prepare for Easter. During Corinne's retreat, her maid shows Oswald her mistress's room. He sees locks of hair of Corinne's mother, father, and sister. That of the sister reminds Oswald of the hair of Lucile Edgermond, his intended fiancée. Oswald feels lost and despairing without Corinne. He spends time wandering in the gardens of various monasteries, and also studies the religion of the country by listening to priests' sermons. On Good Friday, Oswald, who has been left cold by Italian ceremony, is strangely moved by the religious service he witnesses in the Sistine Chapel. Suddenly, he spots Corinne among the worshipers. She is quick to sense Oswald's discomfort at the behavior of her fellow Italians and speaks to him of her religious convictions

Immediately after Easter, Oswald decides to depart for Naples. When Corinne asks to accompany him, she is warned by Erfeuil of the risk she runs in going off unmarried with Oswald. Corinne makes Erfeuil promise not to reveal to Oswald the extent to which she is compromising herself. She informs Oswald that she will reveal her secret only upon their arrival in Naples. They depart, Corinne filled with both hope and fear. At first, Oswald allows himself to relax in the sunny south of Italy, instead of spoiling his pleasure by his reflections and regrets. In Naples, a sailor addresses Corinne as Lady Nelvil when she boards an English ship to attend an Anglican church service. Throughout the service, Corinne thinks of her past unhappiness in England and is happy to set foot on Italian soil once again. Oswald, aware of her agitation, relates to Corinne significant events of his past, during a visit to Mt. Vesuvius.

Oswald grew up completely devoted to his father. Before embracing a military career, he expressed a desire to travel. In 1791, his father reluctantly permitted him to spend six months touring France, a country so different from his own. Much to his surprise, the somber Oswald became seduced by the witty social turbulence of Paris. He also found a devoted friend in Count Raimond and became attracted to Raimond's reserved, calculating widowed sister Mme. d'Arbigny, who soon began to dominate him. When Oswald was called back to England by his father, he departed against Mme. d'Arbigny's wishes and also surprised at the tension existing between brother and sister. After a year spent in Scotland with his father, with whom he now formed a deep and mutual affection, Oswald was sent to London on business. There he received a letter from Mme. d'Arbigny, informing him that her brother had been killed by revolutionaries for his loyalty to the king, and begging Oswald to come and save her from dire poverty. Upon being reunited with Mme. d'Arbigny, Oswald soon discovered that she had lied about her fortune and that her sole aim was to gain control over him by marrying him. He refused to marry her without his father's blessing. Oswald's father then ordered him to come home, assuring his son that he would die of grief if Oswald married Mme. d'Arbigny. Mme. d'Arbigny concocted various excuses to restrain Oswald, not the least of which was that she was pregnant with his child. After vacillating for several months because of his weak character, Oswald finally realized once and for all that Mme. d'Arbigny lied and schemed in every way, and he departed for England, eagerly anticipating his father's pardon. Immediately upon his arrival, however, he learned of his father's death.

Twenty months have passed since then and Oswald's father hovers constantly in the background, like a phantom in pursuit of his son. At the moment of his death, Oswald's father was deeply grieved and fearful that his son would marry a woman whom he would find to be unworthy of him, and who would cause Oswald to lose his reputation in England. In spite of Corinne's attempts to assuage his guilt, Oswald still believes himself to be his father's assassin.

The ascent to the top of Vesuvius deeply troubles both Corinne and Oswald. They return to Naples at once. The next day, Corinne becomes extremely upset when Oswald tells her about Lucile Edgermond. She begs him to wait one more week, the last happy one she may ever have, before hearing her confession. Corinne gives a party in honor of Oswald, during the course of which she improvises a poem inspired by the agitation she feels within her soul. The Italians in attendance are disappointed that her poetic inspiration is so sad, but the English guests are filled with admiration, delighted to hear melancholy sentiments expressed with Italian imagination. Oswald then offers Corinne the wedding ring his father gave to his mother. Corinne is extremely reluctant to accept this ring but finally does so because Oswald becomes so distraught.

At long last, Corinne speaks of her past existence. Her Italian mother died when Corinne was ten years old. Corinne remained in Italy to complete her education; but at the age of fifteen, she rejoined her English father in the remote area of England called Northumberland. Her father, Lord Edgermond, remarried and had a second daughter, Lucile, twelve years Corinne's junior, by his second wife. Corinne's stepmother, Lady Edgermond, a very provincial woman intolerant of foreign ways, dominated her stoic husband. Corinne found it very painful to cope with the stultifying way of life imposed upon her. Her stepmother insisted that a woman existed only to care for her husband's household and her children. Corinne, a young Italian woman of genius and great talent, could not accept this attitude. She spent more than four years feeling like a mechanical doll, her only amusement being to teach her little sister Lucile drawing and Italian.

When Corinne reached the age of twenty, her father wished to select a husband for her. Oswald, whom at this point she had never seen but about whom she had heard many favorable things, was considered to be the leading candidate. However, Oswald's father found Corinne to be too lively and decided against the match, under the pretext that his son was too young for her. (He is eighteen months younger!) Shortly thereafter, when Corinne refused to marry her stepmother's nephew, she was condemned by provincial society.

After the sudden death of her father, Corinne became even more despairing. Then twenty-one years of age, she inherited the money left her by both her parents. In spite of her affection for Lucile, Corinne's desire to return to Italy was so strong that she asked her stepmother to permit her to do so. Lady Edgermond, eager to avoid unfavorable public opinion, consented on the condition that Corinne be declared dead and that she live under an assumed name. After some hesitation, Corinne agreed and departed for Italy in order to live again as Corinne, a name she took from a Greek female friend of Pindar. During the five years which have elapsed between her return to Italy and her first meeting with Oswald, she has lived happily and has established her great reputation in Rome. Twice she has rejected marriage in order to preserve her independence and, before meeting Oswald, believed herself destined never truly to love. However, Oswald's melancholy, uncertainty, and severe opinions have only increased her love for him, while greatly disturbing her. She declares that her fate is in his hands; he is free and will always be, even if he causes her death.

Oswald is greatly troubled and filled with many conflicting emotions after learning of Corinne's past. He finally decides that, in three months, he will return to England to see his father's closest friend in order to find out exactly what his father's reasons were for opposing his marriage to Corinne six years previously. If they are insignificant, he will not marry another woman but will not marry Corinne either.

During the days which follow, both Oswald and Corinne suffer greatly. Oswald is now almost certain that he would be going against his father's wishes if he married Corinne. As for Corinne, she would be happy not to marry Oswald as long as he would stay with her. However, she knows that he would love her less if they remained together unmarried, since legalized domestic bliss is his only concept of true happiness. Once they return to Rome, a painful constraint seems to hamper their relationship. Suddenly, Corinne is stricken with a contagious disease. In spite of her entreaties, Oswald remains with her. When Corinne recovers, they decide to travel to Venice.

The sight of Venice fills Corinne's soul with deep melancholy, so little does it resemble Rome and the south of Italy. Nevertheless, she tries to convince herself that Oswald will not leave her. The adulation of the Venetians no longer pleases Corinne as much as it once did, for now she is attempting to disdain her poetic success in order to resemble the modest and retiring Englishwomen Oswald so admires. All the same, convinced that Oswald loves her and will not be jealous, she lets herself be persuaded to perform in a comic opera.

That very night, Oswald informs her that he must leave immediately for England. His regiment is embarking for certain unnamed islands in a month, and no officer may take his wife with him. Furthermore, news of his liaison with Corinne has reached England. Lady Edgermond refuses to recognize Corinne. Oswald insists upon reestablishing Corinne's reputation before permitting her to return to England. Knowing that they will be separated for a year, Corinne resigns herself to Oswald's departure. She insists that Oswald is everything to her and that she will not live if he fails to return to her, or if he ceases to love her. Oswald, seized with convulsions, prostrates himself before her. Corinne forces herself to maintain a calm exterior until Oswald departs. Then, she nearly loses control of herself because of the enormity of her grief.

As Oswald approaches England, memories of his native country occupy him and diminish his grief. When his regiment's expedition is delayed, the frustrated Oswald resolves to go to Northumberland, determined to persuade Lady Edgermond to acknowledge that Corinne is Lord Edgermond's daughter and to render to Corinne the rank and consideration due her. Lucile, with her delicate and restrained nature, makes a favorable impression upon Oswald. However, Oswald's efforts concerning Corinne have an unfavorable effect upon Lady Edgermond, who becomes so agitated that she asks Oswald to leave. Oswald, filled with fear and guilt, then visits his father's estate in Scotland. Mr. Dickson, his father's friend, arrives and shows Oswald the letter his father wrote to Lord Edgermond seven years earlier when he decided against the marriage of Oswald and Corinne. According to Oswald's father, Corinne is too impetuous and imaginative to be happy as an Englishwoman and, with her ability to enchant, would totally dominate Oswald and cause him to abandon his duties as an Englishman. The father ardently hoped that his son will marry Lucile, who embodies all the good qualities of an English-woman. Oswald, despairing, can no longer doubt that marriage to Corinne would be an offense to the memory of his father.

Meanwhile, Corinne has remained alone in Venice, suffering immeasurably while waiting for word from Oswald. She has a presentiment that her feelings for Oswald will cause her to die. Back in England, Oswald vacillates between two horrible choices: breaking Corinne's heart or failing to respect his father. Furthermore, he still awaits word from his regiment. In his letters to Corinne, he conceals his feelings. Corinne, aware of this, leads a sleepless, tormented existence. Finally, after hearing that Oswald's regiment is to leave in six weeks, Corinne, lucid in her knowledge that she will be struck down by fate, decides to go to England to be with him before his departure.

Meanwhile, Oswald has received no letters from Corinne and believes that she has forgotten him. Corinne becomes ill upon her arrival in England but an English family nurses her back to health. One evening, at the theatre, she sees Lucile Edgermond and Oswald. Corinne immediately understands the attraction Lucile has for Oswald. She subsequently discovers that Oswald visits Lucile and the seriously ill Lady Edgermond every day. Corinne, in her despair, believes that Oswald plans to marry Lucile. In fact, he is helping care for Lady Edgermond and is also attempting to negotiate an inheritance for Corinne, whom he believes to be in Italy. He does, however, take Lucile horseback riding in Hyde Park. Corinne goes there clandestinely and becomes convinced that Oswald truly loves Lucile and that he has forgotten her. Nonetheless, she follows Oswald to Edinborgh, determined to have it out with him.

Oswald is now torn between Lucile and Corinne but believes that Corinne has forgotten him. Corinne falls ill once again, half way to Edinborgh, and is unable to continue on her way for a week. She meets up with Mr. Dickson, who tells her that Lucile and Oswald are in love and, were it not for the commitment Oswald previously made in Italy, Oswald would marry Lucile. Corinne arrives at the Edgermond estate, where a party is in progress. Corinne asks an old man to give to Oswald's servant an envelope containing the ring Oswald once gave her as a symbol of their union. She then falls unconscious at the side of the road.

It is Erfeuil who finds Corinne and cares for her. Corinne reads in the newspaper that Lady Edgermond now recognizes her as a member of the family. At the same time, she learns that Oswald and Lucile are to be married. Corinne, knowing her death to be imminent, resigns herself to despair. On Oswald and Lucile's wedding day, Corinne, now one of the living dead, departs for Italy. She asks Erfeuil to tell the Edgermonds that she disclaims her inheritance. Only at a later date may Erfeuil tell Oswald that she has been in England. Corinne goes to Florence rather than Rome, where memories of her past happiness would torment her too much. Since she has lost all interest in life, her efforts to regain her creative talent prove to be futile. Her devoted friend from her years in Rome, the prince Castel-Forte, comes to stay with her. He receives two letters from Oswald, expressing feelings that would have touched Corinne. However, because of the state of her health, Castel-Forte decides not to show them to her.

In the meantime, when Oswald received the envelope containing his ring, he believed Corinne had been unfaithful and, in spite of the fact that he had already abandoned the idea of marrying her, he felt vindictive and precipitously asked for Lucile's hand in marriage.

Mr. Dickson's arrival inadvertently causes Oswald grief when he tells of the devoted young woman he has met. The stunned Oswald is led to conclude that Corinne is the young woman in question. His deep affliction intensifies after hearing details from Erfeuil. Oswald then sets sail with his regiment; he is filled with such grief and remorse that life is unbearable to him. Lucile is deeply upset by Oswald's departure but, because of her husband's state of depression, she says nothing to him of her pregnancy.

Oswald is away for four years. During this time, Lucile gives birth to a daughter and, little by little, learns everything concerning Corinne and her relationship with Oswald. Lucile, feeling jealousy but also pity for Oswald for abandoning Corinne, fears that he may one day do the same to her.

Oswald returns home a military hero. In time of peril while at sea, he has thought of Corinne more than Lucile. At home, he soon becomes bored with the routine life Lady Edgermond imposes upon them. Unfortunately, he and Lucile are unable to communicate their feelings to each other. Oswald's health also suffers, and his doctor advises a sojourn in Italy. After the death of Lady Edgermond, Oswald, Lucile, and Juliette, their four-year-old daughter, leave Northumberland. They experience very bad weather crossing the mountains into Italy. That winter, everything has the look of death about it. Italy seems covered with a dark veil for Oswald as well as Lucile, who is able to explain Oswald's love for the country only in terms of Corinne. Oswald and Lucile become more ill at ease with each other than ever.

Arriving in Florence, Oswald requests permission to see Corinne in order to justify his past behavior. Corinne refuses; he has hurt her too badly. Oswald then writes a moving letter. In her equally impassioned answer, Corinne forgives him and expresses a desire to see Lucile and Juliette. Without consulting Lucile, Oswald has Juliette visit Corinne every day. The child loves Corinne and makes astonishing progress in Italian and music. This is to be Corinne's legacy to Oswald's child. When Lucile learns of this, she becomes jealous and finally expresses her true feelings to Oswald. Suddenly, Lucile's disposition seems to change; she becomes more animated in conversation and less reserved than usual. A visit to her half sister, during which a frank, open conversation takes place, accounts for the drastic change in her behavior. Corinne, before dying, helps Lucile to understand Oswald's nature and his innermost feelings. Her dying wish is that Oswald find in Lucile and Juliette traces of her influence and thereby remember her.

Corinne wishes to bid a final farewell to Italy and to Lord Nelvil by recalling the time when her genius shone in all its splendor. On a cold winter morning, her poetry is read before the Academy of Florence. Many spectators, including Oswald, are in attendance. Corinne, too weak to perform, sits in the shadows while her verses are recited by a young girl, dressed in white. Corinne dies shortly thereafter, with Oswald and Lucile at her bedside.

Oswald nearly loses his reason and his life. He follows Corinne's funeral procession to Rome and lives there as a recluse for a time. Finally, duty and obligation bring him back to his wife and daughter in England, where he then leads an exemplary domestic life.

Prince d'Amalfi, Mme. d'Arbigny, Aunt of Corinne (unnamed), Banker (unnamed), Prince Castel-Forte, Princess Castel-Forte, Corinne, Mr. Dickson, Edgermond, Lady Edgermond, Lord Edgermond, Lucile Edgermond, Count d'Erfeuil, German Lord (unnamed), Mr. Maclinson, M. de Maltigues, Mother (unnamed) of Corinne, Juliette Nelvil, Lord Nelvil, Oswald Lord Nelvil, Old Man (unnamed), Priest (unnamed), Prince (unnamed), Count Raimond, Mrs. Siddons, Thérésine, Women (two, unnamed).

La Cousine Bette, Balzac, 1846.

Célestin Crevel, a former tradesman and an aging roué, vows that he will avenge himself on his contemporary, the equally lecherous Baron Hector Hulot d'Ervy, by taking as his next mistress none other than the virtuous Baroness Adeline Hulot, Hector's devoted wife. Crevel, whose daughter Célestine has married Victorin Hulot, son of Adeline and Hector, has managed to hinder the proposed marriage of their daughter Hortense, who has no dowry because of her father's outrageous expenditures for his mistresses. The noble Adeline suffers greatly because of her husband's amorous escapades but still adores him with an admiring, maternal, and cowardly devotion. She therefore haughtily rejects Crevel's offer to provide the daughter with a dowry if only the mother will agree to be his mistress.

Adeline Hulot's first cousin, Lisbeth Fischer, is a homely old maid who, while remaining independent, is supported in part by the family and accepted as a member of it. This malevolent creature, long envious and jealous of the beautiful Adeline, is gifted with a cunning which is unfathomable to the somewhat gullible family group she has associated herself with for years. One day, Bette, as they call her, announces quite unexpectedly to Hortense Hulot that she has a young "lover," a Polish refugee, Wenceslas Steinbock, who claims to be an artist. The relationship is actually quite pure, that of a rough but maternal female and a submissive, respectful son. Bette lends Steinbock money until he is able to support himself but obliges him to sign a promissory note. She believes that she has succeeded in gaining complete control over the sensitive young Pole.

Hortense happens by chance to meet Steinbock one day at the art dealer's shop where he is employed; the two fall immediately in love. She buys a sculpture Steinbock has crafted. This, his first sale, leads to his appointment to sculpture for the government the monument of Maréchal Montcornet. An attempt is made to conceal all this from cousin Bette. However, an indiscretion on the part of Valérie Marneffe, a courtesan who is not only Bette's equally cunning neighbor but also Hector Hulot's new mistress, spoils everything for the Hulot family. Without realizing how traumatically her news will be received, Valérie reveals to Bette the impending marriage of Steinbock and Hortense. Her whole frame quivering convulsively, the enraged Bette vows to destroy Adeline, who, in her mind, has caused her to be constantly victimized since childhood. Valérie and Bette pledge complete allegiance to each other, agree to work together and to keep secret the fact that Bette knows everything. All of Bette's psychic energy now goes into heaping misfortune upon the Hulot family.

As a means to this end, Bette goads Crevel into renewing his effort to win over Adeline Hulot. She also encourages him to steal Valérie Marneffe away from Hector. In appearance, Bette plans to play the part of the good angel to the entire Hulot family, whereas in reality she is going to avail herself of every opportunity to cause members of the family suffering, without their ever suspecting that she is the source of it.

Hector, constantly contriving to get money, both for his daughter's wedding and for Valérie Marneffe's new apartment, engages in several shady business deals. Adeline must sell her diamonds to help set up her daughter's new house. Valérie uses all her female wiles on Hector so that she may get an invitation to his daughter's wedding. At the reception, Hector makes it obvious to everyone, by his lack of restraint, what the nature of their relationship is, to the consternation of his family.

Three years pass, during which Hector spends enormous sums of money on Valérie. Crevel, who is still intent upon avenging himself on Hulot for stealing away from him a former mistress, has succeeded in becoming Hulot's rival. The foolish Hector, believing Crevel to be too weak a competitor, constantly invites his enamored contemporary to dine with him and his dear Valérie. Meanwhile, cousin Bette pursues with pitiless logic her scheme to ruin Hector and enrich Valérie. She and Valerie have become such close friends that they now function as a team: Bette makes the plans, Valérie executes them. When Valérie declares to Bette that she is sick of old men lovers and that she lusts for Steinbock, Bette declares that her friend shall have him. She in turn is determined to become Madame la Maréchale by marrying Hector Hulot's older brother, an ex-general about to become Maréchal of France. Meanwhile, Bette secretly delights in the misery of her cousin Adeline, abandoned by her husband and in need of money just to run her household. Hortense Hulot Steinbock is not much better off than her mother. Steinbock's execrable marble statue of Montcornet receives condemning reviews and household funds are dwindling. After leaving the influence of the despotic Bette, Steinbock grows averse to hard work. Hortense, in her excessive love, has made a lazy man of him. She now foresees the hour when beggary will await her, her child, and her husband.

Wenceslas Steinbock, unknown to his wife, meets Valérie Marneffe and cannot resist her many charms. When Hortense finds out that her husband is having a secret affair with Valérie, she stages such a scene that Steinbock is forced to cool his heels. In retaliation, Valérie writes a letter to Steinbock informing him that she is carrying his child and contrives to have Hortense see the letter. The aggrieved and outraged Hortense walks out on Steinbock. At the same time, Valérie also leads Hector and Crevel separately to believe that each is the father of the child. (In fact, the father in a certain Baron Montès de Montejanos, Valérie's Brazilian lover who has just returned to Paris after an absence of three years.) Meanwhile, Hector, in his ardor for his beloved mistress Valérie, not only has exhausted all possibilities for spending money on her, including placing his son and daughter-in-law in a precarious financial situation, but is also on the verge of imprisonment, having exhausted his political influence as well.

Bette has now seen the success of her scheme and her hatred gratified to a large extent. Soon to be Madame la Maréchale, she delights in the anticipated joy of reigning supreme over the family which she believes has looked down upon her for so long.

Baron Hector Hulot has soon sunk so low in his profligate ways that he has swindled the government in order to cater to Valérie's every whim. Baroness Adeline Hulot, reduced to complete despair, makes the ultimate sacrifice by offering herself to Crevel if he will pay her the money needed to repay the government. Crevel, thinking that he has already avenged himself on Hulot by taking Valérie away from him, is only momentarily moved by Adeline Hulot's pleading and then rejects her offer. Furthermore, Valérie Marneffe's threat to cast Crevel aside if he gives the pious Baroness a sou completely discourages the old lecher in his generosity.

Discovering his brother's ignominies proves to be fatal to General Hulot. Hector is forced to retire from his important post at the War Office and stay away from public life altogether. The General heaps contempt on him for his cowardice because he will not commit suicide. To save the family honor, the General accumulates all his personal savings, intended for his heirs, and delivers to the War Office the entire sum his younger brother swindled from the government. Three days later, he is dead. Thus, Bette is thwarted in her attempt to be Madame la Maréchale by death, caused indirectly by her own deeds, with assistance from Valérie Marneffe.

Hulot, who has now caused the death of his brother, ruined his family, mortgaged his children's house over and over, and robbed the government till, all for an unscrupulous mistress, flees to the home of his former mistress Josépha and begs her to help him. Allowing himself to fall immediately under her influence, he takes as his next mistress a poverty-stricken young seamstress, Olympe Bijou. Ten days after deserting his family, Hector Hulot, under the name of Thoul, is established, thanks to the funds of Josépha's current lover and benefactor, at the head of an embroidering business, under the name of Thoul and Bijou.

Adeline Hulot hovers between life and death for more than a month. Fortunately, Victorin Hulot is given a generous gift by the War Minister, out of great respect for the late General Hulot and the Baroness Hulot. This enables Victorin to share his home with his mother, his sister who is still estranged from her husband, and with cousin Bette, who consents to be the housekeeper. Bette sees this as a way of continuing to realize her silent vengeance on these people, each an object of her hatred, which is kept growing by the overthrow of her hope to become Madame la Maréchale. Once a month, she goes to see Valérie, encouraged by Hortense, who seeks news of her unfaithful Wenceslas.

About twenty months of relative tranquillity go by. Nevertheless, Bette's persistent hatred will not allow her to stop upsetting the family. One day, she lets her tongue slip when talking about Valérie Marneffe and arouses the prudent suspicions of Victorin Hulot. He resolves to rid his family of this female demon. With the utmost reluctance, he hires a shady character to be responsible for disposing of Mme. Marneffe. The instrument involved in this person's plan is Valérie's Brazilian lover, Baron Montès de Montejanos— who, upon catching Valérie in a compromising position with Steinbock, becomes so insanely jealous that, urged on by Victorin's agent and her friends, he soon successfully administers to his former mistress and to her new husband, Crevel, a poison so deadly that it hideously disfigures the once-beautiful Valérie and the vain old roué. Both of them die in agony a few days later. However, Valérie repents her foul deeds before dying and espouses Christianity. She bequeathes a sum of three hundred thousand francs to Baron Hulot. Hortense Hulot inherits her father's estate. On the day after the funerals, Victorin Hulot silently places eighty thousand-franc notes in the hand of a mysterious friar who comes to collect.

One day shortly thereafter, while doing charity work, the baroness miraculously discovers her beloved Hector, who is currently living with a fifteen-year-old girl in a squalid section of the city. After three years of depravity with a series of uncaring young mistresses, Hector Hulot is now broken, bent, and totally debased. Nevertheless, he is warmly embraced by his saintly wife and by his family. His son pays off his remaining debts.

Bette, by now afflicted with pulmonary consumption, is so miserable at seeing the family apparently prosperous that she cannot bear it. She dies within a week but manages to keep her hatred secret to the painful, bitter end. Indeed, she has the supreme satisfaction of seeing the entire Hulot family standing in tears around her bed, mourning for her, the angel of the family.

Several happy months then go by, during which Hector Hulot seems to have forsworn the fair sex. His subdued behavior eventually reassures his entire family. Then, one night, Adeline, roused from sleep by some unusual noise, discovers her husband in bed with Agathe, their newly hired kitchen maid. The shock is too great for her. Three days later, the dying baroness tells her husband that she has now given him the only think she has left to offer him, her life. These words of reproach, the only ones she ever uttered in her entire life, are her last. The baron leaves Paris three days after his wife's funeral. Eleven months later, at the end of the legal period of mourning, Mlle. Agathe Picquetard becomes the next Baroness Hulot.

Antonia, Art Dealer (unnamed), Mme. de la Bâtie, Mme. de la Baudraye, Beau-Pied, Beauvisage, Berthier, Dr. Horace Bianchon, Mme. Bijou, Olympe Bijou, César Birotteau, Mlle. Birotteau, Bixiou, Braulard, Bridau, Héloïse Brisetout, Jenny Cadine, Carabine (Séraphine Sinet), Mme. de Carigliano, Chanor, Mme. de la Chanterie, M. Chapuzot, Elodie Chardin, Idamore Chardin, Père Chardin, Mme. Colleville, Coquet, Mme. Coquet, Célestin Crevel, Mme. Crevel, Cydalise, Professor Duval, Marquis d'Esgrignon, Mme. d'Espard, Esther, André Fischer, Johann Fischer, Lisbeth (Bette) Fischer, Pierre Fischer, Mme. Fortin, Théodore Gaillard, Giraud, Mme. de Grandlieu, Pierre Grassou, Grenouville, Grindot, Hannequin, Duke Hérouville, Adeline Hulot, Célestine Crevel Hulot, Hector Hulot (Père Thorec, Thoul, Vyder), Mareschal Hulot (Count de Forzheim), Victorin Hulot, Jean, Joseph, Josépha, Atala Judici, Justice of the Peace (unnamed), Keller, Count Laginski, Dr. Larabit, Lebas, Lebas (Jr.), Lebrun, Lenoncourt, Mme. de Lenoncourt, Léon de Lora, Louise, Lousteau, Maid (unnamed), Malaga, Marguerite, Mariette, Jean-Paul-Stanislas Marneffe, Stanislas Marneffe, Valérie Marneffe, Count Martial de la Roche-Hugon, Massol, Mathurine, Mitouflet, Marquis de Montauran, Count Montcornet, Baron Henri Montès de Montejanos, Mme. de Navarreins, Mme. Nourrisson, Nucingen, Olivier, Benjamin Olivier, Mme. Olivier, Count de la Palférine, Count Paz, Agathe Piquetard, Police Officer (unnamed), Pons, Count Popinot, Mlle. Popinot, Mme. Popinot, Count Eugène de

Rastignac, Mme. de Rastignac, Achille Rivet, Mme. Rivet, Rochefide, Roger, Mme. de Saint-Estève, Samanon, Mme. Schontz, Mme. de Sérizy, Hortense Hulot Steinbock, Wenceslas Steinbock, Wenceslas Steinbock (Jr.), Stidman, du Tillet, Reine Tousard, Maxime de Trailles, Mlle. Turguet, Vautrin, Vauvinet, Baron Verneuil, de Vernisset, Claude Vignon, Vraulard, Maréchal Prince de Wissembourg, Mlle. Zaïre.

L'Education sentimentale, Flaubert, 1869.

Frédéric Moreau, whose dream is to be the Walter Scott of France, is on a steamboat, en route from Paris to Nogent-sur-Seine, where his mother lives. Suddenly, he sees a woman who, to him, is the incarnation of all the women he has read about in romances, the luminous point toward which all things converge. Upon his arrival in Nogent-sur-Seine, he cannot force his mind to stop thinking of Mme. Marie Angèle Arnoux.

Frédéric's best friend from his school days, Charles Deslauriers, comes to visit and informs Frédéric that he cannot afford to live with him in Paris the following year. This is the first of Frédéric's dreams to crumble into dust. Deslauriers, who is passionately interested in politics, encourages his friend to mix with the rich set and pave the way for his own eventual arrival there.

Two months later, Frédéric finds himself in Paris, bored with both his law studies and his extracurricular activities. He sinks into the lowest depths of idleness and depression. Efforts to meet Mme. Arnoux at *L'Art Industriel,* her husband Jacques Arnoux's business establishment, fail. He passes his first-year law examinations indifferently.

One morning, a year later, while witnessing a student demonstration, Frédéric meets Hussonet, who works as a clerk for Jacques Arnoux. Hussonet takes Frédéric to *L'Art industriel,* where he soon begins to make regular appearances in an effort to see Mme. Arnoux. He quickly becomes aware not only of the owner's vulgarity but also of his lack of probity. In addition to acquiring money through suspect political connections, Arnoux supports more than one mistress.

Finally, one evening, Arnoux invites Frédéric home to dinner. All evening long, Frédéric yearns to be an older man in order to be more appealing to Mme. Arnoux. Even after he has left her, he continues to experience the sensation of having been transported into a higher world.

At this moment, Deslauriers arrives in Paris. He and Frédéric believe that the life of which they have long dreamed is now beginning. Frédéric, who has decided to become a painter for the time being, paints exotic scenes while Deslauriers, who still aspires to political power, works as a clerk in a solicitor's office and lends Frédéric money. The latter continues to frequent Arnoux's establishment and follows his advice with docility in order to be invited to the

Arnoux residence for dinner again. During these dinners he scarcely utters a word. Instead, he gazes at Mme. Arnoux and observes every detail about her. Frédéric and Deslauriers have Saturday gatherings in their apartment, inviting friends they have in common. When the day of Frédéric's second-year law examinations arrives, he is ill prepared and fails them. He spends the entire summer in Paris, his melancholy aggravated by a lack of occupation, Mme. Arnoux having left Paris for the summer. When she returns, he continues to dine with her on Thursdays but lacks the courage to declare his love. Curiously enough, he feels in no way jealous of Arnoux nor can he picture Mme. Arnoux undressed; her sex recedes into a mysterious background. Nevertheless, his passion causes his nerves to become unstrung. Deslauriers encourages him to have an affair, but this kind of relationship is distasteful to Frédéric; he declares that he loves only Mme. Arnoux, without mental reservation, without any hope of his love being returned.

The following summer, after spending an afternoon with the Arnoux family, Frédéric dreams that he delivers an impassioned, sublime discourse in court, which prompts Mme. Arnoux to praise him. The next morning, his intellect becomes more active and vigorous than before. Having long since abandoned painting, he buries himself in study until August, at which time he passes his final examination.

Upon his return home to Nogent-sur-Seine for what is intended to be a brief visit, his mother places their situation before him in its true colors. They have very little money left. Frédéric, who has implied to Arnoux that he has a fortune coming to him, feels outraged and humiliated. How can he ever see Mme. Arnoux again? He succumbs to his mother's implorings and remains in Nogent. Months go by as Frédéric spends most of his time daydreaming. He befriends the emotional adolescent Louise and reads romances and dramatic works to her. Just as he is allowing himself to slide into provincial habits and his love to assume a character of mournful sweetness, his rich uncle Barthélémy dies, leaving him a large inheritance. In spite of his aging mother's protests, Frédéric hastens to return to Paris, dreaming of the elegant surroundings in the midst of which he will entertain Mme. Arnoux.

Upon his arrival there, Frédéric discovers to his horror that the Arnoux family has moved and that Arnoux is no longer in the art trade. After a frantic search, he locates them at their new residence, which is above a shop where Arnoux is now a dealer in earthenware. Frédéric is astonished to admit to himself that, in a less elegant environment, Mme. Arnoux has lost some of her fascination. He then discovers not only that Deslauriers has quit his post as law clerk to devote himself to radical politics but also that, having failed his examinations, he is having difficulty surviving. Frédéric barely listens to Deslauriers's impassioned political outbursts; he is too immersed in his own thoughts of what he will buy for himself. One night, he attends a wild, all-night party with Arnoux and, to his surprise, comes away from it with a thirst for women, for licentious pleasure, and all that Parisian life has to offer.

Frédéric immediately pays handsomely for a small mansion which he spares no expense to furnish. Then, eager to become acquainted with Parisian high society, he pays a visit to the respectable, bourgeois Dambreuses, then calls on Rosanette Bron (also known as the Maréchale), hostess of the wild party and the mistress of Arnoux. The following day, Frédéric calls on Arnoux and is pleased to see Mme. Arnoux, in spite of his new feelings toward her. The following Sunday, he invites his old friends, including Deslauriers, to a housewarming. The party is less than successful because of political quarrels and criticism of Frédéric's taste.

Frédéric continues to frequent both the residence of Arnoux and that of Arnoux's mistress, Rosanette. He discovers that he has a strong physical attraction to Rosanette, but she resists his advances. His association with two so very different women causes them to blend gradually with one another in his mind. A letter from his mother reminds him that he has still not decided upon a career. Although his intellectual ambitions have abandoned him once again, he decides to try to use the influence of Dambreuse to find a position, mainly because Mme. Arnoux also encourages him. At a party given by the Dambreuses, Frédéric observes how dull and mechanical the conversation is. Then he happens to visit the Arnoux couple while they are in the midst of a heated dispute, Mme. Arnoux having caught her husband in an act of infidelity and lying about it. Suddenly, Frédéric finds himself in the position of intermediary.

An existence of misery begins for him. He becomes the parasite of the house, finding himself in daily attendance there. Soon, Mme. Arnoux confides in him and relates many details of her life, which she considers to be a failure. Frédéric declares that his own life is also a failure, but he is too fainthearted to tell Mme. Arnoux why. When Frédéric is not with her, he is with Arnoux, whom he wants to hate but cannot, a fact for which he reproaches himself. He finally visits his friend Deslauriers, whom he has long neglected and whom he finds more passionately political than ever. Deslauriers asks Frédéric to use his influence with Dambreuse to get him money to establish a journal. Instead, Frédéric ends up lending the money to Arnoux, now on the brink of financial ruin. Shortly thereafter, Mme. Arnoux visits Frédéric to ask him to use his influence with Dambreuse to save her husband and family. Dambreuse offers the aimless young man a position as general secretary of a corporation of which he is director, but Frédéric fails to keep a necessary appointment with Dambreuse to obtain the post. Instead, he seizes a chance to see Mme. Arnoux alone in the country. Quick to sense his hidden meaning when he broaches the subject of passion, she tactfully but clearly rejects him. Frédéric refuses to accept this and, flattering himself that he will make Mme. Arnoux jealous, goes off to the races with Rosanette. Surprisingly enough, Frédéric finds Mme. Arnoux there. Upon seeing him, she turns pale and quickly disappears. He then feels that an irreparable thing has happened, that this is the end of his great love. And Rosanette, the gay and easy love, is there beside him. Full of conflicting desires, no longer even knowing what he wants, he is possessed by a feeling of infinite sadness, a longing to die.

A few days later, however, Frédéric becomes so enraged when his drunken dinner party host, the Vicomte de Cisy, insults both Rosanette and Mme. Arnoux that he becomes violent and ends up being challenged to a duel. But the duel never takes place, in spite of elaborate preparations, because de Cisy, who is even more terrified than Frédéric, faints. This incident and disputes he has with friends and other social acquaintances cause Frédéric to believe that he has become the laughingstock of society. Feeling an intellectual void in his life, he seeks out his faithful friend, Deslauriers, who embraces him warmly.

In view of Frédéric's sagging finances, Deslauriers, acting as his attorney, encourages him to return home to Nogent to see for himself how good a match he might make with Louise, illegitimate daughter of the wealthy but plebeian Roques. Roques has acquired his wealth by making shady legal investments for his employer, Dambreuse. This possible marital match is applauded by Frédéric's mother. For his part, Roques cherishes the deep-rooted ambition of having his daughter marry into nobility like the Moreau family. A week after Frédéric's return, without any formal engagement being announced, Frédéric is regarded as Louise Roques's "intended."

Meanwhile, during Frédéric's absence, Deslauriers, jealous of his friend, tries unsuccessfully to seduce Mme. Arnoux. He then spitefully informs her that Frédéric is going to be married. Her reaction is so extreme that she is forced to acknowledge to herself that she must love him. Back in Nogent, Louise makes it clear that she is passionately in love with Frédéric. He, feeling pressure on all sides, invents a story in order to return to Paris to reflect, telling everyone, and himself believing, that he will soon go back home.

Upon his arrival in the capital, Frédéric derives no pleasure from life and resolves to engage no more in fruitless passion. However, a chance encounter with Mme. Arnoux rekindles his passion for her. They pour out their hearts to each other. All the precautions they take to hide their love serve only to strengthen it. Finally, Mme. Arnoux agrees to meet Frédéric at an apartment he has rented. The time of the rendezvous arrives, but she fails to appear because her young son is violently ill. Attempts by Frédéric to send a message to her home and receive a reply fail. As a result, his wounded pride takes possession of him and he vows to forget Mme. Arnoux. On this day, an insurrection is taking place in Paris in which friends of Frédéric are participants. Oblivious to this, Frédéric, on impulse, visits Rosanette, whose latest lover has just left her, and, after taking her to the apartment where he intended to make love with Mme. Arnoux, he spends the night with her instead, his physical yearning for Rosanette finally satisfied.

The next morning, Frédéric, roused from sleep by discharges of musketry, finds himself a spectator at one episode in the Revolution of 1848 and joins the throng in rejoicing at the overthrow of Louis-Philippe. Dambreuse, who now fears for his fortune because of his political alliance with the deposed king, convinces Frédéric that he should declare his candidacy for deputy. His appearance at a rally, however, is a disaster, prompting him to abandon the idea. One morning, upon leaving Rosanette's apartment, he encounters Arnoux, now a member of the National Guard, and is quick to find out that Arnoux is seeing Rosanette again, on the sly. When Frédéric insists that Rosanette choose between him and Arnoux, she tells him that she loves only him. During the course of an idyllic trip to Fontainebleau, they hear that a terrible battle has stained Paris with blood and that Frédéric's friend, Dussardier, has been wounded. Suddenly, Frédéric's sense of duty surges to the fore and, in spite of Rosanette's sobs and entreaties, he makes his way back to Paris. At the same time, Roques, accompanied by Louise, has arrived in Paris to serve in the National Guard.

Some time later, Frédéric meets Mme. Arnoux at the Dambreuses'; his passion is quickly reawakened, but she is cool to him. However, Louise, also a guest there, makes open advances to Frédéric and asks him to marry her. He departs in great haste and rushes to Rosanette's house, where he has been spending each night for three months. Upon discovering that Frédéric has a mistress, Louise is heartbroken.

Eventually, Frédéric is asked by Arnoux to pay a call on his wife. He finds Mme. Arnoux alone. In response to a sarcastic remark he makes, she reveals to him why she failed to keep their rendezvous months before. His attempt to embrace her meets with no resistance. This tender scene is suddenly interrupted by the arrival of Rosanette, who insists that Frédéric leave with her. He is crushed to learn that she is pregnant and, once again, sees his hopes with regard to Mme. Arnoux dashed forever. Rosanette becomes a bore to him, so he is eager to attend social events at the Dambreuse mansion in order to be rid of her for a few hours. Political verbiage and good living have their effect on his morality; mediocre though these people may be, Frédéric feels proud of knowing them and longs for bourgeois respectability. As a means to this end, he succeeds in seducing Mme. Dambreuse and finds himself admiring his perversity, since he continues to spend each night with Rosanette.

The impoverished Deslauriers, totally disillusioned by his political experience with the working class, is then taken in by Frédéric, who promises to find him a situation through Dambreuse. Unfortunately, the latter, suddenly taken ill, dies. Mme. Dambreuse now wishes to possess Frédéric and resents the fact that he shares her with Rosanette, who has, meanwhile, given birth to his child, who dies after several months of neglect.

When he hears that Arnoux, who has since become a dealer in religious objects, will be ruined and forced into exile if he cannot procure a large sum of money, Frédéric, fearing that he will never see Mme. Arnoux again, rushes to the rescue. He is too late, however, since Arnoux, his wife, and children have fled Paris. Frédéric turns on Rosanette and makes a definitive break with her. Just before his marriage to Mme. Dambreuse is to take place, Frédéric forsakes her as well; at an auction they attend, she insists upon purchasing a little chest which once belonged to Mme. Arnoux and which evokes within him very dear memories. Frédéric now feels lost amid the wreck of his dreams and ambitions, sick at heart, full of grief, and disappointed. Suddenly, he finds himself longing for the repose of provincial life. He arrives in Nogent-sur-Seine just in time to catch a glimpse of the postwedding procession of Louise and Deslauriers. Vanquished and crushed, he returns immediately to Paris.

Frédéric travels, unceasingly filled with melancholy. He returns home, mingles in society, and conceives attachments to other women, but the constant recollection of his first love makes all of them appear insipid. His intellectual ambitions grow even weaker. Years pass. Frédéric is forced to bear the burden of a life in which his mind is unoccupied and his heart devoid of energy.

Toward the end of March 1867, he receives an unexpected visit from Mme. Arnoux. They discuss their fond memories of each other and their love, even though they never belonged to each other. Frédéric declares to himself that he regrets nothing he has suffered in the past on her account. He is seized with a fierce, desperate desire to possess her, yet does not, partly through prudence, partly through a resolve not to degrade his ideal. She cuts a long lock of her hair, which is now white, and gives it to him, before saying goodbye forever. And this is all.

Toward the beginning of the following winter, Frédéric and Deslauriers, whose wife has eloped with a singer, chat by the fireside, once more reconciled by the fatality of their nature, which has always caused them to reunite and be friends once again. They try to confront their destinies by summarizing their lives. Both have failed, the one who dreamed only of love and the other who dreamed only of power. They relate to each other an experience they shared as adolescents and acknowledge that it was the best time they ever had.

Mme. Alessandri, Alexandre, Mme. Alexandre, Allard, Marquise d'Amaegui, Apollonie, Apothecary (unnamed), Architect (unnamed), Eugène Arnoux, Jacques Arnoux, Mme. Marie Angèle Arnoux, Marthe Arnoux, Georgine Aubert, Augers Sisters (two), Marquis Gilbert des Aulnays, Thérèse Bachelu, Balandard, Barillot, Barthelémy, Hortense Baslin, Beaumont, Mme. Benoît, Berthelmot, Bertinaux, Joseph Boffreu, Bou-Maza, Antenor Braive, Rosanette Bron (la Maréchale), Bugneaux, Jules Burrieux, Catherine, Godefroy Cavaignac, Célestin, Chambrion, Alfred de Cisy, Dr. Colot, Baron de Comaing, Compain, Count (unnamed), Dambreuse, Cécile Dambreuse, Mme. Dambreuse, Clémence Daviou, Delmar, Delphine, Deslauriers, Charles Deslauriers, Mme. Deslauriers, Dr. Des Rogis, Dittmer, Duchess (unnamed), Ducretot, Auguste Dussardier, Eléonore, Félix, Flacourt, Anselme de Forchambeaux, Fumichon, Gamblin, Athanase Gautherot, Paul de Gremonville, Captain Herbigny, Heudras, Hussonnet, Irma, Isidore, Père Issac, Miss John, Jumillac, Adolphe Langlois, Jean-Jacques Langreneux, de Larsilloix, Mme. de Larsilloix, Leboeuf, Lebrun, Lefaucheur, Oscar Lefebvre, Mme. Lombard, Théophile Lorris, Mlle. Loulou, Lovarias, Baptiste Martinon, Saul Mathias, Pierre Paul Meinsius, Mignot, Milliet, Duchess de Montreuil-Nantua, Frédéric Moreau, Mme. Moreau, Moussinot, Negress (unnamed), Michel Evariste Népomucène, de Nonancourt, Charles Jean-Baptiste Oudry, Mme. Oudry, Count de Palazot, Pellerin, Pilon, Pinson, Prouharam, Regimbart, Mme. Regimbart, Mme. de Remoussat, Mme. de Rochegune, Samuel Rondelot, Roque, Elisabeth Olympe Louise Roque, Rosenwald, Mme. de Saint-Florentin, Saint-Valéry, Sainville, Sénécal, Sombary, Spaniard (unnamed), Théodore, Prince Tzernoukoff, Vanneroy, Mlle. Vandael, Mlle. Clémence Vatnaz, Vautier, Vezou, Vourdat, Wine Merchant (unnamed), Woman (unnamed).

Eugénie Grandet, Balzac, 1833.

Enormously wealthy and ferociously avaricious, Félix Grandet has become the most famous citizen of the somber provincial town of Saumur. For obvious reasons, representatives of two prosperous Saumur families, the Cruchots and the Des Grassins, rival each other for the hand of Eugénie, the Grandets' only child, who lives almost as a recluse, reminding one of a flower which is wilting for lack of light. On Eugénie's twenty-third birthday in 1819, both families come to pay their respects but do not fool Grandet, who merely tolerates them in order to use them when it suits his purposes. However, Eugénie, like her oppressed mother, all too innocent and unaware of her father's great wealth, is genuinely touched by the gifts presented to her. The essence of provincial life is depicted during this birthday celebration.

The party is interrupted by the unexpected arrival from Paris of Charles Grandet, Eugénie's first cousin. Charles, attired in the latest fashions of the Paris dandy, contrasts sharply with the slovenliness of the provincials gathered around the lotto table. The unsophisticated Eugénie looks upon her cousin as a creature who has descended from some celestial region. Very abruptly, love illuminates her life and gives it meaning.

Charles's widower father, Victor Grandet, has sent him to Saumur bearing a letter for Félix Grandet, the contents of which are unknown to Charles. In the letter to his brother, the Parisian Grandet announces his bankruptcy and imminent suicide, and begs Félix to be Charles's guardian. Upon hearing of Charles's great misfortune, Eugénie's pity causes her instant love to bloom fully. She enrages her miserly father, already resentful that his nephew has been dumped on him, by insisting that money be spent on Charles that the family has never spent on itself.

In the meantime Grandet, who has already decided that Charles will be sent off to the Indies, determines to trick the Paris creditors and save his dead brother's honor without its costing him or his nephew a penny. As a means to this end, he invites the Cruchots to dinner, at which time he feigns ignorance as a means of getting the Cruchots to discuss at great length how he can redeem the bankruptcy notes. Judge Cruchot offers to go to Paris to settle the matter, but the banker Des Grassins rushes in and steals the job away from Cruchot by offering to go without financial reimbursement. Late that night, Grandet, assisted by Nanon, his blindly devoted servant, loads barrels of gold into a carriage and then goes off into the night in the direction of Angers, where he will sell the gold at a tremendous price.

Eugénie, having heard a moan from Charles's room, is awakened and secretly witnesses her father's departure. Upon entering Charles's room, she discovers two unsealed letters the young man wrote before falling asleep. In the first, Charles breaks off his relations with his mistress because of his current situation. In the second, he asks a friend to take charge of his affairs and get as much as possible for his few remaining worldly possessions. When Charles awakens, Eugénie does not hesitate to offer her cousin her entire savings of valuable gold coins. The enamored young woman fails to understand that Charles's expression of affection for her is not completely without calculation. As the time of his departure draws near, Charles tells Eugénie that he loves her. She insists that she will wait for him to return rather than marry someone else. Eugénie's innocence momentarily sanctifies Charles's love. His departure is a sorrowful one for all except Grandet, who immediately begins a series of sly and ultimately successful maneuvers to reduce his brother's debts.

Eugénie's sorrow over Charles's departure causes her beauty to take on a new character; she is filled with radiance and strength. After several months, her father asks to look once again at her savings, her valuable gold coins. Although terrified at the prospect of having to admit to her father that she has given them to Charles, Eugénie's conscience and, especially, her love give her strength to endure her father's wrath and vengeance. Her refusal to reveal what she has done with the money results in her being confined to her room on a diet of bread and water. Mme. Grandet, already in delicate health, becomes critically ill because of her husband's extreme behavior. Only when he discovers that, if his wife should die, he will have to divide his property with Eugénie, can Grandet, whose monomania has soared to new heights, bring himself to forgive Eugénie. He relents almost too late, for Mme. Grandet dies immediately thereafter. The day after the funeral, Eugénie, prodded by her father, agrees to relinquish her rights to her mother's estate.

Grandet does not delay in initiating his daughter into his miserly ways. Five years go by without a single memorable event to relieve the monotonous existence of Eugénie and her father. Then, Grandet is suddenly stricken with paralysis. Although his death is imminent, the old man's avarice instinctively persists. He dies attempting to seize the gold crucifix the priest puts to his lips. Eugénie is left a thirty-year-old heiress worth millions.

In her case, wealth gives Eugénie neither power nor consolation. The "pack of hounds," particularly the Cruchots, continues its pursuit of Eugénie and her fortune; but, after seven long years, her thoughts are only of Charles. Meanwhile, Charles has made his fortune in the Indies and elsewhere in the world, as a slave trader and by other less than honorable means. His heart is quick to grow cold; soon he feels nothing for Eugénie. On his return crossing to France he negotiates a marriage with a plain young woman of the nobility whose family name he will adopt in exchange for a share of his fortune. Considering Eugénie to be nothing more than a creditor, Charles writes her a letter, breaking the vows he once made and informing her of his plans. Eugénie suffers this deep personal tragedy in silence for the rest of her life but gives immediate proof of her unwavering devotion by paying in full the remaining debts of Charles's father in order that Charles, who has refused to pay them, not be dishonored. She agrees to marry Judge Cruchot de Bonfons, who has sought her hand and fortune for years, imposing upon him the condition that they have a childless marriage. In her heart, she conserves her inextinguishable love for Charles.

At the age of thirty-six, Eugénie finds herself a widow with an enormous annual income. She continues to live alone as she lived in her childhood home, sunless and cold, gloomy and melancholy. This loving woman, created to be a magnificent wife and mother, has neither husband nor children nor family. She lives out her life donating the bulk of her fortune to institutions of charity.

Alphonse, Annette, Mme. d'Aubrion, Mlle. Mathilde d'Aubrion, Marquis d'Aubrion, M. Bergerin, M. de la Bertellière, M. Buisson, Mme. Campan, Duchess de Chaulieu, Cornoiller, Cruchot, Cruchot (de Bonfons), Abbé Cruchot, Fessard, Florine, Marquis de Froidfond, Mme. de la Gaudinière, Mme. Gentillet, Charles Grandet (Carl Sepherd), Eugénie Grandet, Félix Grandet, Mme. Grandet, Victor-Ange-Guillaume Grandet, Des Grassins, Adolphe des Grassins, Mme. des Grassins, Mlle, de Gribeaucourt, Jean, Jean François Keller, M. des Lupeaulx, Merchant (unnamed), Nanon, Baron de Nucingen, Mme. d'Orsonval, Perrotet, Porter (unnamed), Roguin, Souchet.

Germinal, Zola, 1885.

Etienne Lantier, the son of Gervaise Macquart, is a sincere young workman endowed with a strong, if undeveloped, intelligence. After nearly freezing to death in the cold, while searching for a job, he finds work in the Voreux, one of a series of coal mines in Montsou, in northern France. During his first day on the job, he is so outraged by the deplorable working conditions which the dehumanized miners tolerate that he considers going away. Then, something within Etienne determines him to go down again into the mine, to suffer with the miners and to fight the injustice of their situation.

Befriended by the pikeman Maheu, his wife Maheude, and their large family, Etienne becomes a boarder in their dwelling place in the settlement, built by the mining company. This permits Maheude to manage to make ends meet, without begging less than honorable merchants, such as Maigrat, for food and loans in exchange for lovemaking. On the brink of despair, the women of the settlement are often reduced to this in order to save their children from starvation. These pathetic people, with their waxy flesh and their discolored hair, are stunted by degeneration, gnawed by anemia, and tainted with the melancholy ugliness of the undernourished.

Several months go by. Because of the excellent quality of his work, Etienne earns the respect of his fellow workers, with the exception of Chaval, the bullying lover of Maheu's teenage daughter, Catherine. The management of the mine becomes more severe than ever in imposing fines on the workers for the slightest infraction of their unreasonable rules. As life drags on, a deep discontent foments in the pit. Etienne becomes friendly with Souvarine, a young engineman at the Voreux. Souvarine, born of a noble Russian family, has rejected his background and lives in exile as a member of the working class. He and Etienne frequently exchange ideas. Etienne, a Marxist, throws himself into the struggle of labor against capital. He is enthusiastic about the International Working Men's Association, believing that, within months, the workers of the world will rise and unite to assure the laborer that he will receive the bread he has earned. Souvarine, on the contrary, rejects evolution;

he is an anarchist who believes that only by the complete destruction of this rotten world does a better one have a chance of growing up in its place.

Etienne, clinging to his ideals, becomes an obstinate propagandist. As a first step, he convinces his fellow miners of the wisdom of establishing a provident fund. He has books sent to him, among them a medical book entitled *L'Hygiène du mineur,* in which is summed up the evils of which the miners are dying. His somewhat ill-digested reading further excites his brain, and his heart bursts with indignation against the oppressors while he looks forward to the approaching triumph of the oppressed. He believes that one day there will be no more demeaning labor like that which was once a punishment for convicts.

The whole settlement now tends to group around Etienne. The company, feeling threatened, becomes hostile. It suspends output in all the pits. Seized by panic at the growing industrial crisis, it forces its workers to take rest days without pay, thereby economizing out of the miners' pockets. The workers' sense of outrage now reaches the boiling point. The ideas sown by Etienne spring up and expand in a cry of revolt. He declares that, if the company wants a strike, it shall soon have one.

During the week that follows, work goes on suspiciously, in expectation of the conflict. The Maheu family experiences more than one setback during this period. Catherine is forced by Chaval to leave her family and live with him, thereby depriving them of another breadwinner, in addition to the grandfather, nicknamed Bonnemort, now too crippled to work. Then, suddenly, a landslip occurs in the mine, killing one man and crippling one of the young Maheu children, making him unable to earn money. Maheu, the father, becomes seriously ill with fever for a time. It appears that the family will starve to death. Etienne declares that the time is at hand.

The miners strike. Maheu and Etienne plead their case eloquently before Hennebeau, the mine manager, but their words fall on deaf ears. Two weeks pass. The strike becomes even more widespread in the region. Hunger and cold threaten to destroy the settlement. Etienne becomes the strikers' unquestioned leader. He arranges a meeting at which Pluchart, his mentor from Lille, comes to speak. Before the policemen break up the gathering, the coal miners of Montsou vote by acclamation to become members of the International.

Two more weeks pass; the agony of the miners grows even greater. The money sent by the International supplies bread for only three days, and then nothing more arrives. Attempts to negotiate with Hennebeau fail once again. The miners' excess of misery makes them even more obstinate; they resolve to die rather than surrender. At a rally in a nearby glade, Etienne incites them to take action against those miners from nearby pits who have not observed the strike. There is a mad outburst of faith as these people, emptied by famine, see red, and dream of fire and blood in the midst of a glorious apotheosis from which will arise universal happiness.

Meanwhile, the miners at Jean-Bart, a neighboring mine, have decided to resume work, at the urging of Chaval, who has defected from the Voreux pit and who has been led by the manager of Jean-Bart to believe that he will soon be promoted to captain. The Jean-Bart miners soon come to regret their decision because the Voreux men attack their pit, cut the cables, and cause the miners below, including Chaval and Catherine, almost to die of suffocation. The mine is vacated and left in a shambles.

The troop marches on from pit to pit, with Etienne in command, all chanting: "Bread! Bread!" Increasing in number as they go and intoxicated by gin which has been pillaged from a captain's quarters, they become madmen, breaking everything, sweeping away everything, with the force of a torrent which gains strength as it moves. Chaval, taken prisoner by the mob, is nearly killed; Etienne finally decides to let him go free. Continuing their chant, they arrive before the villa of Hennebeau and riddle it with stones. In spite of Etienne's efforts to control them, nobody any longer obeys him. He is finally able to divert the crowd to the shop of Maigrat, the merchant who has exploited them for so long. Maigrat is killed in a fall, while trying to prevent the plundering of his store. His inert mouth is stuffed with dirt, his genitalia torn from his dead body and then paraded about on a stick, like a banner. Only the immediate arrival of the police, summoned by the traitor Chaval, succeeds in dispersing the mob. Warned by Catherine, Etienne and the others flee for their lives.

Two more weeks pass. The military now occupies Montsou. Etienne, denounced by Chaval to the authorities, has been forced into hiding, where he thinks about the difficulty of organizing the workers. He truly wishes to be their leader and to enlarge their horizon, but reflection only makes him feel depressed. Upon paying a visit to Maheu and his family, now in its last agony, he shudders at the sight of these totally destitute people. He experiences the repugnance and discomfort of the workman who has risen above his class, refined somewhat by study and stimulated by ambition. His suggestion that they succumb and go back to work is savagely rejected by Maheude, who wishes that her entire family perish rather than return to their old misery as workers. Alzire, their crippled child, age eight, is the first to die. Etienne despairs even more upon hearing a rumor that the International is losing ground, being slowly destroyed by inner struggles. The idea of death, which has already touched him, fixes itself in his head once again, as a last hope. Death is not long in coming for several of the strikers. A large band of men and women from the settlement arrive at the pit, determined to die rather than allow workers from Belgium, hired as their replacements, to enter the mine.

The last to die in the ensuing skirmish is Maheu, struck in the heart by a soldier's bullet.

After this disaster, the strikers in the settlement turn on Etienne. They blame him for all their misfortune and even throw bricks at him. He is irritated by their lack of intelligence in making him their scapegoat, and also experiences disgust at his own powerlessness to tame these brutes. When the company makes certain concessions to quiet the scandal caused by the bloodshed, Catherine Maheu, abused and abandoned by Chaval, declares to Etienne that she is going down into the Voreux again. Etienne, who has secretly loved Catherine all the while, decides to return to work with her.

Meanwhile, Souvarine, intransigent in his anarchism, executes his plan of destruction. He will, at last, kill the Voreux, that evil beast with ever-open jaws which has swallowed so much human flesh! By creating additional defects in the already unsafe mine, Souvarine is only too successful in his effort. The pit, swallowed whole by an avalanche of earth and a deluge of springs, soon sinks into the abyss.

About twenty miners remain trapped below, among them Catherine and the two men in her life, who find themselves pitted against each other one last time. The inevitable fight to the finish ensues between them. Etienne, beside himself with rage, crushes the sadistic Chaval's skull. Then, resigned to death, Etienne and Catherine lie in wait. Nine days go by. Catherine can endure no more. After lapsing into several hallucinatory fits brought on by inanition, she dies in Etienne's arms. He too has nearly succumbed by the time the miners succeed in rescuing him, fifteen days after the disaster.

Six weeks later, having recovered his health, Etienne leaves the mining community. He is going to Paris, obeying the summons of his mentor, Pluchart. After two and a half months of striking, the miners have returned to the pits, conquered by hunger, and obliged to accept the conditions for which they originally went on strike. But in the farewells Etienne exchanges with them, he feels handshakes both warm with restrained anger and quivering with future rebellion. In that of Maheude, forced by dire necessity to work in the pit, he feels again the long, silent pressure of his mates, giving him a rendezvous for the day when they will begin again. It will be soon and this time it will be the final blow.

It is April. In spite of momentary doubts, Etienne believes that his basic intelligence will sustain him, that he has sown the wild oats of his spite, and that his failure in Montsou was due to a lack of method. He vaguely divines that lawful methods may someday be more effective in fighting the bourgeois. As he walks down the road to catch his train for Paris, the April sun shines in glory and warms the pregnant earth. As the fields are germinating, Etienne envisages an army of men germinating slowly in the furrows, whose germination will soon overturn the earth.

Achille, Annutchka, Bakunin, Bonnemort, Louis Bouteloup, la Brûlée, Captain (unnamed), Carouble, Chaval, Chicot, Commissioner (unnamed), Cook (unnamed), Count de Cougny, Dansaert, la Dansaert, Deneulin, Jeanne Deneulin, Lucie Deneulin, Mme. Désir, Désirée, Baron Desrumeaux, Fleurance, Francis, Cécile Grégoire, Eugéne Grégoire, Félicien Grégoire, Honoré Grégoire, Léon Grégoire, Mme. Grégoire, Hennebeau, Mme. Hennebeau, Hippolyte, Honorine, Abbé Joire, Joiselle, Jules, Etienne Lantier, Legoujeux, Levaque, Bébert Levaque, la Levaque, Philomène Levaque, Alzire Maheu, Catherine Maheu, Estelle Maheu, Guillaume Maheu, Henri Maheu, Jeanlin Maheu, Léonore Maheu, Mme. Maheu (la Maheude), Nicholas Maheu, Toussaint Maheu, Vincent Maheu, Zacharie Maheu, Maigrat, Mme. Maigrat, Mélanie, Mouque, Mouquet, Mouquette, Mme. Négrel, Paul Négrel, Pierron, Lydie Pierron, la Pierronne, Piquette, Pluchart, Quandieu, Abbé Ranvier, Rasseneur, Mme. Rasseneur, Richomme, Rose, Smelten, Souvarine, Dr. Vanderhaghen, Verdonck, Woman (unnamed).

Gil Blas de Santillane, Lesage, 1715-35.

Gil Blas is the major French representative of the *pícaro,* a character firmly established by the anonymous Spanish author or authors of *Lazarillo de Tormes* (1554). The *pícaro* typically is a hero (or antihero) of very humble origin who relates his experiences with a series of masters. These experiences form an episodic framework through which many of the manners and customs of the period are satirized. *Gil Blas de Santillane* is supposedly the autobiography of a certain Gil Blas, who tells the story of his education in (quite literally) the school of "hard knocks."

***

The tone of Gil Blas's relationship with the spiritual and legal offerings of society is set as we follow him on the first of his seemingly endless adventures. At the age of seventeen, after being educated by an ignorant priest, he is sent off on foot to continue his studies at the University of Salamanca. En route, the naïve young man is robbed of his money. Fleeing into the woods, he meets highwaymen who take him to their underground hideout, where he is to serve as their valet.

After a futile attempt at escape, Gil Blas decides to play the hypocrite in order to be allowed to accompany the thieves and eventually get away. His first experience as a highwayman, six months later, fails because he is duped by a monk. Shortly thereafter, the thieves attack a coach, murder four men and capture a young woman who has fainted. Gil Blas feigns illness in order to avoid accompanying them on their next expedition. During the thieves' absence, he and the young woman escape.

The grief-stricken doña Mencia de Mosquera reveals to Gil Blas that her husband was one of the four men murdered by the thieves. Gil Blas is soon arrested, and the judge and his associates rob him of his money. After his release from prison, Gil Blas discovers that doña Mencia has retired to a convent to mourn her husband. She does, however, give him money and clothing, with which he sets out for Madrid.

In Valladolid, Gil Blas is robbed during the night by two people, Camille and don Raphael, who claim to be cousins of doña Mencia. He then meets Fabrice, his old school companion, who convinces him to enter domestic service where he will be able to dupe his master. His first master is to be a canon named Sedillo.

Sedillo is gluttonous and is afflicted with gout. Gil Blas serves him assiduously, hoping to inherit a large sum of money. Sedillo is bled to death by his physician, Dr. Sangrado ("Dr. Bled"). In his will he leaves Gil Blas his library but no money. Gil Blas decides to be the disciple of Dr. Sangrado and soon becomes a famous doctor. One of his patients turns out to be Camille. After serving a prison sentence for attempting to recover his stolen goods from Camille, Gil Blas resumes his medical practice but is soon forced to flee by a town bully whose fiancée he has killed.

Once again en route to Madrid, Gil Blas finds himself in the company of a young barber, Diego de la Fuente, whom he decides to accompany to Olmedo, Diego's birthplace. Diego tells Gil Blas of his life and especially of his situation with a young woman named Mergelina. Gil Blas and Diego meet a man living on bread and water, Melchoir Zapata, a frustrated actor who has just been jeered in Madrid. Gil Blas and Diego arrive at the latter's birthplace just in time to witness the end of a wedding celebration, which includes a bloody dramatic spectacle.

When Gil Blas eventually arrives in Madrid, he finds employment with a mysterious chevalier. He unexpectedly meets up with Rolando, the captain of the troup of highwaymen from whom he escaped. Gil Blas declines Rolando's offer to join up with him again. However, because he has been seen in the company of the notorious Rolando, his master dismisses. him.

Gil Blas then enters the service of don Mathias de Silva, a fop who spends his time in idle pleasures and squandering his money. The valets of don Mathias's friends teach him how to ape his master. Disguised as a young nobleman and assuming the name of his master, Gil Blas courts a young woman who is in fact a soubrette named Laure. Don Mathias and his friends discuss the theatre and especially the actors in the royal troupe. One friend, don Pompeyo de Castro, tells his life story.

Gil Blas's fortunes change once more when don Mathias is killed in a duel. Laure finds him employment as the administrator of the household of Arsénie, a well-known actress. He learns much about the theatrical world, and plunges into it with abandon for a time but soon becomes disgruntled with this way of life.

In order to "save his innocence," Gil Blas seeks employment elsewhere, this time with a rich old nobleman. After making a fool of himself with Aurore, his employer's daughter, Gil Blas agrees to spy on don Luis Pacheco, a libertine to whom Aurore is attracted. After the death of Aurore's father at the hands of his physician, she goes off in pursuit of don Luis, taking Gil Blas with her. They spend two nights at the home of doña Elvira de Pinares, who tells them a story entitled "The Marriage of Vengeance."

Aurore continues her pursuit of don Luis in Salamanca. She and Gil Blas conceive of several schemes to ensure her future happiness with don Luis. They are ultimately successful, whereupon Gil Blas becomes the valet de chambre of don Luis's uncle. He is dismissed before long, however, because his good intentions displease his employer.

Gil Blas's next employer is the mysterious Marquise de Chaves, whose house is frequented by writers of serious works and by many learned and pretentious people. A conflict between Gil Blas and a rival in love soon compels him to leave Madrid.

While taking refuge from a storm in a hermit's cave, Gil Blas meets don Alphonse, a young man who relates how he killed a man without knowing that he was the brother of Séraphine, a young woman whom don Alphonse loves. The hermit and his brother appear and are revealed to be don Raphael and his partner in crime, Ambroise de Lamela. The four travellers decide to join together.

Don Raphael tells his life story in great detail. His entire life has consisted of a series of extraordinary adventures, especially involving his long-lost mother.

Don Raphael, Ambroise, don Alphonse, and Gil Blas attack four thieves and free from their clutches a lady and a nobleman, none other than Séraphine and her father, the Count de Polan.

After leaving the Count de Polan, the four men, disguised as members of the Spanish Inquisition, rob a miserly Jewish merchant of his silver. Don Alphonse and Gil Blas soon become remorseful and part company with don Raphael and Ambroise. After a brief illness, don Alphonse is reunited with his family as well as with Séraphine, whom he soon weds. Gil Blas becomes the superintendent of don Alphonse's estate and is given money which he is to return to the merchant.

Because of personal problems with Seraphine's first lady-in-waiting, Gil

Blas leaves the service of don Alphonse. In Granada, he finds employment as secretary to the archbishop. Through flattery, Gil Blas becomes the archbishop's favorite and begins to have a great deal of influence over him. However, a critical remark about the archbishop's rhetoric brings about another dismissal.

While attending the theatre, Gil Blas is reunited with Laure, now a famous actress named Estelle. Pretending that Gil Blas is her brother, Laure has her current lover, the Màrquis de Marialva, hire him as a secretary. During this period, Gil Blas is reunited with several people from his past.

When circumstances force him to flee Granada, Gil Blas finds himself once again in Madrid. He is joyously reunited with his old friend Fabrice, now a pretentious author. Fabrice finds him employment as the superintendent of the house of a Sicilian count named Galiano. Gil Blas saves the count a great deal of money by spying on the other servants, whom he discovers to be dishonest. He is also obliged to keep vigil around the clock over Galiano's beloved pet monkey. As a result, Gil Blas becomes violently ill. When he recuperates, in spite of his doctors, he discovers that Galiano has abandoned him and returned to Sicily, leaving him barely enough money to pay his medical bills.

Fortune soon begins to smile on the now experienced wanderer. Gil Blas becomes such an esteemed secretary of the Duke de Lerme that he is honored at court. He nearly starves to death, however, because his employer fails to compensate him for his good services. By relating a fable of Pilpay, Gil Blas proves to be extremely successful in making the Duke de Lerme aware of his wretched condition.

With his newly acquired wealth, Gil Blas purchases clothing, a luxurious apartment, and the services of a shrewd valet named Scipion. The latter demonstrates his great talent by finding many people who will pay Gil Blas for the privilege of being introduced to the Duke de Lerme. Soon Gil Blas amasses a huge fortune which he spends lavishly and ostentatiously.

Gil Blas becomes totally corrupted at court. He is charged with finding a mistress for the dauphin of Spain. Scipion finds him Catalina, a woman who leads a double life. A contract of sorts is drawn up, permitting the prince to visit Catalina under certain conditions. Continuing to play the role of great lord at court, Gil Blas is indifferent to news about his family. Fabrice breaks off their friendship.

Out of vanity, Gil Blas has his dear friend and former employer, don Alphonse, named Governor of Granada. Scipion proposes that Gil Blas marry a wealthy goldsmith's daughter. The night before the marriage is to take place, Gil Blas is arrested and taken to Segovia prison. He learns that he has been imprisoned by the king for his role in leading the dauphin to

Catalina. While in prison he listens to the woeful tale of don Gaston de Cogollos.

Thanks to Scipion, the dauphin intercedes on Gil Blas's behalf. He is released on the condition that he stay away from the court. Scipion and Gil Blas return briefly to Madrid to get their money. While there, Gil Blas is reunited once again with don Alphonse, who gives him a piece of land near Valencia. Gil Blas and Scipion head for Oviedo to find Gil Blas's parents and take them to their son's new property.

Upon their arrival, Gil Blas's father utters his last words before dying. At the funeral service, the townspeople turn on Gil Blas, who, consumed with guilt, leaves Oviedo but provides his mother with an annual income.

The luxury which surrounds Gil Blas and Scipion at Gil Blas's estate overwhelms them. Gil Blas resolves to be more economical and have fewer servants. Don Alphonse, whom he visits in Valencia, grants him his requests.

In the street, Gil Blas recognizes the disguised don Raphael and Ambroise de Lamela, who tell how they became Chartrian monks. A few days later the unholy Raphael and Ambroise steal the monks' money and flee.

Upon his return to his estate, Gil Blas falls deeply in love with Antonia, the daughter of his farmer. Their marriage ceremony is temporarily troubled by Scipion and Béatrix, a servant of don Alphonse's wife, Séraphine. The two faint upon recognizing each other as husband and wife. However, they are soon joyously reunited. Gil Blas, Antonia, Scipion, and Béatrix live peacefully together. One day, Scipion is persuaded to tell of the various situations in which he found himself before meeting up with Gil Blas.

Gil Blas and Antonia become parents, but mother and child die shortly thereafter. The disconsolate Gil Blas is urged by Scipion to go to Madrid to seek his fortune with the new king (Philip IV), whom he previously helped.

At court Gil Blas is favorably received by the monarch, who recommends him to the prime minister. After several obstacles have been overcome, Gil Blas gains an audience with the prime minister and ingratiates himself.

Gil Blas learns quickly how to succeed at court. He is amply reimbursed by the prime minister, don Olivarès, for writing a propagandistic document in favor of the current administration and eventually becomes don Olivarès's confidant.

While inspecting a poorhouse, Gil Blas finds his friend Fabrice. He offers to find Fabrice a good position if only he will renounce writing poetry. However, Fabrice finds a patron who engages him to write a tragedy. Even though the tragedy is a flop, Fabrice's patron rewards him handsomely since he too had a hand in its composition.

Meanwhile, Gil Blas's patron, don Alphonse, has fallen into political disfavor. Because of Gil Blas's intervention, don Alphonse is awarded an even more prestigious charge. Gil Blas also obtains important posts for other old friends.

During an official trip to Toledo, Gil Blas witnesses an auto-da-fé. Two of its victims are don Raphael and Ambroise de Lamela. He sees the actress Lucrèce perform, and brings her and her "aunt" back to Madrid to perform before the king. The "aunt" turns out to be Laure (Estelle), whom Gil Blas abandoned in Granada. The two actresses make a very favorable impression upon the king. He falls in love with Lucrèce and has Gil Blas be his go-between. However, Lucrèce has such strict morals that she cannot bear to be the king's mistress. She and Laure flee to a convent.

By now, Gil Blas has been made a nobleman, largely because of his successful effort as governor of the prime minister's newly adopted son. However, the prime minister suddenly loses political favor and is dismissed by the king. Gil Blas and Scipion accompany Olivarès to his country estate, where the inconsolable prime minister soon dies of melancholy and medical treatment.

Gil Blas and Scipion retire to Gil Blas's estate, this time for good. Twenty-two years have passed since the death of Antonia. The two weary travellers meet don Juan de Jutella, who is in love with Séraphine, Scipion's daughter. Gil Blas in turn falls in love with Dorothée, don Juan's sister. A double wedding ceremony takes place, and the now serene Gil Blas becomes the proud father of two children.

don Abel; Alvaro de Acuna; don Louis d'Alcacer; Father Alexis; Louis Aliaga; Marquise de Almenara; Alphonse; Andros; Antonia; Archbishop (unnamed) of Grenada; Arsénie; Bernardo Astuto; Count of Asumar; Augustin; Aurore (don Félix de Mendoce); Sanche d'Avila; Azarini; Père Azarini; Count de Azumar; don André de Baesa; don Baltazar; Barbe; Béatrix (three); Bertrand; Blanche; don Blas de Combados; Gil Blas; Blas de Santillane; Brutandorf; don Vincent de Buena Garra; Fernandez de Buendia; Basile de Buenotrige; Cabaret Owner (unnamed); don Rodrigue de Calderone; Camille; Campario; Inésile de Cantarilla; don Raimond Caporie; Carnero; don Bertrand de Castil Blazo; don Pompeyo de Castro; Catalina; Celinaura; don Antonio de Centellés; Césarino; Marquise de Chaves; don Cherubin Tonto; Chevalier (unnamed); Chilindron; Captain don Annibal Chinchilla; Chrysostome; Clarin; don Antonio Coello; don Gaston de Cogollos; Colifichini; Constable (unnamed); Constance (two); André Corcuelo; don Mathias de Cordel; la Coscolina; Cuchillo; Descomulgado; don Bernard Deslenguado; Diego; Domingo; Dorothée (two); don Enrique; Estelle; doña Estephania; doña Eufrasia; Eugénie; Fabrice; Farrukhnaz; Felicia; Florentine; Florimonde; Vincent Forero; Bertrand de la Fuente;

Diego de la Fuente; Fernand Perez de la Fuente; Nicolas de la Fuente; Pedro de la Fuente; Thomas de la Fuente; Gabriela; Count Galiano; don Georges de Galisteo; doña Helena de Galisteo; don Fernand de Gamboa; Louis Garcias; Gaspard (two); don Gaspard; Dr. Godinez; Marquis de Grana; Grand Duke (unnamed); doña Anna de Guevara; Guyomar; don Gaspar de Guzman, Count d'Olivarès; don Henri-Philippe de Guzman; doña Maria de Guzman; don Ramire Nunez de Guzman; Vincent de Guzman; don Louis de Haro; don Huberto de Horadales; doña Hortensia; Inés; doña Inés; Inésille; don Ignacio de Ipigna; Isménie; Jacinte; Joachim; Julie; don Juan de Jutella; Ambroise de Lamela; don Diègue de Lara; Laure (Estelle); doña Eléonore de Laxarilla; Leganez; Marquis de Leganez; Count de Lemos; Gabriel de Léon; dame Léonarde; Léonor; Duke de Lerme; don Alphonse de Leyva; don César de Leyva; Fernand de Leyva; Martin Ligero; Murcia de la Llana; Arias de Londona; Séphora Lorença; Lucinde; Lucrèce (two); don Valerio de Luna; Mainfroi; Majuelo; don Félix Maldonado; Duke de Mantoue; Marquis de Marialva; don Martin; Mathilde; Mazarini; Duke de Medina Celi; Duke de Medina Sidonia; don Manrique de Medrana; Méhémet; dame Melancia; Mateo Melendez; don Alvar de Mello; Juan Velez de la Membrilla; Pedro de la Membrilla; Mme. Mencia; don Félix de Mendoce; doña Mergelina; don Ambrosio Mesio Carillo; Mogicon; André Molina; don Juan de Moncade; Rodrigue de Mondragon; Margarita de Montalvan; Count de Montanos; don Diègue de Monteser; Luis Morales; Manuel Morales; don Augustin Moreto; doña Mencia de Mosquera; Pedro de Moya; Jérôme de Moyadas; Isabelle Murcia de la Llana; Bertrand Muscada; Theodora Muscoso; Narcissa; Joseph Navarro; Count de Nieblès; Ambrosio de Nisana; Nise; Gregorio de Noriega; Marcos de Obregon; don Augustin de Olighera; Dr. Oloroso; Martin Oñez; Oquetos; Manuel Ordoñez; dame Ortiz (Ximena de Guzman); Duke d'Ossune; don Gonzale Pacheco; don Joseph Pacheco; don Luis Pacheco; don Pèdre; Pédrille; Gabriel de Pedros; Hally Pégelin; Angelica de Penafiel; Gil Perez; Phénice; Philippe IV; doña Elvira de Pinarès; Pedro Placio; Marquise de Pliego; Count de Polan; Porcie (two); Preceptor (unnamed); don Anastasio de Rada; don Roger de Rada; Prince de Radzivill; Ramire; Bernarda Ramirez; don Raphaël (Sidi Hally); don Bertrand Gomez del Ribero; Ricardo; Gregorio Rodriguez; Roger; Rolando; don Jacinte de Romarate; Melchior de la Ronda; Rosimoro; Marquis de Sainte-Croix; Gabriel de Salero; don François de Sandoval; Dr. Sangrado; Scipion; Torribo Scipion; Secretary (unnamed); Sedillo; don Alexo Segiar; Ybagnez de Ségovie; Séraphine (two); Léontio Siffredi; Jérôme de Silva; don Mathias de Silva; Samuel

Simon; Sirena (Catalina); Soliman; don Juan de Solis; doña Margarita de Spinola; Baron de Steinbach; Surgeon (unnamed); Talego; Theodora; don André de Tordesillas; Duke d'Uzède; don Francisco de Valeasar; doña Anna de Velasco; doña Juana de Velasco; Lope de Velasco; Baltazar Velasquez; Gaspard Velasquez; Carlos Alonso de la Ventoleria; Julien de Villanuno; Marquis de Villareal; Sébastien de Villa-Viciosa; Melchior de Villegas; Violante; don Manuel de Xerica; Melchior Zapata; Pedro Zendono; Marquis de Zenette; don Baltazar de Zuñiga; don Francisco de Zuñiga.

Indiana, George Sand, 1831.

Colonel Delmare, a crusty, retired military officer devoid of wit, tact, and education, has married a naïve Creole woman of nineteen who comes from the Ile Bourbon. Delmare retires with his bride Indiana to Lagny, his estate in the country. Three years go by. It is apparent to both Delmare and Indiana's cousin and childhood friend, a seemingly phlegmatic young Englishman named Sir Ralph Brown, that Indiana is greatly depressed. A strange malady seems to be eating away at her.

One night, a young man, unconscious because of a fall from Delmare's park wall, is brought into the house. Indiana helps nurse his injuries as he regains consciousness. Delmare becomes convinced that Noun, Indiana's Creole maid, and the man, Raymon de Ramière, are involved in an amorous intrigue. In fact, Raymon de Ramière is a victim of passion; but, unlike the beautiful Noun, he does not expect the romance to last. After prolonging the affair as long as he can bear to do so, Raymon leaves the area and does not return as he promised Noun he would. The despondent Noun finally writes to Raymon, but he does not answer her letter.

Sometime later, at a ball in Paris, Raymon meets Indiana Delmare and loses his head over her. Determined to see her again, he attempts to curry favor with her snobbish aunt, Mme. de Carvajal. Indiana, who does not love her husband, secretly yearns to love and be loved by a passionate young man. Her fear that her husband might harm Raymon prompts her to avoid him. Raymon, however, pursues her and causes her to succumb rather quickly to his charms. His attempt at lovemaking comes to an abrupt halt when Noun enters the room, forcing Raymon to flee. He soon returns, however, to visit Noun and, because of physical attraction alone, spends the night with her in Indiana's room. Afterward, Raymon feels guilty but does not have the courage to reveal his true feelings to Noun, who is carrying his child.

Suddenly, Indiana bursts in and discovers Raymon attempting to hide in her room. She denounces him as a vile seducer in front of Noun, to whom it is obvious that Raymon loves her mistress and not her. Only the arrival of Sir

Ralph Brown prevents Indiana from publicly denouncing Raymon, who is ordered to leave. Raymon does so, despairing of finding some way to appease Indiana. The following morning, Indiana faints upon discovering Noun's body floating in the stream nearby. The despondent woman has committed suicide.

Two months pass. One day the insensitive Delmare announces to Indiana that he has invited Raymon to breakfast the following day. Unknown to Delmare, Raymon aspires more ardently than ever to Indiana's forgiveness and love. Unable to face Raymon, Indiana feigns illness. However, when the two meet at Sir Ralph Brown's hunting lodge a short time later, Indiana cannot be indifferent to his entreaties. She also explains to the somewhat jealous Raymon the nature of her affectionate relationship with Sir Ralph.

That day, Delmare breaks his leg in a hunting accident and, because of complications, is unable to walk for six months. During this period, Raymon visits them every day. Soon the credulous Delmare comes to believe that Raymon's constant calls are a proof of the interest he takes in his health. Beneath their surface politeness, Raymon and Ralph, who is also a daily visitor, remain not at all fond of each other. The overly scrupulous Ralph regrets not having enlightened Delmare and Indiana concerning the real reasons for Noun's death.

A business house in Belgium, upon which all the prosperity of the Delmare establishment depends, suddenly fails. Colonel Delmare, still in a weakened condition, insists upon going there but will not permit either Indiana or Sir Ralph to accompany him. Raymon seizes this opportunity to be alone with Indiana, persuading her to let him pay her a midnight call in her boudoir. The ever-vigilant Ralph, fully aware of the rendezvous, convinces himself that he must inform Indiana of the true reason for Noun's death. Indiana rejects what he tells her, leaving him in despair that he has had to forfeit her friendship in order to save her.

Indiana is unable to forget Ralph's revelations, since they have confirmed suspicions which she previously chose to set aside. When her would-be lover enters her room, she struggles to surmount her passion and confronts him with the horrible past, eventually extracting from Raymon the fact that he came to her room a year before that night to see Noun and not her. At that moment, Ralph slips a note under Indiana's door, informing her of the sudden arrival of her husband. At Indiana's urging, Raymon flees once again.

At this point, Raymon decides that he no longer loves Indiana but merely wishes to triumph over her. Vowing to be her master and then abandon her, he writes effusive letters which convince the unworldly Indiana of his genuine love for her.

Delmare has returned, having lost his entire fortune. To pay off his debts, he puts Lagny, his estate, up for sale. He and Indiana will spend the winter in Paris, pending their departure for the Ile Bourbon. Sir Ralph, whose offer to his dear friends of his entire estate is refused by Delmare, sells his own estate and follows them to Paris. Raymon too is in Paris, where he is the life of every social event.

As the time to leave France for the Ile Bourbon draws near, Indiana becomes obstinate in her refusal to go there. Early one morning when Raymon returns home from a party, he is shocked to find Indiana, to whom he has been cool, in his bedroom waiting for him. After he insults her and insists that she leave, Indiana wanders aimlessly along the Seine and falls into the river. She is saved by Ophelia, her dog, whose barks bring Ralph to her rescue. Upon her return home, Indiana tells her angry husband that she will accompany him to the Ile Bourbon.

Indiana's hypocritical aunt, Mme. de Carvajal, renounces her upon learning of her scandalous behavior with Raymon. However, Ralph once again remains unswerving in his devotion and begs to be permitted to accompany Indiana and Delmare on their voyage. Before their departure, Indiana receives a letter from Raymon, who wishes to regain her esteem. She breaks its seal only upon reaching their destination and then writes a long letter in response, reproaching Raymon for lacking her exalted feelings, her willpower, and her courage to persevere in spite of society's laws, which are falsely attributed to God. Indiana's one solace is spending each evening walking in the solitary mountains of the island. Ralph, overcome with melancholy, also wanders about alone amidst the wonders of nature. He suppresses his personal thoughts but is always near to protect Indiana whenever necessary.

Meanwhile, the political career of Raymon as a champion of royalist causes is in jeopardy; he is compelled to exile himself in the country for a time. Now that his good fortune seems to have run out, his thoughts turn once more to Indiana. He decides to write to her and make one last effort to win her back and make of her a devoted and submissive mistress. At this particular time, Indiana's suffering is greater than ever. When Delmare discovers letters which she has written but not sent to Raymon, he becomes violent and kicks her in the face. Indiana vows to herself that she will escape from the island. It is at this very moment that Raymon's letter arrives. Indiana secretly enlists the help of a sea captain who, touched by her unprotected condition, agrees to take her on his ship as a stowaway. After four months of insults from the crew, fatigue, seasickness, and other severe discomforts, she surprises Raymon by her sudden arrival at Lagny, which she mistakenly believes he has bought. Laure de Nangy, Raymon's haughty bride, enters suddenly and is quick to set the record straight. Lagny belongs to M. Hubert, a wealthy bourgeois who adopted Laure years before. By marrying Laure, Raymon has obtained not only a beautiful wife of the nobility, but also a considerable fortune. When Indiana recovers the use of her faculties, she finds herself in a carriage, being driven rapidly toward Paris.

Several days later, Indiana is found in a lodging house by Ralph, who has followed her to France to tell her that her husband died the very night of her departure, without ever knowing that she had left him. Ralph now assumes the role of Indiana's guardian, but his efforts to revive her crushed spirit are to no avail. In spite of her pleadings that he not waste any more of his time, Ralph refuses to leave her. Instead, he proposes that they both commit suicide since both of them have experienced nothing but misery in life. After much contemplation, Indiana decides that Ralph is right. The Ile Bourbon, where they spent happy moments as children, is chosen as the place where they will end their lives. The long voyage to their final destination is a surprisingly serene one.

On a warm, beautiful evening, Indiana and Ralph climb the mountain to a ravine where they are to plunge into the waterfall as soon as the moon is high enough. During these last moments, Ralph begs Indiana to listen to the deep, dark secret of his life, his long and terrible battle with his destiny. Suddenly, this man of mediocre talent, who said only commonplace things his entire life, becomes eloquent and convincing as Raymon never quite was. He tells Indiana of his lifelong love for her which he has stifled until now. Indiana finally sees the true Ralph, the man she should have loved instead of Raymon. Their lips meet. Ralph takes her in his arms and bears her away to plunge with her into the torrent. An attack of vertigo prevents them from executing their plan. Ralph chooses to believe that the angel of Abraham and Tobias saved them, in order that they may live again. Initially, both distrust their newfound love and fear the future. However, time, instead of weakening their love, establishes it firmly and gives it added intensity. They live together in harmony, totally unmoved by the criticism of society, which they constantly avoid.

Brown, Edmond Brown, Mistress Ralph Brown, Sir Ralph Brown, Carle, M. de Carvajal, Mme. de Carvajal, Colonel Delmare, Indiana Delmare, Fanny, M. Hubert, Lelièvre, Louis, Laure de Nangy, Narrator (unnamed), Noun, Mme de Ramière, Raymon de Ramière, Captain Random.

Jacques le fataliste, Diderot, 1773.

Jacques and his master wander aimlessly all over eighteenth-century France. Each repeatedly assumes a particular posture, the master being often silent and Jacques frequently pointing out that his captain's motto was that all that happens to us here below, be it good or evil, is preordained.

In order to relieve their boredom, Jacques, his master, and people they meet tell stories. Chief among these is the story of Jacques's love life, which is constantly interrupted by chance events. In addition, the author-narrator frequently injects his own digressions on a wide variety of topics. (From the very beginning, the reader should be aware of the ordered disorder which runs through this entire work. At times, two consecutive sentences of the following summary may appear not to connect. This represents a deliberate attempt to convey to the reader Diderot's ordered disorder.)

As Jacques and his master travel along, Jacques begins to curse a certain innkeeper because the latter's bad wine precipitated a conflict between Jacques and his father. Out of spite, Jacques enlisted in the army, where he was severely wounded in the knee. It is because of this wound that Jacques has a personal love story to tell. Jacques has barely begun his story when night falls. He and his master realize that they are lost. The master begins to whip Jacques. The author-narrator intervenes to tell the reader how easy it is to write a story.

The next morning, they start out again. Jacques continues his love story up to the point where he was placed in a cart because of his knee wound. His story is interrupted by a passing doctor. In his zeal to demonstrate the details of a knee injury, the doctor causes his lady companion to fall off her mount and land on the ground in an embarrassing position. According to Jacques, such a demonstration was preordained. The author-narrator then digresses on what he might have done with the plot at this point.

Jacques continues his story. The cart carrying him stopped at a farmhouse where the farmer's wife took him in. Jacques and his master discuss fatalism; the author-narrator also comments on this subject. Jacques and his master spend the night at an inn where Jacques retaliates when they are mocked by a group of rowdies. After their departure, the two argue about fatality and happiness, with Jacques speaking paradoxically. The author-narrator comments on the possibilities for *Jacques le fataliste* as a novel.

Jacques's story continues. Three surgeons arrived, supposedly to examine Jacques's knee. After drinking several bottles of wine, they disputed as to whether or not Jacques's leg should be amputated. His master accuses him of exaggerating his knee injury and immediately falls off his horse, injuring his own knee. The author-narrator intervenes to comment on realism in the novel. Jacques launches into a discussion of idea-word association.

Jacques's story continues once again. Back at the farmhouse, the farmer reprimanded his wife for having been at the door when Jacques arrived in the cart. He then convinced his spouse to indulge in pleasures of the flesh with him. Jacques's story stops again because he and his master quarrel about women. When a storm breaks out, they take refuge either in a chateau or wherever the reader desires. The author-narrator comments on the novel as a genre.

The next morning, Jacques must return to the inn where he had the encounter with the rowdies, in order to retrieve his master's wallet and watch. After causing a great furor, Jacques is successful in his mission. When Jacques rejoins his sleeping master, he discovers that the latter's horse has been stolen. After offering a fatalistic explanation for the theft, Jacques once again picks up his narration.

He awakened to see a wine-drinking surgeon examining his leg. The surgeon and the farm people were also discussing what to do with Jacques. The author-narrator tells of a poet from Pondichéry. In justifying his digression, the author-narrator reminds the reader that, since he is not reading a novel, he must be constantly reminded of this fact.

Jacques buys a horse from a man they meet in passing. In spite of several interruptions, Jacques manages to tell about his brother, a corrupt monk who fled to Lisbon only to become a victim of that city's famous earthquake. Then, they see a coach decorated completely in black. Jacques believes that the coach bears the body of his beloved captain, whose death he bemoans. The author intervenes to talk to the reader: Who knows where one is going? The master launches into a bombastic discourse on grief.

Jacques, once again attempting to continue his story, explains that he discussed with the doctor how he would pay for medical treatment. However, his master does not listen because he wants Jacques to explain how, by the death of a friend, his captain was deprived of the pleasure of fighting once a week. The reappearance of the funeral train further interrupts Jacques. The group consists not of mourners and the body of Jacques's captain, but of smugglers who chase away Jacques and his master.

The master listens to Jacques describe the reaction of his captain to a slap given him by a beggar. Suddenly, Jacques's horse bolts and stops next to a gallows. Jacques wonders what significance this may have. Nevertheless, he attempts to continue to tell of the eccentric behavior of his captain and his captain's friend, who were extremists: either intimate friends or mortal enemies compelled to fight each other. Before Jacques can finish, his horse dashes off again. The author-narrator assures the reader that the captain's story is true and proceeds to tell the bizarre story of Gousse, whose good side prompted him to sell all his worldly possessions to help two friends in distress but who, on the other hand, never hesitated to forge notes, steal, and totally neglect his family. The author-narrator then reflects upon the relativity of vice and virtue.

Meanwhile, Jacques's head crashes into a door, thanks to his horse. His master buys him a new horse, and they set out to wander once more. The master believes Jacques to be a philosopher comparable to Socrates. They discuss forebodings; Jacques considers fate to be wily at times.

Finally, Jacques resumes his love story. The surgeon and the farm family took most of Jacques's money. He gave what was left to a poor woman in dire need. The landlady brought a roast to the penniless Jacques. The author-narrator once again mentions Gousse, who became imprisoned of his own will.

Jacques and his master arrive at an inn in the midst of a terrible scene being staged by the lady innkeeper. Jacques intervenes and soon finds out from her that the dispute concerns Nicole (who is later revealed to be a dog, not a woman). While Jacques and his master sleep, the author-narrator tells of one more episode in the life of the strange Gousse.

Bad weather forces Jacques and his master to spend another day at the inn. Jacques, attempting once more to continue his love story, is able to relate only that his medical bills were paid by an unknown person who then invited him to stay at his chateau. The lady innkeeper enters and attempts to tell a story of her own. She is thwarted repeatedly by her cantankerous husband and his crony as well as the servants, and is finally forced to postpone telling the story of Madame de la Pommeraye and the Marquis des Arcis, one of the inn guests who abused Nicole, until that evening.

The author-narrator discusses constancy, following which Jacques tells the fable of the sheath and the dagger. Jacques and his master analyze Jacques's mania for talking, which stems from his having been gagged as a child. Jacques tells a story about the friend of his captain. The loquacious lady innkeeper returns with a bottle of champagne in each hand. While they all imbibe, she relates in detail how Madame de la Pommeraye avenged herself on the Marquis des Arcis because his passion for her had cooled. Madame d'Aisnon and her daughter, forced by indigence to become prostitutes, played crucial roles in her scheme. The marquis did manage to rise above the horrible situation in which he found himself, and to have a successful marriage with Mademoiselle d'Aisnon. Jacques, his master, and the lady innkeeper all retire. Before falling asleep, Jacques finishes off the champagne. The author-narrator defends the treacherous deed of Madame de la Pommeraye.

The next morning, the weather is still stormy and Jacques is suffering from the excesses of the night before. Nevertheless, he wishes to continue the story of his love life and is able to relate that he was warmly received by Desglands, the master of the chateau, and also by Jeanne, the head servant, and her daughter Denise. Then, Jacques and his master digress. The master tells the story of the gambler Desglands. The two quarrel over Jacques's status with his master. The lady innkeeper serves as arbiter and decrees that the same obscurity that existed before in their relationship must be reestablished. Jacques declares that his master has the title but that he has the substance.

That afternoon, the weather permits all the travellers to bid a fond farewell to the lady innkeeper. Jacques, his master, the Marquis des Arcis, and the latter's secretary, Richard, travel together for a time. The author-narrator intervenes to discuss vice and virtue. The Marquis des Arcis tells the master the story of Richard, a former monk who finally abandoned the monastic life because he was disgraced in an attempt to bring about the downfall of his superior, a monk named Hudson who imposed severe discipline upon his order while privately enjoying a frenzied love life. The author-narrator makes observations concerning the use of obscenity. At a chateau where the four travellers stay overnight, Jacques and his master discuss painting. The author-narrator wonders what a child born of Hudson and Madame de la Pommeraye would have been like.

The next morning, Jacques and his master set out for somewhere, after bidding farewell to the Marquis des Arcis and Richard. They reflect on the afterlife, with Jacques telling of a man who refused to receive the last rites. Jacques adds one detail pertaining to his love story, which is that Denise was to visit him four times a day. Then, the question of Denise's virginity prompts the master to ask Jacques to tell how he lost his virginity. Jacques relates his accidental encounter in bed with Justine, whose lover was Jacques's friend Bigre. The author-narrator comments on false modesty. Jacques tells how he once schemed to have sex with the wives of two villagers who had made fun of him. He adds an anecdote concerning the ridiculous village vicar who found himself perched on a haystack because he was deprived of the sexual favors Jacques was receiving. The author-narrator again defends the use of obscenity in literature.

As they continue to wander, Jacques nips incessantly from his flask of wine, which he consults whenever a decision needs to be made. The author-narrator extols the virtues of the wine flask. Since Jacques has developed a sore throat and is momentarily unable to talk, the master tells of one of his adventures with the Chevalier de Saint-Ouin, a crook who introduced him to several underworld characters when the master was in need of money. The author-narrator tells a similar story involving a lemonade vendor and then digresses on the ease with which a novel can be created.

The master tells another anecdote concerning him and Saint-Ouin, who was involved in the master's relationship with Agathe, a young bourgeoise he was courting. Jacques and the author-narrator both interrupt him to make comments. Finally, the master is permitted to tell of Saint-Ouin's confession that he had deceived him, whereupon Saint-Ouin planned for the master to avenge himself on Agathe by taking the chevalier's place in bed with her in the darkness. At the very moment in the master's narration when Agathe received the master in her bed, Jacques interrupts and insists that his master tell the story of Desgland's facial plaster. The master begins by giving a detailed portrait of a woman. Jacques again interrupts, telling about the little boy the woman and Desglands conceived out of wedlock; he does this in order to spite his master for giving such a long, boring description. Finally, the master completes the story of Desglands's plaster, which involved duelling a rival and removing bits of plaster from his face each time he drew blood. The last remnant of the plaster was taken off when Desglands killed the rival.

The two wanderers discuss maxims of medicine and morality, the question of personal liberty and the nature of cause and effect. They see a horse harnessed to a plow. It is the master's long-lost horse, which they proceed to buy. Then, they discuss doctrine and deed, God and the devil. Suddenly, the master returns to his story of Agathe and Saint-Ouin. The master and Agathe were discovered in bed and the master was framed. He was obliged to pay a huge settlement in order to avoid marrying Agathe and had to claim as his own and provide for the illegitimate son of Agathe and his friend Saint-Ouin.

The following day, Jacques and his master set out to see Saint-Ouin's illegitimate son. Jacques forewarns his master that his love story is not to be completed but continues to relate it anyway. The surgeon made an incision in Jacques's leg, much to the horror of Denise, who nursed Jacques all the while. Jacques bought her gifts, including a pair of garters. Jacques must stop at this point because they have reached the village where Saint-Ouin's son is being raised. The master falls off his horse while dismounting, becaues Jacques loosened the strap. Angered, the master begins to strike Jacques, who insists that no free will was involved in the deed, merely fatalism. When they arrive at the boy's house, a fight breaks out between the master and Saint-Ouin, with the latter being killed. The master flees, and Jacques is seized and imprisoned.

The author-narrator invites the reader to continue Jacques's story and proposes three endings. The first has Jacques being released and then proving to Denise his tender feelings toward her by not seducing her. The second is from Sterne's *Tristram Shandy* and consists of an argument as to whether or not Jacques kissed Denise's hand. The final and most likely ending has Jacques freed from prison, saving the Desglands chateau from invaders, reunited with his master, marrying Denise and living happily, although there exists the possibility that Jacques may become a cuckold, "if it is written in the stars," courtesy of Desglands and the master.

Abbot (unnamed), Agathe, Mme. d'Aisnon (Mme. Duquesnoi), Mlle. d'Aisnon (Mlle. Duquesnoi), Brother Ange, Marquis des Arcis, M. Aubertot, Marquise du Belloy, Bigre, Bigre (Jr.), Captain de la Boulaye, Mlle. Bridoie, Cabaret Owner (unnamed), Captain (unnamed), Concierge (unnamed), Confectioner (unnamed), Denise, M. Desforges, Desglands, Desglands (Jr.), Executioner (unnamed), Father of Jacques (unnamed), Mathieu de Fourgeot, Friend (unnamed) of Jacques's captain, General (unnamed) of Monastic Order, Géronte, Gousse, M. de Guerchy, M. Hérissant, Father Hudson, Innkeepers (two, one male and one female, unnamed), Intendant (unnamed) with a cello, Mlle. Isselin, Jacques, Jason, Javotte, Jean (two), Jeanne, Justine, Law Official (unnamed), M. LeBrun, M. LePelletier, Lieutenant General (unnamed), Major (unnamed), Man (unnamed), Marguerite (two), Master (unnamed) of Jacques, Merchant (unnamed), Merval, Mistress of Jacques's Master (unnamed), Monk (unnamed), Nanon, Parents of Agathe (unnamed), M. Pascal, Pastry Cook (unnamed), Peasant (unnamed), Peasant Woman (unnamed), Mlle. Pigeon, Plowman (unnamed), Police Commissioners (two, unnamed), Mme. de la Pommeraye, Prémonval, Richard, M. de Rusai, Chevalier de Saint-Ouin, Dame Simion, Surgeons (four, unnamed), Suzanne, André Tissot, Count de Tourville, Tronchin, Valet (unnamed), Village Vicar (unnamed), War Minister (unnamed), Widow (unnamed), Wife (unnamed) of Doctor, Wife (unnamed) of Pastry Cook, Wife (unnamed) of Peasant, Women (four, unnamed).

Les Lettres persanes, Montesquieu, 1721.

A Persian lord by the name of Usbek is the pawn whom Montesquieu uses as the chief protagonist of this work which, while bearing the skeletal form of an epistolary novel, is, in fact, a series of satirical essays on French customs and institutions.

***

Supposedly in pursuit of learning and wisdom, and spurred by a keen desire to learn about other people and their habits, Usbek and his young friend Rica set out for Paris.

Upon his arrival in Turkey, Usbek is distressed to learn, from letters written by members of his harem and also by the chief black eunuch who watches over them, that all has not been well in the seraglio since his departure. In addition, he finds the Turks to be backward and barbaric. Nevertheless, Usbek is determined to persevere. When he learns that in Livorna, the first Christian city he visits, morality has taken the shocking blow of permitting women actually to be gazed upon by men, he becomes all the more anxious to get to Paris in order to pursue his quest for knowledge.

In Paris, the Eastern visitors continue their search for worldly understanding. There the behavior of the French women brings their consciousness of the female role to new heights. In several letters, the Persian travellers revel in their ever-increasing knowledge of the political and social power of debauchery and unrestrained passion. Usbek takes special care to enlighten Roxane, his most recent and favorite wife. In one of his letters, he reminds her of how ferociously she defended her virginity for a full three months after their wedding!

While continuing to pursue their knowledge of the gentler sex, Usbek and Rica do not allow their education to lack balance. They observe and absorb the fine arts of trivial conversation, rude behavior, and total lack of common sense—art forms which the Parisians practice with a high degree of expertise.

The students' letters also turn to the subject of the monarchy and the political foibles of the chauvinistic French. As one might suspect, French politics do not measure up to the high expectations of these two Eastern observers. For example, Usbek and Rica are mystified by that country's absolute monarch, Louis XIV. To them, he is a great magician in exercising his powers, second only to the Pope.

It also comes as no great surprise when our two Persian visitors take on the study of Christian religious practices, which they find to be very curious indeed. For one thing, Christ's kingdom has had more civil wars than any other. The revocation of the Edict of Nantes is another event which they find to be incomprehensible; it has had devastating effects on France, having robbed the country of some of its most valuable citizens.

A course in economics is also included in their educational experience. The state of the French economy appalls Usbek. France experiences so much economic turbulence, particularly among financiers, that it is enough to make one scorn being rich. Rica overhears the tales of woe of several victims of financial ruin. In this area as in all the others, we learn that these students bring a large collection of preconceived notions as well as much critical savoir faire to their search for knowledge.

Montesquieu, having made full use of his novelistic pawns, is now faced with the problem of how to remove them gracefully. A series of letters from the Persian harem would seem to provide an effective resolution. Not long after Usbek's departure, there are indications that his wives have not exactly resigned themselves to his long absence. His chief black eunuch writes to warn him that discipline has broken down in the harem and that his authority is scorned. The eunuch's later plea that Usbek return to restore order in the seraglio goes unheeded. In the meantime, violations occur with increasing frequency. By the time Usbek finally grants the chief black eunuch absolute power, the harem has been reduced to a state of chaos.

Months go by. Usbek waits in vain for further news from the seraglio. He is depressed, homesick, fearful, jealous, and filled with hatred and regret. Only now does he acknowledge that fear for his life accounted for his departure from Persia nearly ten years earlier. Now he wants to risk returning home; but

Rica, who has become an ardent Francophile, finds a thousand pretexts for prolonging their stay.

When Usbek finally hears of recent developments in the seraglio, he loses all hope. Solim, who, after the death of the chief black eunuch, was given the power to implement Usbek's orders, has totally abused this power and thus precipitates the demise of the harem. Several wives complain of the cruel treatment they have received and blame Usbek. Solim announces that even Roxane has been unfaithful and insists that bloodshed is his only recourse. A last letter, written by Roxane just after she has taken a lethal poison, contains a declaration of her hatred of Usbek as well as an admission of her innumerable clandestine violations of his laws.

Anaïs, Aphéridon, Astarté, Ben Josué, Bishop (unnamed), Chief Black Eunuch (unnamed), Fatmé, Gemchid, Geometrician (unnamed), Hagi Ibbi, Hassein, Ibben, Ibbi, Ibrahim, Ismael, Jaron, Nathanaël Levi, Librarian (unnamed), Méhémet-Hali, Mirza, Monk (unnamed), Nadir, Nargum, Narsit, Nessir, *Nouvelliste* (unnamed), Pharan, Rheudi, Rica, Roxane, Rustan, Santon, Solim, Soliman, Suphis, Troglodytes, Usbek, Zachi, Zélis, Zéphis, Zuléma.

Les Liaisons dangereuses, Laclos, 1782.

Before reading a summary of *Les Liaisons dangereuses,* the reader should find it helpful if some of the novel's major characters are identified in advance, since relationships between these characters are often very intricate and complex. The two major protagonists are Mme. de Merteuil and the Viscount de Valmont, who form an alliance in order to avenge an affront suffered by Mme. de Merteuil at the hands of the Count de Gercourt. Although their ultimate victim is to be Gercourt, their immediate victim and sacrificial lamb will be Cécile Volanges, Gercourt's fiancée. Also involved, in spite of themselves, in this act of revenge are two other characters: Danceny, an innocent young nobleman with whom Cécile falls in love; and Mme. de Tourvel, a virtuous woman whom Valmont is attempting to conquer. On the periphery of all this intrigue are Cécile's mother, Mme. de Volanges, and Mme. de Rosemonde, Valmont's elderly aunt, at whose estate much of the intrigue takes place.

***

Vengeance is the name of Mme. de Merteuil's game. She seeks to avenge herself on the Count de Gercourt, a former lover who has insulted her. To achieve her goal, Mme. de Merteuil seeks the help of the Viscount de Valmont, her favorite ex-lover who has remained her ally. During the prolonged absence of Gercourt, Valmont, a handsome and notorious ladies' man, is instructed to seduce Cécile Volanges. Cécile is Gercourt's naïve young fiancée, who has just returned home after having completed her convent education. The extremely clever Mme. de Merteuil has already convinced Cécile and her mother that she is their good friend and that she has Cécile's best interests at heart.

Initially, Mme. de Merteuil experiences difficulty enlisting the services of Valmont because he is currently in hot pursuit of the virtuous and devout Mme. de Tourvel. Valmont is determined to add Mme. de Tourvel to his long list of conquests while he and she are both guests at the country estate of Mme. de Rosemonde, Valmont's elderly aunt.

Meanwhile, Cécile becomes smitten with the equally young and inexperienced Chevalier de Danceny. She also falls very easily under the influence of Mme. de Merteuil. The astute Mme. de Merteuil quickly recognizes that beneath the malleable Cécile's innocent face there is a complete lack of character and principles. She has little difficulty in making Cécile hate Gercourt and also encourages Cécile in her passion for Danceny.

Mme. de Merteuil rejects Valmont's flippant suggestion that he and she become lovers once again before he goes to work for her. Instead, she instructs Valmont to return to her only after he has conquered Mme. de Tourvel and has furnished her with written proof. Mme. de Merteuil also informs Valmont of her delight with her adopted pupil, Cécile, whom she has decided to form in her own fashion before Gercourt's return.

Valmont is successful in his scheme to convince Mme. de Tourvel that he is an honorable, virtuous person. Mme. de Tourvel struggles valiantly to combat her passion for Valmont, but little by little he wears down her resistance to his charms. Valmont boastfully compares himself to a hunter who, lying in wait, forces his prey to bring about her own downfall. Suddenly, however, Mme. de Tourvel asks Valmont to leave Mme. de Rosemonde's estate. She tells Valmont that a friend has urged her to stay away from him because of his reputation. When Valmont discovers that his detractor is Cécile's mother, Mme. de Volange, he vows to get even by seducing Cécile. Now eager to work in partnership with Mme. de Merteuil, Valmont heads for Paris. En route, he writes an impassioned letter to Mme. de Tourvel while in bed with one of his former mistresses.

Valmont experiences frustration in his attempt to ingratiate himself with the unaggressive Danceny. Mme. de Merteuil comes to Valmont's rescue by contriving to have Mme. de Volanges discover that her daughter and Danceny have been exchanging love letters. The outraged mother forbids Danceny to see her daughter again. Mme. de Merteuil then offers to help Cécile in her efforts to be reunited with Danceny. Her goal is to gain complete control over

Cécile's mind. At the suggestion of Mme. de Merteuil, whom she believes to be her dear friend, Mme. de Volanges obliges Cécile to spend time at the country estate of Mme. de Rosemonde. Unknown to Mme. de Volanges, Valmont will return there to play the role of confidant and go-between for Cécile and Danceny.

Upon his arrival, Valmont immediately sets out to gain Cécile's confidence by delivering Danceny's letter to her as well as hers to Danceny. He also continues his ruthless pursuit of Mme. de Tourvel and is determined that she will ultimately come to him on her knees, begging to be loved.

Meanwhile, Mme. de Merteuil discovers that she has been publicly slandered by Prévan, another notorious ladies' man, of whom Valmont is a bit jealous. She vows to avenge herself in no uncertain terms. Responding to Valmont's fears concerning her ability to handle Prévan, the insulted Mme. de Merteuil points out that she is far superior in intelligence to other human beings, even to Valmont. She declares that she was born to avenge women and to control men. Considering herself to be the author of her own destiny, she has never failed to carry out her "principles." Soon thereafter, she concocts an ingenious scheme which succeeds in heaping complete social disgrace upon Prévan.

Valmont, while waiting for the final defeat of Mme. de Tourvel, seeks amusement with Cécile. He enters her room one night and experiences little difficulty in seducing her. However, Cécile is quickly filled with remorse and refuses to admit Valmont the following night. Next, just as Valmont believes himself to be on the brink of triumph with Mme. de Tourvel, she suddenly disappears. Valmont is beside himself; both his vanity and his intelligence have been dealt blows.

Mme. de Merteuil mocks Cécile for feeling remorseful and encourages her to make advances to Valmont. She then informs Valmont that Mme. de Tourvel's flight comes as no surprise to her and criticizes Valmont for his lack of inventiveness. Mme. de Merteuil also declares that she is about to renounce her protégée because of Cécile's severe limitations. She declares that Cécile will turn out to be a mere pleasure machine. She and Valmont must move quickly to complete their work. Valmont will take care of Cécile's body while Mme. de Merteuil will corrupt her mind and thereby bring about Gercourt's disgrace.

Valmont continues to experience frustration because of Mme. de Tourvel, but he is compensated in part by Cécile, who proves herself to be a very apt pupil. Not only does he educate her in the pleasures of the flesh but also, as part of his effort to deprave her, he invents licentious tales about her mother when she was young which delight Cécile. Soon, she is a nightly visitor to Valmont's bedroom. The result of this nocturnal activity is pregnancy and, subsequently, a miscarriage, both of which are able to be kept from Danceny, Mme. de Volange, and Mme. de Rosemonde.

Mme. de Merteuil soon informs Valmont that rumors concerning his love life in the country are spreading through Paris social circles. Since his mission with Cécile has been accomplished, she tells him to renounce his hopeless pursuit of Mme. de Tourvel and return to Paris. Mme. de Merteuil also informs Valmont of her intention to seduce Danceny, whom she considers to be too good for Cécile. Valmont in turn expresses irritation that he and Mme. de Merteuil no longer seem to agree on anything but promises that Mme. de Tourvel will fall very soon. In addition, he asks her to leave Danceny alone.

Upon discovering that his elderly aunt has now become Mme. de Tourvel's confidante, Valmont intercepts letters the two women exchange. As a result, he makes contact with Mme. de Tourvel's confessor. By pretending to be on the verge of confession because of Mme. de Tourvel's influence, Valmont succeeds in having the confessor convince Mme. de Tourvel to see him one last time. At the crucial meeting, Valmont presents himself as a timid, repentant slave, only to emerge as a crowned conqueror. For Valmont, it is by far his most complete victory, the result of an arduous campaign and one decided by skillful maneuvers. However, something has happened that Valmont had not counted on. His oaths of eternal love and devotion have not been empty ones. Without acknowledging it even to himself, he has fallen in love with Mme. de Tourvel.

Mme. de Merteuil, however, is quick to perceive that Valmont loves his virtuous victim. She becomes contemptuous of Valmont and informs him that, if he and she were to renew their old love affair, she would demand sacrifices which he would not, or could not, make. It is also apparent to Mme. de Merteuil that Valmont is deluding himself when he rationalizes staying with Mme. de Tourvel. The sacrifice she demands of Valmont is that he abandon Mme. de Tourvel.

Valmont, torn between his love for Mme. de Tourvel and his need to convince the goading Mme. de Merteuil that he is her equal, forces himself to sacrifice Mme. de Tourvel by deceiving and humiliating her. Consumed with shame and remorse, Mme. de Tourvel retires to a convent, where she slowly dies of grief. Mme. de Merteuil then mocks Valmont for thinking that he could possibly deceive her and also takes credit for directing the blows with which Valmont has struck Mme. de Tourvel. Meanwhile, she has successfully executed her plan to marry Danceny, now madly in love with her. Valmont becomes jealous of Danceny and makes a fatal power play. When he presents Mme. de Merteuil with the ultimatum of becoming his lover or his enemy, she refuses to yield and opts for war.

Valmont prematurely boasts of victory after advising Danceny to abandon the secondhand Mme. de Merteuil for the fresh Cécile. Mme. de Merteuil retaliates by convincing Danceny that Valmont not only has duped and deceived him with Cécile but also has even boasted of it in public. The enraged Danceny challenges Valmont to a duel and mortally wounds him. Before dying, however, Valmont is able to expose Mme. de Merteuil by presenting all of her correspondence with him to Danceny. Danceny, in his indignation, does not hesitate to make the letters public, and thereby brings about the social disgrace of Mme. de Merteuil.

When Cécile hears of Valmont's death and Mme. de Merteuil's treachery, she retreats to a convent to become a postulant. Out of regard for Mme. de Volanges, Danceny turns over all the other letters to Mme. Rosemonde. As for Mme. de Merteuil, her social disgrace is almost immediately accompanied by loss of all her money and her beauty. A severe attack of smallpox causes her to become hideously disfigured. According to one observer, her illness has turned her inside out and now her soul is on her face.

Adelaide, Père Anselme, Roux Azolan, Countess de B... Chevalier de Belleroche, M. Bertrand, M. C..., Sophie Carnay, Chambermaid (unnamed), Countess de ... (unnamed), Chevalier Danceny, Dutchman (unnamed), Emilie, Count de Gercourt, Intendante de... (unnamed), Josephine, Julie, Viscount de M... (unnamed), Viscountess de M... (unnamed), Maréchale de... (unnamed), M. de Merteuil, Marquise de Merteuil, Countess de P..., Mère Perpétue, Philippe, Prévan, Mme. de Rosemonde, Servant (unnamed), Mlle. Tanville, M. de Tourvel, Présidente de Tourvel, Mme. V..., Viscount de Valmont, Victoire, Cécile Volanges, Mme. de Volanges, Vressac.

Madame Bovary, Flaubert, 1857.

Charles Bovary, a plodding, rather obtuse but sincere young man, neglected by his profligate father and pampered by his domineering mother, finally succeeds in passing his medical examinations. He begins to practice medicine in the country village of Tostes. Because of the intervention of his mother, Charles soon marries a forty-five-year-old widow with a healthy income. Like his mother, she is quick to dominate him.

One night, Charles is called upon to ride to a nearby farm to set the broken leg of the farmer, Rouault. While there, he meets the widower Rouault's young daughter, Emma. Charles soon finds himself paying more sick calls than necessary on the farmer. Not long thereafter, his jealous wife, who has lost most of her money and quarreled bitterly with her in-laws, dies quite suddenly. Rouault visits Charles to pay his bill and invites him to visit the farm. The young widower readily accepts. Not many months pass before Charles asks Emma's father for her hand in marriage. They are wed the following spring, after Charles's official period of mourning ends.

Charles discovers what love is, for the first time in his life. Emma, however, is quick to discover that marriage is not the sublime experience she thought it would be. The humdrum life of a country doctor's wife contrasts sharply with the ideal she has clung to since her days in the convent, where she quivered with excitement while singing sentimental ballads and reading equally senti- mental novels. The present deadly calm in which she lives is totally different from the notion of happiness she continues to believe possible. Emma has neither the words nor the opportunity nor the courage to express her innermost thoughts. Charles, whose limited conversation bores her, is incapa- ble of understanding such feelings. She comes to resent his assured tran- quillity, his ponderous peace of mind, and, above all, the very happiness she gives him. Even lovemaking is a habit with Charles, just like everything else.

The monotony of her life is broken momentarily when Emma and Charles are unexpectedly invited to a ball at the home of the Marquis d'Andervilliers. Emma is in another world during their brief sojourn there. Her past life vanishes entirely in the rich glow of the present, which to her is life as she always imagined it to be. However, reality comes tumbling down upon her once more as soon as they return to Tostes. Although Emma attempts to turn her thoughts from all that is close and familiar, she cannot avoid the presence of Charles, the sight of whom fills her with contempt. She waits in vain for something to happen. A year passes and nothing does. Emma becomes openly scornful of things and people around her. Her health also begins to fail. Finally, in the hope of curing Emma of whatever is afflicting her, Charles reluctantly decides to set up practice somewhere else. In the spring, when they leave Charles's beloved Tostes for Yonville-l'Abbaye, Emma is pregnant.

Upon their arrival, they meet, among others, Homais, the sententious, anticlerical, social-climbing pharmacist, and Léon Dupuis, an apprentice law clerk. Emma feels an immediate attraction to the latter because he likes to take long, solitary walks and, especially, because he is a passionate reader of romantic fiction. Before long, she gives birth to her child, who she hoped would be a male, since a man, at least, is free. Her daughter is finally named Berthe, after a young woman who attended the ball, and is then entrusted to the care of a wet nurse.

A bond becomes increasingly strong between Emma and Léon; they continually exchange books and ballads. The credulous Charles, not easily moved to jealousy, seems totally unaffected by this relationship. Although eager to declare his passionate feelings to Emma, Léon lacks the courage to do so. Emma, for her part, is strongly attracted to the young clerk but struggles to conceal it. All the while, her restlessness and contempt for Charles increase. Léon finally becomes sick of loving to no purpose. Bored by Yonville- l'Abbaye and its inhabitants, he decides to move to Paris to prepare for his law examinations.

Emma falls prey to the same sort of dull melancholy and numb despair she experienced upon her return from the ball. To console herself, she indulges her fancies by buying extravagant clothing. Suddenly, one day, she is jarred out of her melancholy upon meeting an elegantly dressed country gentleman who lives on an estate nearby. Rodolphe Boulanger, a man with a coarse nature and a shrewd brain, has seduced many women in his life. He is immediately attracted to Emma, quick to sense her boredom and unhappiness, and determines to add her to his list of conquests. A short time later, as Emma and Rodolphe sit together during the ceremony inaugurating the regional agricultural show, Rodolphe whispers sweet words in her ear. Emma does not withdraw her hand when he seizes it.

Six weeks pass before anything further develops between them because Rodolphe deliberately waits that long before appearing again. Encouraged by the ever-trusting Charles, Emma consents to go horseback riding with Rodolphe. Needless to say, she is quick to succumb to his impassioned implorings, believing that, at last, she is going to enter a marvelous realm where all will be passion, ecstasy, and rapture. They begin to have secret rendezvous on a regular basis. Then, Emma surprises Rodolphe several times by visiting him unexpectedly, in the small hours of the morning. Before too long, Rodolphe begins to tire of her and fails to appear for three successive meetings. He makes no apologies for his behavior and is insensitive to her melancholy sighs. Suddenly, Emma's repentance for her illicit affair knows no bounds and she tries to love her husband. She soon rues this attempt at self-sacrifice, however, when professional disgrace is heaped upon Charles, whose attempt to perform surgery on a servant boy's clubfoot results in the amputation of the patient's leg. Emma falls into Rodolphe's arms that very night. Now her flaming desire for Rodolphe is fanned by her aversion for her husband.

To gratify all her whims, she continues to purchase expensive feminine apparel, as well as a riding crop for Rodolphe, from the merchant Lheureux, who eventually presses for payment. After she becomes upset when Lheureux asks her to return the riding crop, the cunning businessman senses that he has a hold on her and, therefore, decides to lie in wait. Meanwhile, Emma becomes increasingly bold in her behavior and openly shows her contempt for bourgeois propriety, thus losing the respect of many of the townspeople. She pleads with Rodolphe to take her away and convinces herself that their departure is imminent. In her dreams, she envisions a team of horses whirling her and Rodolphe toward a new land, from which they will never return. After Rodolphe delays the date of their departure several times, it is finally set. On the day before they are to flee, Rodolphe writes her a letter in which he announces his departure, alone. Emma is seized with convulsions and becomes delirious. Neglecting all his patients, Charles does not leave her side for weeks. Emma's convalescence is very slow; her detachment from everything becomes complete.

As if Charles does not have enough troubles, the poor fellow also has financial worries. He does not have money to pay Homais for medicine and there is a deluge of other bills as well; Lheureux, especially, harasses him. To make matters still worse, Charles conceives of borrowing money from Lheureux, at a ludicrous interest rate. However, since the time of payment seems far away, he puts these concerns out of his mind.

Emma finally recovers to the point that, at the insistence of Charles, they attend a performance of the opera, *Lucia di Lammermoor,* in Rouen. Emma is enchanted with the opera, which reminds her of the books she read as a girl in the convent; she believes the soprano's voice to be the echo of her own soul. At intermission, Emma is surprised to encounter Léon, who is now living in Rouen. Once again, the credulous Charles suggests that Emma stay a few days longer in Rouen, even though he must leave the next day.

Léon, now a more experienced young man, has gained in self-confidence. Seeing Emma again after three years revives his passion for her. The next day, after he and Emma meet in the Rouen cathedral, the law clerk easily wears down her resistance and, after hiring a cab, makes love with her while the cab is driven aimlessly throughout the city. Upon her return to Yonville-l'Abbaye, Emma convinces Charles to give her power of attorney in their financial matters and insists on going to Rouen to consult Léon. Little does Charles realize that Emma then spends three days behind drawn shutters and locked doors, making love to Léon.

In order to see Léon at least once a week, Emma convinces Charles that she must take piano lessons from a teacher in Rouen. She then begins to pile lie upon lie, using lies at first as a veil to conceal her love. Gradually, however, lying becomes a mania with her, a positive joy. One day, Lheureux runs into her in Rouen, while she is walking arm-in-arm with Léon. Ever quick to seize an opportunity to gain the upper hand, Lheureux persuades Emma to sign promissory notes which plunge her even more deeply in debt to him. To the amazement of Léon, Emma begins to fling herself into a reckless pursuit of pleasure. She soon dominates Léon, forcing him to yield to her every whim as she flaunts her passion to the world. Eventually, they become alienated from each other. He resents the way his personality becomes increasingly submerged by her and finally takes his employer's advice that he stop seeing her. For her part, Emma comes to realize that Léon falls far short of embodying the ideal lover she still imagines to exist. Adultery becomes as banal for her as marriage.

Emma's hand is suddenly called by Lheureux, who relentlessly demands complete payment of all loans she accepted from him. Her declaration that he is driving her to do something desperate leaves the cold-blooded merchant indifferent. Two days later, legal authorities post notices throughout Yonville-l'Abbaye that the contents of the Bovary household are subject to sale. Emma makes frantic efforts to come up with the money, even resorting to prostituting herself, but to no avail. Then, with a heroic resolve, she slips unseen into Homais's pharmacy, steals the key to his drug attic,and, upon finding a jar of arsenic, devours a portion of its contents.

Emma returns home to an overwhelmed Charles, who has just become aware of their situation. After writing and sealing a letter which she tells Charles not to read until the following morning, Emma takes to her bed. During the night, her agony begins. Her death is violent; she vomits blood and her limbs contort. Charles, in even greater agony than Emma, can bear no more. Choked by sobs, he begins to moan and shake all over. Emma dies early in the morning, after receiving the sacraments and uttering a long, loud death rattle.

Charles, whose grief knows no bounds, is left to pay off all the debts contracted by Emma. He refuses to consider selling any of her furniture and becomes violent when his mother, who has come to stay with him, tries to dispute his decision. She packs up and leaves, realizing that her son is a changed man. To please Emma, as though she were still alive, Charles adopts her tastes. He also signs more promissory notes and sells the silver and the parlor furniture. In spite of his frugality, however, he is quite unable to pay off so many debts. The final blow comes when one day by chance, he discovers Emma's love letters from Léon and Rodolphe. Everyone is amazed at the depth of his depression, for he becomes a veritable recluse. Not long thereafter, he is found dead in the grape arbor, with a long lock of Emma's black hair in his hands.

As for his neighbor, the pharmacist Homais, who has prospered while Charles has declined, he is awarded the cross of the Legion of Honor.

Alexandre, Marquis d'Andervilliers, Marquise d'Andervilliers, Mille. d'Andervilliers, Annette, Artémise, Beggar (unnamed), Berthe, Binet, Master Bocage, Boudet, Rodolphe Boulanger, Boulard, Abbe Bournisien, Berthe Bovary, Charles Bovary, Charles-Denis-Bartholomé Bovary, Emma Rouault Bovary, Héloïse Dubuc Bovary, Mme. Bovary, Bridoux, Camus, Dr. Canivet, Mme. Caron, Colonel (unnamed), Derozerays, Mme. Dubreuil, Léon Dupuis, Mme. Dupuis, Dr. Duval, Félicité, Girard, Mlle. Guérin, Guillaumin, Master Hareng, Headmaster (unnamed), Hivert, Homais, Athalie Homais, Franklin Homais, Irma Homais, Mme. Homais, Napoléon Homais, Justin, Langlois, Mme. Langlois, Dr. Larivière, Léocadie Leboeuf, Mme. Lefrançois, Félicité

Lempereur, Leplichey, Catherine-Nicaise-Elisabeth Leroux, Lestiboudois, Lheureux, Liégeard, Lieuvain, Longuemarre, Morel, Nastasie, Peasant (unnamed), M. Roger, Rollet, Mère Rollet, Théodore Rouault, Spinster (unnamed), Hippolyte Tautain, Tellier, Théodore, Thomassin, Tuvache, Lieutenant Tuvache, Mme. Tuvache, Vaufrilard, Vinçart, Watchman (unnamed), Woman (unnamed), Yanoda.

Manon Lescaut, Prevost, 1731.

The narrator, a man of quality, is reunited with a troubled young man of the nobility, to whom he gave money nearly two years before. The young man, the Chevalier des Grieux, insists upon telling his life story in dramatic detail. These revelations form the substance of the rest of the novel.

At the age of seventeen, Des Grieux has just completed his studies in philopsophy in Amiens. His scholarly brilliance, his physical attributes, and the steady, orderly life he has led thus far would seem to augur well for the future.

On the evening preceding his return home, Des Grieux meets and becomes instantly enamored of a beautiful young woman, Manon Lescaut, who tells him that she is being sent against her will to a convent in order to curb her inclination toward pleasure. Des Grieux's vow to free Manon and dedicate his life to making her happy is readily accepted by her. They steal away the next morning at daybreak and head for Paris, where they plan to get married.

Their first days in Paris are characterized by mutual tenderness and ecstasy. Soon, however, Manon becomes greatly upset when Des Grieux expresses a desire to be reconciled with his father, partly for financial reasons. Her insistence that she alone can procure the means to support them both upsets Des Grieux, who begins to notice that they are eating very well and that Manon's wardrobe includes some very costly additions.

Shortly thereafter, Des Grieux discovers that Manon has been having secret meetings with M. de B..., an infamous financier. Des Grieux's tearful beseechings to Manon to explain her situation are abruptly interrupted by the arrival of his father's lackeys, who seize him and take him to his father's estate. Upon his arrival, Des Grieux is mocked and reprimanded by his father, who furnishes him with conclusive proof of Manon's infidelity. For six months, while he is imprisoned in his room, his thoughts alternate between love and hate, hope and despair.

Tiberge, his devoted friend at Amiens, finally convinces Des Grieux to study theology at the Seminary of Saint Sulpice. At the seminary, Des Grieux performs outstandingly. After nearly a year, he believes himself to be cured of his passion for Manon.

But one day, Manon, now more ravishingly beautiful than ever, comes to visit him. In an instant, Des Grieux's passion for her is rekindled and the two lovers flee. Manon and Des Grieux decide to reside in Chaillot, in order to live clandestinely but also to be able to slip into Paris whenever pleasure and need might call them there. Both realize that, in spite of their great passion for each other, the solidity of their relationship depends upon the solidity of their finances. Unfortunately, Manon's passion for material pleasure remains unbridled. Des Grieux knows that she loves wealth too much to sacrifice it out of love for him.

When their house and money are destroyed by fire, the despairing Des Grieux does not tell Manon. Instead, he enlists the help of Lescaut, Manon's dissolute, parasitic brother, who has already been a financial drain on them. With great reluctance, Des Grieux has Lescaut introduce him to an association of trained gambling cheaters. He also decides to ask his devoted friend Tiberge for money. Tiberge complies with the request with the stipulation that he be allowed to visit Des Grieux to try to bring him back to virtuous ways.

Des Grieux masters the art of cheating at the Hôtel de Transylvanie and amasses a large sum of money for Manon and himself. Their affluence is of short duration, however, since they are soon robbed of everything by their servants. The despondent Manon goes off to live with M. de G. M. in order to reestablish their financial prosperity.

Lescaut persuades the distraught Des Grieux to participate in a scheme he and Manon have invented in order to dupe and rob G.M. Des Grieux combats his feelings of shame and remorse before agreeing to do so. That evening, Manon and Des Grieux, disguised as her provincial brother, dine with G.M. and have many laughs at his expense before executing their plan and fleeing. However, G. M. soon realizes what has happened. The police seize Des Grieux and Manon in their bed. Manon is dragged off in one carriage and Des Grieux in another.

Des Grieux is imprisoned at Saint-Lazare, a prison for young people of condition. When G. M. visits him and tauntingly reveals that Manon is a prisoner at the horrible Hôpital, Des Grieux loses control of himself and attempts to strangle the older man. Only the intervention of the kindly father superior spares Des Grieux additional punishment. Des Grieux succeeds in getting Tiberge to visit him. After preaching virtue to Des Grieux, Tiberge agrees to deliver to Lescaut a letter which contains a plan of escape. That night, Lescaut successfully manages to help Des Grieux flee from Saint-Lazare.

In order to ensure the escape of Manon, Des Grieux successfully cultivates the friendship of M. de T..., son of one of the administrators of the Hôpital. The escape takes place without incident the following night and the two lovers are tenderly reunited. Then they witness the murder of Lescaut. Des Grieux and Manon flee to Chaillot, where she vows never to leave him again.

The penniless Des Grieux once again swallows his pride and asks Tiberge and M. de T... for financial assistance. Both friends oblige him. M. de T... pays for Des Grieux's purchases for Manon, after which the two men spend a pleasant evening with Manon in Chaillot.

The next few weeks are relatively happy and calm ones for Des Grieux. Manon plays a cruel joke on an Italian prince who is an admirer of hers. Des Grieux acknowledges the excessiveness of the joke, but his gratitude to Manon for her love far outweighs his disapproval.

One day, the son of G. M., their former victim and persecutor, arrives at their apartment, accompanied by their mutual good friend, M. de T.... M. de T... confirms Des Grieux's suspicion that the wealthy G. M., Jr. is in love with Manon and that he will try to win her over by offering her valuable possessions. When Des Grieux informs Manon of this, she vows to avenge them on the father by duping the son. Des Grieux protests but once again allows himself to be drawn into Manon's scheme. She is to move in with the son of G. M. while Des Grieux finds them new lodging. After she has collected as much money as possible, Manon will have G. M., Jr. take her to the theatre on a certain day. At intermission, she will escape with the money; Des Grieux will be waiting with a carriage.

Instead of meeting Des Grieux, Manon sends to him a pretty young woman with a letter in which she explains that she must postpone their reunion. In the meantime, he should enjoy the young woman. Des Grieux first experiences fury and then grief. Vowing to see Manon, he engages the help of M. de T..., who agrees to detain young G. M. so that Des Grieux may enter his house to be with Manon.

The very sight of Manon causes Des Grieux's anger to subside. His love is stronger than ever. Manon explains that she felt compelled to stay longer in order to acquire more money for them. Des Grieux allows Manon to convince him that they should not leave empty-handed. Suddenly the elder G. M. rushes into the room, accompanied by two law officials. Des Grieux and Manon are arrested and imprisoned separately.

Des Grieux is visited by his father, who, ultimately moved to pity out of paternal love, agrees to meet with the elder G. M. The two fathers arrange for Des Grieux's immediate release from prison and for Manon to be deported as a slave to America. Des Grieux faints upon hearing of Manon's fate. When he regains consciousness, he resolves to devote his life to her deliverance.

Once again, Des Grieux invents a pretext for borrowing money from Tiberge. He then hires four men to attack on the road those who are taking Manon to Havre-de-Grâce (Le Havre). When the cowardly men flee, Des Grieux pleads with the guards to accept him among their number so that he may accompany Manon.

The chief guard agrees to let Des Grieux talk to Manon for a price. In sitting with the weakened and enchained Manon, Des Grieux realizes how much his love has meant to her and how much she cares for him. The greedy guard soon drains Des Grieux of all his money, after which he is no longer permitted to be with Manon. It is at this point that the man of quality (the original narrator) intervenes on Des Grieux's behalf, permitting him to accompany Manon to Havre-de-Grâce.

Once Des Grieux and Manon embark for America, their lot begins to improve. Aboard the ship, the captain proves to be considerate and sympathetic. He provides them with private quarters for the duration of the two-month voyage.

Upon their arrival in New Orleans, Des Grieux and Manon are politely received by the governor, who, assuming that they are married, gives them a cabin all to themselves. Manon's love for Des Grieux now transcends her need for material possessions. They make a rewarding life for themselves and become highly esteemed members of the colony.

Their troubles begin anew when the governor discovers that they are not married. He refuses to marry them because of his nephew Synnelet, who has secretly loved Manon during the nine months she and Des Grieux have been in New Orleans. After pleading in vain with the governor, Des Grieux, in self-defense, kills Synnelet in a sword fight.

Manon insists that they flee together into the desert rather than be separated. They are unable to go far, however, because of Manon's weakened state. During the night, she dies. Des Grieux buries Manon and plans to die by her grave.

The colonists find Des Grieux after two days. He does not wish to live, but is nursed back to health. Peace and tranquillity begin to be reborn within him. Manon's body is carried to holy ground. Des Grieux resolves to return to France to make amends for his past conduct by leading a wise and orderly life.

Several weeks later, a ship arrives from France. One of its passengers is Tiberge, who has undergone many trials in attempting to reach his beloved friend. Des Grieux and Tiberge soon return to France together, where Des Grieux immediately learns of the death of his father. His life story is now completed; he goes off to be reunited with his brother in a neighboring village.

M. de B..., Brother (unnamed) of Des Grieux, Chevalier des Grieux, Father (unnamed) of Des Grieux, Father Superior, M. de G. M., M. de G. M. (Jr.), Governor (unnamed), Italian Prince (unnamed), Lescaut, Manon Lescaut, Marcel, Synnelet, M. de T..., Tiberge.

"Micromégas," Voltaire, 1752.

On one of those planets surrounding the star named Sirius lives a very intelligent young man named Micromégas ("small-large") who is 120,000 kingly feet tall and whose majestic belt is 50,000 kingly feet in circumference.

At the age of 450, he is exiled from the court for eight hundred years for having published a work on small insects which a petty theologian found to be heretical. Micromégas decides to travel from planet to planet in order to complete the development of his mind and his heart. Having arrived on the planet Saturn, he cannot suppress a smile of superiority upon seeing the tininess of the globe and its people. However, Micromégas comes to understand very quickly that a thinking being need not be ridiculous just because he is only six feet tall. He proceeds to cultivate a rewarding friendship with the secretary of the Academy of Saturn.

Micromégas and the secretary discuss several subjects, including the diversity of nature, human anxiety and uncertainty, and the brevity of life, which is five thousand years on Saturn. Micromégas marvels at how the author of nature has spread over the universe a profusion of varieties with, at the same time, an admirable kind of uniformity. He and the secretary resolve to take a philosophical trip together.

The two curious beings depart by jumping on one of Saturn's rings, which they find to be very flat. From there, they go from moon to moon, spend a year on Jupiter, do not stop on Mars because it is too small for them to sleep on, and finally decide to stop on Earth, even though they find it pitifully small. They land on Earth on the northern edge of the Baltic Sea on 5 July 1737. The two travellers go around the earth in thirty-six hours. At first, their search for life is in vain because their eyes and hands are not proportioned to the tiny beings who crawl on earth. Then, it is discovered that the diamonds from Micromégas's broken collar serve as excellent microscopes. Micromégas first seizes a whale and then a ship with philosophers on board. The passengers run all over his hand; and, although they are barely perceptible even with the help of the microscope, Micromégas and the dwarf from Saturn experience great pleasure first in watching these little machines move about and then in discovering that they can speak French.

Upon gaining the confidence of the passengers and discovering that these little creatures possess intelligence, Micromégas marvels that the Eternal Being had no more difficulty creating the infinitely small than he had in creating the infinitely large. Micromégas is led to believe that it is with these intelligent atoms that happiness may be found. One of the little people assures him that, with few exceptions, the inhabitants of Earth are an assembly of wicked, unhappy madmen. Even the little philosophers dispute most issues. They are particularly in disagreement concerning the soul. A little atom wearing a square bonnet interrupts the discussion, declaring to Micromégas and the dwarf from Saturn that all was created for man alone. The two travellers shake so much in attempting to stifle their laughter that they nearly lose the infinitely little but proud creatures.

Micromégas promises that, before his departure, he will write them a book of philosophy in which they will see the scheme of things. The book is soon brought to the Academy of Science in Paris. When the book is opened, all that is to be seen is a completely blank page.

Micromégas, Muphti, Philosophers (unnamed), Secretary of the Academy of Saturn (unnamed).

Les Misérables, Hugo, 1862.

I. Fantine

Bishop Charles François Bienvenu Myriel of Digne is a cleric known throughout the region for his devotion to the poor and for his exemplary humility. The only luxurious items in the bishop's entire residence are six silver spoons and forks, a soup ladle, and two heavy candlesticks of massive silver. Beyond his faith, Bishop Myriel has an excess of love and a serene benevolence which spread over men. His visitations are an inspiration to those who see and hear him.

In October 1815, at which time Bishop Myriel is seventy-five years old, an unknown man of wretched appearance, travelling on foot, enters the little town. He is denied food and lodging at every inn because he is a convict who has just been released from prison after nineteen years at hard labor. Finally, the ex-prisoner, Jean Valjean, is warmly received at the home of Bishop Myriel, where he sleeps in a bed for the first time since he entered prison for having attempted to steal a loaf of bread for his seven starving nieces and nephews. Scarred by society, which has robbed him wholesale, he awakens in the middle of the night and cannot wipe out of his mind the vision of the silver he saw earlier on Bishop Myriel's table. After more than an hour of wrestling with his troubled conscience, Jean Valjean seizes the silver and quickly flees into the night. Upon discovering the theft the following morning, the holy man unperturbedly declares that the silver rightly belongs to the poor. A short time later, when three gendarmes arrive holding Jean Valjean by the collar, the bishop tells them that the silver is a gift from him to Jean Valjean. After the stunned gendarmes depart, Jean Valjean is given Bishop Myriel's two candlesticks as the kindly priest reminds him that he is to employ the money he will receive from them in becoming an honest man; henceforth, Jean Valjean will no longer belong to evil but to good. Deeply moved by such generosity, Jean Valjean walks through the forest like a drunken man. After robbing a boy of a two-franc piece and then trying too late to give it back to him, Jean Valjean is filled with remorse and despair. He sheds tears for the first time in nineteen years. As he weeps, his whole life appears before him, but then his soul is filled with a magnificent radiance by the apparition of Bishop Myriel.

It is now the spring of 1817. Fantine, a beautiful young woman with golden hair and pearly white teeth, is abandoned by her frivolous lover of two years, who does not know that she is pregnant. Ten months pass. Fantine unwisely leaves her infant child, Cosette, in the hands of a tavern keeper and his wife, the vile Thénardiers, while she returns to her native town to find employment. This wicked couple does not hesitate to abuse the child and exploit the mother, who continues to send money each month for her support. Year by year the child grows and so does her wretchedness. At the age of five, she becomes the servant of the house and is dressed in rags.

At the time of Fantine's return to her native town, its major industry has been transformed by the ingenuity of a man of about fifty called Madeleine, who arrived in the town about two years before and immediately distinguished himself by saving the lives of the children of the Chief of Police. Therefore, no one dreamed of asking for his passport. The town now prospers. Most of the wealth M. Madeleine accumulates is spent on the town and on the poor. In 1820, he yields to popular demand and becomes mayor of Montfermeil. By 1821, Madeleine is completely without enemies, so greatly is he venerated. Only one man remains suspicious of him, as if a sort of incorruptible and venerable instinct has kept him on his guard. The name of this grave person is Javert, the police inspector, in whose eyes robbery, murder, and all other crimes are formed of rebellion, which he loathes, and constitute a threat to authority, which he worships. He is absolute in his thinking and admits of no exceptions. One day, Madeleine saves the life of an old man named Fauchelevant by lifting up with his back a cart which is about to crush the old man. Javert declares that only once before, when he was a prison guard, did he see such a display of strength in a man. This person was a galley slave named Jean Valjean. Madeleine turns pale as Javert persists in staring at him.

Fantine, who found work at the factory established by Madeleine, is able to support herself and her child for a time. But eventually, gossips become suspicious of her secret correspondence and, upon discovering that she has an illegitimate child, have her dismissed from her job. For a year, she lives in abject poverty. The next winter, Fantine is obliged to have her beautiful golden hair cut off and her sparkling white front teeth pulled in order to be able to send the Thénardiers money for her child. To make matters worse, a cough she has had for several years begins to become more frequent. Finally, as a last resort, Fantine becomes a prostitute. An incident with a malicious young man brings about her arrest by Javert, who then sentences her to six months in prison. This sentence is revoked by Madeleine, who has been listening unnoticed to Fantine's plea for mercy. He and Javert clash, but the mayor, who has the ultimate authority, frees Fantine and offers to pay her debts and send for Cosette. Fantine, delirious with happiness, can endure no more; she faints at Madeleine's feet.

Fantine's lungs are so diseased that she remains gravely ill. Meanwhile, Thénardier refuses to send Cosette to her. Also, Javert writes to the Prefect of Police in Paris about the incident between Madeleine and himself, accusing the mayor of being Jean Valjean. His is told that he is a madman since Jean Valjean, a man who calls himself Père Champmathieu, has just been recaptured. Javert now insists that the mayor accept his resignation.

After Javert's revelation, Madeleine spends an entire night wrestling with his conscience. For eight years, the double rule of his life has been to hide his name and to sanctify his life. For the first time, the two seem to him to be absolutely at odds with each other. Finally, he resolves to go to Arras, where the trial of Père Champmathieu is being held. Summoning up all the virtue that lies within him, he proves to all assembled in the courtroom that he is Jean Valjean.

Before being arrested, Jean Valjean goes away to accomplish the one thing he must do. However, he is prevented from bringing Cosette to Fantine by the sudden arrival of Javert in Fantine's sickroom. The sight of Javert's terrifying face is too much for Fantine; she is seized with a final convulsion and dies. After placing Fantine's body in a position of tranquillity, Jean Valjean is led by the triumphant Javert to the town jail. That night, however, he escapes and heads for Paris.

II. Cosette

It is the year 1824. Jean Valjean is recaptured three days after his flight but not before withdrawing from Lafitte's bank in Paris a sum of more than half a million francs, which he then succeeds in hiding. He finds himself back at the prison in Toulon, where he previously spent nineteen years as a galley slave. Shortly after his arrival, he falls into the sea while saving a sailor's life. Since his body is not recovered, he is presumed to be dead.

Back in Montfermeil, Cosette, now eight years old, continues to do all the menial chores in the Thénardier household. One night, the terrified child is ordered by Mme. Thénardier to go out into the dark to fetch water from the stream in the woods. Cosette manages to fetch the water, but it is so heavy that she must frequently stop to rest. Suddenly, a man's hand lifts up her bucket. The man carries it for her and, all the while asking Cosette questions, accompanies her to the inn. He stuns the Thénardiers by buying for Cosette a beautiful doll which she has long admired in a neighboring shopkeeper's window. The next morning, the mysterious man, dressed shabbily but carrying a large purse, pays the greedy tavern keepers an outrageous sum of money and leaves the town, accompanied by Cosette, who is wearing her first new dress ever. Thénardier makes an attempt to obtain even more money but finally yields before the man's menacing look.

After a long, exhausting day's journey, Cosette and Jean Valjean arrive in Paris. They seek asylum in the Maison Gorbeau, a wretched garret on the edge of the city, and are able to light this hideous place with love. However, after a few months, the caretaker of the place, known as the "chief lodger," begins to be suspicious of Jean Valjean. Suddenly, the exgalley slave discovers a man spying on him. This man closely resembles Inspector Javert. Forced to take flight, Jean Valjean and Cosette zigzag their way through Paris, closely pursued by the relentless Javert. They are saved from certain arrest by the man whose life Jean Valjean saved at Montfermeil, when he was known as Madeleine. Their savior, Fauchelevant, asks no questions and hides them in his cottage at the convent of Petit-Picpus, where Madeleine got him the post of gardener two years previously. Javert, who comes close to seizing his prey, is eventually forced to return to the prefecture, looking as hangdog as a spy captured by a robber.

Fauchelevant, completely devoted to the man who prevented his body from being crushed under the cart, sees that Jean Valjean and Cosette are well protected and able to live with him indefinitely in his cottage. Jean Valjean is able to pass for Fauchelevant's brother and Cosette for Jean Valjean's granddaughter. The child is cared for by the prioress, who finds a place for her in the convent school. Jean Valjean works every day in the garden, greatly easing Fauchelevant's burden as gardener. Cosette is permitted to spend one hour of each day with him. During the girls' recreation hours, he watches her play and easily distinguishes her glorious laughter from that of the others. Cosette now begins to laugh for the first time in her entire life. God has his inscrutable designs, and the convent contributes, as Cosette does, to reinforce the bishop's influence on Jean Valjean. His heart melts in gratitude, and his love grows and grows. Five years pass thus in these tranquil, holy surroundings.

III. Marius

Marius is the grandson of a haughty bourgeois of royalist sympathies. This venerable gentleman, M. Luke Esprit Gillenormand, considers the husband of his late daughter to be a disgrace to the family because the man, Colonel Georges Pontmercy, a devoted officer under Napoleon, refuses to recognize the reestablished monarchy. Pontmercy lives alone in exile in the provincial town of Vernon because M. Gillenormand imperiously claims Pontmercy's only child, Marius, declaring that otherwise Marius will be disinherited. Pontmercy endures these cruel terms in the belief that he is sacrificing only himself. Marius grows up accepting his grandfather's prejudices and comes to think of his father only with shame. By the time he has reached the age of seventeen, Marius has spent time at college and entered law school. Like his grandfather, he is a fanatic royalist.

One night, upon returning home, Marius is informed that he is to leave for Vernon the following morning in order to see his father, who is seriously ill. Upon his arrival, Marius discovers that his father has just died of a cerebral hemorrhage. He is handed a note written by Colonel Pontmercy in which he bequeathes to his son his title of baron, given him by Napoleon on the field of Waterloo. Baron Pontmercy also requests that his son do whatever he can for a man named Thénardier, a sergeant who saved his life at Waterloo. Upon being made aware of the love and sacrifice of his father for him, Marius undergoes an extraordinary change of political attitude and comes not only to adore his father but also to admire Napoleon. Now a perfect revolutionist, he goes to an engraver's shop and orders one hundred cards bearing the name "Baron Marius Pontmercy." Upon discovering this, M. Gillenormand becomes livid with rage. A clash of two political passions ensues. The grandfather ends by declaring that a baron and a bourgeois can no longer remain beneath the same roof. The banished Marius leaves without saying or knowing where he is going, with only thirty francs, his watch, and some clothes in a carpet bag.

Life becomes extremely difficult for Marius. He is obliged to live on almost nothing, dressing in shabby clothes, eating very little, with no fire to keep himself warm. Through all this, he manages to pass his law examination. By labor, courage, perseverance, and his will, he finally comes to earn a modest annual sum from his work. Tempted by its isolation and cheapness, Marius takes a room at the Maison Gorbeau, the very place where Jean Valjean and Cosette once lived.

Three years pass. Marius is now twenty. He and his grandfather remain on the same terms, without attempting any reconciliation. For some length of time, Marius has been noticing in a deserted walk of the Jardin du Luxembourg a man of about sixty and a young lady of fifteen, seated side by side at the same spot every day. Suddenly, one April day, the young lady raises her eyes to him, and their glances meet. Marius immediately falls head over heels in love. For several days thereafter, he puts on his good clothing and walks past the two, his passion increasing all the while. He then decides to follow the man and young woman to see where they live. He does so several times, then, suddenly, one evening, he finds out that they have moved without leaving a new address. Several months pass during which Marius has only one thought, to see the lovely girl's face once more. He searches everywhere in vain and eventually lapses into a state of deep melancholy.

Toward the middle of the year 1831, Marius discovers that his neighbors, the wretched Jondrette family, are going to be evicted. He makes a financial sacrifice in order to pay their rent. One morning, not long thereafter, he is visited by Eponine, the older Jondrette daughter, a starving, depraved-looking creature of sixteen, who has come in behalf of her father to ask for more help. As the poor creature goes off with his last five-franc piece, Marius notices a triangular hole in the partition separating him from the Jondrette family. By climbing up on his chest of drawers, Marius discovers that he can see what they are doing and what kind of state they are in.

What Marius overhears greatly arouses his curiosity. A "philanthropist" is due to arrive momentarily. Jondrette orders his family to do certain things to make their hovel look even more wretched. Then, to Marius's great surprise, the gentleman in question appears, accompanied by the very young woman he has been seeking all these months. They have brought packages for the Jondrette family but no money. When informed by the conniving Jondrette that he and his family will be evicted that night if their rent is not paid, the man promises to return that evening with the rent money. After he and the young woman have gone away, Marius learns something that fills him with horror. The two are to be the victims of an ambush which Jondrette, who claims to know their identity, has set for them. Marius, indignant at Jondrette's treachery, goes to the police, where he finds Inspector Javert. Measures are taken to arrest Jondrette and his accomplices.

Marius is glued to his position at the partition when the gentleman returns. He and the gentleman see four men arrive silently, one by one. Jondrette then ferociously declares to the gentleman that his real name is Thénardier. Marius becomes weak from shock at the sound of that name. The man who was his father's savior is a monster! Should he be a defaulter to the most sacred duty he has ever taken upon himself, or let a crime be accomplished? Meanwhile, Thénardier, crazed with rage, never ceases to lash with imprecations this "child stealer" who, he insists, is the cause of all his misfortunes. At one point, when Thénardier's back is to him, the man bolts. He nearly succeeds in jumping out the window but is restrained by the other men in the room. After they have tied him to a bed, Thénardier orders him to get two hundred thousand francs and to write what is dictated to him, a letter to the young woman asking her to meet him at this address. Once this has ben done, the letter signed and addressed, Mme. Thénardier goes off in search of her. (The plan is for the young woman to be held captive until the man comes up with the money.) A short time later, Mme. Thénardier returns and announces that the address given is false.

All the while, Marius has been kept nailed to the spot by frightful fascination. He waits for the right moment to give Javert and his men the signal agreed upon. Suddenly, the prisoner leaps forward. He has managed somehow to untie himself, except for one leg. Marius hears Thénardier declare his intention to cut the prisoner's throat. Now Marius knows that he must act immediately. Miraculously, at his feet on his table, a bright moonbeam lights up a sheet of paper, written on in large letters by Eponine, which she earlier dropped there. On the sheet of paper are the words "Here are the cops." In a flash of insight, Marius sees in this note a way to spare the assassin and save the victim. He detaches a lump of plaster from the partition, wraps it up in the paper and throws it through the hole. In the confusion, the thieves all think it came from the window and throw down a rope escape ladder. Their getaway attempt is interrupted by the arrival of Javert and his men, who seize all the thieves, including the Thénardiers. When Javert turns his attention to the prisoner, he discovers that he has escaped through the window, by means of the rope ladder.

IV. The Idyll of the Rue Plumet

The day after this traumatic event, Marius flees from the Maison Gorbeau. He feels a horror for this house because of the social ugliness he witnessed there; furthermore, he does not wish to be involved in the trial and be obliged to give evidence against Thénardier. Marius is also heartbroken because, once again, the two unknown beings who are his only interest in life have vanished into thin air. He spends all his time walking aimlessly, thinking only of "her."

One day, two months after the arrest of Thénardier, Marius is approached by the man's older daughter, Eponine. She has looked for him for six weeks, in order to tell him the new address of the young woman. Marius is barely able to control himself. As the wretched Eponine leads him there, Marius begs her not to tell anyone else this address. It is that of a small, neglected house in the Rue Plumet, largely hidden from the view of passersby. In October 1829, Jean Valjean and Cosette had quietly moved into this long-deserted house.

The reader must now be brought up to date concerning them. Jean Valjean and Cosette leave the Convent of Petit-Picpus after five years. Although happy there, the increasingly paternal Jean Valjean comes to realize that he is doing Cosette a great disservice by obliging her to renounce life, by becoming a nun, before she has had any chance to know life. He determines to leave the convent with Cosette. Old Fauchelevant's death provides him with the opportunity to do so. He tells the prioress that he has inherited from his brother a small property which will enable him to live without working. Out of fear of being caught by the police, Jean Valjean proceeds to acquire three different residences in Paris and spends a few weeks with Cosette at each of them. However, his primary lodging is the Rue Plumet house.

Cosette leaves the convent, at the age of fourteen, her formal education completed. But otherwise she is ignorant of everything. She loves her father (that is to say, Jean Valjean) with all her soul, with a simple, filial passion. Always at his heels, she feels that wherever he is happiness is. Cosette remembers her mother only confusedly but prays for her soul morning and evening. The Thénardiers remain for her two hideous faces in a nightmare. All she remembers of that period in her life is that "one day at night" she went to fetch water in a woods.

From day to day, Cosette becomes more and more beautiful and radiant. Shocked at discovering this, she begins to pay great attention to her dress and appearance and asks Jean Valjean to take her walking. This distresses him because he fears losing her, now that she is fast becoming a young lady. At this point Cosette and Marius exchange that fatal glance in the Jardin du Luxembourg. From that moment on, they adore each other. During this period, she and Marius do not speak and do not know each other; staring at each other in the park is all they require to keep their love strong.

Jean Valjean becomes instinctively aware of Marius's presence and comes to regard him as a threat. When he discovers that Marius has been following them to his lodging in the Rue de l'Ouest, he and Cosette move back to the Rue Plumet. Time passes; Cosette suffers from their separation as much as Marius. Like him, she despairs of their ever seeing each other again. Thus, the lives of Jean Valjean and Cosette gradually become overcast, but they never speak to each other of their innermost feelings. Their one remaining joy is visiting and giving alms to the poor. It is during one such visit that the horrendous incident with the Thénardiers occurs.

Spring arrives once again. It is the year 1832. Their garden at the Rue Plumet property is so beautiful that Jean Valjean encourages Cosette to take frequent solitary walks there. One evening, when Jean Valjean is away, Cosette notices a stone which someone has placed on the garden bench. A letter is under it, a letter from someone in love. Her instincts tell her that it is the young man she longs to see again. The next night, he appears in the garden and gently pours out his declaration of undying love. She responds by declaring that her love is of the same nature. After a long silence, she discovers at long last that his name is Marius and he learns that her name is Cosette. During the nocturnal meetings in the garden which follow, they sit together in admiration and adoration of each other. For a period of about two months, time stands still for Cosette and Marius, with nothing before them, nothing behind them. Little do they know that on the night of 3 June 1832, they, as well as Jean Valjean, are saved from an assault of robbers led by the escaped prisoner Thénardier, because of the intervention of Eponine, who is secretly in love with Marius.

On that very night, a despairing Cosette informs Marius that Jean Valjean has declared his intention of taking her to England. (His desire to leave Paris stems in part from his having seen Thénardier in the area on several occasions. Imminent political turmoil is another factor for this man, who has something to hide from the police.) Marius vows that he will die if they are separated. He determines to prevent this and, after four years, goes to see his grandfather to ask the old man's blessing of his union with Cosette. But, once again, grandfather and grandson fail to communicate. When Marius returns to the garden the next night, Cosette is nowhere to be found. However, Marius hears a voice telling him that he is awaited by his friends at the barricade in the Rue de la Chanvrerie.

It is the moment of the political riots of 1832. Because his grandfather has failed to accept Cosette and because she has disappeared, Marius wishes only to die. Seeing an opportunity offered him, he rushes off toward the Rue de la Chanvrerie. He soon enters the fray and saves the life of little Gavroche, the Thénardiers' long-neglected son. His own life is then saved by someone who stops a bullet meant for him. The bewildered Marius is named chief of the insurgents. After the soldiers have momentarily withdrawn, Marius hears a faint voice calling him. It is that of Eponine Thénardier, who is dying after having saved Marius's life. She delivers a letter from Cosette and then, after asking him to kiss her forehead, dies with her head on his knee. Marius, more despondent than ever upon reading that Cosette is leaving Paris the next day, sends Gavroche to her overnight address in the Rue de l'Homme Armé with a message.

Meanwhile, Jean Valjean discovers that Cosette has written to Marius, telling him of their whereabouts. Such a cloud collects within him that he believes the whole interior of his soul is crumbling because of his hatred for the young man. Mechanically, he moves out into the street, where he happens upon Gavroche and intercepts the letter from Marius to Cosette. In opening the letter, Jean Valjean sees only these words of Marius: ". . . I die; when you read this, my soul will be near you." Initially, Jean Valjean feels infernal joy but cannot sustain this emotion. Suddenly, he becomes gloomy, as if overcome by the change of emotion within him. An hour later, he makes his way toward the barricade in the Rue de la Chanvrerie.

Meanwhile, unknown to Jean Valjean, Javert has been spotted as a spy in the wineshop which the young insurrectionists have made their headquarters in that street. Enjolras and Marius's other companions have bound and tied him and are prepared to kill him at the right moment.

V. Jean Valjean

As daylight begins to appear, the surviving insurgents are both full of hope and prepared to die. Marius, however, has abandoned all hope and, saturated with violent emotions, has buried himself in a visionary stupor. Although he wants to die, he also wishes to save others before his final moment comes. He is astonished to see Jean Valjean (M. Fauchelevant to him) enter the barricade.

The critical moment of the insurrection is not long in coming. As the first cannonball of the artillerymen is fired, Gavroche comes crashing through the barricade, causing more commotion to the insurgents than the artillery fire. It is soon apparent that the barricade cannot hold. Jean Valjean fires two shots to cut asunder the cords attaching a mattress to a nearby window, risks his life to rush out and get it, then place it in the barricade wall where it will be effective. The applause of the insurgents accompanies his action.

Soon, however, it is determined that almost no cartridges are left. Gavroche is spotted in the street, at the foot of the barricade, amid the shower of bullets from the artillerymen. He is carrying a hamper and filling it with full cartridge boxes belonging to the National Guards killed on the slope of the barricade. Defiantly, hands on hips, he sings to the artillerymen who fire at him. Finally, one bullet fells the daring, reckless urchin. Marius rushes out of the barricade and carries in the boy, thinking that he is paying back the son for what the father did for his father, except for the fact that Thénardier brought in his father alive. Marius's face is covered with blood; without his knowing it, a bullet grazed his skull when he stooped over to pick up Gavroche.

As a reward for having secured the mattress, Jean Valjean asks that he be permitted to blow out the brains of the insurgents' captive spy, Javert. When the two are left alone, Javert cold-bloodedly tells Jean Valjean to take his revenge. When Jean Valjean draws his knife, cuts the ropes binding Javert, and tells him that he is free, Javert, for once in his life, cannot suppress his emotion. Jean Valjean then tells Javert where to find him if he survives the impending massacre. After the incredulous Javert has retired slowly, Jean Valjean discharges his pistol in the air, returns to the group, and declares that Javert is dead.

Suddenly, the drums beat the charge and the attack of artillerymen resembles a hurricane. As the assaults rapidly succeed each other, the horror becomes greater and greater. Nearly all of Marius's friends are killed. The wounded insurgents are forced to retreat into the wineshop. Marius remains outside; a bullet breaks his collarbone, and ha feels himself fainting and falling. At this moment, he feels the shock of a powerful hand seizing him and, thinking himself to be a prisoner, faints. Marius is, in fact, a prisoner—the prisoner of Jean Valjean.

The whirlwind of the attack on the wineshop is so violent that no one sees Jean Valjean, supporting the unconscious Marius in his arms, cross the unpaved ground of the barricade and disappear. Their situation appears hopeless, for escape seems impossible. Suddenly, while looking frantically at the ground, Jean Valjean notices an iron grating, made of strong crossbars, about two feet square. Through the bars can be detected an obscure opening. Jean Valjean miraculously manages to pry open the grating and, upon descending, sets foot on a paved surface about ten feet below the earth. All this is executed like something done in delirium, with a giant's strength and the rapidity of an eagle. Jean Valjean and Marius are in the Paris sewer. The burden of carrying Marius, who is dead weight, on his shoulders, while walking in mud among the rats, nearly conquers Jean Valjean. He finally manages to struggle to a grating, only to find it locked. Just as he is about to abandon hope, Jean Valjean hears a raspy voice offering to let him out with a key, for a price. It is Thénardier who does not recognize Jean Valjean and who believes that he is talking to a fellow criminal who has just robbed and then killed. By pretending to play along with Thénardier, Jean Valjean gets himself and Marius out of the sewer. After relocking the grating, Thénardier plunges back into the darkness with the little money both men carried.

A few minutes later, as Jean Valjean is attempting to collect his thoughts and is about to splash Marius's face with water, he has the strange sensation that someone is behind him. It is Javert, who was pursuing Thénardier. Because of Jean Valjean's state, Javert does not recognize him, but the ex-galley slave tells him who he is. Javert seems not to hear but keeps his eyes fixed on Jean Valjean, who asks only that he be permitted to carry Marius home before surrendering. Javert grants this request without hesitation. After Marius has been deposited at his grandfather's, Jean Valjean asks Javert to grant him one thing more—to return home for one precious moment. After a few moments of silence, Javert yields once again. Upon their arrival at the Rue de l'Homme Armé, Javert tells Jean Valjean that he will wait outside. A minute later, upon looking out the second-floor window, Jean Valjean stares below in disbelief. Javert is nowhere to be seen.

Javert, in fact, finds himself unable to cope with what he has done. Jean Valjean's generosity overwhelms him. He cannot bear to have been shown mercy by a convict and, in turn, to have shown mercy to one. His suffering is tremendous because he now sees two roads before him whereas all his life he knew only one straight line. He cannot bear to let a convict go free, nor can he allow himself to arrest this convict. All the axioms which have been the support of Javert's whole life now crumble. His supreme agony is the disappearance of certainty. Since life is now unbearable to him, he ends it by plunging into a whirlpool in the Seine.

Marius remains critically ill for four months, then is declared out of danger. Anticipating another major quarrel with his grandfather, Marius adamantly declares to the old man that he intends to marry Cosette. To Marius's surprise, his grandfather voices no opposition. Grandfather and grandson are tearfully reconciled. Soon thereafter, Cosette and Jean Valjean, who still calls himself M. Fauchelevant, visit Marius and M. Gillenormand. Jean Valjean announces that Mlle. Euphrasie Fauchelevant (Cosette) has 584,000 francs, enough for her and Marius to live comfortably for many years. (This is money from his days as M. Madeleine, the mayor of Montfermeil, which he had kept hidden all these years, along with the bishop's candlesticks.)

Preparations are made for the marriage of Marius and Cosette, which is to take place on 16 February 1833. In advance of this date, Jean Valjean renders everything easy for the couple. He is able to solve the problem of Cosette's civil status, of which only he knows the secret. The huge sum of money is explained as a legacy left to Cosette by a dead person who wished to remain unknown. This legacy, placed in the hands of Jean Valjean (M. Fauchelevant), was to have been handed over to Cosette upon her majority or at the time of her marriage. There are a few unresolved points, but no one chooses to see them. Cosette learns that she is not the daughter of the man whom she has called father for so long. At another moment, this would have grieved her heart, but now it is only a passing cloud. Even though Jean Valjean declares himself to be only a relative, she continues to call him father. She is also enthusiastic about M. Gillenormand, who overwhelms her with presents and attends to her trousseau. Marius, meanwhile, during the little time he is not totally absorbed in Cosette, makes futile efforts to find out about the "unknown" man who saved his life.

A few days before the wedding, an injury to his right hand compels Jean Valjean to wrap it in a bandage and wear his arm in a sling. This prevents him from signing anything; M. Gillenormand, as supervising guardian to Cosette, takes his place, both in signing the marriage contract and in giving his arm to Cosette as she walks down the aisle. Later, when dinner is announced at the wedding banquet, Jean Valjean's chair is empty. He has left a message stating that, because his hand pains him, he begs to be excused from the wedding party, but he promises to call the following day.

In fact, Jean Valjean has simply feigned his injury, in order that his past might never come back to haunt Cosette. He returns home to find complete emptiness, now that Cosette is no longer there. He examines everything of hers that remains, including the clothes she wore, ten years before, when she left the Thénardiers' pothouse with him; these clothes he has kept hidden all these years. All Jean Valjean's precious memories of the past decade, when Cosette had no one else in the world but him, surface at once. Then, his venerable white head falls on the bed, his heart breaking. His head buried in Cosette's clothes, Jean Valjean begins to sob uncontrollably. The same old formidable inner struggle begins anew. How will he behave with regard to the happiness of Cosette and Marius? They possess everything, including wealth, and that is his doing. But now, should he introduce himself quietly into Cosette's house? Should he carry his past into this future, without saying a word? His confusing reverie lasts the entire night, and he remains until daybreak in the same position.

The following day, Jean Valjean, whose conscience compels him to speak candidly, reveals to an astounded Marius that he is an ex-galley slave and still an escaped convict. He asks only that he be permitted to visit Cosette. Marius consents, overwhelmed but understanding at long last why he always found this man to be enigmatic. He is, however, terribly upset by what he has just found out.

The following evening, Jean Valjean returns. He insists, to the dismay of Cosette, that she call him Jean and not father. With great reluctance, she yields to his strange request. Soon, however, the heartbroken man, feeling that Marius does not want him in his house and that he is no longer important to Cosette, stops coming to visit. Then, since he no longer wishes to live, his strength fails him and he is confined to his bed.

Marius has not encouraged Jean Valjean to see Cosette. She, for her part, believes him to be away on a trip. Then, an unexpected visit by Thénardier, ever intent upon taking advantage of other people's misfortunes, enlightens Marius once and for all concerning Jean Valjean. Marius learns that it was Jean Valjean who saved his life one year earlier by carrying him through the Paris sewer and who is now, once again, sacrificing himself for him. After giving Thénardier money to sail for America (where he becomes a slave trader), all the while heaping contempt and scorn upon him, Marius and Cosette rush to the room where, unknown to them, Jean Valjean lies dqing. Upon their arrival, they are both joyously ahd sorrowfully reunited with him. Marius, who now reveres Jean Valjean, begs him for forgiveness. Jean Valjean declares that Cosette and Marius are now one in his heart. Cosette, who is at last told about Fantinc, her real mother, is to inherit his candlesticks, which she now lights for him. He declares that he is dying a happy man and, in his final seconds of life, asks only to be able to lay his hands on their beloved heads. Cosette and Marius fall on their knees, choked with sobs, their hearts breaking, each of them under one of Jean Valjean's hands. Suddenly, these august hands move no more.

At his request, Jean Valjean is buried in an obscure corner of the cemetery of Père-Lachaise, with no name engraved on his tombstone.

Anceau, Count Anglès, Babet, Bahorel, Baloup, Bamatabois, Mlle. Baptistine, Barber (unnamed), Barge, Basque, Blanchevelle, Viscountess de Boischevron, Boulatruelle, Bourgaillard, Bourgeois (unnamed), Boy (unnamed), Brevet, Brujon, Mme. Burgon, Mère Buseaupied, Cashier (unnamed), Père Champmathieu, Marquis de Champtercier, Charcellay, Chenildieu, Pierre Chesnelong, Claquesous, Cochepaille, Combeferre, Cosette, Courfeyrac, Cravatte, Dahlia, Daumont, Demi-liard, Director (unnamed), Doctor (unnamed), Driver (unnamed), Enjolras, Fabantou, Urbain Fabre, Fameuil, Captain Fannicot, Fantine, Favorite, Fauchelevant, Euphrasie Fauchelevant, Père Fauchelevant, Feuilly, G... , Gavroche, M. Géborand, M. Gédéon, General (unnamed), Mère Gerbaud, Gervais, Gibelotte, Luke Esprit Gillenormand, Mlle. Gillenormand, Théodule Gillenormand, Gisquet, Gorbeau, Grantaire, Gribier, Guelemer, Mère Hucheloup, Père Hucheloup, Mother Innocent, Maubert Isabeau, Javert, Jeanne, Joly, Jacques Labarre, Lafitte, Laigle (Bossuet), Guillaume Lambert, Count de Lamothe-Valois, Le Cabuc, Listolier, Landlord (unnamed), Countess de Lô, Louison, Abbé Maboeuf, M. Maboeuf, Mme. Magloire, Magnon, Nicolette Magnon, Mamselle Miss, Marguerite, Marie-Claude, Matelote, Jeanne Mathieu, Mestienne, Montparnasse, Mountebank (unnamed), Paulin Musebois, Musichetta, Bishop Charles-François-Bienvenu Myriel, Navet, Nicolette, Peddler (unnamed), Pépin, Sister Perpétua, Physician (unnamed), Mère Plutarch, Ponchaud (Bigrenaille, Printanier), Georges Pontmercy, Marius Pontmercy, Porter (unnamed), Porter's Wife (unnamed), Portress (unnamed), Prefect (unnamed), Professor (unnamed), Jean Prouvaire, Marquise de R..., Mme. Rousseau, Scaufflaire, Senator (unnamed), Sister Simplice, Surgeon (unnamed), Baroness de T..., Thénardier (Jondrette), Azelma Thénardier, Eponine Thénardier, Gavroche Thénardier, Mme. Thénardier, Thénardier boys (two), Félix Tholomyès, Toussaint, Jean Valjean (M. Madeleine), Mlle. Vaubois, Mère Veuvain, Mme. Victurnien, Jean Vlajean, Woman (unnamed), Zelphine.

Nana, Zola, 1880.

It is opening night at the Théâtre des Variétés. All of Paris is there, the Paris of literature, finance, and pleasure. The producer Bordenave, who refers to the Variétés as his brothel, is presenting to the public his latest discovery, a talentless eighteen-year-old named Nana. Although she can neither act nor sing, Nana, starring in the title role of *Blonde Venus,* is clever enough to capture an audience, with her infectious laugh and her remarkable kick from the hip. By the final act, when she appears totally naked beneath a very thin fabric, Nana has taken possession of the public and every man is her slave. A wave of lust flows from her as from an excited animal; its influence spreads until the whole house is possessed by it.

The next morning, Nana awakens in her third-floor apartment, which smacks of the courtesan who was too early deserted by her first serious protector, who has fallen back on shabby lovers, and who is handicapped by refusals of credit and threats of eviction. This day, however, the doorbell is rung not only by creditors but especially by admirers who seek to win her favor. It seems that all the men who saw her on stage the previous evening are presenting themselves! Nana, aided by her seemingly devoted maid, Zoé, is finally able to dismiss most of them, giving the others only a few minutes of her time, while secretly muttering curses upon the male sex.

At a weekly reception given by the Countess Sabine Muffat de Beuville in her coldly dignified drawing room, the superficial conversation is about contemporary politics. However, there is an undercurrent of excitement among the men, who whisper about a midnight supper to be held at Nana's the following night. The Count Muffat de Beuville and his father-in-law, the Marquis de Chouard, decline an invitation, even though they have already paid a personal call on the courtesan, supposedly on behalf of a religious organization. They assert that the aristocratic classes ought to set a good example.

As for Nana, she wants to celebrate her great success as Venus with a supper which will be the talk of all Paris. It is served to thirty-eight people, far more than her table will hold. The guests consist of other courtesans, many of them fellow actresses at the Variétés, and their latest lovers and would-be lovers, all of whom are wealthy gentlemen of repute. After consuming an abundant quantity of champagne, Nana and her guests pay less and less attention to decorum. The party lasts until dawn, when those guests who have not fallen asleep stagger out the door. Nana has been busying herself almost exclusively with the wealthy German banker Steiner, who verges on apoplexy beside her. Now she informs him that he is going to take her to the Bois de Boulogne to drink milk. After reassuring her current lover, Daguenet, the only person she sleeps with who is not a financial benefactor, she drags off the disappointed banker, who has twice been ruined because of his furious appetite for courtesans.

On the night of the thirty-fourth performance of *Blonde Venus,* Nana is being viewed for the third time by none other than the Prince of Scots, who not only takes her to his apartment after the performance but pays her as well. On this night, the Prince watches the performance with the upright, sexually repressed Count Muffat de Beuville and the latter's dissolute, hypocritical father-in-law, the Marquis de Chouard. Muffat's brain, in particular, is set on fire; this once chaste Catholic would now abjure everything to possess Nana for a single hour.

Meanwhile, Steiner has purchased a country estate in the provinces for Nana. The property, called La Mignotte, happens to be near that of Mme. Hugon, the venerable mother of Nana's extremely ardent admirer, seventeen-year-old Georges Hugon, who became inflamed immediately upon seeing Nana as Venus. Mme. Hugon's guests this late September are her son and Count Muffat de Beuville, his wife the countess, and their daughter Estelle. The timing of the men's arrival is not exactly by chance, for Nana has just arrived at La Mignotte, a fact known by both Georges and Muffat. Georges sneaks away from his mother's estate at night and surprises Nana by his unexpected appearance at her home. Although she has previously treated him like a child, Nana succumbs this night to the lad's bold advances. On subsequent nights, she is barely discreet, even when Steiner is staying there.

On the day after Georges first slips away to spend the night with Nana, Mme. Hugon is quite surprised to find other unexpected guests arriving at her door. Among these are the young theatre critic, Fauchery, and the aristocratic Count de Vandeuvres, afflicted like Georges after seeing Nana on stage. None of the males at dinner that night is deceived as to the reason which brings them together. But of all these men busy following in the tracks of Venus, Muffat is both the most ardent and the most tortured. Since Nana, who for three months has adroitly resisted his advances, has now made a formal promise to him, Muffat resolves to go to La Mignotte that night. He is rebuffed several nights in a row, for Nana is enjoying an idyllic interlude in the country with Georges, in whose arms she feels like a girl of fifteen once more. This charming existence comes to an abrupt halt, however, when, on the weekend, fellow actors from the Variétés pay her a visit. Informed that her understudy is receiving several curtain calls nightly, Nana, though torn, resolves to return to Paris the following day, declaring that she has no wish to die like a beggar. Taking the practical course, she goes to bed that night with Muffat but experiences no pleasure.

By December of that year, Nana has grown tired of Muffat and constantly lies to him about her plans. Muffat finds himself in financial trouble once more and, since he cannot give money, finds himself begging Nana to be with him. One night, feeling hopelessly trapped, she loses her usual good nature and relates to Muffat a rumor that his wife has been having an affair with Fauchery since the time they met at Mme. Hugon's. Feeling already tainted to the marrow and now a cuckold to boot, Muffat becomes momentarily wild and almost crushes Nana by pressing his heel against her head. Then he rushes out into the night and spends hours roaming the streets of Paris, staring at Fauchery's apartment and begging God to comfort him in his despair. At dawn, he mechanically returns to Nana's house, just ahead of Steiner, who has come with the thousand francs she demanded of him if he is ever to sleep with her again. Enraged at being disturbed, she orders both of them to leave. When they beg her to listen to them, she flings open wide the bedroom door and, in the midst of the tumbled bed, the two men catch sight of Fontan. This comic actor at the Variétés, who played the role of Vulcan, god of the cuckolds in *Blonde Venus,* is Nana's latest lover. Outside, on the pavement, the fat, ruined banker and the thin, wasted count shake hands silently as though moved by a mutual sense of fraternity.

Within two weeks, Nana has secretly fled from her creditors by setting up housekeeping with Fontan in another section of Paris. In spite of her many wealthy benefactors, she has not managed to save money. At first, sharing her life with Fontan is a delicious experience, but they soon begin to quarrel and he beats her with increasing regularity and ferocity. Furthermore, neither of them is cast in the current production at the Théâtre des Variétés nor in the one in rehearsal; so they have limited finances. She is vexed to learn that La Mignotte is sold by the nearly bankrupt Steiner for a very low price. Disregarding the advice of friends, Nana remains stubbornly steadfast in her devotion to Fontan, even though his nastiness is always a threat to her well-being. In three months, her savings are exhausted. When Fontan refuses to give her any money, Nana sacrifices herself in order to support them both. She teams up with Satin, her childhood friend, now an experienced street prostitute, and prowls at night in quest of a five-franc piece, just as she did when she was fifteen. Somehow, she always manages to put food on the table. However, her heroic devotion goes unrewarded. At first, Fontan merely takes advantage of her; then he further abuses the privilege and, finally, refuses to let her into their apartment one night. Nana, beside herself with grief, takes temporary refuge at the home of her aunt, Mme. Lerat.

A few weeks later, during November, because a friend named Labordette intercedes in her behalf, Nana is offered the small part of a courtesan in the new production in rehearsal at the Variétés. She sits in on a rehearsal session, then balks at playing a courtesan a second time. She aspires to the part of the honest woman in the show. Labordette has also arranged for Nana to have an interview with Muffat at the theatre. The latter has never gotten over Nana, in spite of her previous behavior; he is hopelessly addicted to her. Since it is his money that is being used to produce the play, Nana makes a business arrangement with him. If he wields his power to get her the part of the respectable woman, she will become his faithful mistress. Unfortunately, a month later, the first night of *Little Duchess* proves disastrous to Nana, who is atrociously bad in a role so ill suited to her. Furious, she vows to force all those who made fun of her lick the ground at her feet one day.

Thereupon, Nana becomes a smart woman, mistress of all that is foolish and filthy in man; she becomes queen among the most expensive of her kind. She and Muffat spare no expense in furnishing the mansion he purchases for her in the Avenue de Villiers. Nana also maps out the terms of their relationship, which Muffat accepts, on the condition that she be faithful. As time goes by, she even influences him in his domestic affairs, giving him good advice. However, to prove to herself that she is still a free woman, she has an affair with the Count de Vandeuvres, again strictly on her own terms. Then she is reunited with young Georges Hugon, who has fled the prison in which his mother has kept him since learning of his affair with Nana. Soon, George's older brother, Philippe, a soldier, is also conquered by her charms and the two brothers become rivals. Muffat is kept in such unquestioning, docile submission that soon all these men are openly about her house, greeting each other like intimate friends.

Nevertheless, in spite of her luxurious life and her sizeable group of courtiers, Nana is nearly bored to death with her existence and feels a great void in her life. One afternoon, while returning home from a concert, she recognizes the shabbily dressed Satin and bears her off in her carriage. From that day on, Satin becomes Nana's vicious foible; her latent attraction for those of her own sex comes to the surface. She tries to keep Satin with her as her lover; but the latter, seized by a longing for air and full of sentimental regret for her old street existence, soon runs away and into the arms of her old lover, a certain Mme. Robert. Nana finally carries Satin off in triumph, but the vengeful Mme. Robert writes anonymous letters to several of her rival's male lovers. Nana, however, forces all these gentlemen with great names and upright tradition to accept Satin as her female lover in residence. One evening, when Satin becomes angry at the men and threatens to leave if Nana will not throw them all out, the latter goes so far as to send Muffat away, refusing him the favor she earlier promised him that night in return for sapphires he gave her.

In June, shortly after Nana has been named the queen of the famous race, the Grand Prix de Paris, in the Bois de Boulogne, because the winning horse was named after her, she finds herself once again with Muffat, who, as usual, has returned servilely to her after sulking for several days. On this night, Nana expresses to Muffat her fear of death and hell with such intensity that both of them become conquered by the same obsession. Two days later, Muffat discovers that Nana has had a miscarriage. However, it is she who ends up comforting him, for Muffat has discovered that his wife has been having a torrid affair with Fauchery. Nana convinces him that it is in the best interests of all parties involved that Muffat take no hostile action against his wife but rather effect a reconciliation, which he reluctantly does. In the meantime, the Countess Sabine Muffat de Beuville, rejuvenated by passion, has become an incredible spendthrift and devours her husband's shrinking fortune by having their home, once full of an atmosphere of religious austerity, totally redecorated. Now everything about the place suggests voluptousness, as if some fleshly wind had swept away the relics of a vanquished epoch. The elderly guests who attend the reception celebrating the signing of the wedding contract between the Muffats' daughter, Estelle, and Daguenet, Nana's former lover, a match Nana helped arrange, are astounded at the metamorphosis which has taken place. In fact, the waltz from *Blonde Venus* is being played by the musicians; it seems to be sounding the knell of an old race amid the suddenly ignited ruins of accumulated wealth. Nana, although unseen, seems to be stretching her limbs above the dancer's heads and sending corruption through their caste.

Not long after this event, Muffat catches Nana in the act of lovemaking with Georges Hugon. She makes excuses this time, but, when surprised by Muffat after that, becomes haughty and orders him to get out of her life if he does not like what he sees. Although Muffat's illusions are totally shattered, he cannot bear to live without her and is thus forced to tolerate her flaunting her other lovers in his face. Nana, more wasteful than ever, is endlessly short of money amid all the luxury that surrounds her. Therefore, she does not hesitate to exchange lovemaking with all of her addicted lovers for the money they procure for her. Philippe Hugon, caught stealing money from his regiment, is dishonored and imprisoned. On those occasions when no one can provide Nana with money immediately, she resorts to a procuress.

Nana's entire situation in the Avenue de Villiers mansion deteriorates very quickly. Her servants turn on her and openly insult her, accusing her, among other things, of sleeping with Julien, her house steward. Charles, her coachman, is fired for calling her a whore. The other servants depart, stealing valuables as they go. Zoé alone remains with Nana; she is planning a secret scheme for the near future. Total debauchery sets in as Nana cheats on Satin, just as she deceives Muffat, by picking up girls on street corners. At the same time, she is hell bent on the financial ruin of all of her once-wealthy lovers. Suddenly, Georges Hugon kills himself, shortly after Nana has mocked him for proposing marriage to her.

Muffat continues to endure every humiliation Nana subjects him to. The rage for debasing people seems inborn in her (or so Zola would have us believe). In his imbecilic state, Muffat is possessed by vaguely remembered stories of saints devoured by vermin who, in turn, devoured their own excrement. His mind snaps completely, however, when he walks into Nana's bedroom and discovers that decrepit old lecher, his father-in-law, the Marquis de Chouard, lying in her bed, wallowing at her bosom. Unable to bear any more, Muffat is led away. He turns again to God; the voluptuous pleasures he used to find with Nana now come from religion.

Shortly after the Muffat-de Chouard incident, Zoé gives Nana notice. Her project, long contemplated, is to be realized at last; she is to take over the establishment of a retiring procuress, Mme. Tricon. Satin too disappears; and, after two weeks, Nana learns that she is about to die in a hospital, Mme. Robert, her former lover, having reduced her to such a damnable state. Nana returns briefly and successfully to the stage, then suddenly vanishes.

Months pass. Rumors circulate that Nana has been up to her old tricks, first in Egypt and then in Russia. Then, she begins to be forgotten. But suddenly, one evening in July, it is discovered that she is back in Paris. Having triumphed among the Egyptian and Russian male elite, Nana comes home to die. She falls victim to smallpox and in no time is fruit for the charnel house.

Venus rots. The poison she assimilated in the gutters, the leaven with which she poisoned a whole people, has climbed to her face and turned it to corruption.

Amélie, Irma d'Anglars, Auguste, Jacqueline Bandu, Barillot, Becker, Clarisse Besnus, Maria Blond, Bordenave, Bosc, Dr. Boutarel, Brebant, Mme. Bron, Simonne Cabiroche, Mme. Chantereau, Charles, Léonide de Chezelles, M. de Chezelles, Marquis de Chouard, Clerk (unnamed), Coachman (unnamed), Duke de Corbreuse, Cossard, Paul Daguenet, Baroness Decker, Mme. Drouard, Hector de la Falaise, Léon Fauchery, Fernande, Fontan, Foucarmont, Baroness de Fougeray, Mlle. de Fougeray, Francis, François, Gaga, Gentleman (unnamed), Gresham, Caroline Héquet, Mme. Héquet, Léa de Horn, Georges Hugon, Mme. Hugon, Philippe Hugon, Mme. de Joncquoy, Jonquier, Joseph, Mme. Jules, Julien, Labordette, Laure, Mme. Lerat, Lili, Louis, Louise, Mme. Maloir, Man (unnamed), Maréchal, Maria, Baron de Mauriac, Auguste Mignon, Charles Mignon, Henri Mignon, Rose Mignon, Miser (unnamed), Count Muffat de Beuville, Countess Sabine Muffat de Beuville, Estelle Muffat de Beuville, Nana, Tatan Néné, Octave, Ollivier, Laure Piédefer, Queen Pomaré, Price, Prince of Scots, Prullière, Mme. Robert, Satin, Blanche de Sivry, Steiner, Lucy Stewart, Super (unnamed), Dr. Tavernier, Mme. Tricon, Count Xavier de Vandeuvres, Théophile Venot, Baron Verdier, Victorine, Louise Violaine, Wallachian (unnamed), Zoé.

Notre-Dame de Paris, Hugo, 1831.

On 6 January 1482, an enormous crowd overflows the Palais de Justice in Paris to see a performance of the poet Pierre Gringoire's morality play. After the arrival of the Cardinal de Bourbon, accompanied by several crude bourgeois Flemish ambassadors, the spectators gradually lose interest in the play. One of the ambassadors proposes that they abandon the play in favor of the ceremony of electing the Pope of the Fools, which is a contest of grimaces. The Parisians enthusiastically support this idea. The unanimous winner of the contest is Quasimodo, the grotesque, hideously deformed hunchback who has been deafened from ringing the bells of Notre-Dame. As soon as he is crowned, the traditional procession of celebration moves outside into the streets of the Ile de la Cité. The few spectators lingering in the Palais de Justice suddenly rush to the windows to watch the dancing of the gypsy girl Esmeralda, thereby completely dashing the hopes of Gringoire, who has insisted that his actors perform his morality play to the bitter end.

Gringoire, despairing and penniless, wanders through Paris in search of lodging and food. He finally comes upon the sinister-looking Place de Grève, with its pillory and gallows. That night it is illuminated by a magnificent bonfire. The same slender, radiant young gypsy woman with large black eyes is dancing and singing in an unknown tongue. Esmeralda's pet goat Djali performs the miraculous stunts her mistress has taught her. Two discordant voices are heard above the applause of the crowd. One is that of a mysterious-looking bald man of austere appearance, and the other belongs to a crazy old woman who lives as a recluse in a neighboring cell known as the Trou-aux-Rats. The man accuses Esmeralda of witchcraft, and the old woman condemns her because she is a gypsy.

As soon as he sees Quasimodo, the man rushes toward him and snatches the Pope of Fools crown from his head. The amazed Gringoire recognizes this person, whom Quasimodo is now following as a slave follows his master, to be Dom Claude Frollo, the bizarre archdeacon of Notre-Dame. Once the two have disappeared, Gringoire decides to follow the gypsy girl. Suddenly, Esmeralda is attacked and nearly abducted by two men. Gringoire receives a hard blow on the head from one of the two, whom he recognizes to be Quasimodo. The police then appear and capture Quasimodo. Esmeralda, after expressing her gratitude to the captain of the guard, slips away into the night. Gringoire, trying to cope with his wounds, guesses that Esmeralda's other assailant, who has fled, is Claude Frollo. While continuing to wander aimlessly through the city, the hungry Gringoire finds himself surrounded by thieves who lead him to their haunt, the Cour des Miracles. He is saved from hanging only by the arrival of Esmeralda, who agrees to take him for a husband. After being led to a shelter and given food by Esmeralda, Gringoire quickly discovers, to his disappointment, that the gypsy girl saved him only out of kindness, not out of love. Even so, a genuine friendship begins to develop between them.

On Quasimodo Sunday 1467, fifteen years before the events of 6 January 1482 which have just been summarized, a foundling, five years of age, is discovered in the Cathedral of Notre-Dame. The child is so monstrous looking that no parishioner wishes to take him in. So the priest Claude Frollo adopts the wretched little creature and destines his foster son to be the bell ringer of Notre-Dame. Frollo himself is known for his intelligence and great dedication to learning in many areas in addition to theology. At the same time, he is also attempting to raise his parentless baby brother, as well as Quasimodo.

Quasimodo's ugliness has deformed his character, making him mischievous and savage. A broken eardrum caused by the thunderous noise of the bells has shut him off from the malice of human beings. The cathedral, whose darkest corners he has fathomed, is his one great love. This magnificent Gothic edifice is not only his entire society but also his entire world. His greatest joy is when he rings the bells on the days of great peals. The only human being to whom Quasimodo remains attached is Claude Frollo, to whom he is extraordinarily grateful. This is still the case in 1482, when Quasimodo is about twenty years old and Claude Frollo about thirty-six.

Discouraged and saddened by the irresponsible behavior of his brother, who has become a dissipated university student, Claude Frollo becomes increasingly morose and ever more deeply absorbed in his studies. His passion for alchemy becomes stronger by the day, thus earning him the distrust not only of lay people but of church officials as well. By the time of the occurrences related in this story, symptoms of a violent moral preoccupation on Claude Frollo's part have become unusually intense. By disposition as well as profession, he has always remained aloof from women; he now seems to dislike them more than ever. His horror of gypsies has also become more pronounced.

In short, both Claude Frollo and Quasimodo are looked down upon by the populace: people mock them but also fear them.

On the morning of 7 January 1482, Quasimodo is brought before the judge to be tried for his attempted abduction of Esmeralda. The deafness of the hunchback exasperates the judge, half-deaf himself; he condemns Quasimodo to be flogged on the pillory of the Grève.

On the Place de Grève, a while later, a crowd gathers near the cell built into the wall of an old house. This cell is the one nicknamed the Trou-aux-Rats, occupied by a recluse who lives on public charity. This recluse is known as Sister Gudule; it is she who previously cursed Esmeralda. Among the crowd are three women of the bourgeoisie who are gossiping. One of them, a visitor from Reims, tells her two Parisian friends the story of a poor woman of Reims, named Paquette la Chantefleurie, whose daughter Agnès was stolen from her sixteen years before by nomad gypsies who substituted for the little girl a hideous, deformed boy. Only one of the little girl's shoes was left behind. Driven mad in her despair, Paquette la Chantefleurie disappeared from Reims. The monstrous child was sent to Paris to be deposited in Notre-Dame. After telling this story the woman from Reims approaches the Trou-aux-Rats and is amazed to discover that the crazed woman in the cell is none other than Paquette la Chantefleurie.

Meanwhile, Quasimodo is brought in to be flogged, jeered at all the while by the crowd. The mob soon begins to laugh and cheer when the torturer arrives and begins to lash the poor hunchback, who writhes in agony and begs for water. After the flogging, the same crowd is suddenly hushed when Esmeralda steps up to the platform and places the neck of a gourd filled with water between Quasimodo's jagged teeth. A big tear is seen trickling from his bloodshot eye, down his deformed face so long contracted by despair. The sight of a beautiful woman offering relief to a deformed man on the pillory is a sublime moment for one and all.

Several weeks elapse; it is now the beginning of March. Esmeralda's thoughts are constantly of the captain, Phoebus de Châteaupers, who saved her from being abducted by Dom Claude Frollo and Quasimodo. She has taught her little goat Djali to arrange in order the letters which spell the name Phoebus. Meanwhile, Dom Claude Frollo's strange interest in Esmeralda has never waned; he watches her in secret each time she performs on the parvis of Notre-Dame. One day, he lures Pierre Gringoire, who as Esmeralda's gypsy husband has become a mountebank, into the cathedral and extracts from him all the information he wishes. Claude Frollo is particularly pleased to hear that Esmeralda remains a virgin; not even Gringoire has touched her. Quasimodo, too, has remained deeply affected by Esmeralda. Since the day she offered him drink on the pillory, his beloved cathedral bells have been relegated to second place in his heart. They ring less jubilantly, to the great disappointment of the populace.

One day, young Jehan Frollo goes to visit his brother at Notre-Dame in the cell where he feverishly pursues his alchemy research. Jehan overhears his brother shrieking at the wall that one fixed idea haunts him and pierces his brain like a red-hot iron. Then, in a moment of extraordinary exaltation, Dom Claude Frollo engraves on the wall in Greek the word "fatality." Beneath it is a word engraved by the same hand, meaning impurity.

Jehan Frollo then observes the visit of Jacques Charmoulue, his brother's disciple in alchemy. Charmoulue, ever eager to bring sorcerers to trial, declares that he is prepared to indict Esmeralda for practicing magic. Frollo nearly loses complete control of himself and, in a menacing tone of voice, calls upon Charmoulue to abandon this scheme. Shortly thereafter, Claude Frollo observes his brother, who has withdrawn unnoticed from the cathedral, in conversation with Phoebus de Châteaupers. Frollo begins to eavesdrop and shudders upon hearing Phoebus boast to Jehan that he has a rendezvous with the gypsy Esmeralda that very night. Insane with jealousy, Dom Claude Frollo follows Phoebus in the darkness to the place of the rendezvous. When Phoebus attempts to take advantage of Esmeralda, just after she confesses her pure, naïve love for him, Claude Frollo leaps upon him and plunges a dagger into his chest. Esmeralda faints. Upon regaining consciousness, she finds herself surrounded by soldiers who declare that she, a sorceress, has stabbed their captain.

At her trial, Esmeralda is accused not only of murder, but of sorcery. Her goat Djali is accused of being an accomplice because of the stunts it performs. Vehemently denying that she killed Phoebus, Esmeralda is sentenced to be tortured. However, she does not have the strength to endure the torture and finally, her spirit broken, confesses to everything the judges wish. Esmeralda is then sentenced to be hanged at the Place de Grève after doing penance on the great porch of Notre-Dame. The day before her hanging, she is visited by Claude Frollo, who, raging and moaning, confesses his love and guilt to her. He proposes to save her, if only she will try to love him. Filled with revulsion, Esmeralda drives him away. The next day, as the execution is in preparation, the hag-recluse of the Trou-aux-Rats becomes exalted upon hearing that the gypsy girl she has hated so much is about to be hanged.

Unknown to both Claude Frollo and Esmeralda, Phoebus miraculously survived his wound. He reappears in Paris on the very day that Esmeralda's execution is to take place and finds himself viewing the ceremony of penance imposed upon her. When Esmeralda is brought onto the parvis to confess her crime before none other than Claude Frollo, she notices Phoebus in the distance standing on a balcony. Both she and Claude Frollo become hysterical, but her cries are ignored. Just as she is about to be led away, another spectator rushes to her aid. Quasimodo fells both of the executioner's assistants, cuts the noose from Esmeralda's neck, grabs her around the waist with one hand and, in one bound, is in the church, shouting in an overpowering voice: "Santuary!" The mob repeats this word and applauds frenetically. The cathedral is a place of refuge; human justice dares not cross its threshold.

The overwrought Dom Claude Frollo rushed away from the scene just before Quasimodo's sudden arrival; he is therefore unaware of what has happened. Nearly insane with passion and despair, he wanders aimlessly through the city. Upon returning to Notre-Dame that night, he sees Esmeralda; but, because he believes her to be dead, he imagines himself to be in the presence of a spectre. Little does he know that Quasimodo has assumed responsibility for Esmeralda's well-being. Gradually, Esmeralda begins to adjust to Quasimodo's deformity; she comes to understand what a beautiful soul is lodged within this hideous body. Nevertheless, her thoughts are almost completely of Phoebus. One day, she sees him entering the house opposite the cathedral. Even though it causes him great personal suffering, Quasimodo is so devoted to the gypsy that he goes off to try to bring Phoebus to her. His great effort proves to be futile, to his chagrin as well as Esmeralda's.

Soon, Claude Frollo is apprised of the fact that Esmeralda is alive and living in Notre-Dame. He shuts himself up in his cell and closes his door to everyone. From the cell window he can watch Esmeralda in her cell-sanctuary and finds himself, to his dismay, jealous even of Quasimodo for being so tender toward the gypsy. Finally, unable to bear it any longer, Claude Frollo rushes to her cell one dark night. He attacks her violently, begging her to love him and cursing her at the same time. Quasimodo intervenes once again and threatens to kill Claude Frollo. Livid with rage, the crazed priest flees to his cell, determined that no human being shall ever have Esmeralda.

Intent that Esmeralda will leave Notre-Dame so that he may be free to dispose of her, Claude Frollo meets up with Pierre Gringoire, whom he convinces that, if he and his band of gypsies do not storm the cathedral and rescue Esmeralda, the court of Parliament will lay hold of her and have her hanged. That night, the gypsies, including Gringoire and also Jehan Frollo, who has become a vagabond, march upon Notre-Dame. They are driven back because of a superhuman effort on the part of Quasimodo, who kills scores of gypsies, including Jehan Frollo. The infuriated gypsies then charge Notre-Dame with increased fury. Quasimodo, realizing that he can not hold them off for long, prays for a miracle to happen. It does, in the form of the king's troups, who rapidly disperse the remaining gypsies. Quasimodo, filled with joy that he has saved his beloved gypsy once again, rushes to her cell, only to find it empty.

Claude Frollo, assisted by Gringoire, who is unaware of Frollo's motives, leads Esmeralda to the Place de Grève, where, one last time, he orders her to choose between loving him and being hanged. When Esmeralda contemptuously rebuffs him, Claude Frollo places her in the hands of Sister Gudule, the hag-recluse of the Trou-aux-Rats, whose hatred for the gypsy girl is well known to him. Claude Frollo then flees, as Gringoire did before him. It so happens that Esmeralda has been wearing a tiny shoe around her neck as a talisman since her infancy. The matching tiny shoe has been in the possession of none other than Sister Gudule, who has constantly clutched to her bosom this reminder of her stolen child. Upon seeing Esmeralda's talisman, Sister Gudule recognizes that she is her long-lost daughter Agnès. As the King's troops close in on the Trou-aux-Rats, the poor woman makes a desperate effort to protect her daughter. But it is too late. Claude Frollo has revealed to the king's executioner where he left Esmeralda. They soon snatch her from her dying mother and lead her to the gallows.

Quasimodo, in despair at Esmeralda's disappearance, notices Claude Frollo climbing to the top of the church tower and decides to follow him. When he finally discovers that Claude Frollo is watching Esmeralda's lifeless body dangling from the gallows and sees a demonic smile on Frollo's face, everything becomes clear to Quasimodo. In a fit of rage and despair, Quasimodo rushes toward Frollo and thrusts him with his two huge hands into the abyss. He then begins to sob, bewailing the loss of the only two people he has ever loved. Immediately thereafter, Quasimodo mysteriously disappears.

About two years later, in the charnel house of Montfaucon, two skeletons are discovered in a singular posture. The one, that of a misshapen male, is in close embrace with the other, a female who has been hanged. When an attempt is made to disengage the male skeleton from the one it holds in its grasp, it crumbles to dust.

Agnès la Herme, Guillaume Alexandre, Andry, Bruno d' Ast, Master Florian Barbedienne, la Bechaine, Mahiet Bellifre, la Boucombry, Cardinal Charles de Bourbon, Marc Cenaine, Bérangère de Champchevrier, François Chanteprune, Master Jacques Charmoulue, Renauld Château, Captain Phoebus de Châteaupers, Master Cheneteau, Diane de Christeuil, Coictier, Jacques Coppenole, Henriet Cousin, Boniface Disome, Guillaume Doulx-Sire, Duke of Egypt, Esmeralda (Agnès, Similar), Robert d'Estouteville, Eustache, la Falourdel, Méhy Fédy, Thibaut Fernicle, Jehan Fourbauld, Dom Claude Frollo, Jehan Frollo, Joannes Frollo de Molendino, Colombe de Gaillefontaine, Gauchère la Violette, Gervaise, Michel Giborne, Gisquete la Gencienne, Dame Aloise de Gondelaurier, Fleur-de-Lys de Gondelaurier, Pierre Gringoire, Sister Gudule (Paquette la Chantefleurie, la Sachette), Henriette la Gaultière, Isabeau La Thierry, Mlle. La Boudrague, Gilles Lecornu, Jehan Lecornu, Mahiet Lecornu, Liénarde, King Louis XI (Tourangeau), Mahiette, Mendicants (unnamed), Guillemette la Mairesse Mistricolle, Robert Mistricolle, Amelotte de Montmichel, Andry Musnier, Oudarde Musnier, Olivier le Daim, Gieffroy Pincebourde, Robin Poussepin, Mahiet Pradon, Quasimodo, Viscount Albert de Ramonchamp, Guillaume Rousseau, Guillaume Rym, Mathias Hunyadi Spicali, Mahiet Targel, Jehanne de la Tarme, Master Thibaut, Pierrat Torterue, Tristan l'Hermite, Clopin Trouillefou, Mlle. Turquant.

La Nouvelle Héloïse, Rousseau, 1761.

The young tutor Saint-Preux, a bourgeois without fortune, has fallen hopelessly in love with his pupil, the lovely and aristocratic Julie d'Etange. His threat to commit suicide because of Julie's silence prompts her to confess the guilt she suffers because she also loves him. In their correspondence, the two exchange impassioned vows of eternal love based on honor and virtue.

Julie and Saint-Preux are soon separated, but the passage of time fails to diminish their passion. Saint-Preux stays on the opposite shore of the lake in order to be near the place where Julie lives. He writes to Julie that he pines away for her in the midst of wild, primitive nature. Julie's reaction to Saint-Preux's despair is so strong that her health becomes seriously affected. Saint-Preux is urged by Claire, Julie's devoted friend, to return immediately. The two lovers struggle to resist the passion that devours them but, in one unguarded moment, succumb to it. Julie, filled with remorse, seeks consolation with Claire. Saint-Preux feels debased and humiliated by Julie's guilt because he believes that they have merely obeyed the purest laws of nature; the tie that binds them lacks only a public declaration. At Julie's urging, Saint-Preux reluctantly moves out of the house before her father finds out about their situation and banishes him. They find it painful to appear together at public gatherings where they must conceal their passion for each other.

Saint-Preux becomes the friend of Lord Edward Bomston, who is also attracted to Julie. Julie assures Saint-Preux that there is no question of marriage between her and Lord Bomston. However, the impetuous Saint-Preux and Lord Bomston quarrel over Julie and threaten to have a duel. Julie condemns such behavior and confesses to Lord Bomston that Saint-Preux is her lover. Lord Bomston shows his magnanimity by publicly retracting his insulting words. As a result, the two men become close friends.

Lord Bomston unselfishly suggests to Julie's father that she and Saint-Preux be married. The haughty Baron d'Etange scornfully rejects this idea. A violent quarrel ensues between d'Etange and his daughter. Julie is forbidden to see Saint-Preux again. She cannot bear to send him away and begs Claire to help her. After a long struggle, Claire convinces Saint-Preux that he must leave in order not to cause Julie's ruin and disgrace.

Lord Bomston informs Julie and Claire of Saint-Preux's agitated, irrational state of mind. He then offers to help Julie flee with Saint-Preux to Yorkshire, where they may live on his country estate. Torn between her love and her family, Julie reluctantly refuses Lord Bomston's generous offer. She could not live with her conscience, were she to abandon her parents. At the same time, Julie implores Lord Bomston to be Saint-Preux's comforter and protector.

Lord Bomston determines that Saint-Preux will await his return from Italy in Paris, after which he will take him to London. When Saint-Preux discovers that Julie has turned down Lord Bomston's generous offer, he is both distraught and enchanted by her sacrifice, and vows to astonish the world by imitating her virtue. Julie, consoled upon hearing of her lover's vow, promises never to marry without the consent of Saint-Preux. The holy love of virtue will inspire her always. Saint-Preux also vows to marry Julie or no one.

While in Paris, Julie and Saint-Preux exchange countless letters. Saint-Preux feels terribly alone in the midst of Parisian society because he sees only masks, not faces, in this wasteland. Julie believes that he is too critical and that he should not make harsh judgments so quickly. When Julie announces the marriage of Claire to a Monsieur d'Orbe, Saint-Preux declares that they should not be envious. Two hearts which glow with a celestial fire find a pure pleasure which is independent of fortune and the rest of the universe. At Julie's request, Saint-Preux gives his impressions of Parisian women, which are quite unfavorable.

Suddenly, Julie's mother discovers her daughter's correspondence with Saint-Preux. Her grief is so all-consuming that the poor woman's health becomes impaired. Claire begs Saint-Preux in the name of virtue to make himself worthy of the guilt-ridden Julie by renouncing her. His soul in agony, Saint-Preux consents to do so. However, Madame d'Etange soon dies. Julie, consumed with remorse, blames Saint-Preux and herself. She asks Saint-Preux to release her from her pledge. Insulted by the threats of the Baron d'Etange, Saint-Preux nevertheless grants Julie permission to marry another.

Julie is suddenly stricken with smallpox. What she later believes to be delirium actually happens: Saint-Preux, overcome with anguish, secretly visits Julie and has to be torn, moaning, from her. Julie recovers but reproaches Claire for nursing her back to health. Since her efforts to erase from her mind the sweet memory of Saint-Preux have been futile, she prefers to die. Saint-Preux, after recuperating from the smallpox he has contracted from his beloved, rejoins Lord Bomston and returns to Paris.

Not long thereafter, Julie marries the Baron de Wolmar. She informs Saint-Preux that her marriage vows were sincere and urges him to follow her virtuous example. No longer his tender mistress, she will never cease to be his faithful friend. Julie also asks Saint-Preux for permission to tell Wolmar of their love affair, but he argues against this. In regard to Julie, Saint-Preux alternates between feelings of admiration and fury.

Time passes. Julie informs Saint-Preux of the serene life she is now leading as the wife of the moderate and rational Wolmar, and requests that he and she no longer write to each other. Saint-Preux attempts to justify committing suicide but is dissuaded from doing so by Lord Bomston, who has secured for Saint-Preux a position on board a ship which is about to embark on a journey around the world. Saint-Preux will have three years in which to try to find peace of mind.

Nearly four years pass and Saint-Preux still has not returned. Julie still feels the need to tell her husband about her love affair with Saint-Preux, but Claire convinces her to wait until Saint-Preux has returned. Saint-Preux, his heart filled with memories, finally arrives home. Wolmar grants his request to see Julie, who now informs her husband of her past relationship. Saint-Preux is overcome at the sight of Julie, which he has both desired and feared. He must soon acknowledge, however, that if his feelings for Julie have not changed their nature, they have at least changed their form. Julie acknowledges that she loves Saint-Preux as tenderly as ever, but not in the same way as before.

Saint-Preux marvels at the order, economy, and harmony which characterize Clarens, the estate of Julie and Wolmar. He is enchanted at the sight of Julie's Elysium, a secluded garden near the house which has been created by nature, under Julie's direction. This lovely garden is the very image of Julie. During a walk, Wolmar, convinced that the three of them will be united in a lasting attachment, discusses his own simple character and natural love of order. He also reveals that, before marrying Julie, he knew that her heart belonged to Saint-Preux. Wolmar then announces his intention of being away from Clarens for a time and, in spite of Julie's reluctance, he insists that Saint-Preux remain there with his family. Claire reassures Julie, urging her to have more self-confidence. Wolmar has explained to Claire that he wishes to engage Saint-Preux's services as tutor to his and Julie's children, and that he has brought Julie and Saint-Preux together in an attempt to make Saint-Preux completely abandon his former image of Julie.

During Wolmar's absence, Julie and Saint-Preux go boating and are caught in a violent storm. Forced to head toward the opposite shore of the lake, they manage to struggle to safety. While waiting for their boat to be repaired, the former lovers visit the spot where Saint-Preux pined away for Julie ten years before. Their sensitive souls communicate once again, but Julie does not allow herself to yield to temptation. Saint-Preux experiences despair and then tenderness. This crisis has convinced him of man's free will and of the value of virtue.

Julie's secret sorrow is that her beloved husband professes to be an atheist. Her belief in God stems from a sentimental response to the universe. She is dismayed that Wolmar can think like an atheist and act like a Christian. Julie, Saint-Preux, and Wolmar now discuss religion and other concerns quite freely with each other. The time for embarrassment is past.

Meanwhile, Claire, recently widowed, is joyously reunited with Julie at Clarens and vows to remain with her dearest friend until death. In addition, Saint-Preux and Julie's father have become completely reconciled. Saint-Preux, overjoyed that he is soon to become the tutor of Julie's children, departs with Lord Bomston for a visit to Italy. En route, he has a dream in which he sees Julie's face covered with a death veil. He unwittingly communicates this fear to Claire. In the meantime, Julie has become aware of Claire's growing attachment to Saint-Preux and, while pointing out the risks involved, expresses the hope that her two beloved friends will marry. Claire acknowledges her fondness for Saint-Preux but questions the advisability of marrying him. She, like Saint-Preux, is unable to dispel her anxiety, brought on by Saint-Preux's dream. Living without Julie is inconceivable to Claire.

In Italy, Saint-Preux has taught his companion the lesson of virtue by helping Lord Bomston overcome his dangerous passion for Laura Pisana, with whom he was on the verge of forming a dishonorable alliance. Saint-Preux is indeed cured of his passion and worthy of being tutor to the Wolmar children, or so he believes.

Before he is able to return to Clarens, Saint-Preux learns that his horrible dream has become a reality. Julie, in saving one of her children from drowning, has lost so much strength that she is unable to recover. She dies at peace with herself, seemingly tranquil in the knowledge that she and Saint-

Preux have purified their passion for each other. Furthermore, her dying statement of faith in a just and merciful God has had its effect on Wolmar, whose conversion is imminent.

In a final letter to Saint-Preux, however, Julie confesses that she has never quite overcome her passion for him and that, through her death, Heaven is protecting her honor. She begs Saint-Preux to live in order that he and Claire, in their insurmountable grief, may preserve each other. Only if they live will all who are dear to Julie be cared for. Julie's spirit will inspire them all and her heart will unite all of theirs.

Claude Anet, George Anson, Babi, Mme. Belon, Lord Edward Bomston, M. du Bosquet, M. du Bosson, Chaillot, Dr. Eswin, Baron d'Etange, Julie d'Etange, Mme. d'Etange, Gustin, Gustin (Jr.), Hans, Mme. d'Hervart, Lord Hyde, Marcellin, Marquise (unnamed), M. de Merveilleux, M. Miol, Claire d'Orbe, Henriette d'Orbe, M. d'Orbe, Laura Pisana, Fanchon Regard, Regianino, Roguin, Saint-Preux, M. Silvestre, Uncle (unnamed) of Julie, Baron de Wolmar.

Paul et Virginie, Bernardin de Saint-Pierre, 1787.

Madame de la Tour finds herself stranded on the island Ile-de-France because of the unexpected death of her adventurous young husband. She seeks refuge in nature, some distance away from a settlement. In such peaceful surroundings, Madame de la Tour begins to cultivate land and raise her infant, Virginie. She also befriends Marguerite, another victim of misfortune, who has an infant son named Paul. An old Frenchman who has retired to the island builds a cabin for each family. Free from the prejudices of Europe, the two women live in perfect harmony. They raise their children side by side, as if each child had two mothers.

Paul and Virginie go through childhood totally devoted to each other. All their efforts are directed to pleasing and helping each other and their mothers. They reach early adolescence in total ignorance of the outside world. Their natural goodness develops day by day. Paul and Virginie possess none of the faults of civilized society; envy, ambition, vanity, and slander are unknown to them. Their terrestrial paradise is enhanced by a magnificent arrangement of trees and flowers, some of which are given names and others of which bear inscriptions. Other than going to mass and to town to sell their produce and handmade wares and to minister to the sick, the two families graciously avoid society, with the exception of their devoted compatriot, the old Frenchman. Their idyllic bliss seems eternal.

However, Virginie suddenly begins to feel agitated in a way which she does not understand. She can no longer bear to have Paul embrace her in his accustomed way. Paul, not yet having reached adolescence, fails to understand Virginie's behavior, but the two mothers do. About the same time, a letter arrives from Madame de la Tour's elderly aunt in France. Formerly unsympathetic to her niece, the invalid spinster now offers to provide Virginie with a good education in France. Pressed by both the governor of the island and her confessor, and also eager to separate Paul and Virginie for a time, Madame de la Tour finally determines that Virginie will go to France. Upon her return, she and Paul will be married. Only the old Frenchman opposes Virginie's departure; he insists that happiness can be found only by preferring the advantages of nature to those of fortune.

After Virginie's departure, Paul lapses into a deep melancholy for a time but eventually asks the old Frenchman to help him acquire knowledge so that he may communicate with Virginie. Nearly two years pass before a letter from Virginie arrives. She is terribly unhappy surrounded by wealth; France is for her the country of savages, totally unlike her beloved Ile-de-France. Paul becomes despondent upon hearing rumors that Virginie is to be married to a wealthy lord. He vacillates between great hope that Virginie will return and great fear that he has lost his loved one forever.

Virginie, constantly at the mercy of her aunt, finally persuades the neurotic old spinster to permit her to return to the island. However, permission is granted at the very worst possible time, the hurricane season. Virginie's ship is wrecked at a very short distance from shore. Paul makes a heroic effort to save Virginie but is too late. The ship is swallowed up by the sea. Virginie's body is recovered; a tiny box containing Paul's portrait is found clutched in her hand.

Virginie is given a magnificent funeral, which all the inhabitants of the island attend in testimony of their great esteem for her. Paul is disconsolate and spends weeks wasting away, wandering about the island visiting all the places where he and Virginie were once happy. The old Frenchman's efforts to help Paul overcome his grief are in vain. Paul survives his beloved Virginie by only two months. Within another month, both mothers have died of grief, soon to be followed by their two servants. Paul and Virginie are buried side by side. Their mothers and servants rest in peace next to them. The two cabins and the garden are left to fall into ruin.

M. Aubin, Aunt (unnamed), M. de la Bourdonnais, Chief of Black Tribe, Confessor (unnamed), Domingue, Frenchman (unnamed), Marguerite, Marie, Negress (unnamed), Paul, Sailor (unnamed), Mme. de la Tour, M. de la Tour, Virginie.

Le Père Goriot, Balzac, 1834.

Eugène de Rastignac, an attractive young provincial eager to achieve success in Paris society, has come to the capital to study law. His family back home valiantly endures severe privations in order to finance this venture.

Eugene takes a room on the fourth floor of the Maison Vauquer, a cheap, seedy boardinghouse in a depressing section of Paris. One of the residents of this petty establishment is a retired vermicelli manufacturer, who is derided by the other boarders and is known as Père Goriot. Mme. Vauquer and the others believe Goriot to be a libertine because of the elegant young women who pay him occasional visits. The truth is that these young women are his two social-climbing daughters who pay calls on their father only when they need money. By the end of his fourth year at Mme. Vauquer's, Goriot is living in abject poverty in her cheapest room, though he initially occupied the most expensive apartment in the boardinghouse.

Our drama begins late one November night in the year 1819. Eugène returns late from his first Paris ball, given by his distant cousin Mme. de Beauséant, to which he managed to get himself invited. Suddenly, he hears a groan coming from the room of Père Goriot. Upon peering through the keyhole, Eugène sees Goriot in the process of packaging a silver breakfast service. The next day, he finds out that this has been done in order to obtain money for Countess Anastasie de Renaud, with whom Eugène was smitten at the ball.

When Eugène calls upon Anastasie that afternoon, her reaction when he mentions Goriot's name makes him aware that some strange relationship exists between the two. He then finds out from Mme. de Beauséant that Anastasie is Goriot's daughter. Both Anastasie and Delphine de Nucingen, Goriot's younger daughter, have taken everything from the old man, who is an embarrassment to his two sons-in-law. Goriot, the devoted father incarnate, has made the great personal sacrifice of banishing himself from the houses of his two daughters, for the sake of their happiness. After relating these facts, Mme. de Beauséant offers to help Eugène succeed in society by letting him make use of her name. At the same time, she proposes to show him the profound corruption of women and the wretched vanity of men. She suggests that he continue his climb up Parisian society's ladder by introducing himself to Delphine de Nucingen, who is of a lower station than her sister and who is very eager to be received in Mme. de Beauséant's drawing room.

Eugène returns to the Maison Vauquer, only too eager to profit from his cousin's help and advice. That evening, he writes to his mother and sisters for more money to enable him to "open his campaign." The adoring females do not hesitate to make even further personal sacrifices for their beloved son and brother.

Eugène soon finds himself engaged in serious conversation with Vautrin, a fellow boarder of about forty years of age whose bearing has always inspired fear and distrust in him. Vautrin, however, has taken a curious liking to Eugène and proceeds to give the young man practical advice on how to succeed in a corrupt world. According to Vautrin: "There are no such things as principles, there are only events; there are no such things as laws, there are only circumstances; and the superior person unites himself with events and circumstances so that they will serve his interests." Although initially horrified, Eugene soon acknowledges to himself that Vautrin has crudely stated exactly the same thing that his cousin couched in more polite terms. In his mind, conscience soon begins to take second place to the desire for success.

When Eugène is introduced by his cousin to Delphine de Nucingen, she does not discourage his flattery. Upon seeing Père Goriot later that night, Eugène informs the old man that he is in love with his daughter. At that moment, Père Goriot strikes Eugène as being sublime, "illumined with the fires of paternal love." From that point on, the relationship between the two men strengthens, Goriot seeing in Eugène a means for him to come a little closer to one of his daughters. Further news from Eugène profoundly disturbs Goriot; Delphine has wept and is forced to gamble because the allowance her husband gives her is not sufficient to permit her to live in the style to which she has become accustomed. Goriot declares that he would sell Father, Son, and Holy Spirit if he could spare his two daughters from shedding a single tear.

Eugène proceeds to throw himself wildly into the dissipated life of Paris society. His gambling losses tempt him to succumb to a plan previously outlined by Vautrin which involves marrying a young woman boarder at the Maison Vauquer after her brother, the original heir to the family fortune, has been killed in a "fixed" duel. He is saved from temptation by the sudden, unexpected arrest of Vautrin, who, as it turns out, is a master criminal bearing the nickname "Cheat-Death."

On this very day, Père Goriot announces to Eugène that he has miraculously been able to finance Eugène and set him up in a bachelor's apartment where they both can be near Delphine. (Goriot will live in the attic.) Eugène overcomes his scruples without great difficulty and accepts with affection Goriot's sacrificial gift. Their plans to leave the Maison Vauquer are short-lived, however. The following day, both Delphine and Anastasie rush in with the catastrophic news that they are penniless and begin to quarrel violently with each other. The destitute Goriot, his morale broken, rages like a lion before being stricken with an attack of apoplexy and collapsing on his bed. Eugène soon understands that Anastasie and Delphine are far more concerned about appearing at Mme. de Beauséant's ball than they are about their dying father. However, the young man now lacks the virtue necessary to express his concern to Delphine and thereby displease her. His "education" has brought him to the point where he is ready to make a sacrifice of his conscience for his mistress. So he accompanies Delphine to the ball, Mme. de Beauséant's last before leaving Paris forever.

The next day, Eugène alone keeps vigil over the dying Père Goriot. In a last burst of energy, the old man rants and raves, expressing love for his daughters and profound agony because they do not come to see him before he dies. By selling his watch, Eugène acquires enough money to pay Père Goriot's funeral and burial expenses. At the cemetery, he sheds the last of his youthful tears. That evening, as a first act in his challenge of society, he goes to dine with Baroness Delphine de Nucingen.

Marquis Adjuda-Pinto, Marchioness d'Aiglemont, Countess d'Ambermesnil, Viscount de Beauséant, Viscountess Clair de Beauséant, Horace Bianchon, Lady Brandon, Mme. Buneaud, Duchess de Carigliano, Marshal de Carigliano, Charles, Christophe, Marshal Clairimbault, Coachman (unnamed), Cogniard, Constance, Mme. Couture, Cuvier, Derville, Director of Police Security (unnamed), Marquise d'Espard, Countess Ferraud, Mme. Firmiani, Colonel Count Franchessini, Princess Galathionne, Gentleman (unnamed), Gobseck, Gondureau, Père Goriot, Grimbert, Grimprel, Jacques, Countess de Kergarouët, Lachapelle, Duchess Antoinette de Langeais, Mme. de Lanty, Marquise de Listomère, Mme. de Marcillac, de Marsay, Duchess de Maufrigneuse, Maulincourt, Maurice, Messenger (unnamed), Mlle. Michonneau, Marquis de Montriveau, Mme. Morin, Muret, Museum Employee, Baron de Nucingen, Delphine de Nucingen, Colonel Piquoisneau, Poiret, Ragoulleau, Agathe de Rastignac, Baron de Rastignac, Chevalier de Rastignac, Eugène de Rastignac, Gabriel de Rastignac, Henri de Rastignac, Laure de Rastignac, Mme. de Rastignac, Count de Restaud, Countess de Restaud, Countess Anastasie de Restaud, Ernest de Restaud, Berthe de Rochefide, Marquis de Ronquerolles, Mme. de Sérizy, Sylvie, Taillefer, Michel (Frédéric) Taillefer, Victorine Taillefer, Thérèse, Tissot, Maxime de Trailles, Vandenese, Baroness de Vaumerland, Mme. Vauquer (Mlle. de Conflans), Vautrin (Jacques Collin).

La Petite Fadette, George Sand, 1849.

In spite of their superstitious parents' concern, Sylvinet and Landry Barbeau, identical twins, grow up not only looking exactly alike but doing everything exactly the same way. Throughout their childhood, they are inseparable and become sad whenever they are forced to be apart. However, at the age of fourteen, Landry is sent off to tend the oxen of Père Caillaud, a neighboring farmer, to the chagrin of his twin brother, who lapses into a state of melancholy. In addition, he becomes jealous upon discovering that his brother enjoys his work as well as the company of Caillaud and his family. The once deep friendship deteriorates to the point of hostility on the part of Sylvinet, who wants his brother to amuse himself with him alone. One day, when he knows that his brother will be home to spend the day with him, Sylvinet deliberately absents himself. Landry begins to worry about his brother's safety and searches in vain for him.

Finally, Landry has the idea of consulting Mère Fadet, known in the region for her ability to come up with remedies for curing ills of all sorts. But, because she and Landry's family have not been on speaking terms, Mère Fadet spurns him. However, her granddaughter Fanchon, known as Fadette, taps Landry on the shoulder as he walks away. The Barbeau family suspects that Fadette, known as the cricket because she is as thin and black as one, will bring them misfortune if the children associate with her. All the same, Landry has never hesitated to tease Fadette and be teased by her. Fadette mockingly insists that she can find Sylvinet. After making him promise to do her a favor one day, Fadette tells Landry where to find his brother. Soon the brothers are tearfully reunited; Sylvinet vows that he will be more reasonable in the future.

Nearly a year goes by. Since Fadette has not asked him for any kind of return favor, the superstitious Landry becomes worried. All is well until one night when Landry tries to return home after dark. Finding it impossible to go beyond the house of Mère Fadet without walking in deep water, he thinks not only that he has lost his way but that he is being pursued by a will-o'-the-wisp. Suddenly Fadette appears and leads the frightened young peasant out of the water. After a series of caustic verbal exchanges, Fadette tells Landry how he may repay this favor as well as the previous one. On the following day, the feast of Saint-Andoche, he will dance all day long with her and her alone. Otherwise, she will brand him as an ingrate, a coward, and a person who does not keep his word. As she runs away, Landry finds her idea extremely irksome since he has already promised to dance with his girl friend Madelon. The next day, he is greatly embarrassed, but complies with the request of the badly groomed Fadette, who is nonetheless a magnificent dancer. As for Fadette, she is thrilled to be dancing with Landry. When people begin to mock her, Landry leaps to her defense and defies them to continue their insults. Fadette expresses her gratitude to Landry before running off.

Later that night, on his way back to Père Caillaud's farm, Landry discovers Fadette lying on the ground, sobbing. She tells Landry that if people were just and reasonable, they would pay more attention to her heart than to her dress and physical appearance. She would like to save humanity without being mocked for the way she looks. At age sixteen, she would leave her grandmother to enter domestic service, were it not for her poor little brother, Jeanet, who is crippled and deformed, and needs her love and care. Landry suddenly feels great love for Fadette and embraces her. She immediately runs away.

The next day, Landry wonders if his great attraction for Fadette was caused by witchcraft. Then when he overhears Fadette telling Madelon to love and respect him while at the same time confessing how much in love with him she herself is, his strong feelings for Fadette return immediately. Fadette, transformed by love, develops into a beautiful young woman. Unable to suppress his love, Landry soon confesses his feelings to her. At first, Fadette, who is accustomed to being ridiculed because of her former ugliness and pugnacious nature, thinks that Landry is mocking her; but she soon becomes convinced of his sincerity. Landry spends all his spare time with Fadette and her little brother, who is quick to respond favorably to the young man's display of affection. Although she is deeply in love with Landry, Fadette forces herself to be prudent in order to give their love a chance to grow.

Nearly a year passes before Sylvinet discovers that Landry and Fadette are in love. His old jealousy returns stronger than ever, but the wretched twin suffers in silence. However, when the equally jealous Madelon, no longer Landry's girl friend, finds out, she attempts to seek vengeance by spreading gossip throughout the countryside. The twins' father, Père Barbeau, who has always been prejudiced against Fadette because of her strange background, is quick to express his disapproval to Landry. When informed of this, Fadette insists upon leaving the area for a year or so in order to gain a good reputation in a new situation. She now openly declares her undying love to Landry and swears to him that she will return in due time.

At first Sylvinet is happy that Fadette is no longer around; he thinks that he will have Landry all to himself and that he can convince him to forget Fadette. When Sylvinet berates Fadette, Landry stops discussing her with his twin and, since he must talk to some one about her, seeks companionship elsewhere. Sylvinet again sinks into deep melancholy, grows weak, and is soon consumed by fever. In an effort to cure Sylvinet, it is decided to separate the twins. Landry is sent to work for several months on another farm owned by Père Caillaud, which is some distance away. Because he wants to help his brother get well, Landry reluctantly goes off.

Three months later, after nearly a year's absence, Fadette returns, upon the death of her grandmother, to claim her inheritance. She and Landry are joyously reunited one night when he surprises her by appearing at her door. For the sake of Sylvinet, Landry agrees to go back to his job the following morning. Fadette promises to do all she can to cure Sylvinet's mind of its sickness. Two days later, she appears at Père Barbeau's door and shrewdly makes the amazed peasant aware of the extent of her inheritance. Barbeau, influenced in part by Fadette's fortune, becomes convinced of her impeccable moral character. Sylvinet, believing that if Landry and Fadette marry he will lose his brother forever, becomes more feverish than ever. Fadette is summoned and succeeds magnificently in using her charms and her candor to rid Sylvinet of his fever.

After Landry is called home, he and Fadette are soon married, with the blessing of everyone, including Sylvinet. Fadette has a small house built where she and her little brother assemble the unfortunate children of the region four hours each day for instruction. She also provides financial help for those little ones who live in dire poverty.

One month after the wedding, Sylvinet announces his intention to enlist in the army. No one, including Landry, is able to dissuade him. A secret conversation between Sylvinet and Fadette convinces her that he is doing the right thing. For the next ten years, Sylvinet enjoys a brilliant military career. Père Barbeau expresses his amazement at the complete change in Sylvinet's nature, but Mère Barbeau understands what has happened. Fadette charmed Sylvinet all too well. In love with his brother's wife, Sylvinet departed because of his great virtue and strong sense of honor.

Jean Aladenise, Etienne Alaphilippe, Pierre Aubardeau, Germain Audoux, la Baigneuse, Landry Barbeau, Mère Barbeau, Nanette Barbeau, Père Barbeau, Sylvinet (Sylvain) Barbeau, Cadet Caillaud, Père Caillaud, Mère Courtillet, Mère Couturier, Mère Fadet, Fadette (Fanchon) Fadet, Mère Fanchette, Père Henri, Jeanet, Landriche, Louise, Lucette, Madelon, Marion, Martin, la Merlaude, Père Naubin, Rosette, Mère Sagette, Solange.

La Princesse de Clèves, Madame de La Fayette, 1678.

To the uninitiated observer, the court of Henri II appears to be a terrestrial paradise. All the inhabitants of this court are extraordinary: the men are extremely handsome and the women are extremely beautiful. However, the essence of court life consists of pleasure, particularly amorous intrigues. These royal subjects all belong to particular cliques, the two most powerful of which are headed by the king's mistress and the queen, who hate each other. In short, politics and passion preoccupy both sexes with equal ardor.

Into this milieu arrives a young woman, Mlle. de Chartres, who immediately attracts the attention of everyone, so perfect is her beauty. Her mother, Mme. de Chartres, has spent several years away from court, seeking to inculcate in her daughter a concept of virtue which would be the guiding force in her life. This rigorous training has resulted in the establishment of Mlle. de Chartres's reputation as a young woman of unassailable virtue.

First and foremost among Mlle. de Chartres's suitors is the prince de Clèves. After several obstacles have been overcome, M. de Clèves, who not only loves Mlle. de Chartres but also respects and esteems her, is free to ask Mme. de Chartres for her daughter's hand in marriage. The mother believes M. de Clèves to be an ideal husband for her daughter. After the marriage, however, M. de Clèves must acknowledge to himself that his wife's feelings for him do not go beyond esteem and gratitude. Nevertheless, M. de Clèves continues to love his wife deeply, taking some consolation in the fact that she gives him no reason to feel jealousy. On the surface, Mme. de Clèves is a perfect wife.

At a marriage ball, Mme. de Clèves meets the Duke de Nemours, who is the handsomest and most attractive man at court but who is also a notorious ladies' man. Mme. de Clèves praises Nemours to her mother in such a way that Mme. de Chartres understands that her daughter has fallen in love with him, even though Mme. de Clèves has not yet admitted this to herself. As for Nemours, his love for Mme. de Clèves is so violent that he no longer has any interest in the ladies whom he has loved and with whom he has kept up a correspondence. His sudden change of attitude and behavior is the talk of the court cliques.

Shortly thereafter, Mme. de Chartres becomes critically ill. On her deathbed she tells her daughter that she is aware of her passion for Nemours, and reminds Mme. de Clèves to think of what she owes her husband and what she owes herself. She beseeches her to avoid the evils of an illicit love affair. Mme. de Chartres prefers to die rather than see her daughter fall like other women.

Mme. de Clèves, inconsolable after her mother's death, is taken by her husband to their country estate. Although genuine affection for her mother accounts in part for her grief, the need she has of her mother to protect her from Nemours is also a factor. She comes to rely more heavily on her husband to play the role of protector. M. de Clèves tells her the story of Sancerre and Mme. de Tournon, an illustration of the consequences of deceit and treachery in love affairs.

Upon her return to court, Mme. de Clèves realizes that her passion for Nemours is stronger than ever. She is determined to conceal her true feelings from Nemours and everyone else at court, bet experiences great inner turmoil in her attempts to do so, particularly upon learning that Nemours has just renounced marrying Queen Elizabeth of England because of his love for another. A love letter mistakenly attributed to Nemours causes Mme. de Clèves to feel tormented by jealousy. When this misunderstanding is clarified, she conveys to Nemours the great joy she experiences.

Soon thereafter, Mme. de Clèves is consumed by guilt and fear. Once again, she flees to Coulommiers, her country home. When she refuses to return to Paris, her husband's persistent questions force her to tell him the truth. She refuses, however, to implicate Nemours, who happens to be hiding in the park and overhears Mme. de Clèves's confession. Overcome with jealousy, M. de Clèves bombards his wife with questions and finally guesses the identity of his rival.

In his glee, Nemours commits the unthinkable error of revealing at court their situation, that a wife has revealed to her husband that she loves another man. Although he withholds the names of the threesome, this bit of gossip spreads rapidly through the court social cliques and serves to intensify the suspicion and uncertainty of M. de Clèves.

Upon discovering that Nemours is making another secret visit to Coulommiers, M. de Clèves sends a servant to spy on his wife and Nemours. Mistakenly believing that his adored wife is unfaithful to him, M. de Clèves is reduced to despair and becomes critically ill. Mme. de Clèves convinces him that she has never been an unfaithful wife. M. de Clèves dies knowing that his wife is worthy of the high esteem in which he has always held her.

Mme. de Clèves is so violently afflicted by the death of her husband that she nearly loses her ability to reason. Several months pass, and she continues to languish. One day, however, she unwittingly finds herself alone with Nemours, whose passion for her has not diminished. They speak openly for the first time and Mme. de Clèves confesses to Nemours her passion for him. However, her confession will lead to nothing because she refuses to marry Nemours, even though external obstacles no longer exist. Her sense of duty to herself and to the memory of M. de Clèves imposes austere rules upon her. In addition, there is another reason for not marrying Nemours, this notorious ladies' man. The fear of being a victim of an amorous intrigue with Nemours is so unbearable to Mme. de Clèves that she cannot bring herself to run this risk. She believes that only the obstacles Nemours has encountered in their relationship have made him constant. In spite of Nemours's protests and implorings, Mme. de Clèves remains resolute. Concern for her enlightened self-interest, sustained by her sense of duty, makes it imperative that she not see Nemours again. Passion may have governed her, but she will not be blinded by it.

Mme. de Clèves leaves Paris and the court. The inconsolable Nemours makes several futile attempts to see her. Time passes and Nemours's passion wanes. Mme. de Clèves spends the rest of her rather short life in solitude and retreat, leaving for posterity an inimitable example of virtue.

Ferdinand Alvarès de Toledo, Duke d'Albe; Mme. d'Amboise; Claude d'Annebauld; Henri I de Montmorency, d'Anville; Claude de Lorraine, Duke d'Aumale; M. de Brézé; Charles de Cossé, Count de Brissac; Charles de France, Duke d'Orléans; François de Vendôme, Vidame de Chartres; Mme. de Chartres; P. de Boscosel, Count de Chastelart; Claude de France; François de Clèves; Jacques de Clèves; Mme. de Clèves; Louis I de Bourbon, Prince de Condé; Edward of Courtenay; Jeanne de Vivonne, Baroness de Dampierre; Diane; Elisabeth de France; Elizabeth; Jean d'Escars; Anne de Pisseleu, Duchess d'Estampes; Alphonse d'Este; d'Estouteville; Alphonse II d'Este, Duke de Ferrare;

François de Valois (François II); François de Lorraine, Chevalier de Guise; François de Lorraine, Duke de Guise; Henri II; Antoinette de La Marck; Philibert de Lignerolles; Mlle. de Longueville; Charles de Guise, Cardinal de Lorraine; Marguerite de France ("Madame"); Marie de Lorraine; Marie Stuart ("the Dauphin Queen"); Countess de Martigues; Catherine de Médicis; Duchess de Mercoeur; Gabriel de Lorges, Count de Montgomery; Anne, Duke de Montmorency; François de Montmorency; Françis de Bourbon, Duke de Montpensier; Mlle. de Montpensier; Antoine de Bourbon, King of Navarre; Queen of Navarre; Jacques de Savoie, Duke de Nemours; François de Clèves, Duke de Nevers; Marguerite de Bourbon, Duchess de Nevers; François Olivier; Mlle. de Piennes; Charles de la Rochefoucauld, Count de Randan; Viscount de Rochefort; Viscountess de Rochefort; Sancerre; Emmanuel-Philibert, Duke de Savoie; Jean, Count de Taix; Mme. de Thémines; François, Cardinal de Tournon; Mme. de Tournon; Viscountess d'Uzès; Diane de Poitiers, Duchess de Valentinois; Nicholas de Neufville, Seigneur de Villeroy; William of Orange.

"René," Chateaubriand, 1802.

René, a young French nobleman living in Louisiana with a tribe of Natchez Indians, is prevailed upon by his only friends, Chactas and the missionary, Father Souël, to reveal the reason for his self-imposed exile. Finally, René forces himself to bare the innermost feelings of his soul.

René's mother died giving birth to him, in France. Neglected by his father, René has as his only companion his sister Amélie, an impassioned soul who shares his love for nature and for poetry. When their father dies, Amélie enters a convent. Left alone, the despondent René rejects the monastic life and decides to travel. Nothing that he sees relieves him of his depression. Seated atop Mt. Etna, René stares first at the barely perceptible Sicilian landscape and then at the entrails of the volcano. These two images symbolize to him his own existence: an immense, imperceptible creation and an open abyss.

René is no less agitated upon his return to France. However, he is determined to profit from his isolation. First, he lives alone in the city but soon tires of that. Then, life amidst the beauties of nature fails to appeal to René for very long. A disgust for existence, which he experienced even as a child, overcomes him more strongly than ever before, and prompts him to contemplate committing suicide. Before doing so, however, he writes a letter to his sister. Amélie can easily read between the lines and surprises René by her sudden arrival.

Having previously been under the false impression that Amélie did not want to be near him, René is ecstatic to be comforted so warmly by his sister.

However, as his spirits begin to soar, Amélie's health begins to deteriorate. One morning, René finds an impassioned note from Amélie, informing him of her retreat to a convent in order to hide a terrible secret. He resolves to follow Amélie there to make her explain herself. En route, René stops to visit his family home, now in ruins, the place where he spent the only happy days of his entire life. He discovers that Amélie too has just been there. His arrival at the convent coincides with the day Amélie is to take her holy vows. René is asked by Amélie to give her away. He alone hears his sister beg God to be kind to her brother, who does not share her incestuous passion. René loses complete control of himself and clasps his agonizing sister in his arms, completely disrupting the ceremony. He is then carried off, unconscious. Upon recovering, he finds unexpected satisfaction in the plenitude of his grief. René no longer wishes to die, now that he is truly unhappy. Instead, he decides to embark for America, where he later learns that Amélie has died heroically while trying to save the lives of others.

Upon hearing René's story, Chactas weeps and sympathizes with the melancholy young Frenchman. Father Souël, however, reproaches René for his excessive indulgence in self-pity and for his presumptuous belief that one can be self-sufficient. Both he and Chactas agree that one's life can have meaning only if it is devoted to serving one's fellow human beings.

Amélie, Caretaker (unnamed), Céluta, Chactas, Father (unnamed) of René, Priest (unnamed), René, Father Souël.

Le Rouge et le noir, Stendhal, 1831.

Julien Sorel, the peasant son of a greedy carpenter who hates him, has grown up in the asphyxiating atmosphere of the ultraconservative provincial town of Verrières. Although he is an ardent admirer of Napoleon, whose soldiers wore red and who is currently condemned politically, the ambitious Julien knows that he must wear the black vestments of the priest in order to succeed in society.

Because of a business deal concluded between his father, whom Julien despises, and M. de Rênal, the crass, pretentious, liberal-hating mayor of Verrières, Julien reluctantly assumes the position of tutor of the mayor's three children. He is immediately both moved and surprised by the kindness and consideration paid him by the naïve, virtuous, and beautiful Mme. de Rênal. She in turn is moved at the sight of the timid and delicately handsome Julien. He proceeds to astound the entire Rênal household as well as their guests, respected members of the bourgeois society of Verrières, by reciting the entire New Testament in Latin. Julien's attitude toward this society, of which he becomes an established part in spite of his social inferiority, is one of hatred.

The inexperienced Mme. de Rênal finds in Julien a sensitivity she did not believe existed in the male sex. Although the two at first feel ill at ease when they are alone together, Julien begins to relax when the Rênal family moves to their summer home in the country. One evening, during a conversation with Mme. de Rênal and one of her friends, Julien inadvertently touches Mme. de Rênal's hand. The next night, Julien's pride conquers his natural timidity; he seizes her hand. She abandons it to him with only slight resistance. Then, attempting to play the role of a Don Juan, Julien brashly enters Mme. de Rênal's bedroom during the night; she ends up by giving herself completely to him. On the verge of revealing to her his special ambitions, Julien bewails the loss of Napoleon to the nation. Mme. de Rênal's sharp reaction reminds Julien once again of the difference in their stations; so he feels distrustful. Nevertheless, he still loves Mme. de Rênal and profits from their relationship by acquiring from her many details which he never learned previously because of his impoverished, ignorant upbringing. When the King of France passes through Verrières, Mme. de Rênal sees to it that Julien plays an important role in the ceremony. This infuriates local citizenry, who continue to remember his social inferiority.

Unfortunately, Elisa, Mme. de Rênal's jealous maid, spreads gossip concerning her mistress and Julien. An anonymous letter is received by M. de Rênal. Julien's friend, the good Abbé Chélan, has also been informed of the nature of the relationship between Julien and Mme. de Rênal. He makes arrangements for Julien to enter the seminary at Besançon. Public opinion is so strong that Mme. de Rênal cannot oppose Julien's departure. Their farewell meeting, when she gives him a lock of her hair, is a sublime moment in their lives.

Julien enters the Besançon seminary filled with dread. His initial encounter with the Abbé Pirard, the director, is a painful one, but he eventually selects Pirard to be his confessor. Julien naïvely observes to himself that since nearly all the seminarians are dull, inferior people, he will reach the top of his chosen profession without difficulty. However, he soon learns from painful experience that one must play the hypocrite inside the seminary as well as outside in order to succeed. Meanwhile, unknown to Julien, the guilt-ridden Mme. de Rênal has written him a farewell letter, declaring that she must stop communicating with him, for the sake of her children. The Abbé Pirard destroys this letter.

Having failed to play the hypocrite convincingly, Julien becomes depressed and feels cut off from the outside world. He also encounters nothing but disaster in his attempts to ingratiate himself with his fellow seminarians; he is too different from them. One day, while working in the cathedral of Besançon, Julien is surprised to notice among the worshippers Mme. de Rênal, who faints upon catching sight of him. Julien is so moved that his is unable to continue to discharge his duties that day.

Meanwhile, Julien has made such a favorable impression upon the Abbé Pirard that he is appointed to the important position of tutor in the New and Old Testaments. Soon, the Abbé Pirard, who has become deeply involved in a lawsuit by favoring an ultraroyalist, the Marquis de la Mole, over his old enemy the Abbé Frilair, loses his position as director of the seminary for political reasons and is transferred to a charge only four leagues from Paris. Because of Pirard's intervention on his behalf, Julien is appointed secretary to the Marquis de la Mole and companion to the latter's son Norbert. En route to Paris, Julien stops in Verrières to pay a clandestine visit to Mme. de Rênal. In spite of a separation of fourteen remorse-filled months, Mme. de Rênal is incapable of resisting him. He spends that night and the entire following day with this courageous woman of the bourgeoisie whom he now not only loves but also greatly respects. M. de Rênal's suspicions finally force Julien to depart for Paris in great haste.

Upon his arrival in the capital, Julien is given very practical advice by the Abbé Pirard concerning his duties as secretary to the capricious Marquis de la Mole. After some initial difficulty because of his provincial gaucheness, Julien begins to find his way at the Hôtel de la Mole. He succeeds in penetrating the political scene and in fully understanding the snobbishness, repression, and mental stagnation which characterize this smug household. In spite of his boredom, Julien also succeeds in being an excellent secretary to the Marquis de la Mole.

Because of a blunder on his part, the peasant Julien ends up duelling with a young nobleman who then befriends him and introduces him to the opera. Julien's climb up the social ladder begins. His protector, the Marquis de la Mole, also facilitates his climb by favoring him. The Marquis's haughty, extravagant daughter, Mathilde, who finds the members of her society a crashing bore, also begins to take a personal interest in Julien. She finds herself strangely attracted to him because of his uncompromising point of view, and also because he scorns her and she cannot find a reason to scorn him in return.

His attitude toward Mathilde begins to change once Julien hears of the tribute she pays annually to her famous ancestor, Boniface de la Mole. The lover of Queen Marguerite de Navarre, Boniface de la Mole was beheaded on 30 April 1574, for having attempted to save his friends who were political prisoners. Each year on 30 April, Mathilde spends the day in mourning. When Mathilde begins to reveal a great deal of herself to Julien, he begins to suspect that she may love him, even though his social station is greatly inferior to hers. In fact, the wildly imaginative Mathilde sees herself and Julien as reincarnations of Queen Marguerite and Boniface de la Mole. After much tension created by the pride of both, the grande dame declares her love to the parvenu.

However, when they finally spend the night together, each realizes that their attraction to each other is something other than true love. For some time thereafter, Mathilde vacillates between wanting to be Julien's slave and, because of her enormous pride, wanting to hurt him for having made her feel like his slave. Her scheme to wound Julien's pride proves to be quite successful.

Upon his return from a secret political mission for the Marquis and his ultraconservative political allies, Julien retaliates by making Mathilde jealous. He pretends to court the foolish, pretentious Mme. de Fervaques. His scheme works only too well; Mathilde soon falls on her knees before him. Fearful of again being scorned by Mathilde, Julien initially forces his head to dominate his heart. However, he eventually abandons himself to the grateful Mathilde, who is now in love for the first time in her life. A few weeks later, she joyously announces to Julien that she is pregnant. At the same time, she is adraid to tell her vain, socially conscious father. In spite of his initial violent reaction and great internal conflict when he discovers that his pride and joy has become pregnant by an employee, the Marquis eventually decides to turn over his estates in Languedoc to Julien and Mathilde. Furthermore, he offers a commission as lieutenant of hussars to Julien, who will henceforth be known as Julien Sorel de la Vernaye. Julien's joy is unbounded; he will have both fame and fortune, and believes the credit for this belongs to him alone. He has contrived to make himself loved by Mathilde, "this monster of pride," whose father cannot live without her nor she without Julien.

Julien's joy is short-lived, however. M. de La Mole suddenly refuses to permit Mathilde to marry Julien. The Marquis has received a letter from Mme. de Rênal in reply to his request for information concerning Julien. In her long and tear-stained letter, dictated by her confessor (as we later find out), Mme. de Rênal denounces Julien as a vile seducer who cultivates the friendship of women only because of their wealth and influence. Beside himself with rage, Julien races immediately for Verrières, walks into the church and shoots Mme. de Rênal while she is attending mass. He is quickly imprisoned.

Mme. de Rênal, who has sincerely longed to die, is not mortally wounded. She would have been happy, however, to die by the hand of Julien. For his part, he also wishes to die, as he no longer has anything left which is worth living for.

Only when Julien learns that Mme. de Rênal is alive does he repent his deed. Curiously enough, he finds that he has lost his lifelong ambition. After much thought, he comes to realize that the truly happy moments in his life were those he spent with Mme. de Rênal. Mathilde arrives and attempts to pull every string in order to save him. Julien feels only a twinge of conscience for having used Mathilde and her father. Ever true to herself, Mathilde imagines herself carrying out extravagant plans in order to save Julien. He, however, is now tired of heroism and lives only for those solitary moments when he can think of Mme. de Rênal and enjoy the ideal life he might have led with her.

Mme. de Rênal writes a letter to each of the thirty-six jurors, pleading for Julien's life. At the trial, in spite of his previous oath to himself that he will say nothing in his defense, Julien is suddenly moved to speak and says everything that is in his heart. He describes himself as a peasant who, not having the honor of belonging to the jurors' class, has risen in revolt against the lowliness of his station. That is his crime, and it will be punished with all the more severity, he states, since he is not being tried by his peers. After deliberating for an hour, the jury sentences Julien to death.

Before Julien is executed, his only wish is to see the one person he truly loves. He thinks only of Mme. de Rênal even when Mathilde is with him. Suddenly, Mme. de Rênal appears before him. Enraptured, they cling to each other, unable to speak. This is the supreme moment of happiness in Julien's life. Mme. de Rênal expresses the wish to die with Julien, but he makes her promise not to attempt suicide.

After Mme. de Rênal's departure, Julien becomes depressed and melancholy. One evening, he even considers taking his own life. Nevertheless, after much introspection, he comes to see clearly into his own heart; if God existed, Julien would fall at his feet and beg him to restore to him the one person he truly loves, for nothing else matters. Refusing to compromise himself and Mme. de Rênal, Julien marches to the guillotine, displaying no lack of courage. Mathilde, true to the memory of her ancestor Boniface de la Mole, carries her lover's head on her knees to its burial place in a little cave in the high mountain overlooking Verrières. Mme. de Rênal is faithful to her promise not to seek to take her life; but, three days after Julien, she dies without a known cause while embracing her children.

Academician (unnamed), Adolphe, Count Altamira, Appert, Prince d'Araceli, Arsène, Balland, Baron Bâton, Charles de Beauvoisis, Chevalier de Beauvoisis, Amanda Binet, Bishop de - (unnamed), Bishop of Agde, Bishop of Besançon, Duke de Bouillon, Don Diego Bustos, Cardinal (unnamed), Abbé Castanède, Count de Caylus, Count Chalvet, Charmier, Abbé Chas-Bernard, Count de Chaulnes, Duke de Chaulnes, Chazel, Abbe Chélan, M. de Cholin, Churchwarden (unnamed), Coachman (unnamed), Convicts (two, unnamed), Cook (unnamed), Marquis de Croisenois, Mme. Derville, Descoulis, Ducros, Duke (unnamed), Duke de ... (unnamed), Durand, Elisa, Falcoz, Count de Fervaques, Maréchale de Fervaques, Duke de Fitz-Folke, Fouqué, Mlle. Fourmont, Abbé de Frilair, General (unnamed), Geronimo,

Giovannone, Grogeot, Gros, Innkeeper (unnamed), Jean, Baron de la
Joumate, Justice of Peace (unnamed), Prince Korasoff, Baron L..., M. de
Lavalette, Mme. de Lavalette, Baron Le Bourguignon, Liévin, Viscount
de Luz, Marquise de M..., Man (unnamed) with Waistcoats, Abbé
Marquinot, Abbé Maslon, Charcot de Maugiron, Mme. de Maugiron,
Abbé Maury, Mme. Michelet, M. de Moirod, Boniface de la Mole,
Marquis de la Mole, Marquise de la Mole, Mathilde de la Mole, Norbert
de la Mole, N..., Duke de N..., Father N..., M. de N..., Napier, M. de
Nerval, Noiroud, Abbé Pirard, Porter (unnamed), Postmaster (un-
named), Priests (two, unnamed), Marquise de R..., Adolphe de Rênal,
Mme. Louise de Rênal, M. de Rênal, Stanislas-Xavier de Rênal, Rivarol,
Countess de Roiville, Marquis de Rouvray, Marquise de Rouvray,
Présidente de Rubempré, Rubigneau, M. Sainclair, Saint-Giraud, M. de
Saint-Giraud, Mlle. de Sainte-Hérédité, Seminarian (unnamed), Sorel,
Julien Sorel, Sorel brothers (two), Surgeon-Major, Tanbeau, Tax Col-
lector (unnamed), Count de Thaler, Baron de Tolly, Valenod, Mme.
Valenod, Philip Vane, Félix Vaneau, Zingarelli.

Salammbô, Flaubert, 1862.

The Mercenaries recruited by Carthage celebrate their latest victory by
indulging in an elaborate feast in the gardens of Hamilcar Barca, the military
leader of Carthage. Men of all nations are gathered here. As the drunkenness
increases, what becomes uppermost in the soldiers' minds is the injustice of
Carthage for not having adequately reimbursed them. They begin to destroy
everything in sight, committing more than one sacrilege. They are suddenly
quieted by the appearance of Hamilcar's daughter, Salammbô, who appears
on the highest terrace of her father's palace. Chanting in a language the
soldiers do not understand, she accompanies her words with gestures that
terrify nearly all of them. Two men in particular watch Salammbô fixedly,
Narr'Havas, a young Numidian chief, and Mâtho, a young Libyan leader of
colossal stature, to whom Salammbô offers a gold cup of wine as a token of
reconciliation with the army, thereby enraging Narr'Havas. Mâtho dashes
toward Salammbô, but she has already vanished.

The Mercenaries leave Carthage two days later, allowing themselves to be
persuaded that they will soon be paid if they go into camp at Sicca. After a
hard journey, they finally arrive there. Mâtho and Spendius, a former slave of
Carthage freed by the Mercenaries, become friendly, and the slave is quick to
ally himself to the Libyan colossus. Mâtho, in agony, confides to Spendius
that he is obsessed by Salammbô, whom he both desires and fears. Meanwhile, weeks go by and money never arrives from Carthage. The soldiers
become increasingly restless. The appearance of the military officer Hanno,

sent to appease the Mercenaries, serves only to enrage them. After forcing Hanno to flee, the Barbarians set out for Carthage, intent on avenging themselves.

In three days, the Barbarian army, bent on destroying Carthage, accomplishes the journey from Sicca. Attacking Carthage is very difficult, since it is well protected physically. Mâtho is jealous of this city, which holds Salammbô, and strives in vain to enter it. He drills his soldiers mercilessly in preparation for combat. Efforts of the Carthaginians to make deals with the Mercenaries fail, partly because of the constant attempt on the part of Spendius to create fresh dissension.

One evening, Mâtho, guided by Spendius, manages miraculously to slip within the walls of Carthage. They then enter the temple of Tanit, where, goaded by Spendius and against his own better judgment, Mâtho steals the Zaïmph, the mysterious veil covering the goddess Tanit, which is guarded by Salammbô. Tanit is believed to be the source of Carthage's greatness. Mâtho, now believing that he no longer fears Salammbô's beauty, insists upon seeing her. She attempts to seize the veil and curses him but, since he possesses the veil of her beloved goddess, she dares not let her servants restrain him. Mâtho and Spendius escape and manage to reenter the Barbarian camp, in possession of the talisman of Carthage.

Upon learning that Mâtho possesses the Zaïmph, Narr'Havas arrives at the Mercenaries' camp and expresses a desire to join them. Mâtho, who is considered head of the army, accepts his proffered alliance, in spite of his personal reservations. Allies begin to arrive from neighboring regions. A plan of attack is formed; the frontier is to be attacked first, then Carthage itself. As for the Carthaginians, they decide to place their fate in the hands of Hanno, but, once again, he proves to be an inept leader. They then come to realize that only one man has the power to save Carthage—Hamilcar Barca, whom the Carthaginians slighted after the last war and for whose return they now feverishly pray.

One morning, Hamilcar's ship is sighted entering the military harbor. Even though the Elders, the Grand Council of Carthage, dislike Hamilcar, they swallow their pride and implore him to lead the troops against the Mercenaries. When Hamilcar insults them, they accuse his daughter, Salammbô, of taking lovers from among the Mercenaries, prompting an exchange of nasty threats between the outraged Hamilcar and the Elders. However, upon inspecting all of his possessions, Hamilcar unearths many additional disasters wrought by the Barbarians. Finally, the sight of his maimed elephants is the last straw. He accepts the command of the Carthaginian forces against the Barbarians.

Hamilcar rallies the Carthaginians, who become as impatient for battle as the Barbarians. His strategy pays off at the battle of the Macar, won by the Punic army. Mâtho is enraged because of the defeat; he and Spendius vow to win the next battle. Meanwhile, Hamilcar unites surrounding regions to his cause. Mâtho and the other chiefs exact an oath of absolute obedience from all the Mercenaries in an attempt to bolster their unstable spirit. This time, the conflict results in a near standoff, with Hamilcar's forces in the more vulnerable situation because their rations become depleted. Back in Carthage, the inhabitants, filled with hatred, turn toward the god Moloch, the man-slayer, and desert Tanit, since she no longer possesses her veil. Blaming all their misfortunes on the rape of the Zaïmph, they even talk of sacrificing Salammbô, since she indirectly participated in the theft of the talisman.

Schahabarim, the high priest of Tanit who is Salammbô's mentor, convinces her that she must go to the Barbarians' camp and bring back the stolen Zaïmph, thereby making reparation for what he calls her crime. The terrified Salammbô makes her way to Mâtho's camp and is instinctively recognized by the young Libyan, even though her face is conceaded by a veil. Entranced, Mâtho leads her to his tent. When Salammbô throws back her veil and tells Mâtho why she is there, he recoils. Then, aroused, he touches the upper part of her bosom with the tip of his finger, causing a sensation which penetrates to the depths of his being. Salammbô allows Mâtho, completely under her spell, to caress her and indulge himself.

Suddenly, a surprise attack on the Barbarian camp obliges its leader to leap out of his tent into battle. Salammbô seizes this opportunity to flee with the Zaïmph in her arms. However, she is surprised not to experience that degree of happiness she thought would be hers upon regaining possession of the veil. As she escapes, a Carthaginian prisoner curses her, calling her a prostitute. At the same time, Mâtho discovers that Narr'Havas has defected to the Carthaginians. When Salammbô rushes into her father's tent with the veil of Tanit, Hamilcar rewards Narr'Havas by giving him his daughter, whom the young Numidian will wed after the war has ended.

Subsequently, the Barbarians suffer a serious defeat. The loss of the Zaïmph conquers them in advance; even those with no real faith in it feel a distress akin to weakness. After a time, however, Spendius somehow succeeds in rallying them once again. As for Hamilcar, he vows to be merciless in the next battle. The return to Carthage of the Zaïmph cements Hamilcar's supreme authority there. No one dares challenge him. With renewed vigor, the Barbarians follow the Carthaginians back to the city and pitch their tents outside the walls, fully resolved to besiege Carthage. Both sides know that a terrible conflict is about to ensue, one which will result in either absolute victory or complete extermination. As a prelude to battle, the skillful, daring ex-slave Spendius destroys the aqueduct of Carthage late one night. Thirst and then famine begin to devour the inhabitants of Carthage, now cut off from the outside. Suddenly, the Barbarians attack and are able to penetrate part of the city. A bloody battle ensues, until night forces the Barbarians to withdraw, exhausted.

The desperate Carthaginian Elders decree that, in order to stave off further disaster, carnal sacrifices of appeasement are to be offered to Moloch, also known as the devourer. A small child from each of the great families is to be offered as a victim. Hamilcar substitutes the child of a slave for his own young son, Hannibal, whom he has kept in hiding for a long time.

As the sacrifice ends, heavy rain deluges Carthage and the Barbarian camp. Hamilcar profits from the confusion caused by the storm to embark the stoutest of his troops and set sail toward the north. Upon discovering this, the infuriated Mercenaries allow themselves to be drawn out from their encampment, in pursuit of Hamilcar, a labor which drags on for several months. Then, Hamilcar ingeniously lures most of the Mercenary troops into the mountain pass of La Hache, whose outlets have been mysteriously barricaded by his troops. These Mercenaries perish of hunger and thirst. Then, the troops commanded by Mâtho are conquered in the battle of Tunis, but not before they have captured and tortured to death the leprous Hanno. Ultimately, however, in spite of their almost superhuman effort, Mâtho's troops are vanquished by the more numerous Carthaginian forces. All the leaders of the Mercenary forces, including Spendius, are killed except for Mâtho, who is seized alive and brought back to Carthage to be tortured to death before the entire populace. After three long years, the war has finally ended!

Uncontrolled, frantic joy reigns in Carthage. In addition to the victory celebration, it is the wedding day of Salammbô and Narr'Havas. Mâtho's death is a feature of the ceremony. As many Carthaginians as can reach his naked body tear at his flesh, inflicting every torture imaginable, until he retains no human feature, except for his eyes. These frightful eyeballs stare at Salammbô, as he falls lifeless to the ground. Salammbô, almost swooning, is cheered by all; they consider Mâtho's death to be her work. As all Carthage convulses in the spasm of a titanic joy, Salammbô, who felt that Mâtho's death would cleanse her, falls to the ground. It is Mâtho, not Narr'Havas, whom she has loved all along.

Thus dies Hamilcar's daughter, for having allowed the veil of Tanit to be stolen.

Abdalonim, Autharitus, Baat-Baal, Hamilcar Barca, Demonades, Elders (unnamed), Garmantian (unnamed), Gaul (unnamed), Giddenem, Gisco, Guide (unnamed), Hannibal, Hanno, Hictamon, Hiero, Hipponax, Iddibal, Istatten, Kapouras, Lutatius, Magdassan, Masgaba, Mâtho, Narr'Havas, Salammbô, Samnite (unnamed), Schahabarim,

Slaves (two, unnamed), Spendius, Subeldia, Taanach, Woman (un-named), Yeoubas, Zarxas, Zaxas.

La Vie de Marianne, Marivaux, 173141.

(Part I) Marianne, a woman of fifty who has come into wealth, yields to the entreaties of a female friend that she tell her life story. She begins by regaling her listener with tha sad tale of her childhood, when she was orphaned at an early age and then, at the age of fifteen, left penniless by her equally unfortunate guardians. After these auspicious beginnings, Marianne is deliv-ered to M. de Climal, a religious hypocrite who manages to scar her young life even further by a compromising purchase of lingerie. Somehow, Marianne's pride and strength of character, she tells her listener, enable her to cope with even this misfortune.

(Part II) At church, Marianne enjoys being the center of attention. By accidentally twisting her ankle after mass, she succeeds in attracting Valville, a dashing young man for whom she felt an inclination in church. She secretly delights in the fact that Valville is able to see her shapely ankle while a physician examines it. Their tender scene is interrupted by the untimely arrival of M. de Climal, who attempts to conceal his passion and jealousy. Marianne and Climal, who is Valville's uncle, hide the fact that they know each other.

(Part III) Although Marianne finds him offensive, M. de Climal insists upon continuing to visit her. He reveals his jealousy by casting aspersions on the morality of his nephew. Then, on bended knee, he attempts to convince Marianne of his love by offering to set her up in more luxurious surroundings. Both of them are surprised by the arrival of Valville, who, shocked at what he sees, turns on his heels and leaves. Incensed at the thought of her reputation being compromised, Marianne turns on Climal, who quickly retreats. Her greatest fear is that Valville will no longer believe her to be virtuous.

A short time later, the distraught Marianne enters a church to pray. Her sobs are heard by a kindly lady who offers to pay her room and board so that Marianne may stay at the convent adjoining the church. The grateful orphan is warmly received by the Mother Superior. A few days later, Valville, disguised as a lackey, delivers a letter but hastily departs upon the arrival of Marianne's benefactress, Mme. de Miran, who happens to be Valville's mother.

(Part IV) Mme. de Miran is accompanied by her dear friend Mme. Dorsin. She tells both Mme. Dorsin and Marianne of her distress concerning her son because Valville now refuses to carry out an arranged marriage with a young woman of birth. He has fallen in love with another young woman whom he met at mass. Marianne, experiencing at the same time shame, concern, and pleasure, reveals to the two ladies that she is the young woman in question. The two ladies are overwhelmed by Marianne's nobility of character; an extremely tender scene ensues.

A plan is soon formulated. Marianne is to persuade Valville to fulfill his marital obligation while pretending that she wishes to become a nun because of her dreadful situation in life. Sad to have to give up Valville but proud and gratified to be loved by such a man, Marianne writes to him, asking that he see her the following day. Their meeting, witnessed by Mme. de Miran, is so moving that the mother can no longer oblige her son to carry out his original marriage plans.

Several days later, Marianne sees Mme. de Miran at a religious ceremony in the convent. Her benefactress is accompanied by Valville and Climal, who pretends not to recognize her. After the ceremony, Mme. de Miran tells the overjoyed Marianne and Valville that, in spite of the prejudices of society, she has yielded to her son's desire to marry Marianne. A few days later, Marianne dines at the home of Mme. Dorsin, where she feels at ease with all the elegant but unaffected guests.

(Part V) A week later Mme. de Miran again has Marianne accompany her to Mme. Dorsin's. Their visit is interrupted by news that M. de Climal has had an attack of apoplexy. The next morning, Marianne is called to Climal's bedside. The dying man confesses before a priest, Valville, and Marianne that he has been a hypocrite and begs God's forgiveness.

Marianne and Valville meet Mlle. de Fare, a delightful young woman, and her mother, whose curiosity proves to be unpleasant for Marianne. Once Mme. de Miran announces that Marianne and Valville plan to be married, Mme. de Fare invites Marianne and Valville to spend the night at her country home just outside Paris.

After spending a pleasant evening, Marianne is rudely awakened the following morning and finds herself being embraced by none other than Mme. Dutour, the laundress with whom she lived before entering the convent. Marianne and Valville are both humiliated. After getting rid of the laundress, Valville pleads with Mlle. de Fare to conserve her esteem and friendship for Marianne and not to hold her obscure birth against her.

(Part VI) Unfortunately, the chambermaid has already told the snobbish Mme. de Fare, who now greets Marianne less warmly. Upon her return to Paris, Marianne insists upon informing Mme. de Miran of her humiliation. Mme. de Miran pledges her unwavering support.

Not long thereafter, Marianne is visited at the convent by an unpleasant-looking woman who claims to be a relative of Mme. de Miran. The woman then has Marianne driven under false pretenses to another convent, where she arrives in great despair. The abbess informs Marianne that wealthy people of great influence, opposed to her marriage to Valville because of her questionable birth, have had her brought there. She must decide whether she wishes to remain permanently at the convent or marry a man selected by these people. Having reluctantly opted for marriage, Marianne is taken the following day to see the influential relatives at the home of a prominent minister. While waiting to see the letter, she meets Villot, the mediocre young man the relatives have chosen to be her husband. He falls in love with Marianne immediately; but she responds coldly to him, in part because he has wounded her pride by referring to her past. When Marianne appears before the minister, he begins to threaten her. At that moment, Valville and Mme. de Miran rush in, looking for Marianne, much to the surprise of everyone.

(Part VII) Mme. de Miran and Marianne speak so eloquently of their great mutual affection that everyone is moved to tears. The minister revokes his order that Marianne marry Villot and permits her to leave with Mme. de Miran. It is decreed by Mme. de Miran that Marianne and Valville will be married shortly, as soon as Valville has concluded a business negotiation.

However, the negotiation seems to drag on. More than a month passes. To her chagrin, Marianne realizes that Valville now shows less tenderness toward her. One evening, upon her return to the convent, accompanied by Valville and Mme. de Miran, Marianne and the others see a young woman faint. Valville's attentions to the young woman seem far to exceed the call of duty. Nevertheless, Marianne and Mlle. Varthon, the young woman, become good friends. Shortly thereafter, Marianne becomes seriously ill. When Valville finally comes to inquire about her, he asks to see Varthon, with whom he has a long conversation.

Valville's visits to see Varthon become more and more frequent. When Marianne recuperates, she confides to Varthon that she feels extremely rejected because of Valville's lack of attention. Varthon bursts into tears and confesses that she loves Valville, who has also deceived her by not saying anything about his involvement with Marianne.

(Part VIII) Varthon tries to dissuade Marianne from wishing to die and vows to reject Valville's advances in the future. However, the next morning, Varthon tells Marianne that Valville has convinced her that he is far less ignoble than Marianne has led her to believe. Valville claims that public persecution has obliged him to renounce his marriage plans. Marianne realizes that Varthon has every intention of continuing to see Valville and that she has justified to herself his innocence. Her grief and rage are now beyond tears; she resolves to act. Marianne deliberately puts Valville in an uncomfortable situation by dining with him, Varthon, and Mme. de Miran at Mme. Dorsin's. As a result, the truth of her situation is made known to Mme. de Miran, to the great embarrassment of Valville.

Several days later, Marianne receives a marriage proposal from a middle-aged officer, a friend of Mme. de Miran who has secretly admired Marianne since the day he witnessed her eloquent self-defense before the minister. Marianne asks for a week to reflect. In the meantime, she has contemplated taking holy vows and has so informed her close friend, a nun at the convent. Before giving her opinion, the nun, Tervire, tells Marianne about her life experiences before she entered the convent.

(Part IX) The infant Tervire's impoverished father died during the course of his first military campaign. Her mother remarried and neglected her, leaving the child to live with her grandmother and her jealous aunts. The grandmother died when Tervire was twelve years old. Tervire, her spirit broken, was sent by her aunts to live with Villot, a farmer in the employ of her family, where she remained for several years.

A religious lady, once the best friend of Tervire's mother, was urged by the latter to persuade Tervire to become a nun. The friend, Mme. de Sainte-Hermières, was only too happy to oblige. Her efforts were thwarted by an unhappy young nun in love with a corrupt young priest who dissuaded Tervire from entering the convent in a state of innocence. Mme. de Sainte-Hermières then imposed upon Tervire a marriage to the infirm but wealthy Baron de Sercour, the uncle of the corrupt young priest. However, the marriage failed to take place because of a wicked scheme of the same priest, who was eager to inherit his uncle's fortune. Tervire was unjustly dishonored and scorned by all except Villot and his wife, who continued to support her. A chambermaid eventually cleared her name.

Tervire's elderly great-aunt, Mme. Dursan, returned to the area to spend her last days. She became extremely fond of Tervire and insisted that her great-niece live with her.

(Part X) Six years later, Mme. Dursan began to grow very weak and wrote her will, making her devoted great-niece her heir. One day, Tervire interrupted a fight between a young man and a guard. The young man was trying to sell a ring which, as it happened, belonged to Mme. Dursan's derelict, forsaken, long-lost son. A friend of Mme. Dursan secretly introduced Tervire to this son, now extremely ill, and his wife, who were the parents of the young man. Tervire conceived of a scheme whereby Dursan and his family would be reunited with his mother. His imminent death precipitated this reunion. Dursan was survived by his mother by only a few weeks. Before her death, Mme. Dursan changed her will. If her grandson married Tervire, he would be her heir. If he did not, then Tervire would inherit one-third of the estate. The grandson's mother opposed both the marriage and the terms of the will. With a great sense of insecurity, Tervire then went to Paris in search of the mother whom she had not seen for many years.

(Part XI) En route to Paris, accompanied by a friend, Mme. Darcire, Tervire lent money to one of her fellow passengers, a woman who was recovering from an illness and who called herself Mme. Darneuil. Upon her arrival in Paris, Tervire discovered that her stepfather had died and that the house had been sold by his son. The whereabouts of Tervire's mother were unknown. Tervire became alarmed when she heard that the mother and son had quarreled and that the mother's current situation was less than comfortable.

Tervire and Mme. Darcire then lent money to a sick woman who was about to be evicted from the inm where she was staying. This woman proved to be none other than Mme. Darneuil. After talking with her, Tervire discovered that they were actually mother and daughter! Their joy at being reunited was soon tempered by the fact that the mother suddenly became paralyzed. Tervire spent most of her time at her mother's side hearing about the past twenty years of her life, including the neglect of her son and the disdain of her daughter-in-law. Tervire then forcefully and reproachfully confronted her sister-in-law in front of dinner guests regarding her behavior and that of her husband.

It is at this point that Tervire's narrative stops. Since Marivaux also chose not to continue the narrative of Marianne, a twelfth part, to complete Marianne's story, was written by Mme. Riccoboni in 1750. It will not be summarized here.

Abbé (unnamed), Abbess (unnamed), Canon (unnamed), Cathos, Cathos, Cavalier (two, unnamed), Chambermaid (three, unnamed), Mme. de Clarville, M. de Climal, Coachman (unnaeed), Confessor (unnamed), Mme. Darcire, Mme. Darneuil (Mlle. de Tresle), Mme. Dorfrainville, Mme. Dorsin, Duke de..., Dursan, Dursan (Jr.), Mme. Dursan, Mme. Dursan (Brunon), Mme. Dutour, Mlle. de Fare, Mme. de Fare, Favier, Fèvre, Innkeepers (two, unnamed), Jeannot, Mme. de Kilnare, Landlady (unnamed), Lord (unnamed), Madelon, Magistrate (unnamed), Mme. de..., Marianne, Marquis (two, unnamed), Marquise (unnamd), Mme. de Miran, M. de..., Nuns (four, unnamed), Peasant (unnamed), Porter (unnamed), Priest (unnamed), Prioress (unnamed), Procurer (unnamed), M. Ricard, Count de Saint-Agne, Father Saint-Vincent, Mme. de Sainte-Hermières, Baron de Sercour, Sister (unnamed) of Priest, Surgeon (unnamed), Tervire, M. Tervire (three), Mlle. de Tresle (two), Mme. de Tresle, Valville, Mlle. Varthon, Mme. Varthon, Villot, M. Villot, Mme. Villot, Vinegrower (unnamed), M. de Viry, Wife (unnamed) of Innkeeper, Wife (unnamed) of Peasant, Woman (five, unnamed).

"Zadig," Voltaire, 1747.

Zadig, a wealthy young man of Babylon, is healthy, handsome, and educated, and has a noble, sincere heart. He therefore believes that he is assured of finding happiness.

The exact opposite turns out to be the case. His fiancée, Sémire, proves to be shallow and abandons him for another. Azora, the woman he marries, is unfaithful to him and obliges Zadig to repudiate her. He is then falsely accused of theft and, even though he clears himself, is heavily fined. Next, he incurs the hatred of his jealous neighbor Arimaze, who accuses him of writing satiric verse against the king.

Suddenly, his fortune takes a turn for the better. Zadig becomes the king's favorite and then his prime minister. His word is respected throughout the kingdom. It is his very merit, however, which causes his next misfortune. The queen Astarté falls in love with Zadig and he with her. Both realize that, because of the king, they must stifle their passion. However, King Moabdar's jealousy is quickly aroused and Zadig narrowly escapes with his life. In flight, the grief-stricken Zadig looks up at the heavenly bodies and, reminded of the tininess of earth, imagines men as insects devouring each other on a little atom of mud.

During his exile, Zadig comes to the rescue of a woman who is being beaten by a man. Zadig is forced to kill the man in self-defense. When the woman turns on him and curses him, Zadig is astonished. Moreover, he is condemned to be a slave for his deed and is sold to an Arabian merchant named Sétoc. Zadig so impresses his master by his intelligence and wisdom that the two become intimate friends. However, Zadig is soon sentenced to be burned to death by priests who resent him. After bidding a tearful farewell to Sétoc, Zadig flees.

Near the Syrian border, Zadig so valiantly defends himself that Arbogad, a master thief, welcomes him into his group. Zadig learns from Arbogad that King Moabdar has been killed and that Babylon is in chaos. Arbogad allows him to leave for Babylon.

En route to Babylon, Zadig sees a fisherman who, in his despair, is about to drown himself. Amazed that someone else is as unhappy as he is, Zadig gives the fisherman money. He thn learns that Astarté has been proclaimed queen of Babylon. Her king is to be the person who emerges from a jousting tournament as the most valiant and then proves himself to be the wisest by explaining a series of riddles.

Zadig meets a hermit who is reading the book of destinies. Zadig cannot understand what he sees on the printed pages of this book. The hermit agrees to accompany Zadig on the condition that Zadig will not leave him, no matter what he does. When the hermit steals valuable goods from a generous lord and then gives them to a miser, Zadig says nothing. However, the hermit then proceeds to set fire to the house of a kind philosopher and causes the nephew of a virtuous woman to drown. Zadig lashes out against the hermit, who suddenly becomes transformed into the angel Jesrad, his body resplendent with light. Upon telling Zadig to bow before the decisions of Providence, the angel takes flight.

Zadig arrives in Babylon. After overcoming several obstacles, he wins the jousting tournament and explains all the riddles. He is proclaimed king and marries Astarté. All those who have treated him well are rewarded. Zadig is blessed by his subjects and Zadig blesses Providence.

Almona, Arbogad, Arimaze, Astarté, Azora, Cador, Cléotofis, Coreb, Cosrou, Fisherman (unnamed), Itobad, Jesrad, Lord (unnamed), Miser (unnamed), Missouf, Moabdar, Ogul, Orcan, Otame, Philosopher (unnamed), Sémire, Sétoc, Widow (unnamed), Yébor, Zadig.

CHARACTERS

A..., Count d'. *La Chartreuse de Parme*. The new name of the French officer Robert as he ascends the military ranks in the service of Napoleon. See also Robert.

A..., Duchess d'. *La Chartreuse de Parme*. One of the most generally admired ladies in Naples, she does foolish things in order to remain Fabrice del Dongo's mistress.

Abbé (unnamed). "Candide." A parasite from Périgord who dupes Candide in Paris.

Abbé (unnamed). *Jacques le fataliste*. A hypocrite and blasphemer with whom Mlle. d'Aisnon has an affair.

Abbé (unnamed). *La Vie de Marianne*. A young priest who specializes in seducing young women.

Abbess (unnamed). *La Vie de Marianne*. The abbess at the convent where Marianne is driven under false pretenses.

Abdalonim. *Salammbô*. The chief intendant in the palace of Hamilcar. He is blamed for the wounds inflicted upon Hamilcar's elephants.

Abel, don. *Gil Blas*. A nobleman and gambler who is one of Scipion's employers.

Academician (unnamed). *Le Rouge et le noir*. A frequent guest at the Hotel de la Mole, he relates to Julien Sorel the circumstances surrounding the beheading of Boniface de la Mole on 30 April 1574.

Achille. *Germinal*. The first illegitimate child of Zacharie Maheu and Philomène Levaque.

Achmet III. "Candide." A dethroned sultan whom Candide meets because he has come to Venice to attend the carnival.

Acuna, Alvaro de. *Gil Blas*. An instructor in the ways of vice for idle young men of the aristocracy.

Adélaide. *Les Liaisons dangereuses*. Mme. de Rosemonde's chambermaid.

Adèle. *L'Assommoir*. A burnisher who runs off with Auguste Lantier, lover of Gervaise.

Adjuda-Pinto, Marquis d'. *Le Père Goriot*. A smug Portuguese man of fashion, he is the lover of the Viscountess de Beauséant.

Adjutant (unnamed). *La Chartreuse de Parme*. A French officer who is suspicious of Fabrice del Dongo's intentions at the battle of Waterloo.

Adolphe. *Adolphe.* A young man who leads a meaningless life and who, because of his inability to take action, is responsible for the death of the woman who loves him.

Adolphe. *Le Rouge et le noir.* The liberal bookseller of Verrières.

Agathe. *Jacques le fataliste.* The mistress of the Chevalier de Saint-Ouin. She and the Chevalier dupe Jacques's master.

Agnès. *Notre-Dame de Paris.* The abducted child of Paquette la Chante-fleurie. She is believed to have been sacrificed to Beelzebub but, in fact, is the gypsy Esmeralda. See also Esmeralda.

Agnès la Herme. *Notre-Dame de Paris.* A widow who comments on the hideousness of the foundling, Quasimodo.

Aiglemont, Marquise d'. *Le Père Goriot.* An elegant Paris society woman.

Aigurande, d'. *A Rebours.* A former friend of Des Esseintes; he makes a very unhappy marriage.

Aisnon, Mlle. d'. *Jacques le fataliste.* Mme. d'Aisnon's daughter who marries the Marquis des Acis. Using the assumed name of Mlle. Duquesnoi, she assists her mother in executing the vengeance scheme of Mme. de la Pommeraye.

Aisnon, Mme. d'. *Jacques le fataliste.* A proprietress of a gambling den, she plays a major role in the vengeance scheme of Mme. de la Pommeraye, under the assumed name of Mme. Duquesnoi.

Aladenise, Jean. *La Petite Fadette.* An admirer of Madelon, Landry's girl friend.

Alaphilippe, Etienne. *La Petite Fadette.* Another admirer of Madelon, Landry's girl friend.

Albe, Ferdinand Alvarès de Tolede, Duke d'. *La Princesse de Clèves.* The proxy sent to France by Philip II of Spain in order to negotiate the latter's marriage to Elizabeth of France.

Alcacer, don Louis d'. *Gil Blas.* A rich and jealous young man who keeps Laure.

Alessandri, Mme. *L'Education sentimentale.* A midwife who keeps the sickly, neglected baby of Rosanette Bron and Frédéric Moreau.

Alexandre. *L'Education sentimentale.* The proprietor of a cafe named after him.

Alexandre. *Madame Bovary.* A resident of Yonville l'Abbaye, from whom Charles buys a filly for Emma.

Alexandre, Guillaume. *Notre-Dame de Paris.* An official recorder of events, he has just rented the Hôtel de Navarre.

Alexandre, Mme. *L'Education sentimentale.* Wife of the cafe proprietor.

Alexis, Father, *Gil Blas.* An old Dominican who finds Scipion employment with Baltazar Velasquez.

Aliaga, Luis. *Gil Blas.* A brother who is exiled by the Count d'Olivarès.

Allard. *L'Education sentimentale.* A former benefactor of Rosanette Bron (la Maréchale).

Almenara, Marquise de. *Gil Blas.* An elderly society woman who marries a young nobleman.

Almona. "Zadig." An Arab woman who, in keeping with custom, once wished to become a saint by publicly burning herself to death over the body of her recently deceased husband. She later saves Zadig's life and becomes the wife of Sétoc.

Alphonse. *Eugénie Grandet.* Charles Grandet's friend who is asked to take care of Charles's affairs.

Alphonse. *Gil Blas.* Named after don Alphonse de Leyva, this son of Gil Blas and Antonia dies in infancy.

Altamira, Count. *Le Rouge et le noir.* A man condemned to death because of his liberal politics. He is greatly admired by Julien and Mathilde de la Mole because he has acted courageously.

Alvizi, Countess. *La Chartreuse de Parme.* One of the well-known ladies at the Court of Parma.

Amaëgui, Marquise d'. *L'Education sentimentale.* An Andalusian who enjoys her life as a courtesan in Paris.

Amalfi, Prince d'. *Corinne.* A handsome Neapolitan whom, it is rumored, Corinne plans to marry.

Amanda. *L'Assommoir.* A music-hall singer whom Gervaise and Lantier go to see perform.

Ambermesnil, Countess d'. *Le Père Goriot.* A boarder for a time at the Maison Vauquer, she cheats Mme. Vauquer out of six months' board and lodging.

Amboise, Mme. d'. *La Princesse de Clèves.* A friend and confidante of Mme. de Thémines.

Amélie. *Nana.* Daughter of the aging courtesan Gaga, young Amélie becomes the mistress of the Marquis de Chouard for the sum demanded by her mother.

Amélie. "René." René's sister who is tormented because of her incestuous love for him.

Anaïs. *Les Lettres persanes.* After her death at the hands of Ibrahim, she enters Paradise and makes Ibrahim suffer for his past cruelty.

Anceau. *Les Misérables.* A merchant whose truck is seized by Gavroche and Bahorel during the insurrection of 1832.

Andervilliers, Marquis d'. *Madame Bovary.* A local politician who breaks the monotony of Emma's existence at Tostes by inviting her and Charles to a ball.

Andervilliers, Marquise d'. *Madame Bovary.* Wife of the person who gives the ball Emma and Charles attend.

Andervilliers, Mlle. d'. *Madame Bovary.* Daughter of the host of the ball Emma attends with Charles.

Andros. *Gil Blas.* A Madrid physician.

Andry. *Notre-Dame de Paris.* One of Pierre Gringoire's potential executioners.

Anet, Claude. *La Nouvelle Héloïse.* A young man who enlists in the military to obtain money for Fanchon Regard, the woman he loves.

Ange, Brother. *Jacques le fataliste.* A devout brother who is the victim of other monks' slander in his order.

Anglars, Irma d'. *Nana.* The current owner of the Château de Chamont, near Orléans. This now religious old woman was once the leading courtesan of her day. The vision of Irma d'Anglars haunts Nana in her moments of reflection.

Anglès, Count. *Les Misérables.* The Prefect of Police who is responsible for getting Javert his position as inspector at Montfermeil.

Aniken. *La Chartreuse de Parme.* The younger daughter of a landlady in Zonders, she falls in love with the wounded Fabrice, imagining him to be a prince.

Annebauld, Claude d'. *La Princesse de Clèves.* Grand Marshal, and then an admiral, of France.

Annette. *Eugénie Grandet.* The worldly mistress of Charles Grandet.

Annette. *Madame Bovary.* The servant of Lheureux.

Annutchka. *Germinal.* The former mistress of Souvarine, she was hanged for her anarchist activities.

Anselme, Father. *Les Liaisons dangereuses.* Mme. de Tourvel's confessor.

Anson, George. *La Nouvelle Héloïse.* A naval officer and an old friend of Lord Bomston.

Antonia. *La Cousine Bette.* A guest at Josépha's party.

Antonia. *Gil Blas.* The beautiful daughter of Basile. Gil Blas falls in love with her at first sight.

Anville, Henri I de Montmorency, Seigneur d'. *La Princesse de Clèves.* The second son of de Montmorency.

Aphéridon. *Les Lettres persanes.* Ibben's friend. He marries Ibben's sister and retires to Smyrna after many adventures.

Apollonie. *L'Education sentimentale.* A former model for Jacques Arnoux, she bacomes a successful courtesan.

Appert. *Le Rouge et le noir.* A Paris inspector who displeases M. de Rênal.

Araceli, Prince d'. *Le Rouge et le noir.* A contemptible ambassador who seeks the extradition of the Count Altamira.

Arbigny, Mme. d'. *Corinne.* Count Raimond's sister who meets Oswald Lord Nelvil just after the death of her elderly husband. She connives unsuccessfully for several years to oblige Oswald to marry her.

Arbogad. "Zadig." An Arab thief who is generous with his friends. He is finally given an honorable rank in King Zadig's army on the condition that he abandon thievery.

Archbishop (unnamed). *Gil Blas.* One of the many employers of Gil Blas, who serves as his secretary.

Arcis, Marquis des. *Jacques le fataliste.* A man of pleasure who becomes the victim of his mistress, Mme. de la Pommeraye, because he tires of her.

Arimaze. "Zadig." Zadig's ugly, wicked neighbor who seeks to ruin him.

Arnoux, Eugène *L'Education sentimentale.* The younger of the two Arnoux children, he is very spoiled.

Arnoux, Jacques. *L'Education sentimentale.* The proprietor of a series of unsuccessful business establishments, this swaggering womanizer is constantly in debt, borrows money from Frédéric Moreau, and is finally forced to flee Paris to escape his creditors.

Arnoux, Mme. Marie Angèle. *L'Education sentimentale.* The woman to whom the eighteen-year-old Frédéric Moreau suddenly becomes obsessively attracted, the day he sees her on a boat. To him, she incarnates the ideal female, the woman he unsuccessfully longs for throughout his life.

Arnoux, Marthe. *L'Education sentimentale.* The daughter of Jacques and Marie Arnoux.

Arsène. *Le Rouge et le noir.* The Marquis de la Mole's domestic who serves Julien.

Arsénie. *Gil Blas.* Don Mathias's actress friend, with whom Gil Blas eventually finds employment.

Art Dealer (unnamed). *La Cousine Bette.* The employer of Steinbock when Hortense Hulot purchases a piece of his sculpture.

Artémise. *Madame Bovary.* The servant of Mme. Lefrançois at the Yonville-l'Abbaye inn.

Ast, Bruno d'. *Notre-Dame de Paris.* A man known to Dom Claude Frollo who was bewitched by a sorceress and who obtained his cure by having the sorceress burned.

Astarté. *Les Lettres persanes.* The sister of Aphéridon, she marries her brother.

Astarté. "Zadig." The Babylon queen who falls in love with Zadig and with whom Zadig is also in love. After many misfortunes, she and Zadig become king and queen of Babylon.

Astuto, Bernardo. *Gil Blas.* Creditor of don Manuel de Xerica, he becomes the second husband of Lucinde.

Asumar, Count d'. *Gil Blas.* An old fogy who is a friend of don Gonzale Pacheco.

Atala. "Atala." A beautiful Indian maiden who is in love with Chactas but who poisons herself rather than marry him because of a vow she once made to her mother.

Aubardeau, Pierre. *La Petite Fadette.* An admirer of Madelon, Landry's girl friend.

Aubert, Georgine. *L'Education sentimentale.* An elderly vaudeville actress whom Frédéric Moreau sees at the races.

Aubertot, M. *Jacques le fataliste.* He refuses to give money to a M. Pelletier and then slaps him.

Aubin, M. *Paul et Virginie.* The captain of the ship on which Virginie returns to the island.

Aubrion, Marquis d'. *Eugénie Grandet.* Gentleman-in-ordinary to King Charles X. Charles Grandet meets him in the West Indies and soon becomes his son-in-law.

Aubrion, Mlle. Mathilde d'. *Eugénie Grandet.* A rather plain young woman whom Charles Grandet marries to gain her family's title.

Aubrion, Mme. d'. *Eugénie Grandet.* A woman of the nobility whose extravagance has reduced her fortune to almost nothing.

Aubry, Corporal. *La Chartreuse de Parme.* A young soldier at the Battle of Waterloo. He gives Fabrice a few instructions in loading and firing a weapon.

Aubry, Father. "Atala." An old missionary who offers shelter and comfort to Atala and Chactas.

Audoux, Germain. *La Petite Fadette.* Still another admirer of Madelon, Landry's girl friend.

Augers, Mlles. *L'Education sentimentale.* Two young ladies of Nogent. Their behavior is considered scandalous by local gossips.

Auguste. *L'Assommoir.* Owner of a cheap wineshop where Gervaise and Coupeau have their wedding dinner.

Auguste. *Nana.* A waiter at a cafe opposite the Théâtre des Variétés.

Augustin. *Gil Blas.* The brother of Jérôme de Mayadas.

Augustine. *L'Assommoir.* Gervaise's apprentice in her laundry shop.

Aulnays, Marquis Gilbert des. *L'Education sentimentale.* The godfather of the Marquis de Cisy, des Aulnays is extremely fond of discussing agriculture.

Aumale, Claude de Lorraine, Duke d'. *La Princesse de Clèves.* Brother of the Duke de Guise.

Aunt (unnamed). *Corinne.* Corinne's aunt who raises the girl in Florence from age ten, when her mother dies, to the day when Corinne is fifteen.

Aunt (unnamed). *Paul et Virginie*. Mme. de la Tour's heartless aunt who is indirectly responsible for Virginie's death.

Aurore. *Gil Blas*. The daughter of Vincent de Guzman. She disguises herself as a man, using the name of don Felix de Mendoce.

Autharitus. *Salammbô*. A member of the Mercenaries, he is commander of an army corps in the attack of Carthage.

Avila, Sanche d'. *Gil Blas*. A friend of Count Galiano.

Azarini. *Gil Blas*. A slave of don Raphaël during the latter's Sidy Hally period.

Azarini, Père. *Gil Blas*. Father of don Raphaël's slave, he and his son are from Livorno, Italy.

Azolan, Roux. *Les Liaisons dangereuses*. Valmont's servant who seduces Mme. de Tourvel's chambermaid and informs his master of Mme. de Tourvel's activities.

Azora. "Zadig." Zadig's first wife. She is attracted to well-built young men and tries to cut off Zadig's nose.

Azumar, Count d'. *Gil Blas*. A friend of don Gonzale Pacheco.

B..., Countess de. *Les Liaisons dangereuses*. A former mistress of Valmont.

B..., General. *La Chartreuse de Parme*. A general of the nobility whose leg is shattered during the Battle of Waterloo and who is accused of having betrayed the emperor.

B..., M. de. *Manon Lescaut*. A famous farmer-general who pays handsomely for Manon's favors and who informs Des Grieux's father of his son's whereabouts.

Baat-Baal. *Salammbô*. One of the Elders of Carthage, he is an owner of gold mines.

Babet. *Les Misérables*. One of four bandits who govern the lowest depths of Paris, from 1830 to 1835. He participates in Thénardier's attempt to ambush Jean Valjean.

Babi. *La Nouvelle Héloïse*. The maid of Mme. d'Etange.

Bachelu, Thérèse. *L'Education sentimentale*. A fashionable vaudeville performer whom Frédéric Moreau sees at the races.

Badinguet. *L'Assommoir*. A drinking companion of Coupeau.

Baesa, don André de. *Gil Blas*. A rival of don Alvar de Mello, he is killed by don Alvar.

Bahorel. *Les Misérables*. A capricious young revolutionary who enjoys turbulence on a grand scale.

Baigneuse, la. *La Petite Fadette*. A woman who, when consulted about a possible cure for Sylvinet's illness, urges that he fall in love with a woman.

Bakunin. *Germinal.* The mentor of the anarchist Souvarine.

Balandard. *L'Education sentimentale.* A solicitor with whom Mme. Arnoux is seen by Frédéric Moreau.

Balbi, Marquise. *La Chartreuse de Parme.* The mistress of the Prince of Parma.

Baldi, Count. *La Chartreuse de Parme.* The handsomest man at the court of Parma and the lover of the ugly virago, the Marquise Raversi.

Balland, M. *Le Rouge et le noir.* A guest at the Hôtel de la Mole, he is a hypocrite who has gained his fortune by marrying two wealthy women.

Baloup. *Les Misérables.* A wheelwright for whom the accused criminal Champmathieu once worked.

Baltazar, don. *Gil Blas.* The unfaithful husband of Violante, he is fatally stabbed by don Raphaël.

Bamatabois. *Les Misérables.* An obnoxious squanderer of money, he jeers at Fantine and causes her to be arrested.

Bandu, Jacqueline. *Nana.* The real name of Blanche de Sivry. See Sivry, Blanche de.

Banker (unnamed). *Corinne.* An Englishman who befriends Corinne when she goes to England to find Oswald.

Baptistine, Mlle. *Les Misérables.* The spinster sister of Bishop Myriel, she is the epitome of respectability.

Baquet, Mère. *L'Assommoir.* The owner of a wineshop frequented by Coupeau and others.

Barbe. *Gil Blas.* A former mistress of Lamela, whom the latter discovers disguised as a religious person.

Barbeau, Landry. *La Petite Fadette.* The second born of identical twins, he falls in love with Fadette, causing his brother Sylvinet to become melancholy and jealous.

Barbeau, Mère. *La Petite Fadette.* The superstitious wife of Père Barbeau, she is concerned because she gives birth to identical twins.

Barbeau, Nanette. *La Petite Fadette.* Two years younger than the identical Barbeau twins, she eventually marries Cadet Caillaud.

Barbeau, Père. *La Petite Fadette.* A peasant farmer who harbors a prejudice against Fadette until he gets to know her through his son, Landry, and discovers that she has inherited a huge sum of money.

Barbeau, Sylvinet (Sylvain). *La Petite Fadette.* The first born of identical twins, he becomes melancholy and jealous whenever his brother Landry pays attention to anyone else, especially Fadette.

Barbedienne, Master Florian. *Notre-Dame de Paris.* A deaf judge who attempts to interrogate the deaf Quasimodo.

Barber (unnamed). *Les Misérables.* The barber whom Gavroche punishes for being unkind to his two little brothers.

Barbone. *La Chartreuse de Parme.* The infamous clerk at the Farnese tower, who vows to kill Fabrice but is killed himself during a revolt.

Barca, Hamilcar. *Salammbô.* The father of Salammbô and the leader of the Carthaginian troops in the war against the Barbarian Mercenaries.

Barge. *Les Misérables.* A returned bailiff who is the receiver of M. Gillenormand's rents.

Bari, Father. *La Chartreuse de Parme.* A priest to whom Prince Ernesto IV awards a pension for restoring nineteen lines of a Greek dithyramb.

Barillot. *L'Education sentimentale.* The co-owner of a circulating library Frédéric Moreau visits.

Barillot. *Nana.* A thirty-year employee in the theater, he is the actors' callboy.

Barone. *La Chartreuse de Parme.* A nobleman at the Court of Parma who is believed to have been killed along with the Crown Prince.

Barthélemy. *L'Education sentimentale.* The rich uncle of Frédéric Moreau, from whom Frederic inherits a large sum of money.

Baslin, Hortense. *L'Education sentimentale.* A young working girl who is under the control of Mlle. Vatnaz.

Basque. *Les Misérables.* M. Gillenormand's fat, cunning valet.

Bâtie, Mme. de la. *La Cousine Bette.* A member of the same charitable organizations as the Baroness Hulot.

Bâton, Baron. *Le Rouge et le noir.* A guest at the Hôtel de la Mole. His name is ridiculed by Mathilde and her circle of friends.

Baudequin. *L'Assommoir.* A depraved draftsman who lives in the same building as Coupeau and Gervaise.

Baudraye, Mme. de la. *La Cousine Bette.* A Paris courtesan who remains almost respectable in spite of her relationship with Lousteau.

Bazouge. *L'Assommoir.* An old drunkard who repels and intimidates Gervaise by speaking constantly of death.

Béatrix. *Gil Blas.* The younger sister of don Raphaël and daughter of Lucinde.

Béatrix. *Gil Blas.* A former soubrette and servant of an actress, she is now employed by Eufrasia.

Béatrix. *Gil Blas.* Seraphine's servant who turns out to be Scipion's long-lost wife.

Beaumont. *L'Education sentimentale.* A notary to whom Arnoux is to give money he owes another person.

Beau-Pied. *La Cousine Bette.* Marechal Hulot's factotum, an old soldier who serves him for thirty years.

Beauséant, Viscount de. *Le Père Goriot.* An indifferent husband who approves of his wife's lover.

Beauséant, Viscountess Claire de. *Le Père Goriot.* Eugene de Rastignac's Parisian cousin. She introduces the young man into society.

Beauvisage. *La Cousine Bette*. A provincial deputy, anxious to copy the style of Parisians. He unwisely imitates Crevel in every way.

Beauvoisis, Charles de. *Le Rouge et le noir*. A fatuous nobleman whom Julien mistakes for a man who grossly insulted him. The two become friends after fighting a duel.

Beauvoisis, Chevalier de. *Le Rouge et le noir*. A cousin of Mme. de Rênal who is with the French embassy in Naples.

Bechaine, la. *Notre-Dame de Paris*. A gossip who witnesses the ceremony of penance Esmeralda is obliged to perform.

Becker. *Nana*. A jeweller from whom Muffat buys sapphires and diamonds for Nana.

"Bec-Salé." *L'Assommoir*. A fellow worker of the blacksmith Goujet and a heavy drinker.

Beggar (unnamed). *Madame Bovary*. A hideous creature near Rouen, whose staring and singing horrify Emma every time he comes near, including the moment preceding her death.

Belleroche, Chevalier de. *Les Liaisons dangereuses*. A young admirer whom Mme. de Merteuil is manipulating.

Bellifre, Mahiet. *Notre-Dame de Paris*. A spectator on the parvis of Notre-Dame where Esmeralda is to do penance before being hanged.

Belloy, Marquise du. *Jacques le fataliste*. A former guardian of Jacques.

Belon, Mme. *La Nouvelle Héloïse*. A social acquaintance of the d'Etange family.

Bénard, M. *L'Assommoir*. A man who lives in the same building as Coupeau and Gervaise, and who fights constantly with his wife.

Bénard, Mme. *L'Assommoir*. A neighbor of Gervaise and Coupeau. She and her husband knock each other about constantly.

Ben-Josué. *Les Lettres persanes*. A Mohammedan proselyte.

Benoît, Mme. *L'Education sentimentale*. A friend and frequent visitor of Mme. Moreau.

Bentivoglio. *La Chartreuse de Parme*. A nobleman and friend of the Marquis Raversi. He becomes the lover of Count Mosca's first wife.

Bergerin, M. *Eugénie Grandet*. The town physician of Saumur.

Bertellière, M. de la. *Eugénie Grandet*. Mme. Grandet's grandfather, from whom she inherits a small fortune which her miserly husband controls.

Berthe. *Madame Bovary*. An elegant woman who attends the ball given by the Marquis d'Andervilliers. Emma names her daughter after Berthe.

Berthelmot. *L'Education sentimentale*. The auctioneer who presides over the sale of Arnoux's furniture.

Berthier. *La Cousine Bette*. A lawyer who oversees the terms of a marriage contract signed by Crevel and Valérie Marneffe.

Bertinaux. *L'Education sentimentale.* A former benefactor of Rosanette Bron (la Maréchale).

Bertrand. *Gil Blas.* The name of Gil Blas's muleteer.

Bertrand. *Les Liaisons dangereuses.* Valmont's business manager.

Besnus, Clarisse. *Nana.* An actress in Bordenave's musical revues at the Théâtre des Variétés, she is also a well-known courtesan.

Bettina. *La Chartreuse de Parme.* The maid of the actress Fausta, she spies on Fabrice for her mistress.

Bianchon, Horace. *Le Père Goriot.* A medical student and friend of Rastignac. He takes his meals at the Maison Vauquer and helps Rastignac care for the dying Père Goriot.

Bianchon, Dr. Horace. *La Cousine Bette.* A famous doctor who confirms that Marneffe will die in a matter of hours. He also attempts to determine what has destroyed Crevel and Valérie Marneffe.

"Bibi-la-Grillade." *L'Assommoir.* The nickname given to a drinking companion of Coupeau.

Bigre. *Jacques le fataliste.* Jacques's godfather and the father of Jacques's good friend.

Bigre (Jr.). *Jacques le fataliste.* The boyhood friend of Jacques.

Bigrenaille. *Les Misérables.* See Ponchaud.

Bijard. *L'Assommoir.* A locksmith who drinks heavily and abuses his family when drunk, first killing his wife and then his eight-year-old daughter, both victims of his drunken rage.

Bijard, Eulalie. *L'Assommoir.* Bijard's maternal young daughter who suffers the same fate as her mother.

Bijard, Henriette. *L'Assommoir.* The infant of the drunkard Bijard and his abused wife.

Bijard, Jules. *L'Assommoir.* An infant who is just weaned at the time his father beats his mother to death.

Bijard, Mme. *L'Assommoir.* A washerwoman who is finally beaten to death by her drunken beast of a husband.

Bijou, Mme. *La Cousine Bette.* The working class-mother of Olympe Bijou, one of Baron Hulot's mistresses.

Bijou, Olympe. *La Cousine Bette.* A child living in dire poverty who becomes one of Baron Hulot's young mistresses for a time.

Binder, Baron. *La Chartreuse de Parme.* The severe Milan chief of police who is intent upon arresting Fabrice.

Binder, Baroness. *La Chartreuse de Parme.* Wife of the Milan chief of police.

Binet. *Madame Bovary.* A priggish tax collector of Yonville-l'Abbaye. His great passion in life is working with his lathe.

Binet, Amanda. *Le Rouge et le noir.* A cafe waitress in Besançon. She and Julien flirt with each other.

Birotteau, César. *La Cousine Bette.* A once-famous banker whose stock has been bought up by Crevel.

Birotteau, Mlle. *La Cousine Bette.* Daughter of César Birotteau. She becomes the bride of Popinot.

Bishop (unnamed). *Les Lettres persanes.* An arrogant man of the cloth who proves himself to be incompetent in discussing the papal bull *Unigenitus.*

Bishop de .... *Le Rouge et le noir.* The uncle of Mme. de Fervaques and one of the men present at the drafting of the Ultras's secret note.

Bishop of Agde. *Le Rouge et le noir.* A nephew of M. de la Mole, he is assisted at a crucial moment by an admiring Julien Sorel in Verrières. Later, in Paris, he attends the secret meeting of the Ultras.

Bishop of Besançon. *Le Rouge et le noir.* The elegant ecclesiastic who, impressed by Julien Sorel's knowledge, sends him a volume of Tacitus.

Bixiou. *La Cousine Bette.* A guest at Héloïse Brisetout's party, he is an artist known for his wild dissipation.

Blanche. *Gil Blas.* The older daughter of Léontio Siffredi, minister of King Roger of Sicily. She is in love with Prince Enrique.

Blanchevelle. *Les Misérables.* A student from Montauban. He is the lover of Fantine's friend Favorite.

Blanès, Abbé. *La Chartreuse de Parme.* An unorthodox priest hired to continue Fabrice's Latin studies. He becomes Fabrice's devoted friend and protector, all the while pursuing his astrology studies.

Blas, Gil. *Gil Blas.* The picaresque hero of the novel bearing his name. His many adventures, from childhood to old age, form the framework of the novel.

Blas de Combados, don. *Gil Blas.* A gentleman of Galicia, he falls in love with doña Helena Galisteo and later dies of wounds inflicted by thieves.

Blas de Santillane. *Gil Blas.* The father of Gil Blas, who never felt any genuine affection for him.

Blond, Maria. *Nana.* A new actress, this thin, vicious creature is invited to Nana's supper party and makes her way in courtesan circles.

Bocage, Master. *Madame Bovary.* Léon Dupuis's employer in Rouen, who urges the young law clerk to break off his relationship with Emma Bovary.

Boche. *L'Assommoir.* A witness for Gervaise at her wedding to Coupeau, he is also doorkeeper of the building they live in.

Boche, Mme. *L'Assommoir.* A gossipy neighbor who befriends Gervaise and later forsakes her.

Boche, Pauline. *L'Assommoir.* The daughter of the Boches and a childhood playmate of Nana.

Boffreu, Joseph. *L'Education sentimentale.* The cousin of de Cisy, he becomes involved in de Cisy's duel with Frédéric Moreau.

Boischevron, Viscountess de. *Les Misérables.* Mlle. Baptistine's childhood friend, with whom she has a voluminous correspondence.

Bomston, Lord Edward. *La Nouvelle Héloïse.* An English gentleman initially attracted to Julie. After being made aware of the great love between Saint-Preux and Julie, he becomes the devoted friend and companion of Saint-Preux.

Bona. *La Chartreuse de Parme.* A recorder who informs Fabrice del Dongo of the death of his father, the Marquis.

Bonnemort. *Germinal.* Nickname given to Grandfather Maheu, who has escaped certain death in the mine several times and whose lungs are diseased from coal dust. See also Maheu, Vincent.

Borda, Canon. *La Chartreuse de Parme.* A young man who, once rebuffed in his attempt to make advances to the Countess Pietranera, turns on her. Later he attempts to make amends by helping Fabrice, even though he is jealous of him.

Bordenave. *Nana.* A producer who consistently casts his latest mistress in his revues at the Théâtre des Variétés, which he refers to as his brothel. Nana, his latest conquest, is the star of his *Blonde Venus.* Eventually he goes bankrupt.

Bosc. *Nana.* An old actor who plays an imbecilic Jupiter in *Blonde Venus,* starring Nana. Later, he becomes paralyzed and helpless.

Bossi, Giuseppe. *La Chartreuse de Parme.* The false name Fabrice assumes in Bologna, as a safety precaution. See also Dongo, Fabrice Valserra del.

Bosson, M. du. *La Nouvelle Héloïse.* The doctor who tends to Julie during her fatal illness.

Bossuet. *Les Misérables.* See Laigle.

Boucombry, la. *Notre-Dame de Paris.* A gossip who witnesses the ceremony of penance Esmeralda is obliged to perform.

Boudet. *Madame Bovary.* A troublesome boy who exasperates the Abbé Bournisien by creating a disturbance in church.

Bouillon, Duke de. *Le Rouge et le noir.* A guest at the Hôtel de la Mole, his name is mocked by Mathilde and her circle of friends.

Boulanger, Rodolphe. *Madame Bovary.* A landed gentleman with a coarse nature and a shrewd brain. He easily seduces the romantic Emma Bovary and then, after convincing her of his eternal love, abandons her.

Boulard. *Madame Bovary.* The bishop's bookseller, he makes up a package of religious books and sends it to the convalescing Emma Bovary.

Boulatruelle. *Les Misérables.* A drunken road mender who lurks about the forest at night looking for a small box Jean Valjean has hidden because he rightly believes that it contains money.

Boulaye, Captain de la. *Jacques le fataliste*. One of Jacques's former masters.

Bou-Maza. *L'Education sentimentale*. A celebrated jockey Frédéric Moreau sees at the races.

Bourbon, Charles, Cardinal de. *Notre-Dame de Paris*. The primate of the Gauls who totally disrupts Pierre Gringoire's morality play by his very presence.

Bourdonnais, M. de la. *Paul et Virginie*. Governor of the island Ile-de-France.

Bourgaillard. *Les Misérables*. The village wheelwright in Heslin who cannot repair the wheel of M. Madeleine (Jean Valjean) quickly enough.

Bourgeois (unnamed). *Les Misérables*. He insists that his young son feed cake to the swans in the Jardin du Luxembourg while the two starving and abandoned Thénardier boys watch from a hiding place.

Bourguignon. *L'Assommoir*. A man for whom the drunken Coupeau fails to do a repair job.

Bournisien, Abbé. *Madame Bovary*. The conservative old priest of Yonville-l'Abbaye, he is oblivious to Emma Bovary's suffering.

Boutarel, Dr. *Nana*. The physician who attends Nana when she lives on the Avenue de Villiers. This young man makes a practice of treating courtesans.

Bouteloup, Louis. *Germinal*. A mine worker who shares the wife of his landlord when the latter is at work in the coal mine, on a different shift.

Bovary, Berthe. *Madame Bovary*. Daughter of Emma and Charles Bovary. Neglected by her mother and father, she is sent to work as a child laborer in a cotton mill after both her parents die.

Bovary, Charles. *Madame Bovary*. A sincere but obtuse young country doctor who deeply loves his fanciful, troubled wife, Emma, in spite of everything she does. After her death, he cannot cope with life and soon follows her to the grave.

Bovary, Charles-Denis-Bartholomé. *Madame Bovary*. Profligate father of Charles Bovary, he fails in every grandiose scheme he invents and dies leaving his family nothing.

Bovary, Emma Rouault. *Madame Bovary*. A fanciful, unstable young woman who has been nurtured on sentimental ballads and novels. She is unable to cope with the humdrum reality of her married life and ends it in agony, after sinking into depravity.

Bovary, Héloïse Dubuc. *Madame Bovary*. Charles Bovary's first wife, a middle-aged widow who is ugly but wealthy. She is a cloying creature who constantly nags at Charles.

Bovary, Mme. *Madame Bovary*. The strong-minded, determined mother of

Charles Bovary, she dotes on her son after she gives up on her husband. Charles finally turns against her, in defense of Emma.

Boy (unnamed). *Les Misérables*. He gives cake to swans while the two starving Thénardier boys watch.

Braive, Anténor. *L'Education sentimentale*. A painter of kings' portraits, he frequents Jacques Arnoux's shop.

Brandon, Lady. *Le Père Goriot*. An elegant Paris society woman.

Braulapd. *La Cousine Bette*. The leader of the claque Olympe Bijou's lover works for.

Brébant. *Nana*. The caterer who plans and serves the midnight supper for Nana, after her success as *Blonde Venus*.

Brevet. *Les Misérables*. An ex-convict at Toulon prison who declares at the trial that Père Champmathieu is Jean Valjean.

Brézé, M. de. *La Princesse de Clèves*. The husband of Diane de Poitiers, Duchess de Valentinois.

Bridau. *La Cousine Bette*. A man of wealth who gets Wenceslas Steinbock out of prison by posting his bail.

Bridoie, Mlle. *Jacques le fataliste*. A clothing merchant who collaborates with usurers.

Bridoux. *Madame Bovary*. The owner of a cafe in Rouen which Homais frequents.

Brisetout, Héloïse. *La Cousine Bette*. One of Crevel's mistresses who gives a sensational housewarming party.

Brissac, Charles de Cossé, Count de. *La Princesse de Clèves*. A master of artillery and a favorite of the Duchess de Valentinois.

Bron, Mme. *Nana*. The portress at the Théâtre des Variétés who runs a bar there.

Bron, Rosanette (la Maréchale). *L'Education sentimentale*. The mistress of the establishment where Frédéric Moreau attends a wild, all-night party with Jacques Arnoux. She later becomes the rival of Mme. Arnoux for Frédéric's affection and gives birth to his child, which soon dies.

Brother (unnamed) of Des Grieux. *Manon Lescaut*. Completely loyal to his father, whom he helps to get Des Grieux out of the apartment the latter shares with Manon.

Brown. *Indiana*. The father of Ralph Brown. He is inconsolable over the loss of his older son Edmond and cold toward Ralph.

Brown, Edmond. *Indiana*. Sir Ralph Brown's older brother, the favorite son who died at the age of twenty.

Brown, Mistress Ralph. *Indiana*. The woman Ralph Brown married in order to serve family sentiments and interests. She felt only aversion for him and died very young.

Brown, Sir Ralph. *Indiana.* A delicate-looking Englishman who is considered dull and phlegmatic. He is, nevertheless, Indiana Delmare's devoted protector and ultimately becomes her husband.

Bru. *L'Assommoir.* A worn-out journeyman painter, unemployed because he is old. He is given food by Gervaise for a time but eventually dies of deprivation.

Brujon. *Les Misérables.* An underworld creature who participates in an attempt to ambush Jean Valjean.

Brûlée, la. *Germinal.* The nickname given to the wild, shrewish mother-in-law of Pierron. A worker in the Voreux pit, she is eventually killed by a soldier during an attack by the workers on the mine.

Bruno. *La Chartreuse de Parme.* A devoted messenger in the employ of Count Mosca and the Duchess Sanseverina.

Brunon. *La Vie de Marianne.* The name given to the wife of Dursan when she serves Dursan's mother disguised as her chambermaid. See Dursan, Mme., Jr.

Brutandorf. *Gil Blas.* A German admirer of Lucinde.

Bubna, General. *La Chartreuse de Parme.* An officer of sound judgment and warm heart who comes to the political rescue of the Count Pietranera and awards him a pension.

Buena Garra, don Vincent de. *Gil Blas.* A vicious nobleman of Toledo. The name is ironic, meaning "with the good claw."

Buendia, Fernandez de. *Gil Blas.* A bookseller who is a neighbor of Mergelina.

Buenotrige, Basile de. *Gil Blas.* A farmer for Gil Blas, and also the father of Antonia.

Bugneaux. *L'Education sentimentale.* A businessman to whom Rosanette Bron pays an installment on a purchase.

Buisson, M. *Eugénie Grandet.* Charles Grandet's tailor.

Bulgarian (unnamed). "Candide." A captain with soft, white skin which Cunégonde compares favorably to Candide's.

Bulot. *La Chartreuse de Parme.* A slain hussar whose uniform is given to Fabrice.

Buneaud, Mme. *La Père Goriot.* The proprietress of a rival boardinghouse, she is detested by Mme. Vauquer.

Burati. *La Chartreuse de Parme.* An ex-lawyer who is now a convict in Genoa.

Burgon, Mme. *Les Misérables.* The new "chief lodger" at the Maison Gorbeau, at the time Marius and the Thénardier family, known as the Jondrettes, live there.

Burrieux, Jules. *L'Education sentimentale.* A frequenter of Jacques Arnoux's art shop, whose sketches popularize the wars in Algeria in the 1840s.

Buseaupied, Mère. *Les Misérables.* A peasant woman who sells vegetables in the town where M. Madeleine (Jean Valjean) is mayor.

Bustos, don Diego. *Le Rouge et le noir.* An admirer of the Maréchale de Fervaques, he fails in his attempt to seduce her.

C..., Dr. *La Chartreuse de Parme.* A liberal, known for his imprudence at the Court of Parma.

C..., M. *Les Liaisons dangereuses.* A shoemaker whom the naïve Cecile Volanges mistakes for her husband-to-be, whom she has never seen.

C..., Signora. *La Chartreuse de Parme.* Fabrice's mistress at the time he decides to study for the priesthood.

Cabaret Owner (unnamed). *Gil Blas.* A cabaret owner who is interrogated by an inquisitor (Ambroise de Lamela), a clerk (don Raphaël), and a mayor (Gil Blas), all three of whom are in disguise.

Cabaret Owner (unnamed). *Jaaques le fataliste.* While drinking wine in the cabaret owner's place, Jacques forgets to tend the horses and as a result receives a beating from his father.

Cabiroche, Simonne. *Nana.* An actress in Bordenave's musical revues, she attends the midnight supper party of her fellow courtesan, Nana.

Cacambo. "Candide." Candide's faithful valet who follows his master all over the world.

Cadine, Jenny. *La Cousine Bette.* The Baron Hulot's mistress when she was in her teens, she is now a famous actress.

Cador. "Zadig." Zadig's young friend who helps him twice, first by duping Azora, Zadig's fickle wife, and later by helping Zadig escape from Babylon.

Caillaud, Cadet. *La Petite Fadette.* Madelon's new boyfriend, Landry's successor, he later becomes Landry's good friend and also his brother-in-law.

Caillaud, Père. *La Petite Fadette.* A farmer who hires the fourteen-year-old Landry to take care of his oxen.

Calderone, don Rodrigue de. *Gil Blas.* The proud secretary of the Duke de Lerme, whom he manipulates and influences greatly.

Camille. *Gil Blas.* The pretended cousin of doña Mencia who dupes Gil Blas. Camille was once the mistress of don Raphaël.

Campan, Mme. *Eugénie Grandet.* A cynical Parisian who worships those who have power and is contemptuous of those who lose it.

Campario. *Gil Blas.* A loud, verbose scholar who never stops talking.

Camus. *Madame Bovary.* A grocer in Yonville-l'Abbaye.

Candide. "Candide." A simple, innocent young man who learns through his experiences that an optimistic view of the world is incompatible with reality.

Canivet, Dr. *Madame Bovary*. A celebrated physician, who laughs with unconcealed scorn upon discovering what has happened to the club-foot, after Charles Bovary's unsuccessful operaion.

Canon (unnamed). *La Vie de Marianne*. A passenger in tha stagecoach with the infant Marianne. He flees when the passengers are attacked by thieves.

Cantarilla, Inésile de. *Gil Blas*. An old woman whose beauty still inspires passion in men, including twenty-five-year-old don Valerio de Luna.

Caporis, don Raimond. *Gil Blas*. Intendant of the Count d'Olivarès.

Captain (unnamed). *Germinal*. A soldier guarding the Voreux pit from attack by the striking miners. He tries in vain to prevent an outbreak of violence.

Captain (unnamed). *Jacques le fataliste*. Jacques's army captain who said that all the good and evil that come to us is written above.

Carabine. *La Cousine Bette*. A guest at Josépha's party, and a notorious courtesan who mocks Valérie Marneffe's Brazilian lover.

Cardinal (unnamed). *Le Rouge et le noir*. An Ultra conspirator who declares that it is impossible to form an armed party in France without the clergy.

Caretaker (unnamed). "René." The grounds keeper of the estate where René and Amélie spent their childhood.

Carigliano, Duchess de. *Le Père Goriot*. An elegant Paris society woman.

Carigliano, Marshal de. *Le Père Goriot*. A prominent member of Parisian society during the Restoration.

Carigliano, Mme. de. *La Cousine Bette*. A member of the same charitable organizations as the ones to which the Baroness Hulot belongs.

Carle. *Indiana*. Raymon de Ramière's manservant.

Carlone. *La Chartreuse de Parme*. A private soldier in the service of the Prince of Parma who is thought to be illiterate but who writes anonymous letters for the Prince.

Carnay, Sophie. *Les Liaisons dangereuses*. Convent companion of Cécile Volanges, with whom she exchanges a lengthy correspondence.

Carnero. *Gil Blas*. First secretary of the Count d'Olivarès.

Caroline. *L'Assommoir*. A girl who works in the artificial flower factory with Nana.

Caron, Mme. *Madame Bovary*. A gossipy townswoman who comes to visit the convalescing Emma Bovary.

Carouble. *Germinal*. A baker in Montsou who is somewhat sympathetic to the miners.

Carvajal, M. de. *Indiana*. Indiana Delmare's late father, a cruel and despised planter on the Ile Bourbon.

Carvajal, Mme. de. *Indiana*. Indiana Delmare's unsympathetic aunt, who survives by dint of shrewd wit, intrigues, and feigned piety.

Cashier (unnamed). *Les Misérables*. A man who sleeps directly under the bedroom of M. Madeleine (Jean Valjean) and hears him pacing during the night.

Castanède, Abbé. *Le Rouge et le noir*. The assistant director of the seminary at Besançon and Julien Sorel's enemy.

Castel-Forte, Prince. *Corinne*. A Roman lord who is highly esteemed because of his mind and his personality. A friend of Corinne, he would also like to be her lover.

Castel-Forte, Princess. *Corinne*. A relative of Prince Castel-Forte and a good friend of Corinne.

Castil Blazo, Bernard de. *Gil Blas*. The mysterious master of Gil Blas in Madrid.

Castro, don Pompeyo de. *Gil Blas*. A relative of don Alexo Segiar.

Catalina. *Gil Blas*. A young woman whom Scipion discovers to be the dauphin's mistress and with whom Gil Blas falls in love. Under the name Sirena, she later reappears as don Rodrigue de Calderanes's mistress, who contrives to get Captain Chinchilla a pension.

Catalina. *Gil Blas*. A relative of Ignacio de Ipigna and also the girl friend of Scipion for a time.

Catena. *La Chartreuse de Parme*. A nobleman at the Court of Parma who is believed to have died with Prince Ernesto IV.

Catherine. *L'Education sentimentale*. Roque's first mistress, a native of Lorraine whose face is marked with smallpox.

Cathos. *La Vie de Marianne*. A servant girl who witnesses a dispute between Mme. Dutour and a coachman.

Cathos. *La Vie de Marianne*. A middle-aged servant who greets Marianne at the minister's residence.

Cavaignac, Godefroy. *L'Education sentimentale*. A worker who dies on the job.

Cavi. *La Chartreuse de Parme*. The name Fabrice del Dongo assumes upon arriving in Lugano, on his way home from Waterloo. See Dongo, Fabrice Valserra del.

Caylus, Count de. *Le Rouge et le noir*. A member of Mathilde de la Mole's gossiping entourage.

Cecchina. *La Chartreuse de Parme*. The Duchess Sanseverina's favorite personal maid.

Célestin. *L'Education sentimentale*. A waiter at the Cafe Alexandre.

Celinaura. *Gil Blas.* An actress friend of Arsénie.

Céluta. "Atala." The Indian bride given to René by Chactas.

Céluta. "René." The neglected Indian wife of René.

Cenaine, Marc. *Notre-Dame de Paris.* A sorcerer whom Master Jacques Charmoulu is having tortured.

Centellés, don Antonio de. *Gil Blas.* A friend of don Mathias de Silva.

Cesarino. *Gil Blas.* An actor slandered by the other guests at Arsénie's party.

Chactas. "Atala." An old Indian of wisdom and understanding who loved the maiden Atala in his youth.

Chactas. "René." A blind old Indian leader who has become René's adopted father.

Chaillot. *La Nouvelle Héloïse.* Claire's worldly governess who has just died.

Chalvet, Count. *Le Rouge et le noir.* The wittiest man of his day, he is frowned upon at the Hôtel de la Mole because of his levity.

Chambermaid (unnamed). *Les Liaisons dangereuses.* Mme. de Merteuil's chambermaid and foster sister.

Chambermaid (unnamed). *La Vie de Mariane.* Mme. Darneuil's servant who remains faithful to her.

Chambermaid (unnamed). *La Vie de Marianne.* Disguised as Mme. de Miran's chambermaid, she accompanies Marianne to another convent under false pretenses.

Chambermaid (unnamed). *La Vie de Marianne.* A woman who confesses her role in the corrupt young priest's scheme and clears Tervire's name.

Chambrion. *L'Education sentimentale.* The tax collector of Nogent-sur-Seine. Frédéric Moreau's mother borrows his horse.

Champchevrier, Bérangère de. *Notre-Dame de Paris.* A child staying at the house of Dame Aloïse de Gondelaurier.

Champion. *L'Assommoir.* A drinking companion of Lantier, with whom he argues politics.

Champmathieu, Père. *Les Misérables.* A thief who, because of circumstantial evidence, is thought to be Jean Valjean.

Champtercier, Marquis de. *Les Misérables.* A rich old miser who contrives to be at once ultra-Royalist and ultra-Voltairean.

Chanor. *La Cousine Bette.* A goldsmith for whom Wenceslas Steinbock works briefly.

Chanteprune, François. *Notre-Dame de Paris.* One of Pierre Gringoire's potential executioners.

Chantereau, Mme. *Nana.* Wife of an ironmaster and a guest at weekly receptions given by the Countess Sabine Muffat de Beuville. Later, she is scandalized by the changes which have taken place in the Muffat household.

Chanterie, Mme. de la. *La Cousine Bette*. The founder of a Catholic charitable organization devoted to promoting marriages between persons
who have formed a voluntary but illicit union. She enlists the help of
the Baronness Hulot for her organization.

Chapuzot, M. *La Cousine Bette*. The head of one of the branches of the
central police. He is unwilling to help Victorin Hulot in his vengeance
scheme.

Charcellay. *Les Misérables*. A resident of Montfermeil, he complains that a
leaking gutter from a neighbor's house is undermining the foundation
of his house.

Chardin, Elodie. *La Cousine Bette*. The sluttish sister of a parasite who ruins
the embroidery business of Baron Hulot and Olympe Bijou. She steals
Hulot from Olympe and leads him further down the path of degradation.

Chardin, Idamore. *La Cousine Bette*. The great-nephew of Père Chardin. He
is a parasite who lives off women, including Olympe Bijou.

Chardin, Père. *La Cousine Bette*. A mattress picker who carries messages
from Baron Hulot to Bette.

Charles. *L'Assommoir*. A butcher with whom Gervaise and Coupeau do
business for a time.

Charles. *L'Assommoir*. The porter at the washhouse where Gervaise does her
laundry.

Charles. *Nana*. The coachman hired when Nana lives on the Avenue de
Villiers. He is eventually fired for calling his mistress a whore.

Charles. *Le Père Goriot*. A young painter with a caustic wit who takes his
meals at the Maison Vauquer.

Charles-Edouard. "Candide." The pretender to the English throne. Candide
meets him at the carnival in Venice.

Charles de France, Duke d'Orléans. *La Princesse de Clèves*. The third son of
François I and brother of King Henri II.

Charmier. *Le Rouge et le noir*. A notorious cuckold of Verrières.

Charmoulue, Master Jacques. *Notre-Dame de Paris*. The king's proctor in the
Ecclesiastical Court and Dom Claude Frollo's disciple in alchemy.
Excited by trials for witchcraft, he wishes to indict Esmeralda for
practicing magic.

Chartres, François de Vendôme, Prince de Chabanois, Vidame de. *La
Princesse de Clèves*. Uncle of Mme. de Clèves, he is involved in
amorous court intrigues.

Chartres, Mlle. de. *La Princesse de Clèves*. Maiden name of Mme. de Clèves.
See Clèves, Mme. de.

Chartres, Mme. de. *La Princesse de Clèves*. Confidante of her devoted
daughter. She instills a very strong sense of virtue in her.

Chas-Bernard, Abbé. *Le Rouge et le noir*. Director of the Besançon cathedral. He teaches religious eloquence to the seminarians and is impressed by Julien Sorel.

Chastelart, P. de Boscosel, de. *La Princesse de Clèves*. A court favorite of M. d'Anville.

Château, Renauld. *Notre-Dame de Paris*. Keeper of the seal of the Chatelet of Paris, he is the only spectator who remains to watch Pierre Gringoire's morality play.

Châteaupers, Captain Phoebus de. *Notre-Dame de Paris*. The libertine Captain of the Archers of the King's Ordinance, he rescues Esmeralda from the clutches of Quasimodo and Claude Frollo. Esmeralda then falls madly in love with him.

Chaulieu, Duchess de. *Eugénie Grandet*. A snobbish friend of the Marquis d'Aubrion.

Chaulnes, Count de. *Le Rouge et le noir*. The son of M. de la Mole's old friend, the Duke de Chaulnes.

Chaulnes, Duke de. *Le Rouge et le noir*. A man who shares M. de la Mole's love of noble titles.

Chaval. *Germinal*. A pikeman in the mine. His instinctive hatred of Etienne Lantier leads to his death at the hands of the latter, when both are trapped in the mine with Catherine Maheu, whom they quarrel over.

Chaves, Marquise de. *Gil Blas*. A woman of renown who loves elegant conversation and in whose employ Gil Blas remains for a time.

Chazel. *Le Rouge et le noir*. A clever seminarian at Bescançon, one of the few to distinguish himself by his talent.

Chélan, Abbé. *Le Rouge et le noir*. A liberal priest of eighty who teaches Latin to his young disciple, Julien Sorel.

Cheneteau, Master. *Notre-Dame de Paris*. A spectator who chatters instead of listening to Pierre Gringoire's play.

Chenildieu. *Les Misérables*. A convict who testifies at the trial that Champmathieu is his former fellow convict, Jean Valjean.

Cherubin Tonto, don. *Gil Blas*. A stupid monk with a deceptive appearance.

Chesnelong, Pierre. *Les Misérables*. A carter who nearly drives over Mère Buseaupied and her child.

Chevalier (unnamed). *Gil Blas*. A parasite who dupes Gil Blas.

Chevalier (unnamed). *La Vie de Marianne*. A middle-aged gentleman who escorts Mme. de Miran to a religious ceremony at the convent where Marianne is staying.

Chevalier (unnamed). *La Vie de Marianne*. A man who, after witnessing the reunion of Marianne and Mme. de Miran at the minister's, proposes marriage to Marianne.

Chezelles, Léonide de. *Nana.* A convent friend of the Countess Muffat de Beuville and her weekly guest. She deceives her husband quite openly.

Chezelles, M. de. *Nana.* A magistrate whose wife deceives him openly.

Chicot. *Germinal.* A pikeman in the pit who dies after being engulfed in a landslip.

Chief of Black Tribe (unnamed). *Paul et Virginie.* He acknowledges the goodness of Paul and Virginie by helping them.

Chilindron. *Gil Blas.* The valet of don Luis Pacheco.

Chinchilla, Captain don Annibal. *Gil Blas.* An elderly captain whom Gil Blas meets in Madrid. Very proud and concerned about his honor, he is bitter because the government will not grant him a pension.

Cholin, M. de. *Le Rouge et le noir.* An old fool who gets the post of director of the lottery office in Verrières, at Julien's whimsical request.

Chouard, Marquis de. *Nana.* A hypocritical old lecher who, beneath his mask of respectability, actively pursues young women. He is caught by his son-in-law, the Count de Beuville, Nana's chief benefactor, wallowing over her naked body.

Christeuil, Diane de. *Notre-Dame de Paris.* A companion of Fleur-de-Lys de Gondelaurier.

Christophe. *Le Père Goriot.* Mme. Vauquer's dull handyman.

Chrysostome. *Gil Blas.* A hermit who befriends the nine-year-old Scipion and then proceeds to rob him.

Churchwarden (unnamed). *Le Rouge et le noir.* M. de Rênal's sentimental friend.

Cisy, Alfred de. *L'Education sentimentale.* A pretentious aristocratic acquaintance of Frédéric Moreau, who is contemptuous of de Cisy's feeble intellect.

Clairimbault, Marshal. *Le Père Goriot.* Maternal grandfather of the Viscountess de Beauséant and an ancestor of Eugène de Rastignac.

Clairon, Mlle. "Candide." An actress on the Parisian stage whom Candide admires.

Claquesous. *Les Misérables.* One of four bandits who govern the lowest depths of Paris, from 1830 to 1835. He participates in Thénardier's attempt to ambush Jean Valjean.

Clarin. *Gil Blas.* Valet of don Alexo Segiar.

Clarville, Mme. de. *La Vie de Marianne.* A friend of Mme. de Sainte-Hermières.

Claude de France. *La Princesse de Clèves.* Second daughter of Henri II and Catherine de Medicis.

Clémens, Mlle. *L'Assommoir.* An ironer who is considered by gossips to be a young woman of loose morals.

Clerk (unnamed). *Nana.* A chief clerk at the Office of the Ministry of the Interior, he attends *Blonde Vanus,* starring Nana, with his mistress Mme. Robert, who in reality prefers women.

Clèves, François de. *La Princesse de Clèves.* Older brother of Jacques de Clèves, husband of the Princess de Clèves.

Clèves, Jacques de. *La Princesse de Clèves.* Younger son of the Duke de Nevers, he becomes the husband of Mlle. de Chartres (the Princess de Clèves), in spite of the fact that his love for her is unrequited.

Clèves, Mme. de *La Princesse de Clèves.* Née Mlle. de Chartres, wife of Jacques de Clèves. Her passion for the Duke de Nemours and her accompanying guilt bring great unhappiness to her, Nemours, and her husband.

Climal, M. de. *La Vie de Marianne.* A religious hypocrite who lusts after Marianne but, on his deathbed, repents his sins.

Cléotofis. "Zadig." The jealous young man who beats his mistress Missouf and whom Zadig kills in self-defense.

Clock Maker. *L'Assommoir.* The shopkeeper opposite Gervaise's laundry shop. Gervaise respects him greatly.

Coachman (unnamed). *A Rebours.* The person who drives Des Esseintes from the Sceaux railroad station to a British bookstore and restaurant in Paris.

Coachman (unnamed). *Nana.* A taciturn little man who drives Nana and her guests to and from the estate in the country which the banker Steiner has purchased for her.

Coachman (unnamed). *Le Père Goriot.* A servant who drives Eugène de Rastignac from one fashionable Parisian lady's house to another.

Coachman (unnamed). *Le Rouge et le noir.* The servant of the Chevalier de Beauvoisis who steals his master's calling cards. He also grossly insults Julien Sorel.

Coachman (unnamed). *La Vie de Marianne.* He and Mme. Dutour engage in a heated dispute because she has paid him so little.

Cochepaille. *Les Misérables.* A convict who testifies at the trial that Père Champmathieu is his former fellow convict Jean Valjean.

Coello, don Antonio. *Gil Blas.* Supposedly a captain, later the deceased husband of Laure (Estelle).

Cogniard. *Le Père Goriot.* A convict who, like Vautrin, circulates in society under a false name.

Cogollos, don Gaston de. *Gil Blas.* A knight of the order of Calatrava. Gil Blas befriends him while they are both prisoners in the Segovia tower and listens to the story of his life.

Coictier. *Notre-Dame de Paris.* The personal physician of King Louis XI. One day he pays a call on Dom Claude Frollo and they argue, Frollo proclaiming his faith in alchemy.

Colifichini. *Gil Blas.* Lucinde's third husband.

Colleville, Mme. *La Cousine Bette.* A famous Paris courtesan who yields to the pleasure of a genuine passion and to hard necessity.

Collin, Jacques. *Le Père Goriot.* The real name of the escaped convict who lives at the Maison Vauquer under the name of Vautrin. See also Vautrin.

Colombe. *L'Assommoir.* Owner of the bar "L'Assommoir" ("The Bludgeon") where Coupeau and others become helpless alcoholics.

Colonel (unnamed). *Madame Bovary.* Head of the National Guard from a neighboring town who participates in the Yonville-l'Abbaye agricultural show.

Colot, Dr. *L'Education sentimentale.* The Arnoux family doctor who pronounces that the seriously ill Eugène Arnoux is out of danger.

Comaing, Baron de. *L'Education sentimentale.* A jovial blade of thirty whose social ideal is the unintelligent de Cisy. He is also a former lover of Rosanette Bron.

Combeferre. *Les Misérables.* A young revolutionary known for his gentleness and also for his philosophical bent, who is killed during the insurrection of 1832.

Commissioner (unnamed). *Germinal.* The officer of the law who attempts to disperse the meeting of the Montsou workers with Pluchart.

Compain. *L'Education sentimentale.* A friend of Regimbart, he tells Arnoux of Frédéric's supposed duel with de Cisy.

Concierge (unnamed). *Jacques le fataliste.* The caretaker of the Desglands's chateau, who dies and is replaced by Jacques, according to one ending of the work.

Condé, Louis I de Bourbon, Prince de. *La Princesse de Clèves.* A prominent prince at the court of Henri II.

Condillac, Abbé de. *La Chartreuse de Parme.* The incompetent tutor to the Crown Prince of the Court of Parma.

Confectioner (unnamed). *Jacques le fataliste.* One of the young women Father Hudson has seduced.

Confessor (unnamed). *Paul et Virginie.* The priest who convinces Mme. de la Tour that Virginie should depart for France to study for a time.

Confessor (unnamed). *La Vie de Marianne.* The priest who hears the deathbed confession of Mme. Dursan's son.

Conflans, Mlle. de. *Le Père Goriot.* The maiden name of Mme. Vauquer. See Vauquer, Mme.

Constable (unnamed). *La Chartreuse de Parme.* The officer who attempts to arrest General Fabio Conti.

Constable (unnamed). *Gil Blas*. A man who marries Blanche even though she does not love him.

Constance. *Gil Blas*. An actress friend of Arsénie.

Constance. *Gil Blas*. The niece of Roger, King of Sicily, and daughter of Mathilde, the king's sister.

Constance. *Le Père Goriot*. Anastasie de Restaud's maid.

Contarini, Countess. *La Chartreuse de Parme*. Clélia Conti's aunt, with whom Clélia takes refuge after her father is dismissed from his post at the Farnese prison.

Conti, don Cesare. *La Chartreuse de Parme*. The brother of Fabio Conti and uncle of Clélia Conti. He is chaplain at the Farnese prison.

Conti, Clélia. *La Chartreuse de Parme*. The beautiful daughter of General Fabio Conti. She falls in love with Fabrice del Dongo when he is imprisoned in the Farnese tower. Only later does she yield to her passion and become Fabrice's devoted but fearful mistress.

Conti, General Fabio. *La Chartreuse de Parme*. Count Mosca's chief enemy at the Court of Parma. He is governor of the Farnese prison, where liberal prisoners, among them Fabrice del Dongo, serve their prison terms.

Convicts (unnamed). *Le Rouge et le noir*. Two fellow inmates whom Julien Sorel invites into his cell to share a bottle of champagne.

Cook (unnamed). *Germinal*. The cook at the Hennebeau residence. She worries about her elaborate dinner preparation while the starving coal miners rage outside the house.

Cook (unnamed). *Le Rouge et le noir*. Mme. de Rênal's cook who protects Julien.

Coppenole, Jacques. *Notre-Dame de Paris*. A cruel Flemish ambassador to Paris in 1482, and a hosier from Ghent.

Coquet. *La Cousine Bette*. An employee in the War Office whom Hulot wants to replace with Marneffe.

Coquet, Linguerlot. *L'Assommoir*. A child neglected by his family who is nearly burned to death.

Coquets. *L'Assommoir*. A family evicted from the building where Gervaise and Coupeau live.

Coquet, Mme. *La Cousine Bette*. The wife of a chief clerk in Hulot's office.

Corbreuse, Duke de. *Nana*. The owner of a horse entered in the Grand Prix de Paris.

Corcuelo, André. *Gil Blas*. An innkeeper at Penaflor who dupes Gil Blas.

Cordel, don Mathias de. *Gil Blas*. A nobleman of Toledo. The name is ironic, meaning "with the rope."

Coreb. "Zadig." The King's minister who has fallen into disgrace and about whom Zadig speaks with kindness.

Corinne. *Corinne.* The most famous woman of Italy, a poet whose spontaneity contrasts sharply with the English reserve of her lover Oswald, Lord Nelvil. Their love, doomed from the beginning, destroys this gifted and extremely sensitive woman.

Cornoiller. *Eugénie Grandet.* A farmer on Grandet's land who marries Nanon after she inherits money from Eugénie.

Coscolina, la. *Gil Blas.* The gypsy mother of Scipion.

Cosette. *Les Misérables.* The abused daughter of Fantine. She later becomes the wife of Marius, and adopted daughter of Jean Valjean. She brings joy and sorrow to the latter, who lives his last years only for her, and offers love and devotion to young Marius.

Cosrou. "Zadig." A young widow who builds a tomb for her dead husband near a stream, vows to remain near the tomb as long as the water of the stream flows near it, and then changes the direction of the stream.

Cossard. *Nana.* The humpbacked prompter at the Théâtre des Variétés.

Coudeloup. *L'Assommoir.* A baker whose bread is criticized by Lantier.

Cougny, Count de. *Germinal.* A mining competitor of Desrumeaux, who merges with him and Joiselle in 1760.

Count (unnamed). *L'Education sentimentale.* A nobleman whom Jacques Arnoux is forced to reimburse for a counterfeit picture.

Countess de... *Les Liaisons dangereuses.* A friend of Valmont.

Coupeau. *L'Assommoir.* The zinc worker whom Gervaise marries. He is an honest man until idleness sets in after an accident. After this, he succumbs to the temptations of drink and destroys not only himself but also his weak-willed wife.

Coupeau, Anna (Nana). *L'Assommoir.* Neglected child of Gervaise and Coupeau, who abandons her drunken parents at the age of fifteen to become a woman of the streets.

Coupeau, Mme. *L'Assommoir.* Coupeau's elderly mother, once a maker of waistcoats. She moves in with her son and Gervaise, where she lives until her death.

Courfeyrac. *Les Misérables.* The leader of the group of young revolutionaries who offers Marius friendship and lodging after the latter has been banished by his grandfather. He is killed during the insurrection of 1832, along with most of his companions.

Courtenay, Edward de. *La Princesse de Clèves.* Lover of Elizabeth of England. He is exiled by Queen Mary, who is jealous of Elizabeth.

Courtillet, Mère. *La Petite Fadette.* A village gossip.

Cousin, Henriet. *Notre-Dame de Paris.* Assistant to Tristan l'Hermite, Louis XI's executioner.

Couture, Mme. *Le Père Goriot.* Widow of a commissary-general in the time of the Republic. She is a boarder at the Maison Vauquer, where she lives with and cares for Victorine Taillefer.

Couturier, Mère. *La Petite Fadette.* A village gossip.

Cravatte. *Les Misérables.* A notorious brigand who, upon repenting, sends to Bishop Myriel ecclesiastical articles he and his band previously stole.

Crescentini. *La Chartreuse de Parme.* An older man who considers himself to be the actress Marietta's father.

Crescenzi, Giulia. *La Chartreuse de Parme.* Sister of Clélia Conti's suitor. It is at her wedding party that Clélia and the Duchess make important moves to ensure Fabrice's escape from prison.

Crescenzi, Marquis. *La Chartreuse de Parme.* A rich but weak nobleman at court whom Clélia Conti marries at her father's request.

Crevel, Célestin. *La Cousine Bette.* An aging roué, and a former tradesman and shopkeeper, whose obsession with young mistresses finally destroys him.

Crevel, Mme. *La Cousine Bette.* Silly, ugly, and vulgar, she gives her husband no pleasure other than that of paternity. Happily for him, she dies at an early age.

Croisenois, Marquis de. *Le Rouge et le noir.* A member of Mathilde de la Mole's gossiping entourage, who is eventually killed in a duel while attempting to defend Mathilde's honor.

Cruchot. *Eugénie Grandet.* A notary in Saumur who looks after M. Grandet's usurious loans and who wants his nephew to marry Eugénie for her inheritance.

Cruchot (de Bonfons). *Eugénie Grandet.* Nephew of the notary Cruchot and presiding judge of the civil court of Saumur. He finally succeeds in marrying Eugénie Grandet three years before his death.

Cruchot, Abbé. *Eugénie Grandet.* Brother of the notary. He is a dignitary of the chapter of Saint-Martin de Tours and is eager to gain possession of the Grandet money.

Cuchillo, *Gil Blas.* A colleague of Dr. Sangrado. Gil Blas gets into a fight with him.

Cudorge, Mmes. *L'Assommoir.* Two owners of an umbrella shop, neighbors of Gervaise.

Cunégonde. "Candide." The plump, lascivious young daughter of Baron Thunder-ten-tronck. Because of his passion for Cunégonde, Candide travels all over the world searching for her.

Cuvier. *Le Père Goriot.* A professor in the School of Medicine which Bianchon, Eugene de Rastingnac's friend, attends.

Cydalise. *La Cousine Bette.* A young girl who is hired to attract the attention of Valérie Marneffe's lover, Baron Montès de Montejanos.

Daguenet, Paul. *Nana.* Nana's sometime lover, a pretty fellow who goes through huge sums of money in pursuit of women. As a favor to her ex-lover, Nana exercises her influence over Muffat de Beuville to assure that the marriage of Daguenet and Estelle Muffat de Beuville takes place.

Dahlia. *Les Misérables.* A grisette who is the mistress of Listolier.

Dambreuse. *L'Education sentimentale.* A wealthy aristocrat who is influential. Frédéric Moreau attempts to take advantage of his influence when it suits his fancy.

Dambreuse, Cécile. *L'Education sentimentale.* Supposedly the niece of Dambreuse, she is actually his illegitimate daughter.

Dambreuse, Mme. *L'Education sentimentale.* Social-minded young wife of the wealthy businessman and aristocrat, she becomes the possessive mistress of Frédéric Moreau shortly before her husband's death.

Dampierre, Jeanne de Vivonne, Baroness de. *La Princesse de Clèves.* Lady-in-waiting of Marguerite de France, sister of King Henri II.

Danceny, Chevalier. *Les Liaisons dangereuses.* A naïve young man who falls in love with Cécile Volange and is manipulated by Mme. de Merteuil. Later, he kills Valmont in a duel, after he discovers what Valmont has been doing to Cécile.

Dansaert. *Germinal.* Head captain of the Voreux. He is accused of sleeping with the wife of one of the workers and is fired.

Dansaert. *Germinal.* Sister of the head captain of the Voreux, she defends her brother when he is accused.

Darcire, Mme. *La Vie de Marianne.* A friend of Mme. Dorfrainville who accompanies Tervire to Paris.

Darneuil, Mme. *La Vie de Marianne.* A woman whom Tervire meets in a carriage en route to Paris and to whom she lends money. She turns out to be Tervire's own mother, née Mlle. de Tresle.

Daumont. *Les Misérables.* A name assumed by Javert when he is on the trail of Jean Valjean. See Javert.

Daviou, Clémence. *L'Education sentimentale.* Deslaurier's mistress, an embroideress whom he mistreats.

Decker, Baroness. *Nana.* A mistress of the Marquis de Chouard.

Delmar. *L'Education sentimentale.* A performer at the music hall Frédéric Moreau and his friends visit. He later becomes an actor and one of Rosanette Bron's lovers.

Delmare, Colonel. *Indiana.* A retired military officer who has married a very young wife, whom he abuses.

Delmare, Indiana. *Indiana.* The nineteen-year-old bride of Colonel Delmare. She is unhappy in her marriage with the ill-tempered old officer and also in her romantic attachment to Raymon de Ramière. At long last, she unexpectedly finds true happiness with Ralph Brown.

Delphine. *L'Education sentimentale*. Rosanette's maid.

Demi-liard. *Les Misérables*. An underworld creature who participates in the attempt to ambush Jean Valjean.

Demonades. *Salammbô*. Slave to Hanno who prepares his master's baths for treatment of an ulcerous skin disease.

Deneulin. *Germinal*. Owner of Vandame, a coal pit neighboring the Voreux. He barely manages to keep going before the miners' strike and is ruined when it occurs.

Deneulin, Jeanne. *Germinal*. Naïve daughter of Deneulin who is raised in ignorance by her overly protective father.

Deneulin, Lucie. *Germinal*. Daughter of Deneulin. Like her sister, she is oblivious to the suffering of the miners and their families.

Denise. *Jacques le fataliste*. The great love of Jacques's life.

Derozeroys. *Madame Bovary*. The president of the jury at the Yonville-l'Abbaye agricultural show.

Derville. *Le Père Goriot*. A Parisian lawyer whom Père Goriot knows. He is also the legal adversary of the bankrupt Baron de Nucingen.

Derville, Mme. *Le Rouge et le noir*. A close friend and relative of Mme. de Rênal. She despairs upon seeing her friend fall in love with Julien Sorel.

Dervish (unnamed). "Candide." A resident of the area in Turkey where Candide and his followers have their farm. He refuses to philosophize with Candide and Pangloss.

Descomulgado. *Gil Blas*. A usurer from whom don Mathias borrows huge sums of money.

Descoulis, M. *Le Rouge et le noir*. A bald guest who is mocked by Mathilde de la Mole.

Des Esseintes. *A Rebours*. See Esseintes, Jean des.

Desforges, M. *Jacques le fataliste*. A friend of Jacques's master.

Desglands. *Jacques le fataliste*. The lord who requests Jacques's presence at his chateau and warmly receives him there. He also once wore a significant plaster mask on his face.

Desglands (Jr.) *Jacques le fataliste*. The spoiled illegitimate son of Desglands.

Des Grassins. *Eugénie Grandet*. See Grassins, des.

Des Grieux, Chevalier. *Manon Lescaut*. A young man of the nobility whose steady, orderly life undergoes a metamorphosis when he falls hopelessly in love with Manon Lescaut.

Désir, Mme. *Germinal*. A fat matron who manages the ballroom of the establishment where the miners' annual fair always concludes.

Désirée. *Germinal.* The second illegitimate child of Zacharie Maheu and Philomène Levaque.

Deslauriers. *L'Education sentimentale.* Charles Deslauriers's embittered father who mistreats his son.

Deslauriers, Charles. *L'Education sentimentale.* Frédéric Moreau's best friend during his school days. Afterwards, in Paris, in spite of their many differences, the two inevitably become reconciled, largely because of the many adolescent experiences they shared.

Deslauriers, Mme. *L'Education sentimentale.* The long-suffering mother of Charles Deslauriers. She is ill treated by her husband and dies of cancer.

Deslenguado, don Bernard. *Gil Blas.* A misanthropic author who slanders everyone.

Des Rogis, Dr. *L'Education sentimentale.* A doctor who, enraged at not having made a name for himself, writes a book of medical pornography. He attends wild parties as well.

Desrumeaux, Baron. *Germinal.* An intelligent, persistent seeker of coal. He was the founder of the Montsou Mining Company.

Diane. *La Princesse de Clèves.* An illegitimate daughter of Henri II.

Dickson, M. *Corinne.* A good friend of Oswald's father who shows Oswald the letter his father wrote about Corinne.

Diego. *Gil Blas.* The Archbishop of Toledo's cook who takes care of Scipion.

Director (unnamed). *Les Misérables.* Director of the hospital adjoining the episcopal palace of Digne. He is shocked when Bishop Myriel insists that the episcopal palace become the hospital because it is so much larger than the actual hospital.

Director (unnamed) of Police Security. *Le Père Goriot.* An official who enlists the help of Poiret and Mlle. Michonneau to capture Vautrin.

Disome, Boniface. *Notre-Dame de Paris.* A shopkeeper near the Place de Grève.

Dittmer. *L'Education sentimentale.* A painter of oriental landscapes, he frequents Jacques Arnoux's art shop.

Doctor (unnamed). *L'Assommoir.* The chief doctor at the Asylum of Sainte-Anne, where Coupeau dies of alcoholism.

Doctor (unnamed). *A Rebours.* A physician who visits Des Esseintes after the latter has fainted from the overwhelming odor of frangipani, but who fails to understand the cause of the illness.

Doctor (unnamed). *Les Misérables.* The physician who attends the dying Fantine.

Domestics (unnamed). *A Rebours.* A husband and wife, formerly in the employ of Des Esseintes's mother and father. They are brought by Des

Esseintes to his new abode to lead the same cloistered existence as before.

Domingo. *Gil Blas.* An old black man in the service of Captain Rolando.

Domingue. *Paul et Virginie.* Marguerite's hard-working slave.

Dongo, Ascanio del. *La Chartreuse de Parme.* The older del Dongo son, heir to the paternal fortune and worthy of his father in every way.

Dongo, Fabrice Valserra del. *La Chartreuse de Parme.* Second son of the Marquis del Dongo. He is a daring, adventurous, romanesque soul whose escapades with his aunt, the Duchess Sanseverina, his beloved Clélia Conti and many others, comprise the substance of the novel.

Dongo, Gina del. *La Chartreuse de Parme.* Sister of the Marquis del Dongo. She is famous for her love of excitement and her passion for her nephew, Fabrice. See also Sanseverina-Taxis, Duchess.

Dongo, Marquis del. *La Chartreuse de Parme.* A loathsome aristocrat who hates and fears the invading army of Napoleon. He becomes the head of the conservative government in Milan. He and his son Fabrice hate each other.

Dongo, Marquise del. *La Chartreuse de Parme.* The timid, long-suffering, but devoted mother of Fabrice del Dongo.

Dongo, Mlle. del. *La Chartreuse de Parme.* The younger sister of Fabrice. She marries poorly, unlike her sister, who marries a duke from Milan.

Doorkeeper (unnamed). *L'Assommoir.* Predecessor of Boche as doorkeeper of the building where Gervaise and Coupeau live.

Dorfrainville, Mme. *La Vie de Marianne.* Friend of Mme. Dursan and Tervire.

Dorothée. *Gil Blas.* The travelling companion of Laure.

Dorothée. *Gil Blas.* Sister of don Juan de Jutella, she becomes the second wife of Gil Blas.

Dorsin, Mme. *La Vie de Marianne.* A woman who befriends Marianne. She is noted for her warmth and intelligence.

Doulx-Sire, Guillaume. *Notre-Dame de Paris.* Pierre Gringoire's landlord, to whom the poet owes money.

Driver (unnamed). *Les Misérables.* Driver of the carriage in which Javert takes away Jean Valjean and Marius, who have just emerged from the Paris sewer.

Drouard, Mme. *Nana.* An elderly actress who plays the role of Juno in *Blonde Venus,* starring Nana.

Dubreuil, Mme. *Madame Bovary.* A townswoman who becomes to visit the convalescing Emma Bovary.

Duchess (unnamed). *L'Education sentimentale.* Daughter of a companion of the Count d'Artois. This little old lady is treated well by the socially ambitious Mme. Dambreuse.

Ducretot. *L'Education sentimentale.* A man with a stutter, a priest, an agriculturist, and author of a novel entitled *Manures,* who tries in vain to speak at a political gathering.

Ducros. *Le Rouge et le noir.* A childhood friend whom M. Rênal has renounced because of political differences.

Dugnani. *La Chartreuse de Parme.* The vicar of San Paolo and the confessor of General Rassi.

Duke (unnamed). *Le Rouge et le noir.* A member of the Ultras's conspiracy, Julien's contact in the countryside.

Duke de... (unnamed). *Le Rouge et le noir.* A member of the political committee which entrusts Julien Sorel with a secret mission because of his extraordinary ability to memorize.

Duke de... (unnamed). *La Vie de Marianne.* Father-in-law of Tervire's step-brother.

Dupuis, Léon. *Madame Bovary.* A young law clerk who falls in love with Emma Bovary in Yonville-l'Abbaye but is too timid to declare himself. Three years later, when he is more experienced, he has a passionate love affair with her in Rouen.

Dupuis, Mme. *Madame Bovary.* Mother of Léon Dupuis. She is concerned about her son's liaison with Emma Bovary.

Duquesnoi, Mlle. *Jacques le fataliste.* See Aisnon, Mlle. d'.

Duquesnoi, Mme. *Jacques le fadaliste.* See Aisnon, Mme. d'.

Durand. *Le Rouge et le noir.* The town clothier in Verrières.

Durati. *La Chartreuse de Parme.* A convict in Genoa.

Dursan. *La Vie de Marianne.* Son of Mme. Dursan who has incurred the wrath of his mother by marrying a woman of a low-class family.

Dursan (Jr.). Grandson of Mme. Dursan who falls in love with Tervire but is inconstant in his affection.

Dursan, Mme. *La Vie de Marianne.* Great-aunt of Tervire, she takes her in and treats her as a daughter.

Dursan, Mme., Jr. *La Vie de Marianne.* Daughter-in-law of Mme. Dursan, she comes to her disguised as a chambermaid named Brunon.

Dussardier, Auguste. *L'Education sentimentale.* A young shop employee who is arrested during a student riot and is then aided by Frédéric Moreau. The two become good friends after this.

Dutchman (unnamed). *Les Liaisons dangereuses.* A short, fat man on whom Valmont plays a sadistic trick.

Dutour, Mme. *La Vie de Marianne.* A laundress who takes in Marianne on the recommendation of M. de Climal.

Duval, Dr. *Madame Bovary.* A Rouen physician whose treatise Charles Bovary devours before performing the operation on Hippolyte Tautain's clubfoot.

Duval, Professor. *La Cousine Bette*. A professor of medicine who does an analysis of the poisoned blood of Valérie Marneffe and Crevel.

Edgermond. *Corinne*. Cousin of Lucile Edgermond and a believer in the established order of things. He urges Oswald not to marry Corinne.

Edgermond, Lady. *Corinne*. Lord Edgermond's second wife, a narrow-minded, provincial Englishwoman.

Edgermond, Lord. *Corinne*. Father of Corinne by his first marriage, to an Italian woman, and of Lucile by his second marriage, to an Englishwoman.

Edgermond, Lucile. *Corinne*. The young English girl whom Oswald's father destined to be Oswald's wife one day. Oswald eventually marries her but is still in love with Corinne.

Egypte, Duke d'. *Notre-Dame de Paris*. An old gypsy beggar who is Esmeralda's protector and claims that she is a lost child seeking her parents.

Elders (unnamed). *Salammbô*. The members of the Grand Council of Carthage. They oppose Hamilcar Barca but reluctantly support him because they have no choice.

Eléonore. *L'Education sentimentale*. The handsome young mistress of Roques who gives birth to his illegitimate child Louise and then dies at an early age.

Elisa. *Le Rouge et le noir*. Mme. de Rênal's chambermaid who first loves Julien and then hates him because of his relationship with her mistress.

Elisabeth de France. *La Princesse de Clèves*. Daughter of King Henri II and Catherine de Médecis. She becomes queen of Spain upon her marriage to Philip II.

Elizabeth. *La Princesse de Clèves*. Queen of England, who is considering marriage to the Duke de Nemours.

Ellénore. *Adolphe*. A beautiful Polishwoman, several years Adolphe's senior, who becomes his mistress and eventually dies when she discovers that he no longer cares for her.

Emilie. *Les Liaisons dangereuses*. A former mistress of Valmont.

Enjolras. *Les Misérables*. A young revolutionary of a priestly and warlike nature whose only passion is justice, as he defines it. He is killed during the insurrection of 1832.

Enrique, don. *Gil Blas*. Son of Mainfroi and brother of don Pèdre.

Erfeuil, Count d'. *Corinne*. A valiant Frenchman who is also a snob and a vicious gossip. He accompanies Oswald to Italy, where the two become friends in spite of their differences.

Ernesto IV. *La Chartreuse de Parme*. The severe, cruel Prince of Parma whose court thrives on intrigue, which he encourages. He nearly causes Fabrice's death.

Ernesto V. *La Chartreuse de Parme*. The timid Crown Prince of Parma, who admires the Duchess Sanseverina's beauty. Later, when he becomes monarch, he invites her to come out of exile and return to the court and, then, to become his mistress and prime minister.

Escars, Jean d'. *La Princesse de Clèves*. A court favorite of King Henri II.

Esgrignon, Marquis d'. *La Cousine Bette*. One of the lovers of the singer Josépha.

Esmeralda. *Notre-Dame de Paris*. A vivacious, beautiful gypsy girl who has lost her parents. She is loved by the hunchback Quasimodo, who protects her, and by the tormented priest, Dom Claude Frollo, who wishes to have her executed because he considers her to be evil. As for Esmeralda, she loves only Phoebus de Chateaupers.

Espard, Marquise de. *Le Père Goriot*. An elegant Paris society woman.

Espard, Mme. d'. *La Cousine Bette*. A member of the same charitable organizations as the Baroness Hulot.

Esseintes, Jean des. *A Rebours*. The last descendant of a rich and noble family. This neurotic man of thirty becomes disgusted with society and retreats to a solitary existence. In this hermetic atmosphere, he cultivates the artificial in his search for rare and refined sensations. However, his neurosis pursues him to the point where he is reluctantly obliged to renounce this close confinement.

Esseintes, M. des. *A Rebours*. The solitary father of Jean des Esseintes, who rarely saw him. He died when his son was an adolescent.

Esseintes, Mme. des. *A Rebours*. The melancholy, distracted, extremely nervous mother of Jean des Esseintes. She died when her son was barely an adolescent.

Estampes, Anne de Pisseleu, Duchess d'. *La Princesse de Clèves*. The mistress of François I at the time of his death and the hated rival of Diane de Poitiers, Duchess de Valentinois.

Este, Alphonse d'. *La Princesse de Clèves*. Royal prince at Henri II's court.

Estelle. *Gil Blas*. Name assumed by Laure when she becomes an actress. See also Laure.

Estephania, doña. *Gil Blas*. The beautiful wife of don Anastasio de Rada who is stabbed by her insanely jealous husband.

Esther. *La Cousine Bette*. Former mistress of the Baron Nucingen, whose fortune she depletes.

Estouteville, d'. *La Princesse de Clèves*. Deceived lover of Mme. de Tournon.

Estouteville, Robert d'. *Notre-Dame de Paris*. Councillor who sentences Quasimodo to be flogged at the pillory of the Place de Grève.

Eswin, Dr. *La Nouvelle Héloïse*. Lord Bomston's physician.

Etange, Baron d'. *La Nouvelle Héloïse*. Inflexible, prejudiced father of Julie. He refuses to allow her to marry Saint-Preux because the latter is not of the nobility.

Etange, Julie d'. *La Nouvelle Héloïse*. A virtuous young woman in love with Saint-Preux. Later, however, she spares no effort to stifle her passion for him, in order to be faithful to her husband, the Baron de Wolmar.

Etange, Mme. d'. *La Nouvelle Héloïse*. Loving, long-suffering mother of Julie.

Eufrasia, doña. *Gil Blas*. A young woman loved by don Gonzale. She wants to get the old man's money.

Eugénie. *Gil Blas*. Wife of Gabriel de Salero.

Eulalie. *L'Assommoir*. A fish huckster who is the girl friend of "Bec-Salé," one of Coupeau's drinking pals.

Eunuch, Chief (unnamed). *Les Lettres persanes*. The chief black eunuch who is in charge of Usbek's harem.

Eustache. *Notre-Dame de Paris*. Son of Mahiette who is seeing the sights of Paris with his mother.

Executioner (unnamed). *Jacques le fataliste*. A man who aids Jacques after the latter hits his head on a door.

Fabantou. *Les Misérables*. The disguised name used by Thénardier to beg for money from Jean Valjean. See also Thénardier.

Fabre, Urbain. *Les Misérables*. The name assumed by Jean Valjean after he and the thirteen-year-old Cosette leave the convent of Petit-Picpus. See also Valjean, Jean.

Fabrice. *La Chartreuse de Parme*. See Dongo, Fabrice Valserra del.

Fabrice. *Gil Blas*. Son of a barber and school companion of Gil Blas. He and Gil Blas are later joyously reunited in Madrid, by which time Fabrice has become a mediocre poet.

Fadet, Mère. *La Petite Fadette*. A woman supposedly endowed with the power to cure all illnesses. She is regarded with suspicion by the superstitious country folk.

Fadette (Fadet, Fanchon.). *La Petite Fadette*. Grand-daughter of Mère Fadet. She is known as the cricket because she is dark and thin as a young girl, but she suddenly becomes transformed by love (for Landry) into a beautiful and altruistic young woman.

Falaise, Hector de la. *Nana*. The not overly intelligent cousin of the journalist-critic Fauchery. This young provincial has come to Paris to complete his formal education. He is wildly enthusiastic about Nana; and, after he comes into an inheritance, flatters himself that she will be his mistress, but Nana only mocks him.

Falcoz. *Le Rouge et le noir.* A fellow traveller in the stagecoach which takes Julien Sorel to Paris, and a fellow admirer of Bonaparte. M. de Rênal has repudiated Falcoz for political reasons.

Falourdel, la. *Notre-Dame de Paris.* An old woman at whose establishment Phoebus de Chateaupers has a fatal rendezvous with Esmeralda.

Fanchette, Mère. *La Petite Fadette.* Fadette's relative and godmother, who comes to care for Fadette's grandmother and little brother after Fadette goes away.

Faneuil. *Les Misérables.* A student from Limoges, the lover of Fantine's friend, Zelphine.

Fannicot, Captain. *Les Misérables.* Commander of a company of suburban National Guards. He has the Rue de la Chanverie, where Marius and his comrades are fighting, decimated on 6 June 1832.

Fanny, *Indiana.* The maid who replaces Noun, after the latter's suicide.

Fantine. *Les Misérables.* The abandoned mistress of Félix Tholmyès, who lives only for her daughter Cosette. She sells her hair and teeth to obtain money for her child's care. Fantine dies, hearing Jean Valjean promise that he will take care of Cosette.

Fare, Mlle. de. *La Vie de Marianne.* A friendly young woman whom Marianne meets at the home of the dying M. de Climal.

Fare, Mme. de. *La Vie de Marianne.* An empty-headed, inquisitive woman who finds Marianne to be socially unacceptable because of her low birth.

Farrukhnaz. *Gil Blas.* The harem favorite of Soliman. She takes a liking to Gil Blas.

Father (unnamed) of Adolphe. *Adolphe.* A timid man, who believes that his son does not care for him. In reality, Adolphe misjudges him as aloof.

Father (unnamed) of Des Grieux. *Manon Lescaut.* A man who has Des Grieux abducted from the apartment where he is living with Manon and then mocks his son for believing that Manon is faithful to him.

Father (unnamed) of Jacques. *Jacques le fataliste.* A man whose son Jacques, because of a beating given him by his father, enlists in the military out of spite.

Father (unnamed) of René. "René." A man who dislikes his son René because of the fact that René's mother died while giving birth to him. Later, he dies in René's arms.

Father Superior (unnamed). *Manon Lescaut.* The head priest at Saint-Lazare prison who tries to make Des Grieux see the error of his ways.

Fatmé. *Les Lettres persanes.* A member of Usbek's harem.

Fauchelevant. *Les Misérables.* The name assumed by Jean Valjean after the death of Père Fauchelevant. See Valjean, Jean.

Fauchelevant, Euphrasie. *Les Misérables.* The name given Cosette from the time she enters the Petit-Picpus convent with Jean Valjean until she marries Marius. See Cosette.

Fauchelevant, Père. *Les Misérables.* An old carter whose life is saved by Jean Valjean (M. Madeleine). He later saves the lives of Jean Valjean and Cosette, when they are fleeing Javert, by giving them refuge at the convent.

Fauchery, Léon. *Nana.* A journalist-critic who socializes in Nana's circle of friends and becomes the lover of her rival, Rose Mignon. Later, he becomes the lover of the once cold and austere Countess Sabine Muffat de Beuville, wife of Nana's chief benefactor.

Fauconnier, Mme. *L'Assommoir.* Proprietress of a laundry shop who hires Gervaise as a laundress before and after Gervaise has her own laundry shop. The second time, however, she is forced to fire her.

Fauconnier, Victor. *L'Assommoir.* The son of Gervaise's washerwoman employer, and later a boyfriend of Nana.

Fausta F.... *La Chartreuse de Parme.* A capricious singer with whom Fabrice momentarily falls in love.

Favier. *La Vie de Marianne.* Chambermaid of Mlle. de Fare. She gossips about Marianne's unexpected and embarrassing encounter with Mme. Dutour.

Favorite. *Les Misérables.* A friend of Fantine and the mistress of Blanchevelle.

Féhy, Méhy. *Notre-Dame de Paris.* A fellow soldier with whom Phoebus de Chateaupers has supposedly had a skirmish.

Felicia. *Gil Blas.* Servant of doña Helena de Galisteo. She helps don Gaston woo her mistress.

Félicité. *Madame Bovary.* The young girl Emma hires to replace her fired servant, Nastasie. Félicité is trained to become Emma's personal maid.

Felino, Marquis di. *La Chartreuse de Parme.* Count Mosca's predecessor at the Court of Parma.

Félix. *L'Education sentimentale.* Rosanette Bron's servant.

Fernande. *Nana.* A chorus girl in *Blonde Venus,* starring Nana.

Fernicle, Thibaut. *Notre-Dame de Paris.* A shopkeeper near the Place de Grève.

Ferrare, Alphonse II d'Este, Duke de. *La Princesse de Clèves.* A courtier of Henri II.

Ferraud, Countess. *Le Père Goriot.* An elegant Paris society woman.

Fervaques, Count de. *Le Rouge et le noir.* A guest at the Hôtel de la Mole.

Notorious for his insolence, he is outdone in this regard by Mathilde de la Mole, to whom he falls victim.

Fervaques, Maréchale de. *Le Rouge et le noir.* A late arrival at M. de la Mole's salon. Her eyes and expression remind Julien of Mme. de Rênal. Later he flirts with her in order to make Mathilde jealous.

Fessard. *Eugénie Grandet.* A Saumur merchant.

Feuilly. *Les Misérables.* A self-educated orphan who becomes a learned young revolutionary known for his eloquence.

Fèvre. *La Vie de Marianne.* The chambermaid of Mme. Dursan.

Firmiani, Mme. *Le Père Goriot.* An elegant Paris society woman.

Fischer, André. *La Cousine Bette.* A laborer from Lorraine and the father of the Baroness Hulot.

Fischer, Johann. *La Cousine Bette.* The youngest of the three Fischer brothers, uncle of both Adeline Hulot and Bette Fischer. He commits suicide in Algeria because Baron Hulot has caused him to be dishonored.

Fischer, Lisbeth (Bette). *La Cousine Bette.* A middle-aged spinster who is extremely jealous and envious of her more beautiful cousin, Adeline Hulot. She is relentless in her clandestine efforts to destroy the entire Hulot family, whom she despises.

Fischer, Pierre. *La Cousine Bette.* Father of Lisbeth (Bette) Fischer and uncle of Hortense Hulot.

Fisherman (unnamed). "Zadig." A despairing man on the verge of drowning himself. He makes Zadig realize that other people are equally miserable. Zadig later reestablishes his small fortune.

Fitz-Folke, Duke de. *Le Rouge et le noir.* A young dandy who invites Julien Sorel to dinner in London.

Flacourt. *L'Education sentimentale.* A former benefactor of Rosanette Bron (la Maréchale).

Fleurance. *Germinal.* A worker who dies in her bed. Because of the intervention of Maheu, she is replaced by Etienne Lantier.

Florentine. *Gil Blas.* The daughter of Jérôme de Mayadas.

Florimonde. *Gil Blas.* An actress who is a friend of Arsénie.

Florine. *Eugénie Grandet.* A pretty Parisian actress with whom the provincial banker des Grassins becomes infatuated.

Fontan. *Nana.* A comic actor of talent who performs in *Blonde Venus* with Nana. Later, he becomes Nana's lover for a time, then begins to abuse her, and finally throws her out of their apartment.

Fontana. *La Chartreuse de Parme.* The aide-de-camp of the Prince of Parma.

Footman (unnamed). *La Chartreuse de Parme.* A man from whom the fugitive Fabrice steals a horse.

Forchambeaux, Anselme de. *L'Education sentimentale.* A bald young man who is mocked by de Cisy because he is about to get married.

Forero, Vincent. *Gil Blas.* The owner of a magnificent hotel where Gil Blas rents an apartment.

Fortin, Mme. *La Cousine Bette.* Mother of an illegitimate child who will grow up to be Valérie Marneffe.

Foscarini. *La Chartreuse de Parme.* A favorite in the Marquis Crescenzi's drawing room.

Foucarmont. *Nana.* One of Nana's many lovers, whom she ruins.

Fougeray, Baroness de. *Nana.* A woman who is so overcome when her eldest daughter takes the veil that she takes to her bed.

Fougeray, Mlle. de. *Nana.* A young woman who has decided to take the veil. This is the talk of all Paris.

Fouqué. *Le Rouge et le noir.* Julien's devoted friend, a young merchant who stands by him to the bitter end.

Fourbauld, Jehan. *Notre-Dame de Paris.* An artist whose paintings are on display during Epiphany, 1482.

Fourgeot, Mathieu de. *Jacques le fataliste.* A usurer with whom Jacques comes into contact.

Fourmont, Mlle. *Le Rouge et le noir.* A young woman at a ball who pouts because Mathilde de la Mole is more beautiful than she is.

Franchessini, Colonel Count. *Le Père Goriot.* The person hired by Vautrin to kill Michel Taillefer in a duel.

Francis. *Germinal.* The coachman of the Grégoire family.

Francis. *Nana.* Nana's hairdresser. He is fond of her and attempts to dissuade her from continuing her unfortunate liaison with Fontan.

François. *L'Assommoir.* The elderly proprietor of a wineshop where Coupeau sometimes idles away the day drinking.

François. *Nana.* Husband of Victorine and the porter and footman at Nana's residence on the Avenue de Villiers.

François de Valois (François II). *La Princesse de Clèves.* Oldest son of King Henri II, he is the future King François II.

Frenchman (unnamed). *Paul et Virginie.* The old man who narrates the story of Paul and Virginie and who builds the cabins for their two families.

Friend (unnamed) of Adolphe. *Adolphe.* A man who, by having a love affair, interests Adolphe in having one.

Friend (unnamed) of Ellénore. *Adolphe.* Female friend who destroys their friendship by siding with Adolphe during an argument.

Friend (unnamed) of Jacques's Captain. *Jacques le fataliste.* Fellow officer who shares the Captain's passion for duelling for sport.

Frilair, Abbé de. *Le Rouge et le noir.* A politically powerful cleric to whom

Valenod is indebted, and who fails Julien Sorel on an examination because Julien is the Abbé Pirard's favorite.

Froidfond, Marquis de. *Eugénie Grandet.* An impoverished young nobleman who is forced to sell his estate to Grandet. Later, he is considered a possible husband for Eugénie.

Frollo, Dom Claude. *Notre-Dame de Paris.* A tormented priest whose perverse love for the gypsy Esmeralda destroys not only both of them but also Quasimodo, his foster son, who cannot live without Esmeralda and him.

Frollo, Jehan. *Notre-Dame de Paris.* Claude Frollo's younger brother, whom he cares for as a parent and who disappoints him by becoming a reckless libertine.

Frollo de Molendino, Joannes. *Notre-Dame de Paris.* A young clerk-scholar who impatiently awaits the start of Pierre Gringoire's morality play.

Fuente, Bertrand de la. *Gil Blas.* The uncle of Diego, the barber.

Fuente, Diego de la. *Gil Blas.* A young barber whom Gil Blas accompanies en route to Madrid.

Fuente, Fernand Pérez de la. *Gil Blas.* The grandfather of the young barber, Diego.

Fuente, Nicolas de la. *Gil Blas.* The father of Diego and also a barber.

Fuente, Pedro de la. *Gil Blas.* The poet who is the uncle of Diego, the barber, Gil Blas's friend.

Fuente, Thomas de la. *Gil Blas.* Another uncle of Diego. He is a schoolmaster.

Fulgenzio. *La Chartreuse de Parme.* The Duchess Sanseverina's old boatman from Grianta.

Fumichon. *L'Education sentimentale.* A manufacturer whose conservative zeal scandalizes Frédéric Moreau.

G.... *Les Misérables.* An old conventionalist, condemned by the populace after the restoration of the monarchy. Just before his death, he has a significant encounter with Bishop Myriel.

Gabriela. *Gil Blas.* A goldsmith's daughter whom Gil Blas is to marry.

Gaga. *Nana.* An older courtesan who was the delight of Paris under Louis-Philippe. She is the mistress of La Faloise for a time.

Gaillard, Théodore. *La Cousine Bette.* A proprietor of an important political newspaper in Paris, and a social butterfly.

Gaillefontaine, Colombe de. *Notre-Dame de Paris.* A companion of Fleur-de-Lys de Gondelaurier.

Galathionne, Princesse. *Le Père Goriot.* The woman for whom de Marsay is abandoning Delphine de Nucingen.

Galeazzo. *La Chartreuse de Parme*. Duke of Milan during the life of Fabrice's ancestor, Vespasiano del Dongo.

Galiano, Count. *Gil Blas*. A Sicilian lord who engages the services of Gil Blas to be his overseer and whose favorite living creature is his pet monkey Cupidon.

Galisteo, don George de. *Gil Blas*. The father of doña Helena, the beloved of don Gaston de Cogollos.

Galisteo, doña Helena de. *Gil Blas*. A noblewoman who becomes the wife of don George, whom she loves, after the death of her husband, whom she despises.

Gamblin. *L'Education sentimentale*. A friend of Frédéric's mother, Mme. Moreau.

Gamboa, don Fernand de. *Gil Blas*. A dissipated friend of don Mathias.

Garcias, Louis. *Gil Blas*. A young priest on the outs with the archbishop. Gil Blas succeeds in reestablishing him.

Garmantian (unnamed). *Salammbô*. A Mercenary who decapitates the captive Carthaginian, General Gisco.

Gaspard. *Gil Blas*. A valet of don Fernand who befriends Gil Blas.

Gaspard. *Gil Blas*. The servant boy of Samuel Simon. He does not hesitate to denounce his master to the supposed members of the Spanish Inquisition.

Gaspard, don. *Gil Blas*. Seraphine's brother who is killed by don Alphonse.

Gatonax. *A Rebours*. A dentist who extracts one of Des Esseintes's teeth.

Gauchère la Violette. *Notre-Dame de Paris*. A widow who comments on the hideousness of the foundling Quasimodo.

Gaudinière, Mme. de la. *Eugénie Grandet*. The mother-in-law of Grandet, from whom he inherits a fortune.

Gaudron. *L'Assommoir*. A guest at the wedding reception of Gervaise and Coupeau who resides in the same building.

Gaudron (Jr.). *L'Assommoir*. A seventeen-year-old carpenter, one of the Gaudrons' sons.

Gaudron, Mme. *L'Assommoir*. A corder of mattresses who is nearly always pregnant.

Gaul (unnamed). *Salammbô*. A Mercenary soldier who declares to Mâtho that, since Salammbô already offered Mâtho a drink, she is now offering him her couch.

Gautherot, Athanase. *L'Education sentimentale*. A sheriff's officer who threatens to seize Rosanette Bron's personal possessions because of her debts.

Gavroche. *Les Misérables*. See Thénardier, Gavroche.

Géborand, M. *Les Misérables*. A usurer who, after hearing one of Bishop

Myriel's sermons, begins to give a coin each week to six old beggars. This is an attempt to buy his way into paradise.

Gédéon, M. *Les Misérables.* The prefect of Digne and frequently the dining companion of Bishop Myriel.

Gemchid. *Les Lettres persanes.* The cousin of Usbek and the dervish of the monastery of Tauris.

General (unnamed). *La Chartreuse de Parme.* One of the generals in Napoleon's army at Waterloo whom Fabrice mistakenly caused to be soaked with muddy water.

General (unnamed). *Les Misérables.* The brother of Bishop Myriel. Unlike his brother, he was a supporter of the Emperor.

General (unnamed). *Le Rouge et le noir.* A former general under Napoleon who becomes a turncoat and attends the conspiratorial meeting of the Ultras.

General (unnamed) of the Friars Minor. *La Chartreuse de Parme.* A dull cleric whom Fabrice is obliged to talk to at a court festivity.

General (unnamed) of Monastic Order (unnamed). *Jacques le fataliste.* A Jansenist who wishes to incriminate his enemy, Father Hudson.

Genevan (unnamed). *La Chartreuse de Parme.* A phlegmatic young man from Geneva with whom the impetuous Fabrice picks a fight.

Gentillet, Mme. *Eugénie Grandet.* Mme. Grandet's maternal grandmother, from whom Grandet inherits a fortune.

Gentleman (unnamed). *L'Assommoir.* An eccentric rich old man from Plassens. He has Gervaise send her son Claude to school there, at his expense.

Gentleman (unnamed). *L'Assommoir.* A button manufacturer who pursues the fifteen-year-old Nana and becomes her first benefactor.

Gentleman (unnamed). *Nana.* A tall and mysterious guest at Nana's midnight supper party.

Gentleman (unnamed). *Le Père Goriot.* An old man, a prefect during the Napoleonic era who is now in dire need. Eugène gives him a gambling tip.

Geometrician (unnamed). *Les Lettres persanes.* A smug, opinionated, egocentric creature whom Rica meets in Paris.

Gerbaud, Mère. *Les Misérables.* A poor woman to whom Bishop Myriel gives fifteen sous.

Gercourt, Count de. *Les Liaisons dangereuses.* The fiancé of Cécile Volanges and the object of Mme. de Merteuil's vengeance.

Geronimo. *Le Rouge et le noir.* A famous Neapolitan singer who visits the Rênal family to obtain papers which will enable him to be received at the court.

Géronte. *Jacques le fataliste.* A rigid but tenderhearted innkeeper, the husband of a chatty woman who loves to tell stories.

Gervais. *Les Misérables.* A little Savoyard whose two-franc piece is seized by Jean Valjean, who feels remorseful shortly thereafter and tries in vain to return the coin.

Gervaise. *L'Assommoir.* See Macquart, Gervaise.

Gervaise. *Notre-Dame de Paris.* A Parisian woman who is accompanying friends on a sightseeing tour of Paris and leads them to Paquette la Champfleurie.

Ghisleri, Marquise. *La Chartreuse de Parme.* The Grand Mistress of the Princess of Parma, she is replaced by the Duchess Sanseverina.

Ghisolfi. *La Chartreuse de Parme.* A singer with a harsh voice at the Court of Parma.

Ghita. *La Chartreuse de Parme.* The devoted old servant of the Abbé Blanès. She also loves Fabrice.

Gibelotte. *Les Misérables.* An exhausted, oppressed servant-girl who works at "Corinth."

Giborne, Michel. *Notre-Dame de Paris.* An actor ready to play the role of Jupiter in a morality play by Pierre Gringoire. He attempts in vain to quiet and appease the impatient crowd.

Giddenem. *Salammbô.* The governor of Hamilcar Barca's slaves.

Giletti. *La Chartreuse de Parme.* Marietta's raging, jealous lover whom Fabrice kills in a fight, an act which proves to have grave consequences for him.

Gillenormand, Luke Esprit. *Les Misérables.* Marius's grandfather, a haughty old bourgeois. He finally conquers his pride and accepts his rebellious grandson and the latter's bride, Cosette.

Gillenormand, Mlle. *Les Misérables.* The wealthy spinster daughter of Luke Esprit Gillenormand and aunt of Marius. She is a prude with an acute nose and an obtuse intellect.

Gillenormand, Théodule. *Les Misérables.* A pompous lancer who is the great-great-nephew of Luke Esprit Gillenormand.

Giovannone. *Le Rouge et le noir.* The San Carlino Opera House director who hires Geronimo.

Girard. *Madame Bovary.* The plowboy of Rodolphe Boulanger. He is the bearer of his master's farewell letter to Emma Bovary.

Giraud. *La Cousine Bette.* A government official who occasionally spends the evening at Valérie Marneffe's.

Giroflée, Brother. "Candide." A Theatine monk who is extremely unhappy with his lot. He is the sexual companion of Paquette.

Gisco. *Salammbô.* General in the Army of the Republic of Carthage, who commands the Mercenaries before their revolt. Later, he suffers horrible torment as the Mercenaries' prisoner before being decapitated.

Gisquet. *Les Misérables.* Javert's severe superior at the prefecture in Paris.

Gisquette, la Gencienne. *Notre-Dame de Paris.* One of two young gossips who converse about the morality play with Pierre Gringoire.

G. M., M. de. *Manon Lescaut.* A sensual old man with whom Manon goes off, abandoning Des Grieux for a time, in order to reestablish their fortune. After being duped by Manon and Des Grieux, he has them arrested.

G. M. (Jr.). *Manon Lescaut.* A man who follows in his father's footsteps and also becomes enamored of Manon. An attempt by Manon and Des Grieux to get his money results in their imprisonment.

Gobseck. *Le Père Goriot.* A money lender to whom Père Goriot sells a piece of silver plate in order to obtain money for one of his daughters. Goriot's daughter, Anastasie de Restaud, sells her mother-in-law's diamonds to Gobseck.

Godinez, Dr. *Gil Blas.* Known as the cleverest pedant of Oviedo, he teaches a bit of Greek and Latin to Gil Blas.

Gondelaurier, Dame Aloïse de. *Notre-Dame de Paris.* A wealthy lady who is appalled at the sight of the foundling Quasimodo. She lives opposite the cathedral.

Gondelaurier, Fleur-de-Lys de. *Notre-Dame de Paris.* The young daughter of Dame Aloise de Gondelaurier.

Gondureau. *Le Père Goriot.* An agent for the Minister of Justice, he helps implement the plan to capture Vautrin.

Gonzo. *La Chartreuse de Parme.* A coarse, comic courtier who obtains, through the influence of the Marquise Crescenzi, a magnificent post at the Court of Parma. He serves as Clélia Conti's informant concerning Fabrice and Annette Marini.

Gorbeau. *Les Misérables.* A lawyer, formerly named Corbeau, who once owned the building where Jean Valjean and Cosette—and, later, Marius—live for a time.

Goriot, Père. *Le Père Goriot.* A former manufacturer of vermicelli who made a small fortune. He sacrifices all his worldly possessions and, ultimately, his life for his two selfish daughters who bleed him to death. Goriot is a monomaniac; his love for his daughters is his sole reason for existence.

Goujet. *L'Assommoir.* A bashful blacksmith and neighbor of Gervaise, whom he secretly loves. This unselfish man lends her the money to purchase her laundry shop and then mourns in silence as she goes steadily downhill.

Goujet, Mme. *L'Assommoir*. A lace mender who lives with her adoring son in the apartment next to that of Gervaise and Coupeau.

Gousse. *Jacques le fataliste*. A striking individual whose behavior is either virtuous or vicious but never moderate.

Governor (unnamed). *Manon Lescaut*. Governor of the New Orleans colony to which Des Grieux follows Manon. He treats them well until he learns that they are unmarried and that his nephew Synnelet loves Manon.

Grana, Marquis de. *Gil Blas*. The ambassador of the Emperor of Austria to the Court of Spain while Gil Blas is in Madrid.

Grand Duke (unnamed). *Gil Blas*. The Prince of Tuscany, whom don Raphaël visits in Florence.

Grandet, Charles. *Eugénie Grandet*. Eugénie's shallow cousin from Paris. He is sent to Saumur by his bankrupt father, just before the latter commits suicide. Eugenie loves Charles deeply, and he professes to care for her; but, once he regains his fortune in the Indies, he becomes corrupted and renounces her.

Grandet, Eugénie. *Eugénie Grandet*. A naïve, loving, and devoted young woman whose life is destroyed by the limitations of provincial life, by her father's avarice, and, ultimately, by her beloved Charles's betrayal of her.

Grandet, Félix. *Eugénie Grandet*. A wealthy farmer and businessman of Saumur. His greed destroys the lives of those closest to him.

Grandet, Mme. *Eugénie Grandet*. A woman who is first reduced to a state of serfdom by her avaricious husband and is eventually destroyed by him.

Grandet, Victor-Ange-Guillaume. *Eugénie Grandet*. The bankrupt father of Charles Grandet. He commits suicide after sending his son to live with the avaricious Félix Grandet.

Grandlieu, Mme. de. *La Cousine Bette*. A member of the same charitable organizations as the Baroness Hulot.

Grantaire. *Les Misérables*. A young revolutionary known for his skepticism. He carefully avoids believing in anything and anyone, except in Enjolras, the most rigid, resolute member of the group.

Grassins, Des. *Eugénie Grandet*. The richest banker in Saumur. The avaricious Grandet sometimes shares discreetly in his profits. Des Grassins eventually flees to Paris to pursue a young actress he has fallen in love with.

Grassins, Adolphe des. *Eugénie Grandet*. The son of the banker, who wants him to marry Eugénie for her inheritance money. Adolphe eventually flees to Paris to lead the same dissolute life as his father.

Grassins, Mme. des. *Eugénie Grandet*. The gossipy, ambitious wife of the banker. She is abandoned in Saumur by both her husband and her son.

Grassou, Pierre. *La Cousine Bette*. The favorite painter of many members of the bourgeoisie, including Célestin Crevel.

Grégoire, Cécile. *Germinal*. The only child of the Léon Grégoires, she is doted upon by her loving parents. By a quirk of fate, she is strangled by the crazed Bonnemort, when she gets too close to him and begins to stare at him.

Grégoire, Eugène. *Germinal*. The son of Honoré Grégoire and the grandfather of Léon Grégoire.

Grégoire, Félicien. *Germinal*. The father of Léon Grégoire.

Grégoire, Honoré. *Germinal*. The steward of the Baron Desrumeaux and the great-grandfather of Léon Grégoire. He wisely invests his savings in the Montsou Mining Company.

Grégoire, Léon. *Germinal*. A complacent shareholder in the Montsou Mining Company. He has invested his entire fortune in the Voreux pit but refuses to give any money to the starving workers.

Grégoire, Mme *Germinal*. The Voreux pit owner's complacent wife, who is totally indifferent to the plight of the mine workers.

Grémonville, Paul de. *L'Education sentimentale*. A diplomat whom Frédéric Moreau meets at a ball.

Grenouville. *La Cousine Bette*. A rich tradesman whom Olympe Bijou marries after she abandons Baron Hulot.

Gresham. *Nana*. An English jockey at the Grand Prix race who rides a losing horse owned by the desperate Vandeuvres.

Gribeaucourt, Mlle. de. *Eugénie Grandet*. A resident of Saumur whose living room is a center for provincial gossip among followers of the Cruchots.

Gribier. *Les Misérables*. The gravedigger who replaces the deceased Mestienne, to the horror of Fauchelevant, who must trick Gribier in order to save Jean Valjean.

Grillo. *La Chartreuse de Parme*. The jailor who attends the imprisoned Fabrice in the Farnese tower.

Grimbert. *Le Père Goriot*. The head of the office for the *Messageries royales* in the small provincial town where Eugène de Rastignac's family lives.

Grimprel. *Le Père Goriot*. Mme. Vauquer's physician.

Grindot. *La Cousine Bette*. A once-popular architect whose work is admired by Crevel.

Gringoire, Pierre. *Notre-Dame de Paris*. A poet and writer of morality plays who unwittingly becomes involved in the lives of Dom Claude Frollo and Esmeralda.

Grogeot. *Le Rouge et le noir*. An ordinary citizen of Verrières.

Gros. *La Chartreuse de Parme*. A young painter of Milan who draws a mock portrait of the Austrian Archduke.

Gros. *Le Rouge et le noir*. A geometrician, one of the few tolerable people Julien Sorel meets at dinner parties in Verrières. Later, Julien unknowingly victimizes him.

Gudule, Sister. *Notre-Dame de Paris*. See Paquette la Chantefleurie and Sachette, la.

Guelemer. *Les Misérables*. One of four bandits who govern the lowest depth of Paris, from 1830 to 1835. He participates in Thénardier's attempt to ambush Jean Valjean.

Guerchy, M. *Jacques le fataliste*. A French soldier.

Guérin, Mlle. *Madame Bovary*. A young woman whose nervous depression resembles that of Emma, according to her servant, Félicité.

Guevara, doña Anna de. *Gil Blas*. The nurse of the royal family of Spain and the employer of Catalina and Scipion.

Guide (unnamed). *Salammbô*. The slave who leads Salammbô to Mâtho's tent so that Salammbô may recover the Zaïmph, the stolen veil.

Guillaumin. *Madame Bovary*. A lawyer in Yonville-l'Abbaye. Léon Dupuis serves as an apprentice under him for a time.

Guise, François de Lorraine, Chevalier de. *La Princesse de Clèves*. One of the many handsome young men at court. He is attracted to Mlle. de Chartres, the future Mme. de Clèves.

Guise, François de Lorraine, Duke de. *La Princesse de Clèves*. A prince at the court of Henri II, renowned for his military and business accomplishments.

Gusman, Ximena de. *Gil Blas*. The assumed name of Dame Ortiz. See Ortiz, Dame.

Gustin. *La Nouvelle Héloïse*. Julie's gardener at Clarens.

Gustin (Jr.). *La Nouvelle Héloïse*. The son of Julie's gardener.

Guyomar. *Gil Blas*. A drunken professor of philosophy.

Guzman, don Gaspar de, Count d'Olivarès. *Gil Blas*. The Duke de Lerme's successor as prime minister, upon the ascension of Philippe IV to the Spanish throne.

Guzman, don Henri-Philippe de. *Gil Blas*. The adopted son of Guzman, Count d'Olivarès. He is perhaps the latter's illegitimate son.

Guzman, doña Maria de. *Gil Blas*. The only daughter of Guzman, Count d'Olivarès.

Guzman, don Ramire Nunez de. *Gil Blas*. The young nobleman whom Guzman, Count d'Olivarès has selected to marry his daughter and be his heir.

Guzman, Vincent de. *Gil Blas*. A rich old nobleman who is an employer of Gil Blas. He rambles when relating his military exploits.

Hagi Ibbi. *Les Lettres persanes.* A pilgrim who sings the praises of Mohammed.

Hally, Sidi. *Gil Blas.* A name given to don Raphaël after he becomes a Mahometan. See Raphaël, don.

Hannequin. *La Cousine Bette.* General Hulot's notary.

Hannibal. *Salammbô.* The young son of Hamilcar Barca, he is zealously protected by his father, who keeps the boy in hiding.

Hanno. *Salammbô.* A government official of Carthage. This grotesque, leprous creature consistently fails in his attempts to be a valiant, victorious military leader. He is always the fool, up to the time of his death by torture.

Hans. *La Nouvelle Héloïse.* A servant employed by Claire.

Hareng, Master. *Madame Bovary.* A lawyer whose signature is affixed to the documents ordering Emma to appear in court for failing to pay off her loans.

Haro, don Louis de. *Gil Blas.* Another suitor of doña Maria de Guzman, daughter of Guzman d'Olivarès.

Hassein. *Les Lettres persanes.* A dervish with whom Usbek corresponds.

Hayez. *La Chartreuse de Parme.* An artist who paints a portrait of Fabrice, at the request of Annetta of Marini.

Headmaster (unnamed). *Madame Bovary.* Head of the school which the boy Charles Bovary enters.

Hennebeau. *Germinal.* The general manager of the Voreux mine, who finds his wife's infidelities almost unbearable.

Hennebeau, Mme. *Germinal.* The wife of the general manager of the Voreux pit. She is rightly suspected of making a cuckold of her husband. Her latest lover is her nephew.

Henri, Père. *La Petite Fadette.* A village gossip.

Henri II. *La Princesse de Clèves.* King of France (1547-59). Most of the action of the novel takes place during the last months of his reign. His most significant feature in the novel is his devotion to his older mistress, Dianne de Poitiers, Duchess de Valentinois.

Henriette la Gaultière. *Notre-Dame de Paris.* A widow and religious sister who comments on the hideousness of the foundling Quasimodo.

Henriot, Captain. *La Chartreuse de Parme.* An officer killed during the battle at Waterloo.

Héquet, Caroline. *Nana.* A courtesan possessing a cold type of beauty, she attends the opening performance of *Blonde Venus,* starring Nana.

Héquet, Mme. *Nana.* Caroline's mother, a woman of a worthy demeanor who looks as if she were stuffed with straw.

Herbigny, Captain. *L'Education sentimentale.* An old man who leads a depraved life and attends the same all-night party that Frédéric Moreau does.

Hérissant, M. *Jacques le fataliste.* A former master of Jacques.

Hérouville, Duke d'. *La Cousine Bette.* An admirer of the singer Josépha, who renounces the Baron Hulot for him and becomes his devoted mistress.

Hervart, Mme. d'. *La Nouvelle Héloïse.* A social acquaintance of the d'Etanges family.

Heudras. *L'Education sentimentale.* A social acquaintance of Mme. Moreau.

Hictamon. *Salammbô.* One of the important men in Hamilcar's party.

Hiero. *Salammbô.* The ruler at Syracuse who sends cattle and wheat to Carthage for political reasons.

Hippolyte. *Germinal.* The Hennebeaus' footman.

Hippolyte. *Madame Bovary.* See Tautain, Hippolyte.

Hipponax. *Salammbô.* A merchant of Samos who has supposedly advised the Barbarian soldiers to keep close watch over Gisco and the other Carthaginian captives.

Hivert. *Madame Bovary.* The driver of the stagecoach from Rouen to Yonville-l'Abbaye.

Homais. *Madame Bovary.* The smug, opiniated chemist of Yonville-l'Abbaye. He epitomizes the social-climbing, provincial bourgeois.

Homais, Athalie. *Madame Bovary.* An unruly child of Homais. Her name represents an act of homage on the part of her father to Racine's immortal masterpiece.

Homais, Franklin. *Madame Borary.* An unruly child of Homais. He is named after Benjamin Franklin, a symbol of liberty to Homais.

Homais, Irma. *Madame Bovary.* Another unruly child of Homais. Her name is a concession to the romantic spirit.

Homais, Mme. *Madame Bovary.* The rather listless wife of the sententious pharmacist of Yonville-l'Abbaye.

Homais, Napoléon. *Madame Bovary.* Still another unruly child of Homais. He is named after the Emperor of France.

Homosexual (unnamed). *A Rebours.* A young man whom Des Esseintes once encountered by chance and with whom he had an affair which lasted for months.

Honorine. *Germinal.* The housemaid of the Grégoire family.

Hordalès, don Huberto de. *Gil Blas.* Doña Estephania's cousin who falls in love with her and then seeks revenge when she rejects his advances.

Horn, Léa de. *Nana.* A courtesan who attends Nana's midnight supper party.

Hortensia, doña. *Gil Blas.* A widow of an officer of the King's guard. She declares her love to don Pompeyo de Castro.

Hubert, M. *Indiana.* A wealthy manufacturer who purchases Lagny, the estate Colonel Delmare sells for the benefit of his creditors.

Hucheloup, Mère. *Les Misérables*. The bearded, ugly wife of the owner of the wineshop named "Corinth." She lets the shop degenerate after her husband dies.

Hucheloup, Père. *Les Misérables*. The proprietor of "Corinth," the inn where the young revolutionary friends of Marius congregate.

Hudson, Father. *Jacques le fataliste*. A wily Father Superior who is very successful in leading a double life.

Hugon, Georges. *Nana*. A young truant from a boarding school. He falls in love with Nana upon seeing her in *Blonde Venus,* pursues her, and becomes one of her lovers. Later, after Nana mocks him for proposing marriage to her, the despondent young man kills himself.

Hugon, Mme. *Nana*. The widow of a notary and the mother of two sons who are obsessed with Nana. She is left to grieve over both of them, for one commits suicide and the other is imprisoned bcause of their obsession.

Hugon, Philippe. *Nana*. A lieutenant in a garrison at Bourgues. He falls under the spell of Nana and is imprisoned for stealing money for her.

Hulot, Baroness Adeline. *La Cousine Bette*. The long-suffering wife of Baron Hulot. Her devotion to such an unworthy husband is so unwavering that it ultimately destroys her.

Hulot, Célestine Crevel. *La Cousine Bette*. Daughter of Crevel the womanizer. She becomes the insignificant, moneyed bride of Victorin Hulot and dutifully comforts her family in time of need.

Hulot, Baron Hector. *La Cousine Bette.* An aging government official whose addiction to young women, particularly Valérie Marneffe, heaps disgrace upon him, kills his long-suffering wife, and nearly destroys his entire family.

Hulot, Maréchal. *La Cousine Bette.* The Baron Hulot's older brother, a military hero whose courage has brought him renown and the title Count de Forzheim. His brother's disgrace, however, deals him a fatal blow.

Hulot, Victorin. *La Cousine Bette*. The son of Hector and Adeline Hulot. He is a devoted son and father who seeks to destroy Valérie Marneffe and, thereby, rehabilitate his family.

Hussonnet. *L'Education sentimentale*. A young man who works as a clerk in Jacques Arnoux's art shop but who aspires to make his fortune in the theatre.

Hyde, Lord. *La Nouvelle Héloïse*. A friend of Lord Bomston.

Ibaraa y Figueora y Mascarenes y Lampourdos y Souza, don Fernando d'. "Candide." The wealthy, haughty governor of Buenos Aires who is inflamed upon seeing Cunégonde and insists upon having her as his mistress.

Ibben. *Les Lettres persanes.* A friend and correspondent of Usbek and Rica.

Ibbi. *Les Lettres persanes.* A eunuch who accompanies Usbek on his journey.

Ibrahim. *Les Lettres persanes.* A jealous man who, because of his abuse of members of his harem, is made to suffer by Anaïs, one of the injured parties.

Iddibal. *Salammbô.* Hamilcar's robust old servant who, disguised as an old woman, protects Hamilcar's son.

Inès. *Gil Blas.* The lady-in-waiting and confidante of doña Mencia de Mosquera.

Inès, doña. *Gil Blas.* Violante's friend, in whose house the rendezvous between Violante and Gil Blas takes place.

Inésille. *Gil Blas.* The niece of Dame Jacinte.

Innkeeper (unnamed). *Jacques le fataliste.* The owner of the wretched inn where thieves cause Jacques and his master great difficulty.

Innkeeper (unnamed). *Jacques le fataliste.* The garrulous, cordial hostess of an inn where Jacques and his master spend the night. She tells them the story of Mme. de la Pommeraye's revenge.

Innkeeper (unnamed). *Le Rouge et le noir.* The hostess of a hotel in Besançon. She is attracted to Julien Sorel.

Innkeeper (unnamed). *La Vie de Marianne.* A sinister innkeeper who exploits the innocent, fifteen-year-old Marianne.

Innkeeper (unnamed). *La Vie de Marianne.* A coldhearted man who tries to evict Mme. Darneuil because she is unable to pay her bill.

Innocent, Mother. *Les Misérables.* The prioress at the Petit-Picpus Convent. She unwittingly assists Jean Valjean because Fauchelevant claims that Jean Valjean is his brother.

Inquisitor (unnamed). "Candide." A holy man who shares Cunégonde with the Jew, don Issachar, and orders an *auto-da-fe* both to ward off the earthquake and to intimidate his rival.

Intendant (unnamed) with a cello. *Jacques le fataliste.* A schemer whose plan to have the pastry cook jailed backfires.

Intendante de.... *Les Liaisons dangereuses.* The woman for whom Gercourt abandons the Marquise de Merteuil.

Ipigna, don Ignacio de. *Gil Blas.* The pedant, tutor, and professor emeritus who becomes Scipion's employer for fifteen months.

Irma. *L'Education sentimentale.* A friend of Rosanette who has a well-to-do protector.

Isaac, Père. *L'Education sentimentale.* An employee of Arnoux. His specialty consists of attaching the signatures of the great masters to paintings by other artisits.

Isabeau, Maubert. *Les Misérables.* The baker from whom Jean Valjean steals a loaf of bread, in order to feed his sister's starving family. Because of this theft, he is sentenced to nineteen years in prison.

Isabeau la Thierrye. *Notre-Dame de Paris.* A prostitute whose company Jehan Frollo enjoys.

Isidore. *L'Education sentimentale.* The manservant of Frédéric Moreau's mother.

Ismael. *Les Lettres persanes.* One of Usbek's black eunuchs, who dies.

Isménie. *Gil Blas.* An actress slandered by the other guests at Arsénie's party.

Isotta, Princess. *La Chartreuse de Parme.* The middle-aged cousin of the Prince of Parma. Count Mosca pretends to be interested in her for a time.

Issachar, don. "Candide." A Jewish banker who shares Cunégonde with the Inquisitor.

Isselin, Mlle. *Jacques le fataliste.* A former mistress of Jacques.

Istatten. *Salammbô.* One of the important men in Hamilcar's party.

Itobad. "Zadig." A very rich lord who participates in the jousting tournament. He attempts to rob Zadig of his victory but is foiled by him.

Ivan. "Candide." A dethroned Russian monarch who has come to attend the carnival in Venice, where Candide meets him.

Jacinte. *Gil Blas.* Sedillo's governess who is after his money.

Jacopo. *La Chartreuse de Parme.* A prison official at the Farnese tower.

Jacques. "Candide." An altruistic Anabaptist who helps Candide and Pangloss. He is later killed during the Lisbon earthquake.

Jacques. *Jacques le fataliste.* The fatalistic ex-soldier who wanders about eighteenth-century France with his master, telling and listening to stories which are almost always interrupted.

Jacques. *Le Père Goriot.* Mme. de Béauseant's valet.

Jailer's Wife (unnamed). *La Chartreuse de Parme.* The woman who, for money, releases Fabrice from prison and gives him the uniform of a dead hussar.

Jaron. *Les Lettres persanes.* A black eunuch who initially accompanies Usbek on his voyage west but who is soon sent back to Ispahan.

Jason. *Jacques le fataliste.* Jacques's grandfather, a dealer in secondhand goods. He almost never uttered a word.

Javert. *Les Misérables.* The rigid police inspector who relentlessly pursues Jean Valjean for years. Javert ultimately commits suicide because he cannot accept the fact that the ex-galley slave saved his life when he had a good opportunity to kill him instead.

Javotte. *Jacques le fataliste.* The young woman from the inn who takes Jacques's purse.

Jean. *La Cousine Bette.* Josépha Mirah's manservant.

Jean. *Eugénie Grandet.* A workman on Grandet's property.

Jean. *Jacques le fataliste.* One of the servants of the innkeeper and hostess.

Jean. *Jacques le fataliste.* The older brother of Jacques who becomes a depraved monk.

Jean. *Le Rouge et le noir.* The nephew of the Abbé Chelan who cares for his aged uncle upon the latter's retirement.

Jeanet. *La Petite Fadette.* Fadette's little brother, known as the grasshopper because of his crippled walk.

Jeanne. *Jacques le fataliste.* Denise's mother, who is helped by Jacques.

Jeanne. *Les Misérables.* Jean Valjean's widowed, poverty-stricken sister. It is for her seven children that he steals a loaf of bread, which results in his long imprisonment.

Jeannot. *La Vie de Marianne.* The son of Mme. Dutour.

Jesrad. "Zadig." The angel who is sent in the guise of a hermit to enlighten the worthy Zadig and to teach him to submit to the will of Providence.

Jesuit Superior (unnamed). *La Chartreuse de Parme.* The Superior of the Jesuit College at Milan. He compromises himself by awarding undeserved prizes to Fabrice because of the influence of Fabrice's aunt.

Joachim. *Gil Blas.* The cook at Gil Blas's house in Valencia. Like Gil Blas, he loves Antonia.

John, Miss. *L'Education sentimentale.* The governess of Mlle. Dambreuse.

Joire, Abbé. *Germinal.* The fat, indifferent priest of the coal miners' community. He is eventually replaced and sent elsewhere, much to his relief.

Joiselle. *Germinal.* A competitor of Desrumeaux and de Cougny. He merges with them to form the Montsou Mining Company.

Joly. *Les Misérables.* A medical student who belongs to the group of young revolutionaries whom Marius eventually joins.

Joncquoy, Mme. de. *Nana.* An elderly, conservative guest at the Countess Muffat de Beuville's reception.

Jondrette. *Les Misérables.* The name Thénardier assumes during the time he lives in the Maison Gorbeau with his wife and two daughters. See Thénardier.

Jonquier. *Nana.* A former benefactor of Rose Mignon, at a time when he was also supporting another woman, Laure.

Joseph. *La Cousine Bette.* An Italian stove fitter known to Baron Hulot when the latter is in hiding.

Joséph. *Nana.* The talkative gardener who looks after La Mignotte, the country estate which the banker Steiner purchases for Nana.

Josépha. *La Cousine Bette.* A former singer who was Crevel's mistress until she jilted him for Baron Hulot, whom she in turn rejects for a wealthier patron.

Josephine. *Les Liaisons dangereuses.* A sister at the convent where Cécile Volanges was a resident.

Josse, Mlle. *L'Assommoir.* The proprietress of the school where Gervaise sends her unruly six-year-old Nana.

Joumate, Baron de la. *Le Rouge et le noir.* A short, ugly creature who has nothing to say about anything. The Marquise de la Mole wants her daughter Mathilde to marry him.

Judici, Atala. *La Cousine Bette.* A fifteen-year-old Italian girl who takes up with Baron Hulot while the latter is in hiding from his debtors.

Jules. *Germinal.* A sympathetic sentry at the Voreux pit after the miners' uprising. Etienne Lantier attempts to communicate with him shortly before Jules is senselessly killed by young Jeanlin Maheu.

Jules, Mme. *Nana.* Nana's dresser who always has a supply of straight pins where her heart should be.

Julie. *Gil Blas.* The younger sister of Séraphine.

Julie. *Les Liaisons dangereuses.* Mme. de Tourvel's chambermaid who is also the mistress of Valmont's huntsman.

Julien. *Nana.* The smiling, becurled butler of Nana while she lives in the house given her by the Count de Muffat. He is accused by the other servants of sleeping with Nana.

Jumillac. *L'Education sentimentale.* A former benefactor of Rosanette Bron (la Maréchale).

Justice of the Peace (unnamed). *La Cousine Bette.* An official sent to arrest Baron Hulot, who is caught in a compromising position. He offers Hulot some practical advice.

Justice of the Peace (unnamed). *Le Rouge et le noir.* A former liberal who is forced to turn conservative in order to survive.

Justin. *Madame Bovary.* Homais's nephew who works in his uncle's pharmacy when he is not loitering around Emma Bovary's house. He goes there as often as possible in order to sneak a look at Emma, whom he secretly loves.

Justine, *Jacques le fataliste.* A young seamstress with whom Jacques and his friend Bigre both fall in love.

Jutella, don Juan de. *Gil Blas.* A young nobleman of Valencia who marries Séraphine, the goddaughter of Gil Blas.

Kapouras. *Salammbô.* An illustrious merchant who is one of the elders of Carthage.

Keller. *La Cousine Bette.* A banker who is the lover of Mme. Colleville and was once the lover of Josépha.

Keller, François. *Eugénie Grandet.* Head of a prosperous banking house in Paris who is involved in the liquidation of the Guillaume Grandet estate.

Kergarouët, Countess de. *Le Père Goriot.* An elegant Paris society woman.

Kilmare, Mme. de. *La Vie de Marianne.* A social hostess to Valville and Mlle. Varthon.

King (unnamed) of Eldorado. "Candide." The monarch who welcomes Candide and Cacambo to his country and also helps them to leave, albeit with reluctance.

Kings (two, unnamed) of Polaques. "Candide." Two dethroned Polish kings who have come to attend the carnival in Venice.

Korasoff, Prince. *Le Rouge et le noir.* A fatuous young Russian gentleman who tells Julien Sorel how one must behave in society, particularly with women.

L..., Baron. *Le Rouge et le noir.* A guest at the Hôtel de la Mole.

L..., Count. *La Chartreuse de Parme.* One of the liberals unjustly hanged at the Court of Parma.

Labarre, Jacques. *Les Misérables.* A highly respected innkeeper in Digne.

Labordette. *Nana.* A tall young man whose company Nana enjoys because he does not ask her for sexual favors. He eventually buys "La Mignotte" for his mistress, Caroline Héguet.

La Boudrague, Mlle. *Notre-Dame de Paris.* A resident of the Place de Grève area.

Lace Mender (unnamed). *L'Assommoir.* A young girl whom Goujet is supposed to marry. He cannot do so because of his deep love for Gervaise.

Lachapelle. *Le Père Goriot.* A recorder for police security in Paris.

Lafitte. *Les Misérables.* A banker in Paris. It is at his bank that Jean Valjean initially keeps his money.

Laginski, Count. *La Cousine Bette.* A Polish exile living in Paris. He attends the wedding of Hortense Hulot and Steinbock, and is a guest at Josépha's party.

Laigle (Boussuet). *Les Misérables.* Called Bossuet by his comrades, this bald young revolutionary is known for his merriment.

La Marck, Antoinette de. *La Princesse de Clèves.* The granddaughter of the Duchess de Valentinois.

Lambert, Guillaume. *Les Misérables.* The name Thénardier gives to Jean Valjean when he is questioned by Javert.

Lamela, Ambroise de. *Gil Blas.* A thief disguised as a valet, he accompanies
Gil Blas from Burgos to Madrid and later reappears as a hermit, along
with don Raphaël. He is finally hanged, as is don Raphaël.

Lamothe-Valois, Count de. *Les Misérables.* M. Gillenormand's rival at the
salon of the Baroness de T....

Landlady (unnamed), *La Chartreuse de Parme.* The owner of the Woolcomb
Inn in Zonders. Assisted by her daughters, she nurses Fabrice back to
health and helps him escape.

Landlady (unnamed). *La Vie de Marianne.* The proprietress of the hotel
where Tervire stays. She gives money to help Mme. Darneuil.

Landlord (unnamed). *Les Misérables.* A man who turns away the ex-convict
Jean Valjean, refusing him food and a bed.

Landriani, Father. *La Chartreuse de Parme.* The Archbishop of Parma, a
man of learning and intelligence who is extremely timid, especially in
the presence of nobility. He becomes very fond of Fabrice del Dongo.

Landriche. *La Petite Fadette.* Landry's godfather, before whom Landry's
relationship with Fadette is discussed.

Lange, Colonel. *La Chartreuse de Parme.* Fabio Conti's successor as general
of the Farnese prison.

Langeais, Duchess Antoinette de. *Le Père Goriot.* An elegant Paris society
woman who is the Viscountess de Beauséant's best friend.

Langlois. *Madame Bovary.* A man who buys a small property belonging to
Charles Bovary. It is sold to him by Lheureux, acting as Emma's agent.

Langlois, Adolphe. *L'Education sentimentale.* A notary who informs Mme.
Dambreuse of the contents of her husband's will.

Langlois, Auguste. *A Rebours.* A sixteen-year-old youth whom Des Esseintes
once met on the street and whom he took to a house of prostitution for
his own perverse reasons.

Langlois, Mme. *Madame Bovary.* A townswoman who visits the convalescing
Emma Bovary.

Langreneux, Jean-Jacques. *L'Education sentimentale.* A political revolutionary who proposes in 1848 that a monument be raised in memory of the
martyrs of Thermidor.

Lantier, Auguste. *L'Assommoir.* The selfish, irresponsible lover of Gervaise
Macquart and the father of Etienne and Claude Lantier. He is a
parasite who lives on the income of the women he seduces.

Lantier, Claude. *L'Assommoir.* The older son of Gervaise Macquart and
Auguste Lantier. He is sent to Provence to attend school where he lives
with a benefactor.

Lantier, Etienne. *L'Assommoir.* The younger son of Gervaise Macquart and
Auguste Lantier. At the age of twelve the unhappy boy is sent to Lille,
where he becomes an engineer's apprentice.

Lantier, Etienne. *Germinal.* An engine man and an admirer of Karl Marx. He is the catalyst and leader of the striking miners of Montsou. In spite of the disaster that results there, he remains optimistic in his belief that the working class will one day inherit the earth.

Lanty, Mme. de. *Le Père Goriot.* An elegant Paris society woman.

Lapidary (unnamed). *A Rebours.* A collector of stones who sells Des Esseintes precious gems, with which the latter decorates the shell of a tortoise.

Lara, don Dïègue de. *Gil Blas.* The late husband of Séraphine.

Larabit, Dr. *La Cousine Bette.* A doctor called in as a consultant to diagnose Adeline Hulot's illness.

Larivière, Dr. *Madame Bovary.* Charles Bovary's old teacher from Rouen. He is called for consultation by Charles when Emma becomes seriously ill after the departure of her lover, Rodolphe Boulanger, and again just before her death from poisoning.

La Rose. *La Chartreuse de Parme.* One of the wounded soldiers in Colonel Le Baron's command.

Larsilloix, M. de. *L'Education sentimentalee.* A prefect under Louis-Philippe and a friend of M. Dambreuse.

Larsilloix, Mme. de. *L'Education sentimentale.* The frightened wife of a prefect under Louis-Philippe.

Laure. *Nana.* A large woman who has Jonquier as her benefactor, thanks to the procurer Mignon, whose wife is also a mistress of Jonquier.

Laure (Estelle). *Gil Blas.* Arsénie's servant who later disguises herself as a young widow and becomes an actress named Estelle. Gil Blas encounters her on several occasions.

Laure, Mme. *A Rebours.* The madam of a house of ill repute where Des Esseintes takes young Auguste Langlois.

Lavalette, M. de. *Le Rouge et le noir.* An innocent convict who escapes from prison. Fouqué attempts to compare him to Julien Sorel.

Lavalette, Mme. de. *Le Rouge et le noir.* The woman who, unlike Mathilde de la Mole, was able to save her beloved from the guillotine.

Law Official (unnamed). *Jacques le fataliste.* A friend of the pastry cook, whom he refuses to jail.

Laxarilla, doña Eleonor de. *Gil Blas.* The aunt of don Gaston de Cogollos.

Le Baron, Colonel. *La Chartreuse de Parme.* A wounded officer whose spirit has been broken. He feels compassion for Fabrice when the latter is wounded.

Lebas. *La Cousine Bette.* A counselor whose son's proposed marriage to Hortense Hulot is hindered by Crevel.

Lebas (Jr.). *La Cousine Bette.* A young counselor who is the unsuccessful suitor of Hortense Hulot.

Leboeuf. *L'Education sentimentale.* Co-owner of a manufacturing mill.

Leboeuf, Léocadie. *Madame Bovary.* The young woman whom the notary Léon Dupuis marries after Emma Bovary's death.

Le Bourguignon, Baron. *Le Rouge et le noir.* A favorite guest of the Marquis de la Mole. He has been promoted from subprefect to prefect because of his twenty years of assiduous attendance at the Marquise's dinner parties.

Lebrun. *La Cousine Bette.* A division head in the War Office headed by Baron Hulot.

Lebrun. *L'Education senimentale.* A social acquaintance of Mme. Moreau.

Lebrun, M. *Jacques le fataliste.* A usurer with whom Jacques has dealings.

Le Cabuc. *Les Misérables.* The name which Claquesous apparently assumes after murdering someone in cold blood. See Claquesous.

Lecornu, Gilles. *Notre-Dame de Paris.* The master furrier of the King's robes, he is mocked by the populace because of his name.

Lecornu, Jehan. *Notre-Dame de Paris.* The Provost of the King's household. Like his brother Gilles, he is mocked because of his name.

Lecornu, Mahiet. *Notre-Dame de Paris.* First porter of the wood of Vincennes. Like his sons Gilles and Jehan, he is mocked because of his name.

Lefaucheur. *L'Education sentimentale.* A lawyer who is a guest of the Arnoux family at Saint-Cloud.

Lefebvre, Oscar. *L'Education sentimentale.* A banker who knows that Jacques Arnoux is not solvent.

Lefrançois, Mme. *Madame Bovary.* The innkeeper at Yonville-l'Abbaye.

Leganez. *Gil Blas.* The rebellious companion of don Raphaël when both were twelve years old.

Leganez, Marquis de. *Gil Blas.* The father of don Raphaël's companion.

Legoujeux. *Germinal.* Pluchart's associate in the International.

Lehongre. *L'Assommoir.* A grocer of whom Lantier disapproves.

Lehongre, Mme. *L'Assommoir.* A grocer's wife who makes a cuckold of her husband.

Lelièvre. *Indiana.* The factotum of Colonel Delmare's household.

Lemos, Count de. *Gil Blas.* The Duke de Lerme's nephew whom the Duke wishes to succeed him as prime minister.

Lempereur, Félicité. *Madame Bovary.* A piano teacher in Rouen from whom Emma Bovary is supposedly taking lessons.

Lenoncourt. *La Cousine Bette.* A guest at Josépha's party.

Lenoncourt, Mme. de. *La Cousine Bette.* A member of the same charitable organizations as the Baroness Hulot.

Léon, Gabriel de. *Gil Blas.* A grand old man of letters who becomes involved in an argument concerning the *Iphigénie* of Euripides.

Léonarde. *Gil Blas.* The cook for the thieves who imprison Gil Blas in their cave hideout.

Léonie. *L'Assommoir.* A girl who works in the artificial flower factory with Nana and who exercises a bad influence on her.

Léonor. *Gil Blas.* A coquettish widow who lives opposite the house of don Alphonse and his parents.

Le Pelletier, M. *Jacques le fataliste.* A citizen of Orléans who, after giving all his money to the poor, is forced to become a beggar.

Leplichey. *Madame Bovary.* A citizen of Yonville-l'Abbaye who attends the Agricultural Show.

Lerat, Mme. *L'Assommoir.* Copeau's older sister, a widow who tries in vain to look after her niece, Nana, by getting her a job at the artificial flower factory where she is employed.

Lerat, Mme. *Nana.* Nana's aunt, who retrieves her niece's child Louis for her and keeps the sickly boy in return for presents from her niece.

Lerme, Duke de. *Gil Blas.* The Prime Minister of Spain under Philip III. He becomes Gil Blas's employer.

Leroux, Catherine-Nicaise-Elisabeth. *Madame Bovary.* A shy old farm woman who is awarded a silver medal at the Agricultural Show for her fifty-four years of uninterrupted service on the same farm.

Lescaut. *Manon Lescaut.* The dissolute, parasitic brother of Manon. His lack of moral values leads him to suggest any scheme to Des Grieux and Manon to obtain money for the three of them.

Lescaut, Manon. *Manon Lescaut.* An extremely beautiful young woman of the lower class whose inclination toward pleasure and love of material possessions bring repeated misfortune both to her and to her devoted lover, Des Grieux.

Lestiboudois. *Madame Bovary.* The curator of Yonville-l'Abbaye and the town's sexton and grave digger.

Levaque. *Germinal.* A mine worker whose wife sleeps all day with their boarder, who works on a different shift.

Levaque, Bébert. *Germinal.* An urchin of twelve who works in the Voreux coal pit. He is killed by soldiers who are defending the pit against the enraged strikers.

Levaque, la. *Germinal.* A woman who sleeps with two men, her husband by night and their lodger by day.

Levaque, Philomène. *Germinal.* The eldest Levaque child. She is the mistress of Zacharie Maheu, by whom she, at age nineteen, has already had two children.

Lévi, Nathanaël. *Les Lettres Persanes.* A Jewish doctor with whom Rica corresponds concerning the rational and the supernatural.

Leyva, don Alphonse de. *Gil Blas.* A young man pursued by police. He is
helped by Gil Blas, who later has him named Governor of Valencia and
gives him the title of Viceroy of Aragon.

Leyva, don César de. *Gil Blas.* The true father of don Alphonse, who is finally
reunited with him.

Leyva, Fernand de. *Gil Blas.* The abductor of Julie, younger sister of
Séraphine, because her hand in marriage was refused him. He is also
the nephew of don César de Leyva.

Lheureux. *Madame Bovary.* The cunning draper and dealer in fancy goods in
Yonville-l'Abbaye. He tempts the naïve Emma Bovary and the credulous Charles into sinking deeper and deeper into debt to him.

Librarian (unnamed). *Les Lettres persanes.* He comments on the contents of
the various volumes while showing Rica through the Bibliothèque de
St.-Victor.

Liégeard. *Madame Bovary.* Owner of the property on which the Agricultural
Show banquet is served.

Liénarde. *Notre-Dame de Paris.* One of two young gossips who converse
about Pierre Gringoire's morality play with the author.

Lieutenant General (unnamed). *Jacques le fataliste.* A friend of Jacques's
master.

Lieuvain. *Madame Bovary.* A counselor of the prefecture who replaces the
prefect at the Agricultural Show, where he makes a bombastic speech.

Liévin. *Le Rouge et le noir.* A former lieutenant and fencing partner who
agrees to be Julien Sorel's second in a duel.

Ligero, Martin. *Gil Blas.* The pretentious dancing teacher of don Henri-
Philippe de Guzman.

Lignerolles, Philibert de. *La Princesse de Clèves.* A court favorite who is the
confidant of the Duke de Nemours.

Lili. *Nana.* The nineteen-year-old daughter of Gaga. She is dragged everywhere by her mother, an aging courtesan.

Limercati. *La Chartreuse de Parme.* A rich young man whom Gina Pietranera
(la Sanseverina) reduces to despair because he has refused to avenge
her husband's murder.

Listolier. *Les Misérables.* A student from Cahors who is the lover of Fantine's
friend, Dahlia.

Listomère, Marquise de. *Le Père Goriot.* An elegant Paris society woman.

Llana, Murcia de la. *Gil Blas.* An incompetent physician.

Lô, Countess de. *Les Misérables.* A distant relative of Bishop Myriel. She is
constantly preoccupied with her sons' future inheritance.

Lombard, Mme. *L'Education sentimentale.* A friend of Rosanette Bron.

Londona, Arias de. *Gil Blas.* The head of a placement service for lackeys.

Longuemarre. *Madame Bovary.* A friend of young Boudet, this boy is also disruptive in church, to the consternation of the Abbé Bournisien.

Longueville, Mlle. de. *La Princesse de Clèves.* An attendant who helps carry the wedding dress of "Madame" during the marriage ceremony.

Lopez, Philippe. "Atala." An old Castillian settler in St. Augustine. He takes in the young Chactas and brings him up with great care. Lopez is also the father of Atala.

Lora, Léon de. *La Cousine Bette.* A guest at Héloïse Brisetout's housewarming party and an artist known for his wild dissipations.

Lord (unnamed). *La Vie de Marianne.* The gentleman who marries the widowed mother of Tervire when Tervire is about eighteen months old.

Lord (unnamed). "Zadig." A generous but vain gentleman who is robbed of valuable possessions after having fed and lodged Zadig and the hermit (the angel Jesrad).

Lord, German. *Corinne.* A rejected suitor of Corinne.

Lorença, Séphora. *Gil Blas.* The first lady-in-waiting of Séraphine. She falls in love with Gil Blas and is then offended by him.

Lorilleux. *L'Assommoir.* Coupeau's sly, malicious brother-in-law who makes gold chains for a company in his leprous-looking attic apartment.

Lorilleux, Anna. *L'Assommoir.* Coupeau's younger sister, with whom he takes his meals before his marriage to Gervaise. She despises her new sister-in-law and spares no effort to humiliate her. Anna (Nana) Coupeau is named after her.

Lorraine, Charles de Guise, Cardinal de. *La Princesse de Clèves.* Brother of François de Lorraine, Duke de Guise, he is known as the Cardinal de Lorraine.

Lorris, Théophile. *L'Education sentimentale.* A poet who, along with Frédéric Moreau, attends a dinner party at the Arnoux residence.

Louis. *Indiana.* M. Delmare's gardener.

Louis. *Nana.* Illegitimate child of Nana, born when she is sixteen, left first in the care of a nurse and then with Nana's aunt, Mme. Lerat. The sickly child, visited only occasionally by his mother, dies of smallpox when he is only four years old.

Louis XI. *Notre-Dame de Paris.* The aged, sickly King of France who is in his last year on earth when he orders the hanging of Esmeralda and other gypsies.

Louis, Mère. *L'Assommoir.* The proprietress of a wineshop which Coupeau, Lantier, and others frequent.

Louise. *La Cousine Bette.* The maid of Hortense and Wenceslas Steinbock.

Louise. *Nana.* An actress at the Palais-Royal who is invited to attend Nana's supper party.

Louise. *La Petite Fadette.* A country maiden who is a neighbor of Fadette.

Louison. *Les Misérables.* The young girl who is the dishwasher at the "Café Musain."

Loulou, Mlle. *L'Education sentimentale.* A celebrated dancer at one of the public halls frequented by Frédéric Moreau.

Lousteau. *La Cousine Bette.* A guest at Héloïse Brisetout's housewarming party and the lover of Mme. de la Baudraye.

Lovarias. *L'Education sentimentale.* A mystic artist who frequents Jacques Arnoux's art shop.

Lucette. *La Petite Fadette.* A country maiden who is a neighbor of Fadette.

Lucinde. *Gil Blas.* A Madrid actress who is the mother of don Raphaël. She later turns up in Algiers as her son's captive and tells him the story of her life during the twelve years they have been apart.

Lucrèce. *Gil Blas.* Loved by the Grand Duke of Tuscany, she is also wooed by don Raphaël.

Lucrèce. *Gil Blas.* A famous fourteen-year-old actress who is the fruit of the union between Laure (Estelle) and the Marquis de Marialva.

Ludovico. *La Chartreuse de Parme.* One of the Duchess Sanseverina's coachmen. He proves his loyalty to her by helping Fabrice escape from the Farnese tower.

Luna, don Valerio de. *Gil Blas.* A young nobleman whose violent passion for his mother, Inésile de Cantarilla, drives him to suicide.

Lupeaulx, M. des. *Eugénie Grandet.* A dishonorable Parisian who is in a position of power.

Lutatius. *Salammbô.* An enemy of Carthage, he exacts an enormous sum of money from the Republic.

Luz, Viscount de. *Le Rouge et le noir.* A member of Mathilde de la Mole's gossiping entourage.

M..., Count. *La Chartreuse de Parme.* A haughty nobleman who is the jealous lover of the capricious singer Fausta F... at the time Fabrice del Dongo meets her.

M..., Marquise de. *Le Rouge et le noir.* An admiring spectator at Julien Sorel's trial.

M..., Viscount de. *Les Liaisons dangereuses.* A cuckold whose wife spends the night with Valmont.

M..., Viscountess de. *Les Liaisons dangereuses.* One of Valmont's many conquests.

Maboeuf, Abbé. *Les Misérables.* The worthy priest who befriends the exiled soldier Georges Pontmercy. He is the brother of the botanist Maboeuf.

Maboeuf, M. *Les Misérables.* The brother of the Abbé Maboeuf. This
compassionate botanist is also the churchwarden at Saint-Sulpice. He
tells Marius of the great love his father always had for the young man
and remains Marius's friend for the rest of his life. He dies, penniless,
while participating in the 1832 insurrection.

Maclinson, Mr. *Corinne.* The nephew of Corinne's stepmother whom the
latter proposes as a husband for Corinne. She refuses to marry him.

Macquart, Gervaise. *L'Assommoir.* The mistress of the parasite Lantier, then
the wife of the drunkard Coupeau, and also the mother of Claude and
Etienne Lantier and Nana Coupeau. This weak-willed woman slowly
deteriorates and lives long enough to see her whole world destroyed by
alcohol.

Madame de .... *La Vie de Marianne.* Mme. de Miran's relative who attempts
to force Marianne to marry a dull, young bourgeois.

Madeleine, M. *Les Misérables.* The name assumed by Jean Valjean from the
time he leaves Bishop Myriel's house until he denounces himself at the
Champmathieu trial in order to save an innocent man. See Valjean,
Jean.

Madelon. *La Petite Fadette.* A niece of Père Caillaud who seems destined to
become engaged to Landry before the latter falls in love with Fadette.

Madelon. *La Vie de Marianne.* The servant girl of Mme. Dutour.

Madinier. *L'Assommoir.* A manufacturer of cardboard boxes whose business
is failing. He serves as Coupeau's witness at the latter's wedding to
Gervaise.

Magdassan. *Salammbô.* One of the Elders of Carthage, a provincial governor, and a lieutenant of Hanno.

Magistrate (unnamed). *La Vie de Marianne.* A close friend of M. de Climal
who visits the dying man.

Magloire, Mme. *Les Misérables.* Bishop Myriel's housekeeper and the waiting woman of his sister Mlle. Baptistine. She is a busy little person who
is always short of breath.

Magnon. *Les Misérables.* A girl who is closely connected with the Thénardiers
and the Paris underworld. She serves as a messenger for all of them.

Magnon, Nicolette. *Les Misérables.* The name of the former maid maidservant of M. Gillenormand. She sends the octogenarian two babies she
claims he has sired by her.

Maheu, Alzire. *Germinal.* The tiny nine-year-old child of Toussaint Maheu
and la Maheude who is an invalid with a humpback. Alzire dies of
starvation during the miners' prolonged strike.

Maheu, Catherine. *Germinal.* The undernourished fifteen-year old daughter
of Toussaint Maheu and la Maheude. She works as a wheeler of coal in

the Voreux pit. Catherine is torn between Chaval, her lover, and Etienne Lantier, to whom she is attracted, up to the time of her death, nine days after being trapped in the mine.

Maheu, Estelle. *Germinal.* The infant daughter of Toussaint Maheu and la Maheude. She is scarcely three months old and starves to death.

Maheu, Guillaume, *Germinal.* The grandfather of Bonnemort (Vincent Maheu). He discovered the rich coal at Requillart, the Montsou Mining Company's first pit.

Maheu, Henri. *Germinal.* The four-year-old son of Toussaint Maheu and la Maheude.

Maheu, Jeanlin. *Germinal.* The eleven-year-old child of Toussaint Maheu who is obliged to work in the coal mine. Crippled for life by a landslip in the mine, he lives by his wits after that.

Maheu, Lénore. *Germinal.* The six-year-old child of Toussaint Maheu and la Maheude.

Maheu, Mme. (la Maheude). *Germinal.* The strong-willed wife of Toussaint Maheu and the mother of seven children. She despairs of ever being able to make ends meet, and lives to see her husband and three children killed.

Maheu, Nicolas. *Germinal.* The father of Bonnemort. He died at an early age in the coal pit because of an accident.

Maheu, Toussaint. *Germinal.* The son of Bonnemort and the father of Catherine, Zacharie, and five other children. He struggles, like his ancestors before him, to survive the horrible conditions in the Voreux mine. He is eventually felled by a soldier's bullet when he leads the strikers' charge on the military.

Maheu, Vincent. *Germinal.* The miner father of Toussaint Maheu and the grandfather of Catherine, Zacharie and others. He ends his life with crippled legs and in an imbecilic state of mind. See also Bonnemort.

Maheu, Zacharie. *Germinal.* The oldest of the undernourished children of Toussaint Maheu. He is a pikeman in the Voreux mine, where he dies while trying to rescue his sister, Catherine, after the mine explosion.

Maheude, la. *Germinal.* See Maheu, Mme.

Mahiette. *Notre-Dame de Paris.* A woman from Reims who, while sightseeing in Paris, tells the story of Paquette la Chantefleurie.

Maid (unnamed). *La Cousine Bette.* Josépha Mirah's maid.

Maigrat. *Germinal.* A merchant who is owed money by the Maheus and other mining families. In return for sexual favors, he lends money to women. Later, the women avenge themselves by grossly abusing his dead body.

Maigrat, Mme. *Germinal.* A pitiful creature who is constantly beaten and deceived by her lecherous husband.

Mainfroi. *Gil Blas.* A brother of Roger, King of Sicily.

Major (unnamed). *Jacques le fataliste.* An officer who spies on Jacques's captain while disguised as a peasant, and also on his friend, the Commandant.

Majuelo. *Gil Blas.* A greedy inkeeper whom Gil Blas encounters in Burgos.

Malaga. *La Cousine Bette.* A guest at Josépha's party.

Maldonado, don Félix. *Gil Blas.* A mayor's son who falls in love with the actress, Laure.

Maloir, Mme. *Nana.* Nana's old friend, chaperone, and companion, known for her extravagantly quaint hats. She leads a mysterious existence at night.

Maltigues, M. de. *Corinne.* A conniving relative of Mme. d'Arbigny, who confides all of her schemes to him.

Mammaccia. *La Chartreuse de Parme.* An elderly actress in Marietta's troupe of actors and actresses.

Mamselle Miss. *Les Misérables.* An Englishwoman, a very clever gallicized English thief who becomes a celebrated criminal.

Man (unnamed). *L'Assommoir.* A scraggy young man who is with Nana at a cheap public ball room.

Man (unnamed). *Jacques le fataliste.* A man whose refusal to take final rites is mentioned by Jacques.

Man (unnamed). *Nana.* A sickly looking, light-haired man who bears one of the greatest names in France. He arrives at Nana's midnight supper party in the small hours of the morning.

Man (unnamed) with waistcoats. *Le Rouge et le noir.* One of the speakers at the meeting of conspiring Ultras which Julien Sorel attends with the Marquis de la Mole.

Mantoue, Duke de. *Gil Blas.* The former governor of Portugal who accuses Olivarès of causing all the misfortune which has fallen upon Spain because of the Portuguese rebellion.

Marcel. *Manon Lescaut.* A valet who helps Manon Lescaut escape from the Hôpital and who then becomes the devoted servant of Des Grieux and Manon.

Marcellin. *La Nouvelle Héloïse.* One of Julie's two sons by M. de Wolmar. Julie dies after rescuing Marcellin from the water.

Marcillac, Mme. de. *Le Père Goriot.* Eugène de Rastignac's aunt.

Maréchal. *Nana.* A shady bookmaker with whom the Count de Vandeuvres deals, thereby ruining himself.

Maréchale, la. *L'Education sentimentale.* See Bron, Rosanette.

Maréchale de.... *Les Liaisons dangereuses.* A society woman at whose residence Mme. de Merteuil meets Prévan.

Marescot. *L'Assommoir.* The miserly landlord of the building where Gervaise establishes her laundry shop. He later evicts Gervaise from her quarters.

Margot. *La Chartreuse de Parme.* A canteen keeper who tries to dissuade Fabrice del Dongo from fighting at Waterloo.

Marguerite. *La Cousine Bette.* Old Johann Fischer's servant.

Marguerite. *Jacques le fataliste.* The village joker's wife who seduces Jacques.

Marguerite. *Jacques le fataliste.* The daughter of a friend of the innkeeper.

Marguerite. *Les Misérables.* An old woman who gives Fantine lessons in indigent living.

Marguerite. *Paul et Virginie.* An abandoned young woman who, disgraced, leaves France to settle on the island Ile-de-France, and raise her son Paul there.

Marguerite de France. *La Princesse de Clèves.* The daughter of François I and the sister of Henri II. She is known as Madame.

Maria. *Nana.* A chorus girl in *Blonde Venus* who nearly falls flat on the stage.

Marialva, Marquis de. *Gil Blas.* A portuguese Marquis who takes Estelle (Laure) as his mistress.

Marianne. *La Vie de Marianne.* The heroine of Marivaux's novel who, at the age of fifty, relates her many youthful experiences to a female friend.

Maric. *Paul et Virginie.* The faithful slave of Mme. de la Tour, she marries Marguerite's slave, Domingue.

Marie-Claude. *Les Misérables.* A farmer's wife and the neighbor of Jean Valjean's sister and her children, who borrow milk from her.

Marie de Lorraine. *La Princesse de Clèves.* Married to James V, King of Scotland, and the mother of Marie Stuart, the "dauphin queen."

Marie Stuart. *La Princesse de Clèves.* The daughter-in-law of Henri II. She is known as the "dauphin queen," then becomes queen when her husband ascends to the throne, under the name of François II.

Marietta. *La Chartreuse de Parme.* A young actress with whom Fabrice del Dongo falls in love. This causes him to flee Parma for a time.

Mariette. *La Cousine Bette.* The Baroness Hulot's maid.

Marini, Annetta. *La Chartreuse de Parme.* The young daughter of a cloth merchant. She falls madly in love with Fabrice del Dongo upon hearing him preach a sermon.

Marini, Giacomo. *La Chartreuse de Parme.* The former master of the Abbé Blanès.

Marion. *La Petite Fadette.* A country maiden who is the neighbor of Fadette.

Marneffe, Jean-Paul-Stanislas. *La Cousine Bette.* A head clerk at the War Office headed by Baron Hulot. This depraved young man and his equally depraved wife. Valérie, will stop at nothing to obtain money.

Marneffe, Stanislas. *La Cousine Bette.* The Marneffes' neglected child.

Marneffe, Valérie. *La Cousine Bette.* The illegitimate daughter of one of Napoleon's officers and Bette Fischer's partner in crime. She makes her way in life by taking men for all they are worth. Her chief victim is Baron Hulot, to whose family she causes great suffering.

Marquinot, Abbé. *Le Rouge et le noir.* A Jansenist priest from Dijon whom the Abbé Frilair accuses Mme. de Rênal of seeing for confession.

Marquis (unnamed). *La Vie de Marianne.* Tervire's mother's second husband.

Marquis (unnamed). *La Vie de Marianne.* The ungrateful son of Tervire's mother by her second husband.

Marquise (unnamed). *La Nouvelle Héloïse.* Lord Bomston's former mistress, whom he abandons for Laura Pisana.

Marquise (unnamed). *La Vie de Marianne.* A disdainful woman who will have nothing to do with her mother-in-law, Tervire's mother.

Marsay, M. de. *Le Père Goriot.* Delphine de Nucingen's lover, a smug Parisian dandy who is bored with her.

Marsoullier. *L'Assommoir.* The keeper of the squalid Hôtel Boncoeur, where Gervaise and Lantier live before he suddenly abandons her.

Martial de la Roche-Hugon, Count. *La Cousine Bette.* Baron Hulot's successor at the War Office.

Martigues, Marie de Beaucaire, Countess de. *La Princesse de Clèves.* The Vidame de Chartres's mistress.

Martin. "Candide." A confirmed pessimist who becomes Candide's chosen travelling companion because Candide considers him to be the most unhappy of all the men he has interviewed.

Martin. *La Petite Fadette.* The eldest son of Père Barbeau, he has entered into domestic service.

Martin, don. *Gil Blas.* The father of doña Mencia de Mosquera.

Martinon, Baptiste. *L'Education sentimentale.* A childhood classmate of Frédéric Moreau. Although Frédéric finds Martinon's life to be dull, the individual becomes a successful businessman.

Masgaba. *Salammbô.* A Gaetulian brigand whose attempt to stir the Numidian states to revolt against the Barbarians has disastrous results for him.

Maslon, Abbé. *Le Rouge et le noir.* The ultraconservative young vicar of Verrières. He replaces Julien Sorel's friend, the Abbé Chélan.

Massa-Carrara, Prince de. "Candide." The old woman's fiancé when both were very young. He was poisoned by a jealous woman.

Massol. *La Cousine Bette.* The Master of Appeals in the government. He fills Hulot's seat in the Council of State after the Baron is forced to retire. Like Hulot, he is a great womanizer.

Master (unnamed) of Jacques. *Jacques le fataliste.* Jacques's travelling companion who often says nothing and who is less intelligent than his servant Jacques.

Matelote. *Les Misérables.* An ugly servant girl employed at the wineshop "Corinth."

Mathias, Saul. *L'Education sentimentale.* A celebrated art dealer from London who makes Jacques Arnoux an offer for a Ruysdaël painting.

Mathieu, Jeanne. *Les Misérables.* Jean Valjean's mother, who died when he was very young.

Mathilde. *Gil Blas.* The sister of Roger, King of Sicily.

Mâtho. *Salammbô.* A young libyan chief of colossal stature. He falls insanely in love with Salammbô at first sight and steals the sacred veil of the goddess Tanit. When Salammbô arrives in his camp to retrieve the veil, he makes love to her. He is ultimately tortured to death by the citizens of Carthage who use him as a scapegoat for the outrages of his fellow Mercenaries. After his death, Salammbô, who loves him, commits suicide.

Mathurine. *La Cousine Bette.* A pious relative whom Bette brings to Paris to be Valérie Marneffe's cook.

Maufrignac, Duchess de. *Le Père Goriot.* An elegant Paris society woman.

Maugiron, Charcot de. *Le Rouge et le noir.* The subprefect of the district in which Verrières is located.

Maugiron, Mme. de. *Le Rouge et-le noir.* The wife of the subprefect.

Maulincourt. *Le Père Goriot.* A smug man of fashion in Parisian society.

Mauriac, Baron de. *Nana.* The starter for the big horse race, the Grand Prix de Paris.

Maurice. *Le Père Goriot.* Anastasie de Restaud's snobbish footman.

Maury, Abbé. *Le Rouge et le noir.* A bishop whose talent Mathilde de la Môle admires.

Mayor (unnamed). *L'Assommoir.* The official who delays the wedding of Gervaise and Coupeau because he arrives late to marry them.

Mazarini. *Gil Blas.* The husband of Lucrèce.

Médicis, Catherine de. *La Princesse de Clèves.* The ambitious queen of Henri II, King of France.

Medina Celi, Duke de. *Gil Blas.* An admirer of Lucinde, mother of don Raphaël.

Medina Sidonia, Duke de. *Gil Blas.* A nobleman who is the poet Fabrice's patron.

Medrana, don Manrique de. *Gil Blas.* Baltazar Velasquez's successor as the employer of Scipion.

Méhémet. *Gil Blas.* The leader of the pirates who capture don Raphaël.

Méhémet-Hali. *Les Lettres persanes.* The divine Mollak, who is the son-in-law and successor of Mohammet. Usbek seeks his advice.

Meinsius, Pierre Paul. *L'Education sentimentale.* The last representative of the "grand" school of painting. He is invited, along with Frédéric Moreau, to a dinner party at the Arnoux household.

Melancia, dame. *Gil Blas.* A governess, supposedly a dragon of virtue, but actually a hypocrite.

Mélanie. *Germinal.* The cook in the Grégoire household.

Melendez, Mateo. *Gil Blas.* A cloth merchant who lodges Gil Blas in Madrid.

Mello, don Alvar de. *Gil Blas.* The young husband of doña Mencia de Mosquera. He is falsely reported to be dead.

Membrilla, Juan Velez de la. *Gil Blas.* The father of the young man whom Jérôme de Mayadas's daughter is to marry.

Membrilla, Pedro de la. *Gil Blas.* The young man who is supposed to marry Florentine, daughter of Jérôme de Moyadas.

Mencia, Mme. *Gil Blas.* An attractive older woman who is supposedly the aunt of Catalina.

Mendicants (unnamed). *Notre-Dame de Paris.* Beggars by day, thieves by night, who relentlessly pursue the poet Pierre Gringoire.

Mendoce, don Félix de. *Gil Blas.* The assumed name of the disguised Aurore. See Aurore.

Merchant (unnamed). *Eugénie Grandet.* Grandet's nearest neighbor, a cloth merchant who covets Grandet's gold.

Merchant (unnamed). *Jacques le fataliste.* A strolling vendor who sells small merchandise, including the watch of Jacques's master.

Mercoeur, Jeanne de Savoie, Duchess de. *La Princesse de Clèves.* The sister of the Duke de Nemours.

Mergelina, doña. *Gil Blas.* A doctor's wife who falls in love with Diego.

Merlaude, la. *La Petite Fadette.* A nurse Père Barbeau wants to hire for his identical twins.

Merteuil, Marquis de. *Les Liaisons dangereuses.* The deceased husband of Mme. de Merteuil.

Merteuil, Marquise de. *Les Liaisons dangereuses.* The cousin of Mme. de Volanges. She connives artfully to avenge herself of an insult suffered at the hands of the Count de Gercourt by depraving Gercourt's fiancée, who happens to be Mme. de Volanges's daughter, Cécile. She succeeds all too well in her scheme. To the Marquise de Merteuil, life is a deadly game which the person with the superior intellect—i.e., herself—wins.

Merval. *Jacques le fataliste.* A usurer whom Jacques encounters.

Merveilleux, M. de. *La Nouvelle Héloïse.* A recruitment officer who, out of generosity, discharges Claude Anet.

"Mes-Bottes." *L'Assommoir.* The nickname of a big drinker at "L'Assommoir," along with Coupeau and others.

Mesio Carillo, don Ambrosio. *Gil Blas.* An old Marquis who becomes the second husband of doña Mencia de Mosquera.

Messenger (unnamed). *Le Père Goriot.* Delphine de Nucingen's messenger.

Mestienne. *Les Misérables.* A grave digger and a drunkard who is a friend of Fauchelevant. He dies just when Fauchelevant needs his help.

Meyer. *L'Assommoir.* The proprietor of a Viennese bakery in Gervaise's neighborhood.

Michelet, Mme. *Le Rouge et le noir.* The name of Mathilde de la Mole's maid, whose passport Mathilde uses in order to visit Julien Sorel in prison without being recognized.

Michonneau, Mlle. *Le Père Goriot.* A covetous spinster who is a fourth-floor tenant at Mme. Vauquer's boardinghouse. She is responsible for the capture of Vautrin.

Micromégas. "Micromégas." A very intelligent young man from the planet Sirius who is 120,000 feet tall. He decided to educate himself by travelling from planet to planet.

Midwife (unnamed). *L'Assommoir.* The young woman who assists in the delivery of Gervaise's baby, Nana.

Mignon, Auguste. *Nana.* The parasitic husband of the musical revue star, Rose Mignon. He encourages his wife's liaison with the banker Steiner, among others, while working as her procurer.

Mignon, Charles. *Nana.* The child of Rose and Auguste Mignon. He attends boarding school.

Mignon, Henri. *Nana.* Another child of Rose and Auguste Mignon. Like his brother, he attends boarding school.

Mignon, Rose. *Nana.* Bordenave's reigning comic actress-singer, who is jealous of the star billing given to Nana. She is encouraged in her liaisons by her parasitic husband. Often inheriting Nana's discarded lovers, Rose is eager to avenge herself on Nana; but, when Nana dies, she sees to it that she is buried properly.

Mignot. *L'Education sentimentale.* A patriot who sues Jacques Arnoux for having illegally sold shares of stock. He forces Arnoux and his family to flee Paris.

Milliet. *L'Education senimentale.* Co-owner of a mill.

Miol, M. *La Nouvelle Héloïse.* A friend of M. de Wolmar.

Miran, Mme. *La Vie de Marianne.* Valville's mother, a virtuous woman who becomes so devoted to Marianne that the loving, grateful Marianne regards her as her mother.

Mirza. *Les Lettres Persanes.* A good friend of Usbek and Rica in Ispahan.

Miser (unnamed). *Nana.* A tradesman of very economical tendencies from the Faubourg Saint-Denis. He pays, albeit reluctantly, to sleep with Nana. She discards him after her success in *Blonde Venus.*

Miser (unnamed). "Zadig." A disagreeable man who treats Zadig and the hermit badly but who is given a luxurious golden bowl for his behavior by the hermit (the angel Jesrad in disguise).

Missouf. "Zadig." A beautiful and capricious young Egyptian whom Zadig defends against her jealous lover and who curses him for it.

Mistress (unnamed) of Jacques's Master. *Jacques le fataliste.* The woman for whom the Master borrows money from corrupt usurers.

Mistress (unnamed) of Washhouse. *L'Assommoir.* A delicate woman with sore eyes who silently watches the violent fight between Gervaise and Virginie.

Mistricolle, Guillemette la Mairesse. *Notre-Dame de Paris.* Wife of Robert Mistricolle.

Mistricolle, Robert. *Notre-Dame de Paris.* The grave and learned Prothonetary of the King. He contemplates burning the hideous foundling Quasimodo at the stake.

Mitouflet. *La Cousine Bette.* The Prince of Wissembourg's groom of the chambers.

Moabdar. "Zadig." The King of Babylon, who, upon discovering that his queen Astarté and Zadig are in love, tries to have them both killed. He later becomes insane and dies ignominiously.

Mogicon. *Gil Blas.* The valet of don Antonio Centellés.

Moirod, M. de. *Le Rouge et le noir.* A candidate for the post of First Deputy to the Mayor (M. de Rênal) in Verrières.

Mole, Boniface de la. *Le Rouge et le noir.* Mathilde de la Mole's famous ancestor, the beheaded lover of Queen Marguerite de Navarre. His beloved gained possession of his head and buried it herself. Mathilde pays tribute to this event annually by wearing mourning clothes every 30 April and, finally, by doing for Julien Sorel what Marguerite de Navarre did for Boniface de la Mole.

Mole, Marquis de la. *Le Rouge et le noir.* The governor of the province of which Verrières is a part, and the father of Mathilde. He is known for his capricious nature and large temper, as Julien Sorel discovers while he is in the employ of the Marquis.

Mole, Marquise de la. *Le Rouge et le noir.* A haughty, empty-headed woman who is excessively proud of her ancestors.

Mole, Mathilde de la. *Le Rouge et le noir.* The daughter of the Marquis de la Mole. This haughty, bored, extravagant young woman comes to love Julien Sorel because he evokes heroic admiration in her and reminds her of her illustrious ancestor, Boniface de la Mole.

Mole, Norbert de la. *Le Rouge et le noir.* The vacuous, unambitious son of the Marquis de la Mole. Julien Sorel is hired to become Norbert's companion.

Molina, André. *Gil Blas.* The witty governor of the pages at the residence of the Marquise de Chaves.

Moncade, don Juan de. *Gil Blas.* A dissipated young man who idles away his life.

Mondragon, Rodrigue de. *Gil Blas.* A ruffian who frequents the tennis court at Valladolid and frightens everyone.

Monime, Mlle. "Candide." An actress who is denied the right of Christian burial because of her profession. Candide is horrified to learn this.

Monk (unnamed). *Jacques le fataliste.* A brother who accompanies Richard when both are tricked by Father Hudson.

Monk (unnamed). *Les Lettres persanes.* The guardian of a library who is incapable of discussing the books which surround him.

Monsieur de .... *La Vie de Marianne.* The minister who attempts to force Marianne to marry a young bourgeois whom he has chosen for her.

Montalvan, Margarita de. *Gil Blas.* A woman of moderation who visits the Marquise de Chaves.

Montanos, Count de. *Gil Blas.* The employer of Manuel Morales.

Montauran, Marquis de. *La Cousine Bette.* A member of the old French nobility, who further distinguishes General Hulot's funeral by his attendance.

Montchevrel. *A Rebours.* The elderly cousin and guardian of Des Esseintes until the latter reaches his majority.

Montcornet, Count. *La Cousine Bette.* Valérie Marneffe's father who sired her out of wedlock and died without leaving her anything.

Montejanos, Baron Henri Montès de. *Le Cousine Bette.* Valérie Marneffe's Brazilian lover who unexpectedly comes back to Paris three years after he returned to Brazil. Crazed by jealousy, he fatally poisons Valérie and her new husband, Crevel.

Monteser, don Diègue de. *Gil Blas.* In charge of collecting the revenue of the Duke de Lerme. He becomes Gil Blas's superior.

Montgomery, Gabriel de Lorges, Count de. *La Princesse de Clèves.* The Captain of the Scotch Guards under Henri II, who unwittingly kills the king at a tournament.

Montmichel, Amelotte de. *Notre-Dame de Paris.* A female companion of Fleur-de-Lys de Gondelaurier.

Montmorency, Anne, Duke de. *La Princesse de Clèves.* High Constable of France under Henri II.

Montparnasse. *Les Misérables.* One of a quartet of bandits who govern the lowest depths of Paris, from 1830 to 1835. He participates in Thénardier's ambush attempt on Jean Valjean.

Montpensier, François de Bourbon, Duke de. *La Princesse de Clèves.* One of Mlle. de Chartres's suitors, considered to be a good marriage prospect.

Montpensier, Mlle. de. *La Princesse de Clèves.* One of the young women at court who help carry "Madame's" wedding dress during the marriage ceremony.

Montreuil Nantua, Duchess de. *L'Education sentimentale.* An old dowager who is a guest of the Dambreuse family.

Montriveau, Marquis de. *Le Père Goriot.* A man of fashion in Paris society. He is the lover of the Duchess de Langeais for a time but soon tires of her.

Morales. Luis. *Gil Blas.* A thief disguised as a cantor who becomes the travelling companion of don Raphaël.

Morales, Manuel. *Gil Blas.* Luis Morales's older brother.

Moreau, Frédéric. *L'Education sentimentale.* A young man who yearns to become the Walter Scott of France but whose dreams do not correspond with reality. Consequently, his wasted, sterile life is filled with melancholy and emptiness.

Moreau, Mme. *L'Education sentimentale.* Frédéric Moreau's highly respected mother. She is from an old family of nobility and is now a widow trying to keep up social appearances while entertaining great ambitions for her unambitious son.

Morel. *Madame Bovary.* One of Léon Dupuis's friends. He is the son of a businessman from whom Léon tries to acquire money for Emma.

Moreto, don Augustin. *Gil Blas.* A young poet, not without talent but somewhat crazed.

Morin, Mme. *Le Père Goriot.* A woman found guilty at her trial, during which Poiret appears as a witness for the defense.

Mosca, Count. *La Chartreuse de Parme.* The Minister of War and Finance at the Court of Parma, and a former squadron commander under Napoleon. He falls madly in love with Gina Pietranera and establishes her at court as his mistress, the Duchess Sanseverina.

Mosca, Countess. *La Chartreuse de Parme.* The Duchess Sanseverina's title after she finally marries Count Mosca. See Sanseverina-Taxis, Duchess.

Mosquera, doña Mencia de. *Gil Blas.* A young woman whom Gil Blas helps to escape from thieves.

Mother (unnamed) of Corinne. *Corinne.* Corinne's Italian mother who dies when Corinne is ten years old.

Mountebank (unnamed). *Les Misérables.* A man condemned to death who is comforted and made to feel radiant at the moment preceding his execution, thanks to Bishop Myriel.

Mouque. *Germinal.* The groom of the horses in the Voreux pit and the father of Mouquet and Mouquette. He lives on after the death of his two children.

Mouquet. *Germinal.* The brother of Mouquette. He is employed as a lander in the pit and is killed during the striking miners' rebellion against the soldiers brought in by the company management.

Mouquette. *Germinal.* A putter girl whose enormous breasts and flanks cause quite a sensation among her many lovers. She is good-hearted and sacrifices her life for the miners' cause.

Moussinot. *L'Education sentimentale.* Dussardier's employer, a lawyer.

Moya, Pedro de. *Gil Blas.* A poor, dirty author who has written a tragedy for Arsénie and her friends but who is scorned by them.

Moyadas, Jérôme de. *Gil Blas.* A credulous old man, first rescued by don Raphaël and Luis Morales and then duped by them.

Muffat de Beuville, Count. *Nana.* A chamberlain in the government and a devoutly religious man until he sees Nana in *Blonde Venus.* Yearning to have her be his mistress, he spends his entire fortune to realize this desire. Then he allows himself to be subjected to every degradation imaginable in order to hang onto Nana, who ultimately causes him to lose his mind.

Muffat de Beuville, Estelle. *Nana.* The slight, lanky, awkward sixteen-year-old daughter of the Count and Countess Muffat de Beuville. She and Daguenet, Nana's former lover, engage in a marriage of convenience, largely because of the influence Nana has over the bride's father.

Muffat de Beuville, Countess Sabine. *Nana.* The seemingly cold, austere wife of the sexually repressed Muffat de Beuville. She suddenly becomes voluptuous after having a torrid love affair with the journalist Fauchery and then indulges herself completely in all that is profane.

Muphti. "Micromégas." A doctor of theology who condemns the work of Micromégas on theology as being heretical.

Murcia de la Llana, Isabelle. *Gil Blas.* A young woman who is in love with don Luis Pacheco.

Muret. *Le Père Goriot.* The merchant who buys out Goriot's vermicelli business.

Muscada, Bertrand. *Gil Blas.* The son of a grocer from Oviedo who tells the indifferent Gil Blas about his family.

Muscoso, Théodora. *Gil Blas.* The sickly aunt of don Manrique de Medrana.

Musebois, Paulin. *Les Misérables.* The locksmith of Digne.

Museum Employee (unnamed). *Le Père Goriot.* A boarder at the Maison Vauquer.

Musichetta. *Les Misérables.* A mistress of Laigle of Meaux who is perhaps shared with his friend Joly.

Musnier, Andry. *Notre-Dame de Paris.* A bookseller who is intimidated by the crowd at the cathedral.

Musnier, Oudarde. *Notre-Dame de Paris.* The wife of Andry Musnier.

Myriel, Bishop Charles François Bienvenu. *Les Misérables.* The humble, devoted Bishop of Digne. He plays the crucial role in Jean Valjean's transformation from hardened convict to confirmed humanitarian by giving the ex-convict the massive silver candlesticks which Jean Valjean attempted to steal from him.

N.... *Le Rouge et le noir.* A member of the Marquis de la Mole's secret political group. He has been the recent victim of a misfortune.

Duke de N.... *Le Rouge et le noir.* Mathilde de la Mole's uncle who fought at Wagram.

Father N.... *Le Rouge et le noir.* A priest whose acquittal is secured by the political Abbé Frilair.

M. de N.... *Le Rouge et le noir.* The uncle of Tanbeau, he is a member of the Academy of Inscriptions who frequents the Hôtel de la Mole, where he seeks to test Julien Sorel's knowledge of Latin.

Marquise de N.... *La Chartreuse de Parme.* A society woman of Parma. She announces the imprisonment of Fabrice del Dongo to his aunt, the Duchess Sanseverina.

Nadir. *Les Lettres persanes.* A white eunuch who enters the room of Zachi, wife of Usbek.

Nana (Anna Coupeau). *Nana.* The latest discovery of the showman Bordenave. This eighteen-year-old girl of the streets, the daughter of Gervaise and Coupeau, has no musical or acting talent. However, she is clever enough to captivate an audience, as she does in *Blonde Venus.* She quickly becomes the most fashionable courtesan of all Paris and ruins many once-wealthy lovers, particularly Count Muffat de Beuville. Nana seems to have within her the rage not only for ruining men financially but for debasing them. Only a hideous disease is able to destroy her.

Nangy, Laure de. *Indiana.* A pretty young woman with whom Raymon de Ramière enters into a marriage of convenience.

Nani, Count. *La Chartreuse de Parme.* The adoring admirer Gina Pietranera (Duchess Sanseverina) uses in her scheme to reduce Limercati to despair.

Nanon. *Eugénie Grandet.* The miser Grandet's devoted workhorse of a servant who, out of gratitude to her master for having hired her, allows him to exploit her in feudal fashion. She is also devoted to Eugénie, even after she is married to Cornoiller.

Nanon. *Jacques le fataliste.* Servant of the innkeeper.

Napier. *Le Rouge et le noir.* A frequent guest at the Hôtel de la Mole. He is mocked by Norbert de la Mole, who calls him a spy.

Narcissa. *Gil Blas.* The actor Melchior Zapata's coquettish wife. She was formerly the mistress of the Marquis de Marialva.

Nargum. *Les Lettres persanes.* A Persian envoy to Moscow who corresponds on occasion with Usbek.

Narrator (unnamed). *Indiana.* The guest of Sir Ralph Brown and Indiana in their cabin by the ravine. He learns from Ralph of Ralph's and Indiana's new life together.

Narr'Havas. *Salammbô.* An untrustworthy young Numidian chief who eventually deserts the Mercenaries to fight against them with Carthage. As a result, he is offered the hand of Salammbô in marriage.

Narsit. *Les Lettres persanes.* Usbek's oldest slave who temporarily assumes command of the seraglio, upon the death of the chief black eunuch.

Nastasie. *Madame Bovary.* The maid in the employ of Charles Bovary and his first wife. She is fired by Emma Bovary for no valid reason, after the latter's return from the Marquis d'Andervillier's ball.

Naubin, Père. *La Petite Fadette.* A village gossip.

Navarre, Antoine de Bourbon, King of. *La Princesse de Clèves.* One of the many extraordinary princes at the court of Henri II.

Navarre, Queen of. *La Princesse de Clèves.* The mother of Henri IV and the leader of one of the women's cliques at court.

Navarreins, Mme. de. *La Cousine Bette.* An active member of the same charitable organizations as the Baroness Hulot.

Navarro, Joseph. *Gil Blas.* The nephew of don Melchoir de la Ronda and the head servant of don Baltazar de Zuniga. He befriends Gil Blas and finds him employment.

Navet. *Les Misérables.* A young lad who is Gavroche's good friend.

Négrel, Mme. *Germinal.* The long-suffering mother of Paul Négrel. She once lived on bread and water so that her son could attend the Ecole Polytechnique. Her son, an engineer with the Montsou Mining Company, now provides well for her.

Négrel, Paul. *Germinal.* The nephew of Hennebeau and the engineer at the Voreux pit. He is engaged to marry Cécile Gregoire but is his aunt's lover.

Negress (unnamed). *L'Education sentimentale.* The nurse of little Marthe Arnoux.

Negress (unnamed). *Paul et Virginie.* A runaway slave whom Paul and Virginie attempt to help.

Nelvil, Juliette. *Corinne.* The daughter of Oswald and Lucile Edgermond Nelvil, she bears a marked resemblance to Corinne.

Nelvil, Lord. *Corinne.* Oswald's father. He haunts his son after his death.

Nelvil, Oswald Lord. *Corinne.* A melancholy Englishman who is torn between his love for Corinne and his background and upbringing, which stand in opposition to his marrying Corinne.

Nemours, Jacques de Savoie, Duke de. *La Princesse de Clèves.* The most handsome of all the handsome noblemen at the court of Henri II. The fatal consequences of the mutual passion of Nemours and Mme. de Clèves form the substance of the novel.

Néné, Tatan. *Nana.* The most finely developed female discovery in the musical revue world, she becomes a well-known courtesan. Up to the age of twenty, she herded cows in Champagne.

Népomucène, Michel Evariste. *L'Education sentimentale.* An ex-professor who, at a political gathering in 1848, asserts that the European democracies should adopt unity of language.

Nerval, M. de *Le Rouge et le noir.* The French Minister of Foreign Affairs who is a frequent guest at the Hôtel de la Mole and is scorned by Julien Sorel.

Nessir. *Les Lettres persanes.* A close friend of Usbek who lives in Ispahan.

Nevers, François de Clèves, Duke de. *La Princesse de Clèves.* An outstanding prince at the court of Henri II. He is the father of M. de Clèves and is known as the Duke de Nevers.

Nevers, Marguerite de Bourbon, Duchess de. *La Princesse de Clèves.* The wife of François de Clèves, the mother of Jacques de Clèves, and the mother-in-law of Mme. de Clèves.

Nicolette. *Les Misérables.* The latest of the many maidservants of M. Gillenormand, all of whom he insists upon calling Nicolette.

Nieblès, Count de. *Gil Blas.* The oldest son of the Duke de Medina Sidonia and a suitor of doña Maria de Guzman.

Nisana, Ambrosio de. *Gil Blas.* An old benefactor of Laure.

Nise. *Gil Blas.* The lady-in-waiting of Blanche.

Noiroud. *Le Rouge et le noir.* The avaricious jailer of Verrières who is feared by many.

Nonancourt, M. de. *L'Education sentimentale.* An old man with the air of a mummy preserved in cold cream. He visits the Dambreuse family on occasion.

Noriega, Gregorio de. *Gil Blas.* A stupid bourgeois who is mocked by the decadent youth who surround him.

Noun. *Indiana.* Indiana Delmare's foster sister and Creole maid. She commits
suicide because Raymon de Ramière no longer loves her but now loves
Indiana.

Nourrison, Mme. *La Cousine Bette.* The assumed name of Mme. de Saint-
Estève. See Saint-Estève, Mme. de.

Nourrisson, Mme. *La Cousine Bette.* The proprietress of a house, the rooms
of which are rented to lovers such as Valérie Marneffe and Wenceslas
Steinbock.

Nouvelliste. *Les Lettres persanes.* A society member whose letter Rica reads.
It reveals the laziness, arrogance, and delusions of grandeur of the
group.

Nucingen, Baron de. *La Cousine Bette.* A wealthy banker who attends social
events where courtesans are to be found.

Nucingen, Baron de. *Eugénie Grandet.* A wealthy banker whose party
Charles Grandet attends in Paris.

Nucingen, Baron de. *Le Père Goriot.* A rich banker who makes a show of
loyalism. He is also the cold, unloving husband of Père Goriot's
younger daughter, Delphine.

Nucingen, Delphine de. *Le Père Goriot.* The selfish younger daughter of
Goriot who becomes the mistress of Eugène de Rastignac.

Nun (unnamed). *La Vie de Marianne.* A melancholy sister who is in love with
a priest.

Nun (unnamed). *La Vie de Marianne.* A relative of Tervire's mother. She tries
to seduce the young Tervire into becoming a nun.

Nun (unnamed). *La Vie de Marianne.* The sister who cares for the ill
Marianne in the convent.

Nun (unnamed). *La Vie de Marianne.* A nun who discovers Marianne
sobbing in the church

Obregon, Marcos de. *Gil Blas.* The guitar teacher and friend of Diego, the
barber.

Octave. *Nana.* The lover of Blanche de Sivry.

Officer (unnamed). *La Chartreuse de Parme.* The police officer who arrests
Fabrice del Dongo.

Official (unnamed). *La Chartreuse de Parme.* A passport official who permits
Fabrice del Dongo to pass through customs, not knowing that Fabrice
has just killed Giletti, the official's good friend.

Ogul. "Zadig." The sick master of a group of female slaves who are seeking a
basilisk in order to cure him of gluttony.

Old Man (unnamed). "Candide." A wise old man of Eldorado. He informs
Candide and Cacambo of the beliefs of that country.

Old Man (unnamed). "Candide." A farmer whom Candide and his associates visit. He does not inform himself of world events and merely contents himself with cultivating his garden.

Old Man (unnamed). *Corinne.* The messenger who bears the envelope containing the ring which Corinne is returning to Oswald.

Old Woman ("la Vieille") "Candide." An old servant to Cunégonde. She claims to be the daughter of Pope Urbain X and the Princess of Palestine. Among the many atrocities she has been subjected to is the loss of her left buttock, which was eaten by hungry soldiers.

Olighera, don Augustin de. *Gil Blas.* The nephew of don George de Galisteo who intends to marry don George's daughter, doña Helena.

Olivier. *La Cousine Bette.* The porter in the building where Bette Fischer lives. He later becomes porter of the building in which Valérie Marneffe's sumptuous apartment is located.

Olivier, Benjamin. *La Cousine Bette.* The eldest of three Olivier children. He is declared exempt from military service because of Mme. Marneffe's influence over Baron Hulot.

Olivier, François. *La Princesse de Clèves.* The Chancellor of France under Henri II. He is banished by the Duchess de Valentinois.

Olivier, Mme. *La Cousine Bette.* Wife of the building porter.

Olivier le Daim. *Notre-Dame de Paris.* King Louis XI's proud and arrogant barber.

Ollivier. *Nana.* Son of Lucy Stewart and an eighteen-year-old pupil at the Ecole de Marine.

Oloroso, Dr. *Gil Blas.* An elderly doctor who is the husband of doña Mergelina.

Oñez, Martin. *Gil Blas.* A surgeon who treats Sedillo.

Oquetos. *Gil Blas.* A Madrid doctor.

Orator (unnamed). "Candide." A speaker for the Protestant Church on the subject of charity. He denies Candide charity because Candide does not declare that the pope is the Antichrist.

Orbe, Claire d'. *La Nouvelle Héloïse.* Julie's beloved friend and confidante. Her lifelong devotion to Julie knows no bounds.

Orbe, Henriette d'. *La Nouvelle Héloïse.* Claire's only child.

Orbe, M. d'. *La Nouvelle Héloïse.* Claire's fiance and then husband who dies at an early age.

Orcan. "Zadig." A despicable man of Babylon who steals the wife of a cream-cheese merchant and his money as well.

Orderly (unnamed). *La Chartreuse de Parme.* The orderly to Robert, a young French officer. He helps Robert patch up his uniform and shoes.

Ordoñez, Manuel. *Gil Blas.* The administrator of a poorhouse and the employer of Fabrice.

Oreillons. "Candide." An Indian tribe of the Upper Amazon that wishes to eat
Candide and Cacambo because it believes them to be Jesuits.

Orsonval, Mme. d'. *Eugénie Grandet.* A resident of Saumur. Her living room
is a center for provincial gossip.

Ortiz, Dame. *Gil Blas.* A maidservant of Aurore.

Ossune, Duke d'. *Gil Blas.* A nobleman whose gentleman-in-waiting is an
admirer of Lucinde.

Oswald. *Corinne.* See Nelvil, Oswald Lord.

Otame. "Zadig." A participant in the jousting tournament who conquers four
combatants and is Zadig's final and most challenging opponent.

Oudry, Charles Jean-Baptiste. *L'Education sentimentale.* A lawyer who is a
neighbor of the Arnoux family at Saint-Cloud. He is a lecherous old
man who, late in life, marries Rosanette Bron (la Maréchale).

Oudry, Mme. *L'Education sentimentale.* A neighbor of the Arnoux family at
Saint-Cloud who is survived by her lecherous husband.

Outalissi. "Atala." An Indian warrior who is the father of Chactas.

P..., Count de. *Adolphe.* A friend of Adolphe's family. He loses Ellénore, his
mistress of ten years, to Adolphe.

P..., Countess de. *Les Liaisons dangereuses.* A victim of Prévan's slander.

P..., General. *La Chartreuse de Parme.* The devoted Commander of the
Prince's Guard at the Court of Parma.

P..., Mme. *La Chartreuse de Parme.* A famous singer at the Court of Parma.

Pacheco, don Gonzale. *Gil Blas.* The excessively thin uncle of don Luis.

Pacheco, don Joseph. *Gil Blas.* The father of don Luis.

Pacheco, don Luis. *Gil Blas.* A young nobleman who is loved by Aurore.

Palanza, Count David. *La Chartreuse de Parme.* A nobleman who is executed
because of the influence of the evil Razzi, a Chief Justice at the Court
of Parma.

Palazot, Count de. *L'Education sentimentale.* A guest at an all-night party
which Frédéric Moreau attends.

Palestrine, Princess of. "Candide." Supposedly the mother of the old woman
(la Vieille).

Palférine, Count de la. *La Cousine Bette.* A guest at Josépha's party.

Palla, Ferrante. *La Chartreuse de Parme.* A poet who is considered to be a
lunatic by all at the Court of Parma except the Duchess Sanseverina.
Devoted to her, Palla helps her get Fabrice del Dongo out of the
Farnese prison tower and then, to avenge the Duchess, he assassinates
Ernesto IV, Prince of Parma.

Pangloss. "Candide." The "oracle" of the Baron Thunder-ten-Tronck's chateau, where Candide grows up. He is, in fact, a ludicrous figure who clings stubbornly to his irrational optimistic beliefs and who "reasons" incessantly.

Paolina, Clara. *La Chartreuse de Parme*. The extremely unhappy Princess of Parma who is deceived by her husband, Prince Ernesto IV. The Duchess Sanseverina-Taxis befriends her.

Paquette. "Candide." A pretty servant girl from whom Pangloss gets syphilis and who later appears as the mistress of Brother Giroflée, a Theatine monk.

Paquette la Chantefleurie. *Notre-Dame de Paris*. A woman whose child was stolen by gypsies, which caused her to become crazed and live as a recluse in the "Trou aux Rats." Known as Sister Gudule, she is later revealed to be the mother of the of the gypsy-girl Esmeralda. See also Sachette, la.

Parents (unnamed) of Agathe. *Jacques le fataliste*. Two who collaborate with their daughter and the Chevalier de Saint-Ouin to dupe Jacques's master.

Parolignac, Marquise de. "Candide." The proprietress of a gambling den in Paris. She yearns to possess Candide's diamonds.

Partana, Duchess of. *La Chartreuse de Parme*. The political bride of the King of Naples.

Pascal, M. *Jacques le fataliste*. The Advocate General of Toulouse. He is one of Jacques's former masters.

Pastry Cook (unnamed). *Jacques le fataliste*. A man whose wife's lover tries to get him imprisoned.

Paul. *Paul et Virginie*. The virtuous son of Marguerite. He loves Virginie from childhood on and is unable to survive his beloved for long.

Paz, Count. *La Cousine Bette*. A Polish exile living in Paris who attends the wedding of Hortense Hulot and Wenceslas Steinbock.

Peasant (unnamed). *La Chartreuse de Parme*. A peasant at whose house Fabrice del Dongo pays to stay overnight.

Peasant (unnamed). *Jacques le fataliste*. The ill-tempered husband of the woman who nurses the wounded Jacques.

Peasant (unnamed). *Madame Bovary*. Rodolphe Boulanger's hired man. When he comes to see Dr. Charles Bovary in order to be bled, his master meets Emma Bovary.

Peasant (unnamed). *La Vie de Marianne*. The husband of the woman who is the infant Tervire's wet nurse.

Peasant Woman (unnamed). *Jacques le fataliste*. The travelling companion of a peasant-surgeon who falls head over heels and exposes the bottom half of her body.

Peddler (unnamed). *Les Misérables.* A guest at Thénardier's inn whose horse needs water. As a result, a terrified little Cosette must go out into the dark night to fetch some. This is when she meets Jean Valjean for the first time.

Pèdre, don. *Gil Blas.* The son of Mainfroi, brother of Enrique.

Pédrille. *Gil Blas.* A former servant of the Duke de Chinchilla. He is then in the employ of don Rodrigue de Calderone, first secretary of the Duke de Lerme.

Pedros, Gabriel de. *Gil Blas.* A friend of don Luis Pacheco.

Pégelin, Hally. *Gil Blas.* A Greek renegade with whom don Raphaël's mother, Lucinde, falls in love.

Pellerin. *L'Education sentimentale.* A fifty-year-old painter, befriended by Frédéric Moreau. He constantly changes his style in a futile effort to produce a masterpiece.

Penafiel, Angelica de. *Gil Blas.* A learned lady who frequents the house of the Marquise de Chaves.

Pépin. *Les Misérables.* A grocer in the Faubourg St.-Antoine. He sends ammunition for the 6 June 1832 insurrection in which Marius participates.

Peppe. *La Chartreuse de Parme.* The Duchess Sanseverina's first footman. He goes off in search of Fabrice del Dongo, who is in hiding after killing Giletti.

Péquignot. *L'Assommoir.* A friend of Lorilleux who is in the furniture business.

Perez, Gil. *Gil Blas.* A monk who is the uncle of Gil Blas. He attempts, without great success, to educate both his nephew and himself.

Pernice. *La Chartreuse de Parme.* The principal valet of Prince Ernesto IV. He often confides in Count Mosca.

Perpétua, Sister. *Les Misérables.* A rough, harsh, clumsy sister of charity.

Perpétue, Mother. *Les Liaisons dangereuses.* The Mother Superior of the convent where Cécile Volanges was a resident.

Perrotet. *Eugénie Grandet.* One of Grandet's tenant farmers who is behind in his rent payments.

Pharan. *Les Lettres persanes.* One of Usbek's black slaves who prefers death to becoming a eunuch.

Phénice. *Gil Blas.* Florimonde's former servant who becomes an actress and persuades Laure to become one also.

Philippe. *Les Liaisons dangereuses.* One of Valmont's servants.

Philippe IV. *Gil Blas.* The Dauphin of Spain. Gil Blas finds a mistress (Catalina) for him.

Philosopher (unnamed). "Zadig." A wise man who has retired from the world and who plays the gracious host to Zadig and the hermit (the angel Jesrad). As a token of his esteem and affection, the hermit sets fire to the philosopher's house.

Philosophers (unnamed). "Micromégas." Little earth people who are seized in a ship by Micromégas. They express to him their views on the nature of the soul.

Physician (unnamed). *A Rebours.* Renowned for his successful treatment of nervous maladies, he is summoned by Des Esseintes, whom he orders to return to Paris and live an ordinary mode of existence, if he wishes to survive.

Physician (unnamed). *Les Misérables.* The doctor who looks in on the dying Jean Valjean and realizes that no medicine can cure him; only the sight of a loved one can.

"Pied-de-Céleri." *L'Assommoir.* The nickname of one of Coupeau's big drinking companions.

Piédefer, Laure. *Nana.* The lesbian proprietress of a disreputable establishment for women in difficulty.

Piennes, Mlle. de. *La Princesse de Clèves.* One of the ladies-in-waiting of Catherine de Médicis.

Pierron. *Germinal.* A mine worker whose wife, with his permission, sleeps with Dansaert, captain of the Voreux pit, in order to maintain a well-kept home and, during the strike, to get bread.

Pierron, Lydie. *Germinal.* One of the Pierron children. She works in the Voreux pit and is killed during a confrontation of the miners with soldiers.

Pierronne, la. *Germinal.* The wife of Pierron. By sleeping with Dansaert, who pays her for the pleasure, she is financially much better off than the other inhabitants of the miners' settlement.

Pietranera, Count. *La Chartreuse de Parme.* A person of great wealth and high birth. His marriage of convenience to Gina del Dongo establishes her at the Court of Parma. Pietranera is soon killed during the course of a political argument.

Pietro-Antonio. *La Chartreuse de Parme.* The husband of Theolinda. He assists her in helping Fabrice del Dongo escape.

Pigeon, Mlle. *Jacques le fataliste.* The student whom the schoolteacher Permonval loves very much.

Pilon. *L'Education sentimentale.* A peasant from whom Frédéric Moreau tries in vain to rent a vehicle.

Pinarès, doña Elvira de. *Gil Blas.* An elderly noblewoman who lodges Gil Blas, Aurore, and their friends in her chateau near Avila.

Pincebourde, Gieffroy. *Notre-Dame de Paris.* One of the vagabonds who participate in the assault on the cathedral.

Pinson. *L'Education sentimentale*. The co-owner of a circulating library which Frédéric Moreau visits.

Piquetard, Agathe. *La Cousine Bette*. The rough-tongued kitchen maid in the Hulot household. She becomes the second Baroness Hulot as soon as possible after the death of the first, Adeline Hulot.

Piquette. *Germinal*. The owner of the inn where Catharine and Chaval live after Catharine goes off with him.

Piquoisneau, Colonel. *Le Père Goriot*. An officer killed in battle whose widow is to become a lodger at Mme. Vauquer's.

Pirard, Abbé. *Le Rouge et le noir*. The director of the seminary at Besançon. He is a friend of the Abbé Chelan and becomes Julien Sorel's good friend and benefactor.

Pisana, Laura. *La Nouvelle Héloïse*. Lord Bomston's former mistress in Rome.

Placio, Pedro. *Gil Blas*. A merchant from Segovia who befriends Gil Blas.

Pliego, Marquise de. *Gil Blas*. A witness at the baptism of Alphonse, son of Gil Blas.

Plowman (unnamed). *Jacques le fataliste*. The farmer from whom Jacques's master buys back his horse.

Pluchart. *Germinal*. Etienne Lantier's former foreman at Lille. He is admired by Etienne because he is a socialist leader who advocates unionization of the miners.

Plutarch, Mère. *Les Misérables*. M. Maboeuf's devoted maidservant.

Pococurante. "Candide." A wealthy Venetian whom Candide visits. He seemingly has everything but is disgusted with everything he possesses.

Poiret. *Le Père Goriot*. A tenant at Mme. Vauquer's boardinghouse. He is a sad-looking creature who resembles a machine because of the way he carries himself.

Poisson. *L'Assommoir*. The quiet, dedicated policeman married to Virginie, who makes a cuckold of him.

Polan, Count de. *Gil Blas*. The father of Séraphine and Julie. He is rescued from thieves by Gil Blas, don Raphaël, don Alphonse, and Ambroise.

Police Commissioner (unnamed). *Jacques le fataliste*. A friend of Father Hudson who helps him trick Richard and another monk.

Police Commissioner (unnamed). *Jacques le fataliste*. An officer who discovers Jacques's master and Agathe in bed.

Police Officer. "Candide." An officer for the Inquisition who has Pangloss hanged and Candide thrashed during an auto-da-fé.

Police Officer (unnamed). *La Cousine Bette*. A watchdog who comes to arrest Baron Hulot.

Pomaré, Queen. *Nana*. Now an old ragpicker who rakes in the gutters but once a splendid beauty about whom all Paris raved. The sight of her frightens Nana, who sees in Pomaré a prefiguration of what is to happen to her.

Pommeraye, Mme. de la. *Jacques le fataliste.* A wealthy, proud woman who seeks revenge on her lover when his passion for her cools.

Poncet. *La Chartreuse de Parme.* The assumed name of the poet Ferrante Palla while he is in hiding in France.

Ponchaud. *Les Misérables.* A dangerous criminal with whom Thénardier (Jondrette) schemes to rob Jean Valjean. Ponchaud is also known as Printanier and Bigrenaille.

Pons. *La Cousine Bette.* Two brothers, once embroiderers to the Imperial Court of Napoleon. Lisbeth Fischer once worked with them, doing gold and silver lacework.

Pontmercy, Georges. *Les Misérables.* Marius's father, who was a general under Napoleon, whom he continues to admire. He lives his life in solitude in the country, after the fall of Napoleon, because of political differences with his father-in-law, M. Gillenormand. During the battle of Waterloo, Thénardier, the marauder, once inadvertently saved Pontmercy's life.

Pontmercy, Marius. *Les Misérables.* Disinherited by his grandfather, M. Gillenormand, after defending his father politically, this handsome young man manages to survive as a young lawyer. He falls deeply in love with Cosette and eventually plays a major role in her life and that of Jean Valjean.

Popinot, Count. *La Cousine Bette.* A former druggist who has become the Minister of Commerce.

Popinot, Mlle. *La Cousine Bette.* Daughter of the Minister of Commerce. She is considered as a possible match for the Lebas's son.

Popinot, Mme. *La Cousine Bette.* The wife of the Minister of Commerce and a member of the same charitable organizations as the Baroness Hulot.

Porcie. *Gil Blas.* The younger daughter of Léontio Siffredi, a minister of Roger, King of Sicily.

Porcie. *Gil Blas.* Maidservant of the Marquise de Chaves. Gil Blas becomes attracted to her and, as a result, is challenged to a duel.

Porter (unnamed). *Eugénie Grandet.* A servant who tells Grandet that his money is silver, not copper.

Porter (unnamed). *Les Misérables.* A Bonapartist who loses his job because he persists in ridiculing Louis XVIII. He and his family are saved from starving in the streets because of the kindness of Bishop Myriel, a Royalist, who appoints him beadle to the cathedral.

Porter (unnamed). *Le Rouge et le noir.* A young seminarian whose countenance Julien Sorel finds abhorrent.

Porter (unnamed). *La Vie de Marianne*. The person who informs Tervire of the death of her stepfather.

Porter's Wife (unnamed). *Les Misérables*. The woman who brings food and water to the infirm Jean Valjean, just before his death.

Portress (unnamed). *Les Misérables*. The only servant of M. Madeleine (Jean Valjean) at Montfermeil.

Postillion (unnamed). *La Chartreuse de Parme*. An old smuggler and devoted servant in the Duchess Sanseverina's employ.

Postmaster (unnamed). *Le Rouge et le noir*. A man who lies to Julien Sorel, at that moment a messenger for the Ultras, by telling him that there are no fresh horses.

Poussepin, Robin. *Notre-Dame de Paris*. A young clerk-scholar who awaits with impatience the start of the morality play.

Pradon, Mahiet. *Notre-Dame de Paris*. The uncle of Paquette la Chantefleurie who has left her a small piece of property in Rheims.

Preceptor (unnamed). *Gil Blas*. The instructor of Leganez. He whips Gil Blas in order to intimidate Leganez.

Prefect (unnamed). *Les Misérables*. One of Bishop Myriel's brothers. He is an ex-prefect living in Paris.

Prémonval. *Jacques le fataliste*. A schoolteacher who is helped by his friend Gousse.

Prévan. *Les Liaisons dangereuses*. An arrogant but handsome ladies' man. When he slanders the Marquise de Merteuil, she makes him pay dearly for his remarks.

Price. *Nana*. The English jockey who rides the horse named Nana in the Grand Prix de Paris.

Priest (unnamed). *L'Assommoir*. The cleric who argues with Coupeau over the fee to be paid for his marrying Coupeau and Gervaise.

Priest (unnamed). *Corinne*. A priest who blesses Corinne's house in order to preserve it from contagion.

Priest (unnamed). "René." The priest who officiates when Amélie takes her final vows.

Priest (unnamed). *Le Rouge et le noir*. The Jansenist priest who is Julien Sorel's prison confessor.

Priest (unnamed). *Le Rouge et le noir*. An intriguing priest who tries to make a name for himself by praying aloud in the street for Julien Sorel's salvation.

Priest (unnamed). *La Vie de Marianne*. The elderly country priest who takes in the orphaned child, Marianne.

Prina. *La Chartreuse de Parme*. A former minister of the King of Italy and a man of great merit, whose life could have been saved by the Marquis del Dongo's confessor.

Prince (unnamed). *Corinne.* A rejected Italian suitor of Corinne.

Prince, Italian (unnamed). *Manon Lescaut.* A victim of a practical joke on the part of Manon Lescaut, who lures him into her apartment, knowing that he is attracted to her.

Prince of Scots, Charles. *Nana.* One of Nana's lovers during her engagement as *Blonde Venus.* When she sees him eighteen months later, he has become stouter.

Printanier. *Les Misérables.* See Ponchaud.

Prioress (unnamed). *La Vie de Marianne.* The head of the convent where Marianne stays under the auspices of Mme. de Miran.

Procurer (unnamed). *La Vie de Marianne.* A man in the employ of Mme. Darcire.

Professor (unnamed). *Les Misérables.* An old, brutal, and boastful instructor of mathematics. He is the father of Favorite, who is born out of wedlock.

Prosper, Dom. *A Rebours.* The great-granduncle of Des Esseintes, who has inherited his library. As a result of this, Des Esseintes learns much about theology.

Prouharam. *L'Education sentimentale.* A solicitor for whom Frédéric Moreau becomes a clerk for a time, at his mother's insistence.

Prouvaire, Jean. *Les Misérables.* A gentle young poet, one of the young insurrectionists of 18 June 1832 who are killed in battle.

Prullière. *Nana.* A favorite of burlesque audiences who performs with Nana in *Blonde Venus.* Although he loves Nana and tries to help her when she is down on her luck, she always dismisses him when he makes his amorous feelings known to her.

Putois, Mme. *L'Assommoir.* An employee of Gervaise in her laundry shop.

Quandieu. *Germinal.* The septuagenarian doyen of the Montsou captains who prevents the striking miners from cutting the cables of his pit, Mirou.

Quasimodo. *Notre-Dame de Paris.* The deaf, hunchbacked, hideously deformed bell ringer of Notre-Dame. His pure love for the gypsy-girl Esmeralda and his devotion to the tormented priest Dom Frollo, his foster father, are sublime but make his difficult life tragic in the end.

R..., Marquise de. *Les Misérables.* A kind woman who gives the ex-convict Jean Valjean a little money and advises him to knock on the door of Bishop Myriel to seek food and lodging.

R..., Marquise de. *Le Rouge et le noir*. M. de Rênal's only living relative. She is old, senile, and wicked.

Rada, don Anastasio de. *Gil Blas*. A nobleman of Granada who is insanely jealous of his wife.

Rada, don Roger de. *Gil Blas*. A young Granada nobleman who seeks the protection of the Duke de Lerme because of an affair of honor.

Radzivill, Prince de. *Gil Blas*. In love with doña Hortensia, he is jealous of don Pompeyo de Castro.

Ragotski. "Candide." A former sovereign in whose house Cunégonde is a slave.

Ragoulleau. *Le Père Goriot*. The adversary of a Mme. Morin in a trial case in which Poiret participates.

Raimond, Count. *Corinne*. Oswald Lord Nelvil's devoted French friend who is killed during the French Revolution because of his loyalty to the king.

Rambo. *La Chartreuse de Parme*. A physician who reports that Fabrice del Dongo's lungs are diseased.

Ramière, Mme. de. *Indiana*. Raymon de Ramière's well-meaning mother who, in her excessive generosity, has only helped make her son extremely selfish.

Ramière, Raymon de. *Indiana*. A passionate nobleman who, because of his fickleness, causes the death of Noun and nearly causes the death of Indiana.

Ramire. *Gil Blas*. The valet of don Gaston de Cogollos.

Ramirez, Bernarda. *Gil Blas*. The hostess at a Salamanca hotel.

Ramonchamp, Viscount Albert de. *Notre-Dame de Paris*. A student to whom the dissolute Jehan Frollo administers a beating.

Randan, Charles de la Rochefoucauld, Count de. *La Princesse de Clèves*. A colonel in the French infantry. He is sent by Henri II to compliment Queen Elizabeth I upon her ascension to the throne in 1558.

Random, Captain. *Indiana*. The captain of the ship *Eugène*. He agrees, for personal reasons, to carry Indiana Delmare on board his ship as a stowaway so that she may return to her lover, Raymon de Ramière.

Ranvier, Abbé. *Germinal*. Abbé Joire's replacement as priest to the miners. He defends the striking miners and attacks the middle class, in order to convert the workers to his beliefs.

Raphaël, don. *Gil Blas*. A professional thief who is supposedly the first cousin of doña Mencia de Mosquera. Gil Blas becomes a part of his gang for a time. Don Raphaël is eventually hanged, the victim of an auto-da-fé, along with Ambroise de Lamela. See Hally, Sidi.

Rasseneur. *Germinal*. A former pikeman in the Voreux pit. He was dismissed

by the company after the last strike and then became the proprietor of
an inn next to the pit, where he heads the opposition to the company
until the arrival of the more militant Etienne Lantier.

Rasseneur, Mme. *Germinal.* The inn owner's wife who is more radical in her
politics than her husband. She is sympathetic to Etienne Lantier's
beliefs.

Rassi. *La Chartreuse de Parme.* The sniveling, conniving, vicious Minister of
Justice of the Court of Parma. He is enamored of titles and power.

Rassi, Giacomo. *La Chartreuse de Parme.* The eldest son of the Minister of
Justice. He becomes engaged to Annetta Marini, who then spurns him
because she has fallen in love with Fabrice del Dongo.

Rastignac, Agathe de. *Le Père Goriot.* Eugene de Rastignac's younger sister.

Rastignac, Baron de. *Le Père Goriot.* Eugène's father, a nobleman of modest
means. Secrets concerning gifts sent to Eugène in Paris are kept from
him by the female members of his family.

Rastignac, Chevalier de. *Le Père Goriot.* Eugène's great-uncle who married
the de Marcillac heiress.

Rastignac, Eugène de. *Le Père Goriot.* A young man from Angoulême who
comes to Paris, supposedly to study law, and boards at the Maison
Vauquer at first. During his climb up the Paris social ladder, the
socially ambitious Eugène becomes involved in the lives of Père Goriot
and his two selfish daughters.

Rastignac, Count Eugène de. *La Cousine Bette.* Currently Undersecrtetary of
State, Eugène has now arrived at the top of the Paris social ladder. He
is invited to Josépha's party, along with other members of high society.

Rastignac, Gabriel de. *Le Père Goriot.* Eugène's younger brother.

Rastignac, Henri de. *Le Père Goriot.* Eugène's other young brother.

Rastignac, Laure de. *Le Père Goriot.* The older of Eugène's two young sisters.

Rastignac, Mme. de. *Le Père Goriot.* Eugène's devoted, self-sacrificing
mother.

Rastignac, Mme. de. *La Cousine Bette.* The wife of Eugène de Rastignac. She
is an active member of the same charitable organizations as the
Baroness Hulot is.

Raversi, Marquise. *La Chartreuse de Parme.* A rich, intriguing woman who is
the head of the Liberal Party at the Court of Parma. She is also the
niece of the Duke Sanseverina and is especially anxious to discredit
Count Mosca and his mistress, the Duchess Sanseverina.

Regard, Fanchon. *La Nouvelle Héloïse.* A very poor young woman who is
saved from poverty by Julie, who hires her as a maidservant.

Regianino. *La Nouvelle Héloïse.* Lord Bomston's valet at Vevey and a music
instructor.

Regimbart. *L'Education sentimentale.* A former painter who frequents Arnoux's art shop. He leads an aimless existence and lets his wife, a dressmaker, support their family.

Regimbart, Mme. *L'Education sentimentale.* The dressmaker of Mme. Dambreuse and others. She valiantly supports her idle painter-politician husband and their children.

Remanjou, Mlle. *L'Assommoir.* A doll maker who lives in the same building as Coupeau and Gervaise.

Remoussat, Mme. de. *L'Education sentimentale.* A fashionable actress whom Frédéric Moreau sees at the races.

Rênal, Adolphe de. *Le Rouge et le noir.* Oldest of the three de Rênal sons.

Rênal, Mme. Louise de. *Le Rouge et le noir.* The dutiful, virtuous wife of the Mayor of Verrières, and a loving mother as well. However, once she falls in love with Julien Sorel, she remains steadfast in her devotion to him for the rest of their lives, which are short.

Rênal, M. de. *Le Rouge et le noir.* The smug, self-centered bourgeois conservative who is the mayor of the provincial town of Verrières.

Rênal, Stanislas-Xavier de. *Le Rouge et le noir.* The youngest of the de Rênal children. He adores his tutor, Julien Sorel.

René. "Atala." A young Frenchman driven by passion and misfortune to exile himself in America with the Natchez Indian tribe whose sage, Chactas, adopts him as a son.

René. "René." A young Frenchman living in exile in Louisiana among the Natchez. He is a victim of pathological boredom and melancholy throughout his life.

Restaud, Count de. *Le Père Goriot.* The cold, indifferent husband of Anastasie, Goriot's older daughter. He even approves of his wife's lover.

Restaud, Countess de. *Le Père Goriot.* The dowager whose diamonds are sold by her daughter-in-law, Anastasie, who is in constant need of money.

Restaud, Countess Anastasie de. *Le Père Goriot.* The self-centered older daughter of Père Goriot. She is in constant need of money, which she spends frivolously. She hastens the death of her devoted father, who cannot bear to see her so unhappy.

Restaud, Ernest de. *Le Père Goriot.* The only legitimate child of Anastasie de Restaud.

Rhedi. *Les Lettres persanes.* The nephew of Ibben, he corresponds with Usbek while spending time in Venice, where he has gone in an effort to broaden his knowledge.

Ribero, don Bertrand Gomez del. *Gil Blas.* The treasurer in the government of Phillippe IV. He employs Fabrice to write verse.

Rica. *Les Lettres persanes.* Usbek's young travelling companion who becomes an ardent Francophile, to the dismay of the more mature Usbek.

Ricard, M. *La Vie de Marianne.* One of Mme. Dutour's tenants.

Ricardo. *Gil Blas.* An actor friend of Arsénie.

Richard. *Jacques le fataliste.* Now the secretary to the Marquis des Arcis. He was once a monk who failed in his attempt to incriminate the wily priest, Father Hudson.

Richomme. *Germinal.* A captain at the Voreux pit who is killed during the confrontations of miners and soldiers.

Riscara. *La Chartreuse de Parme.* A cavalier who is a political ally and the former lover of the Marquise Raversi.

Rivarol. *Le Rouge et le noir.* A writer and old friend of the Marquis de la Mole.

Rivet, Achille. *La Cousine Bette.* A businessman who buys the Pons establishment and for whom Bette Fischer works for several years.

Rivet, Mme. *La Cousine Bette.* Wife of Achille Rivet.

Robert. *La Chartreuse de Parme.* An impoverished young French officer who must wear makeshift shoes. He is befriended by the Marquise del Dongo.

Robert, Mme. *Nana.* A lady who enjoys a good reputation because she has only one male lover at a time. In reality, she is a lesbian who sleeps with men only for practical purposes. When Nana steals Satin, her female lover, Mme. Robert sets out to avenge herself on both of them.

Rochefide. *La Cousine Bette.* A guest at Josépha's party.

Rochefide, Berthe de. *Le Père Goriot.* The young woman whom the Marquis d'Ajuda-Pinto is about to marry.

Rochefort, Viscount de. *La Princesse de Clèves.* Henry VIII's brother who is accused of being Anne Boleyn's lover.

Rochefort, Viscountess de. *La Princesse de Clèves.* The Viscount's jealous wife.

Rochegune, Mme. de. *L'Education sentimentale.* A friend of Rosanette Bron.

Rodriguez, Gregorio. *Gil Blas.* An intendant of don Mathias de Silva who lives by his wits.

Roger. *La Cousine Bette.* A friend of Baron Hulot at the War Office. He urges the Baron not to press for Marneffe's appointment as head clerk there.

Roger. *Gil Blas.* The King of Sicily, who is visited by Gil Blas and others.

Roger, M. *Madame Bovary.* The Latin teacher at the school which the young Charles Bovary attends.

Roguin. *Eugénie Grandet.* The bankrupt notary of Victor-Ange-Guillaume Grandet.

Roguin. *La Nouvelle Héloïse.* An officer who offers Saint-Preux a company in the regiment which he is assembling for the King of Sardinia.

Roiville, Countess de. *Le Rouge et le noir*. A vulgarian whom Mathilde de la Mole scorns.

Rolando. *Gil Blas*. The captain of the thieves who imprison the young Gil Blas in a cave and try to make him their apprentice.

Rollet. *Madame Bovary*. An impoverished peasant who is the husband of Berthe Bovary's wet nurse.

Rollet, Mère. *Madame Bovary*. The wet nurse of Emma Bovary's infant, Berthe.

Romarate, don Jacinte de. *Gil Blas*. A man of letters who argues about the *Iphigénie* of Euripides.

Ronda, Melchoir de la. *Gil Blas*. The elderly valet de chambre of the Archbishop of Grenada. He describes to Gil Blas the archbishop and all the hypocrites in his employ.

Rondelot, Samuel. *L'Education sentimentale*. A law professor who is greatly venerated at the time Frédéric enrolls as a law student in Paris.

Ronquerolles, Marquise de. *Le Père Goriot*. A smug man of fashion in Paris society, he is an admirer of Anastasie de Restaud.

Roque. *L'Education sentimentale*. A peculiar resident of Nogent-sur-Seine, near Frédéric Moreau's mother's estate. He lives in curious relations with his mistresses and his one child. This cunning peasant lends money to Mme. Moreau, in the hope that she will agree to the marriage of Frédéric and his daughter, Louise.

Roque, Elisabeth Olympe Louise. *L'Education sentimentale*. Roque's illegitimate daughter who falls in love with Frédéric Moreau and is devastated when he fails to marry her.

Rose. *Germinal*. The housemaid of the Hennebeaus.

Rosemonde. Mme.de. *Les Liaisons dangereuses*. Valmont's octogenariar aunt who is a good friend of Mme. de Tourvel, the woman Valmont intends to conquer.

Rosenwald. *L'Education sentimentale*. A composer who, along with Frédéric Moreau, attends a dinner party at the Arnoux residence.

Rosette. *La Petite Fadette*. The aunt of the identical twins, Sylvinet and Landry.

Rosimiro. *Gil Blas*. An actor friend of Arsénie.

Rouault, Théodore. *Madame Bovary*. A farmer, the father of Emma Bovary. Charles meets Emma when he comes to the farm to set Rouault's leg.

Rousseau, Guillaume. *Notre-Dame de Paris*. A leader among thieves at the Cour des Miracles.

Rousseau, Mme. *Les Misérables*. The proprietress of the very modest restaurant where the nearly indigent Marius takes his meals for a time.

Rouvray, Marquis de. *Le Rouge et le noir*. A young man who has entered into a marriage of convenience with Mathilde de la Mole's cousin.

Roxane. *Les Lettres persanes.* Usbek's most recent acquisition in the seraglio. She is his prize possession but ultimately betrays him.

Rubempré, Présidente de. *Le Rouge et le noir.* An elderly Besançon benefactress who vows that she will bequeath her valuable worldly goods to the church.

Rubigneau. *Le Rouge et le noir.* A dinner guest of Valenod. He asks Julien Sorel to recite passages from the New Testament from memory, which Julien proceeds to do.

Rusai, M. de. *Jacques le fataliste.* A Sorbonne professor.

Rusca, Count. *La Chartreuse de Parme.* A singer with a harsh voice who is omnipresent at the Court of Parma.

Rustan. *Les Lettres persanes.* Usbek's dear friend who has remained in Ispahan.

Rym, Guillaume. *Notre-Dame de Paris.* A Flemish envoy to Paris in 1482.

Sachette, la. *Notre-Dame de Paris.* The nickname given to a crazy old woman (Paquette la Chantefleurie), living as a recluse in the Trou aux Rats, who curses the gypsy Esmeralda. She was also known as Sister Gudule. See also Paquette la Chantefleurie.

Sagette, Mère. *La Petite Fadette.* The wet nurse who helps bring the identical twins, Sylvain (Sylvinet) and Landry, into the world.

Sailor (unnamed). "Candide." A vicious man who is saved from drowning by the Anabaptist Jacques, but who leaves everyone else to drown. He, Candide, and Pangloss are the only survivors of the shipwreck caused by the Lisbon earthquake.

Sailor (unnamed). *Paul et Virginie.* A valiant man who tries in vain to save Virginie's life before the ship sinks.

Sainclair, M. *Le Rouge et le noir.* A liberal who visits the Hotel de la Mole to curry favor.

Saint-Agne, Count de. *La Vie de Marianne.* A middle-aged officer of birth who, after hearing of Valville's infidelity to Marianne, offers the young woman a marriage contract.

Saint-Estève. Mme. de. *La Cousine Bette.* A greedy old spinster who plans to destroy the marriage of Crevel and Valérie Marneffe, in exchange for a large sum of money, to be paid her by Victorin Hulot.

Saint-Florentin, Mme. de. *L'Education sentimentale.* A friend of Rosanette Bron.

Saint-Giraud. *Le Rouge et le noir.* A fellow traveller in the stagecoach which transports Julien Sorel to Paris. He is fleeing the countryside because he refuses to succumb to pressure to become involved in politics.

Saint-Giraud, M. de. *Le Rouge et le noir.* The bureau chief of a district bordering Verrières.

Saint-Ouin, Chevalier de. *Jacques le fataliste.* The supposed friend of Jacques's master, he dupes him out of a huge sum of money.

Saint-Preux. *La Nouvelle Héloïse.* Julie's young tutor whose passion for her is unbridled at first. Later, he must try to overcome this passion, in the name of virtue, when Julies marries Baron de Wolmar.

Saint-Valéry. *L'Education sentimentale.* A former benefactor of Rosanette Bron (la Maréchale).

Saint-Vincent, Father. *La Vie de Marianne.* The priest in Paris to whom the country priest's sister confides young Marianne. He first places the girl in the care of M. de Climal.

Sainte-Croix, Marquis de. *Gil Blas.* A nobleman with whom Gil Blas's friend, Fabrice, talks.

Sainte-Hérédhté, Mlle. de. *Le Rouge et le noir.* Mathilde de la Mole's cousin, with whom she exchanges gossip.

Sainte-Hermières, Mme. de. *La Vie de Marianne.* Once the best friend of Tervire's mother. This woman befriends Tervire and tries to persuade her to become a nun.

Sainville. *L'Education sentimentale.* An actor admired by Hussonnet.

Salammbô. *Salammbô.* The daughter of Hamilcar Barca. She casts a spell over the Libyan chief Mâtho, then goes to his tent to recover the sacred veil of the goddess Tanit, which Mâtho has stolen, and finds herself responding to his passion. She commits suicide after Mâtho is tortured to death because she cannot rid herself of the passion she feels for him.

Salero, Gabriel de. *Gil Blas.* A goldsmith whose daughter Gil Blas is to marry.

Samanon. *La Cousine Bette.* A usurer to whom Baron Hulot owes money.

Samnite (unnamed). *Salammbô.* The last Mercenary to be killed in the final battle with the Carthaginian army, except for Mâtho, who is captured alive and then tortured to death.

Sancerre. *La Princesse de Clèves.* The ill-fated lover of Mme. de Tournon.

Sandoval, don François de. *Gil Blas.* The original name of the Duke de Lerme. See Lerme, Duke de.

Sandrino. *La Charteuse de Parme.* The illegitimate child of Clélia Conti and Fabrice del Dongo. He dies as a child because of a caprice on the part of his father.

Sangrado, Dr. *Gil Blas.* A barbaric doctor for whom Gil Blas works as an associate for a time.

Sanseverina-Taxis, Duke. *La Chartreuse de Parme.* A rich old man with whom Count Mosca concludes a marriage contract. The Duke becomes an ambassador and receives the Grand Cordon, his fervent ambition, on the condition that he never again set foot in Parma. This arrangement enables the Duchess Sanseverina, the former Gina del Dongo, to become the enamored Mosca's mistress.

Sanseverina-Taxis, Duchess. *La Chartreuse de Parme.* Gina del Dongo Pietranera's title at the Court of Parma, after her marriage to the Duke, at which time she is established as the mistress of Count Mosca. See also Dongo, Gina del.

Santon. *Les Lettres persanes.* Usbek's brother, a Mohammedan monk.

Sarasine. *La Chartreuse de Parme.* A Parma apothecary whose wife is the mistress of Ferrante Palla.

Sarasine, Mme. *La Chartreuse de Parme.* Mistress of the poet Ferrant Palla. She bears five children.

Satin. *Nana.* An eighteen-year-old prostitute who was once a classmate of Nana. Satin and Nana eventually become lovers for a time, but the relationship ends badly, especially for Satin.

Savoie, Emmanuel-Philibert, Duke de. *La Princesse de Clèves.* The prospective husband of Marguerite de France, sister of King Henri II.

Scaufflaire. *Les Misérables.* A Flemish resident of Montfermeil who rents horses and gigs by the day.

Schahabarim. *Salammbô.* The high priest of Tanit who has educated Salammbô. He orders her to go to Matho's tent to retrieve the veil of Tanit. Later, he defects to the god Moloch, only to be rejected because he is a eunuch.

Schalischim. *Salammbô.* The name Mâtho's comrades give him when they ask him to be commander in chief of their troops in fighting Carthage. See Mâtho.

Schontz, Mme. *La Cousine Bette.* A well-known courtesan who is a guest at Josépha's party.

Scipion. *Gil Blas.* The crafty valet of Gil Blas, who hires him while he is in the service of the Duke de Lerme. Scipion remains his devoted companion and confidant.

Scipion, Torribo. *Gil Blas.* The father of Scipion.

Scotti, Colonel. *La Chartreuse de Parme.* A former lover of Gina del Dongo Pietranera.

Secretary (unnamed). *Gil Blas.* A man in the employ of the Marquise de Chaves. He challenges Gil Blas to a duel and wins.

Secretary (unnamed) of the Academy of Saturn. "Micromégas." An intelligent individual who is a popularizer of science and speaks of it by making flowery comparisons.

Sedillo. *Gil Blas.* An old canon who becomes the employer of Gil Blas.

Segiar, don Alexo. *Gil Blas.* A friend of don Mathias de Silva.

Ségovie, Ybagnez de. *Gil Blas*. A wardrobe dealer who buys Scipion's stolen costume for much less than it is worth.

Seminarian (unnamed). *Le Rouge et le noir*. A young man from Verrières who, on Julien Sorel's first day at the Besançon seminary, offers to be Julien's friend.

Sémire. "Zadig." Zadig's beloved fiancée who leaves him for another man when she is led to believe that Zadig will be one-eyed.

Senator (unnamed). *Les Misérables*. A powerful, antireligious man who declares to Bishop Myriel that believing in God is only for the poor, who have nothing else to fall back on.

Sénécal. *L'Education sentimentale*. A mathematics tutor whose misfortunes lead him to become a political fanatic, first a champion of the working class, then a reactionary conservative who shoots down insurgents in 1848.

Sepherd, Carl. *Eugénie Grandet*. The name Charles Grandet assumes in the United States as a speculator and slave trader, in order not to compromise his name. See Grandet, Charles.

Séraphine. *Gil Blas*. A lovely young woman whom don Alphonse de Leyva meets in her castle during a storm and whom he eventually marries.

Séraphine. *Gil Blas*. The name given to the daughter of Scipion and Béatrix. She is named after doña Séraphine de Leyva.

Sercour, Baron de. *La Vie de Marianne*. A sickly but wealthy man who wishes to marry Tervire, until she is dishonored by his corrupt nephew, a dissipated abbot.

Sergeant (unnamed). *La Chartreuse de Parme*. An incompetent officer who, mistaking Fabrice del Dongo for General Fabio Conti, attempts to arrest him.

Sérizy, Mme. de. *La Cousine Bette*. The owner of Presles, an estate which Crevel eventually buys for Valérie Marneffe and himself.

Sérizy, Mme. de. *Le Père Goriot*. An elegant Paris society woman.

Servant (unnamed). *La Chartreuse de Parme*. An old soldier who serves Fabrice when the latter attempts to join Napoleon's army.

Servant (unnamed). *La Chartreuse de Parme*. A servant of Count Mosca and the lover of Cecchina, the Duchess Sanseverina's favorite personal maid.

Servant (unnamed). *Les Liaisons dangereuses*. Mme. de Tourvel's servant who spies on Valmont.

Sétoc. "Zadig." An Arab merchant who buys Zadig as a slave and who becomes a wiser man because of Zadig's influence on him.

Siddons, Mrs. *Corinne*. An English actress whom Oswald Lord Nelvil compares with Corinne.

Siffredi, Léontio. *Gil Blas.* A minister of King Roger of Sicily and then of King Enrique.

Silva, Jérôme de. *Gil Blas.* The husband of Porcie and the father of doña Elvira de Pinarès.

Silva, don Mathias de. *Gil Blas.* A young dandy who lives for the pleasure of the moment and gambles heavily. He is one of Gil Blas's masters in Madrid.

Silvestre, M. *La Nouvelle Héloïse.* An acquaintance of Saint-Preux in Paris.

Simaghan. "Atala." The chief of a tribe of Muskogee Indians who capture Chactas.

Similar. *Notre-Dame de Paris.* The name Phoebus de Châteaupers gives to Esmeralda. See Esmeralda.

Simion, Dame. *Jacques le fataliste.* A religious hypocrite who is in reality a procuress.

Simon, Samuel. *Gil Blas.* A miserly merchant who is duped by Gil Blas and his associates.

Simplice, Sister. *Les Misérables.* A sister of charity whose most characteristic feature is that she has never told a falsehood. She tells her first when she lies to Javert about the whereabouts of Jean Valjean (M. Madeleine).

Sinet, Séraphine. *La Cousine Bette.* See Carabine.

Sirena. *Gil Blas.* See Catalina.

Sister (unnamed) of priest. *La Vie de Marianne.* The virtuous, devoted spinster who becomes Marianne's foster mother for thirteen years, after the child has lost her parents.

Sivry, Blanche de. *Nana.* A courtesan who attends the opening performance of *Blonde Venus,* starring Nana, and who also attends Nana's midnight supper party. She was also known as Jacqueline Bandu.

Slave (unnamed). *Salammbô.* A man who disguises himself as a soldier while attempting to obtain money from Carthage, and who is beheaded for his deed.

Slave (unnamed). *Salaambô.* The faher of thd child whom Hamilcar Barca substitutes for his own son, to be a sacrifice to the god Moloch.

Smelten. *Germinal.* A banker in Montsou, somewhat sympathetic to the miners' plight.

Solange. *La Petite Fadette.* The curious, sly youngest daughter of Père Caillaud. She is suspicious of the identical twins, Sylvinet and Landry.

Soldier (unnamed). *La Chartreuse de Parme.* A soldier with whom Fabrice fights while acquiring a horse.

Solim. *Les Lettres persanes.* The chief black eunuch's replacement as commander of Usbek's seraglio. He abuses his power and precipitates the demise of the harem.

Soliman. *Gil Blas.* A Turkish provincial government leader in Algeria.

Soliman. *Les Lettres persanes.* Usbek's friend whose daughter is rejected by her new husband, supposedly because she was not a virgin when he married her.

Solis, don Juan de. *Gil Blas.* A former bon vivant student who becomes a hermit named Brother Jean.

Sombary. *L'Education sentimentale.* A caricaturist who frequents the art shop of Jacques Arnoux.

Sophie. *L'Assommoir.* A gossipy girl who works in the artificial flower factory with Nana.

Sorel. *Le Rouge et le noir.* Julien Sorel's uneducated, crude, but cunning peasant father who despises his delicate son.

Sorel, Julien. *Le Rouge et le noir.* A sensitive but ambitious young man who attempts to rise above his lowly backround by hiding his true feelings and desires, and by playing the hypocrite. Only at the end of his rather short life does he see clearly into his heart, because of his genuine, pure love for Mme. de Rênal.

Sorel brothers (two, unnamed). *Le Rouge et le noir.* Formidable in size and strength, they are scornful of their delicate younger brother, Julien.

Souchet. *Eugénie Grandet.* The bankrupt broker of Victor-Ange-Guillaume Grandet.

Souël, Father. "René." A French missionary who listens to René's long confession and then reprimands him.

Souvarine. *Germinal.* An anarchist who works in the Voreux pit. He remains true to his principles by destroying the pit.

Spaniard (unnamed). *L'Education sentimentale.* A patriot from Barcelona who rails incomprehensibly at a club political gathering attended by Frédéric Moreau.

Spendius. *Salammbô.* A Greek slave of Carthage who is set free by the rebellious Mercenaries and who provides them with leadership in their ensuing war with Carthage. He seeks vengeance to the full, up to the moment of his death in battle.

Spicali, Mathias Hunyadi. *Notre-Dame de Paris.* A gypsy who is one of the thieves' leaders in the Cour des Miracles.

Spinola, doña Margarita. *Gil Blas.* A former mistress of Guzman, Count d'Olivarès. She gives birth to a son fathered either by him or by don Francisco de Valeasar.

Spinster (unnamed). *Madame Bovary.* A woman who came to Emma's convent for a week each month in order to repair the linen, and who sang sentimental love songs as she plied her needle, to the excitement of Emma and others.

Steinbach, Baron de. *Gil Blas*. A German officer who adopts don Alphonse de Leyva.

Steinbock, Hortense Hulot. *La Cousine Bette*. The daughter of Baron Hulot. Her guileless passion for the artist Wenceslas Steinbock incites jealous cousin Bette to seek revenge upon the entire Hulot family. Her marriage to Steinbock causes her much personal grief.

Steinbock, Wenceslas. *La Cousine Bette*. A young Polish artist with whom Bette Fischer has fallen in love. He unwittingly unleashes the old maid's hatred and desire for revenge by falling in love with and marrying Hortense Hulot, Bette's cousin.

Steinbock, Wenceslas (Jr.). *La Cousine Bette*. The offspring of Wenceslas and Hortense Hulot Steinbock.

Steiner. *Nana*. A banker who has twice been ruined because of his furious appetite for courtesans before he meets Nana, who ruins him financially once again. Nevertheless, this resourceful German manages once more to recuperate and continue his profligate ways.

Stewart, Lucy. *Nana*. A plain woman o;f forty who, nevertheless, does not lack charm. She attends the opening performance of *Blonde Venus,* starring Nana.

Stidman. *La Cousine Bette*. A goldsmith for whom Wenceslas Steinbock works briefly. He is also a guest at the courtesan Héloïse Brisetout's housewarming party.

Subeldia. *Salammbô*. One of the important men in Hamilcar Barca's party.

Super (unnamed). *Nana*. An extra, a pastry cook, called upon to play the role of Pluto in *Blonde Venus,* starring Nana. He is also an old lover of the prostitute Satin.

Suphis. *Les Lettres persanes*. A young man who rejects his bride, claiming that she was not a virgin on their wedding day.

Surgeon (unnamed). *L'Assommoir*. The house surgeon at Saint-Anne Asylum who diagnoses Coupeau's final bout with delirium tremens.

Surgeon (unnamed). *Gil Blas*. A medical man who arrives clandestinely at night to nurse Séphora Lornça's wound.

Surgeon (unnamed). *Jacques le fataliste*. A surgeon who causes trouble by wishing to demonstrate how a leg is injured.

Surgeon (unnamed). *Les Misérables*. The physician who attends the unconscious Marius after Jean Valjean has the young man brought to M. Gillenormand's home.

Surgeon (unnamed). *La Vie de Marianne*. Tha physician who examines Marianne's twisted abkle in Valville's house.

Surgeon-Major (unnamed). *Le Rouge et le noir.* Julien Sorel's cousin and friend who nurtured Julien's admiration for Napoleon.

Surgeons (three, unnamed). *Jacques le fataliste.* Three incompetent surgeons who drunkenly argue about whether or not Jacques's leg should be amputated.

Suzanne. *Jacques le fataliste.* The village joker's wife who seduces Jacques.

Sylvie. *Le Père Goriot.* The cook at Mme. Vauquer's boardinghouse.

Synnelet. *Manon Lescaut.* The violent young nephew of the governor of New Orleans. He loves Manon and is determined to marry her. As a result, he and Des Grieux fight and Synnelet is killed. This event leads to the death of Manon.

T..., Baron de. *Adolphe.* A minister to Poland and a friend of Adophe's father. He attempts to advise Adolphe concerning his liasison with Ellénore.

T..., Baroness de. *Le Misérables.* The proprietress of a salon frequented by M. Gillenormand and the boy Marius.

T..., M. de. *Manon Lescaut.* The son of one of the administrators of the Hôpital. Des Grieux enlists his help in the escape of Manon, and the two men become good friends.

Taanach. *Salammbô.* Salammbô's devoted slave-nurse.

Taillefer. *Le Père Goriot.* Victorine Taillefer's cruel father, who disowns her as his legitimate daughter.

Taillefer, Michel (Frédéric). *Le Père Goriot.* Victorine Taillefer's uncaring brother, whom Vautrin proposes to have killed in a duel so that Eugène de Rastignac may marry Victorine for her money.

Taillefer, Victorine. *Le Père Goriot.* A second-floor boarder at Mme. Vauquer's boardinghouse. This timid young woman's father will not admit her legitimacy. Later, Vautrin suggests that Eugène de Rastignac marry her for her newly acquired inheritance, if he agrees to Vautrin's scheme.

Taix, Jean, Count de. *La Princesse de Clèves.* The Master of Artillery who is disgraced by the Duchess de Valentinois.

Talego. *Gil Blas.* A peasant farmer of don Mathias de Silva. He is in conspiracy with Rodriguez and is caught in the act by Gil Blas.

Tanbeau. *Le Rouge et le noir.* Julien's envious rival as secretary in the de la Mole household. He is also the nephew of the Marquis de la Mole's friend, the academician.

Tanville, Mlle. *Les Liaisons dangereuses.* A convent classmate of Cécile Volanges.

Targel, Mahiet. *Notre-Dame de Paris.* A student whose gown is torn in a skirmish with the incorrigible Jehan Frollo.

Tarme, Jehanne de la. *Notre-Dame de Paris.* A widow and religious sister who comments on the hideousness of the foundling Quasimodo.

Tautain, Hippolyte. *Madame Bovary.* The stable man at the inn owned by Mme. Lefrançois. His club foot is operated on by Charles Bovary, with disastrous results.

Tavernier, Dr. *Nana.* An old doctor whom Georges Hugon claims to be consulting while, in fact, Georges is in bed with Nana.

Tax Collector (unnamed). *Le Rouge et le noir.* A dinner guest of the Valenod family.

Tellier. *Madame Bovary.* The proprietor of a cafe in Yonville-l'Abbaye. His establishment rivals that of Mme. Lefrançois.

Teodolinda. *La Chartreuse de Parme.* The owner of a small restaurant. He helps Fabrice del Dongo escape from the police.

Tervire. *La Vie de Marianne.* The unhappy nun who tells Marianne much of her life story.

Tervire, M. *La Vie de Marianne.* Tervire's father, who is killed during her infancy.

Tervire, M. *La Vie de Marianne.* Tervire's grandfather, a provincial gentleman who opposes the marriage of his son and Mlle. de Tresle.

Tervire, M. *La Vie de Marianne.* Tervire's uncle who is eager to inherit the fortune of his aunt, Mme. Dursan, but is inept in his attempt to do so.

Thaler, Count de. *Le Rouge et le noir.* A Jew of enormous wealth who is jeered at by Mathilde de la Mole and her friends. He eventually slanders Mathilde and Julien, and is challenged to a duel.

Thémines, Mme. de. *La Princesse de Clèves.* The mistress of the Vidame de Chartres.

Thénardier. *Les Misérables.* A marauder with a black soul who once saved the life of Marius Pontmercy's father. He causes Jean Valjean and Cosette much grief by constantly harassing them because he wants to make money at the expense of their lives.

Thénardier, Azelma. *Les Misérables.* The younger, long-suffering daughter of the Thénardiers. She eventually follows her evil father to America, after her mother and older sister have died.

Thénardier, Eponine. *Les Misérables.* The older daughter of the Thénardiers. She locates Cosette for the enamored Marius and then sacrifices her miserable life for the young man, whom she secretly loves.

Thénardier, Gavroche. *Les Misérables.* An urchin who, when disowned by his vile parents, roams the streets of Paris and manages to survive for some years. He meets his death defiantly while participating with Marius, Jean Vajean, and others in the insurrection of 1832.

Thénardier, Mme. *Les Misérables.* A stout, wicked woman who loves only her two daughters and loathes the small child, Cosette, whom she is paid to care for by Fantine.

Thénardier sons (two, unnamed). *Les Misérables.* Abandoned by their uncaring parents, without food, clothing, or shelter, they are protected by Gavroche, who does not know that they are his brothers.

Theodora. *Gil Blas.* An old woman who is the best friend of Felicia, the servant to doña Helena.

Théodore. "Candide." An impoverished, once-imprisoned king who has come to Venice to attend the carnival, where Candide meets him.

Théodore. *L'Education sentimentale.* The waiter in Vauthier's restaurant who regards Regimbart with hero worship.

Théodore. *Madame Bovary.* The servant of the lawyer Guillaumin, he courts Emma Bovary's maid, Félicité.

Thérèse. *Le Père Goriot.* Delphine de Nucingen's maid.

Thérèse. *L'Assommoir.* A former neighbor of the Lorilleux couple who dies of consumption.

Thérésine. *Corinne.* Corinne's Italian chambermaid who devotedly follows her to Scotland and then back to Italy.

Thibaut, Master. *Notre-Dame de Paris.* The Rector of the University of Paris in 1482.

Tholomyès, Félix. *Les Misérables.* A student from Toulouse and the frivolous lover of Fantine. He callously abandons her in order to return to respectability in the provinces.

Thomas. *L'Assommoir.* The owner of a Montmartre wineshop frequented by Coupeau.

Thomassin. *Madame Bovary.* The editor of Homais's favorite newspaper, the *Fanal de Rouen.*

Thorec, Père. *La Cousine Bette.* One of the names which Baron Hulot assumes while he is in hiding. See Hulot, Baron Hector.

Thoul. *La Cousine Bette.* Another assumed name of Baron Hulot while Olympe Bijou is his mistress. See Hulot, Baron Hector.

Thunder-ten-tronckh, Baron de. "Candide." One of the most powerful noblemen in Westphalia and probably the uncle of Candide. He dismisses Candide from his chateau by means of kicks in the buttocks because Candide has touched his daughter, Cunégonde.

Thunder-ten-tronckh, Baron de (Jr.). "Candide." In every way like his father, the Baron's son turns out not to have been killed by the Abares and appears later as a Jesuit priest in South America, where Candide supposedly kills him a second time, because of his noble pride.

Thunder-ten-tronckh, Baroness de. "Candide." A three-hundred-fifty-pound woman who attracts great attention because of her size.

Tiberge. *Manon Lescaut.* The devoted friend of Des Grieux. His ardor and generosity in friendship cannot be surpassed.

Tillet, du. *La Cousine Bette.* A former employee in César Birotteau's shop, now a famous banker and a frequenter of courtesans.

Tissot. *Le Père Goriot.* The editor of a radical newspaper, *La Pilote.*

Tissot, André. *Jacques le fataliste.* A doctor who learns from Jacques that white wine encourages urination.

Titreville, Mme. *L'Assommoir.* The proprietress of the artificial-flower factory where Nana works for a time.

Toinon. *La Vie de Marianne.* The shop girl in the employ of Mme. Dutour. She becomes jealous of Marianne.

Tolly, Baron de. *Le Rouge et le noir.* A guest at the Hôtel de la Mole. He has come to public attention in recent elections, which he won by illegal means.

Tombone. *La Chartreuse de Parme.* A banker known for his miserliness.

Tordesillas, don André de. *Gil Blas.* A former gentleman of the Archbishop of Granada, he becomes the keeper of the Segovia prison tower. Later he appears in Madrid with don Gaston de Cogollos. Even later, Gil Blas has him appointed Governor of the Royal Prison of Valladoloid.

Torterue, Pierrat. *Notre-Dame de Paris.* The torturer and executor of the Châtelet prison. He flogs the bare back of Quasimodo before a cheering crowd.

Toto. *La Chartreuse de Parme.* A groom at the Court of Parma.

Tour, M. de la. *Paul et Virginie.* A young man who comes to the Ile-de-France to seek his fortune but who dies shortly after his arrival with his wife and their young daughter.

Tour, Mme. de la. *Paul et Virginie.* A young widow who decides to cultivate land in the wilderness on the Ile-de-France and raise her daughter, Virginie, there.

Tourangeau. *Notre-Dame de Paris.* An unknown man accompanying the King's physician, Coictier, on a visit to the priest, Claude Frollo. He soon reveals himself to be King Louis XI in disguise. See Louis XI.

Tournon, François, Cardinal de. *La Princesse de Clèves.* The Archbishop of Embrun. Banished from court by the Duchess de Valentinois, he returns after the death of Henri II.

Tournon, Mme. de. *La Princesse de Clèves.* A deceitful widow at the court of Henri II.

Tourvel, M. de. *Les Liaisons dangereuses.* The absent husband of the Présidente de Tourvel.

Tourvel, Présidente de. *Les Liaisons dangereuses.* A devout, sincere woman of principle who falls victim to the Viscount de Valmont and becomes his most recent conquest. The humiliation of being deceived by him destroys her.

Tourville, Count de. *Jacques le fataliste.* A former master of Jacques.

Tousard, Reine. *La Cousine Bette.* Mme. Marneffe's personal maid who betrays her mistress for a price.

Toussaint. *Les Misérables.* A rustic old woman who is the domestic for Jean Valjean and Cosette at the Rue Planet residence. She is saved from wretchedness by Jean Valjean.

Trailles, Maxime de. *La Cousine Bette.* A guest at Josépha's party and a playboy of Paris society.

Trailles, Maxime de. *Le Père Goriot.* A smug, arrogant young man of fashion in Paris society. He is the unscrupulous lover of Anastasie de Restaud.

Tresle, Mlle. de. *La Vie de Marianne.* Tervire's mother. See Darneuil, Mme.

Tresle, Mlle. de. *La Vie de Marianne.* A jealous, greedy aunt of Tervire.

Tresle, Mlle. de. *La Vie de Marianne.* Another greedy aunt of Tervire.

Tresle, Mme. de. *La Vie de Marianne.* The maternal grandmother of Tervire, the nun. She raises her granddaughter until the time of her death.

Tricon, Mme. *Nana.* A procuress for Nana and others. She eventually retires and sells her business to Zoé, Nana's maidservant.

Tristan L'Hermite. *Notre-Dame de Paris.* King Louis XI's heartless chief executioner.

Troglodytes. *Les Lettres persanes.* Barbaric people who, after becoming nearly extinct, finally prosper bdcause of their awareness that virtue is the first condition of good government.

Tronchin. *Jacques le fataliste.* A famous doctor who cxamines the Marquis des Arcis.

Trouillefou, Clopin. *Notre-Dame de Paris.* A mendicant and thief who disrupts the performance of Pierre Gringoire's morality play. Also the King of the Cour des Miracles, he threatens to hang Gringoire.

Turquant, Mlle. *Notre-Dame de Paris.* A resident of the Place de Grève.

Turquet, Mlle. *La Cousine Bette.* A famous courtesan of Paris, she is diminished by Carabine.

Tuvache. *Madame Bovary.* A wealthy lawyer who is the mayor of Yonville-l'Abbaye.

Tuvache, Lieutenant. *Madame Bovary.* An officer in Binet's company of firemen at the Agricultural Show.

Tuvache, Mme. *Madame Bovary.* The gossipy wife of the mayor of Yonville-l'Abbaye.

Tzernoukoff, Prince. *L'Education sentimentale.* One of Rosanette Bron's many benefactors.

Uncle (unnamed) of Julie. *La Nouvelle Héloïse.* The kindly father of Claire. He is also devoted to his niece.

Urania, Miss. *A Rebours.* An American trapeze artist who is a former mistress of Des Esseintes.

Urbain X. "Candide." An imaginary pope who is supposedly the father of the old woman (la Vieille).

Usbek. *Les Lettres persanes.* The Persian lord who leaves his harem to travel and broaden his knowledge. He makes many observations about life in other cultures, during the course of a lengthy stay in France.

Uzède, Duke d'. *Gil Blas.* The Duke de Lerme's son who has fallen into disfavor with his father because he has become the king's favorite. He is later exiled by Count Guzman d'Olivarès.

Uzès, Viscountess d'. *La Princesse de Clèves.* A well-known woman at the court of Henri II.

V..., Duchess. *La Chartreuse de Parme.* Fabrice del Dongo's sister who marries a wealthy duke from Milan. See Dongo, Mlle.de.

V..., Mme. *Les Liaisons dangereuses.* A society woman who is acquainted with the Volanges family.

Valeasar, don Francisco de. *Gil Blas.* Superintendent of the court police who pays for the favors of doña Margarita Spinola.

Valenod. *Le Rouge et le noir.* The ambitious director of the poor house in Verrières, and Mayor de Rênal's social and financial rival. Valenod epitomizes crass, bourgeois mentality. He is eventually made a baron and replaces M. de Rênal as mayor of Verrières.

Valenod, Mme. *Le Rouge et le noir.* The masculine-looking wife of Valenod.

Valentinois, Diane de Poitiers, Duchess de. *La Princesse de Clèves.* Henri II's longtime mistress, twenty years the king's senior. She exercises great power at court.

Valet (unnamed). *Jacques le fataliste.* The lord of the castle's servant, he comes to take Jacques there.

Valjean, Jean. *Les Misérables.* A galley slave for nineteen years, this hardened criminal is miraculously transformed into a loving, self-sacrificing man. He spends the rest of his life helping others, especially Fantine, Cosette, and Marius, while fleeing the relentless Inspector Javert, who is intent upon persecuting him.

Valmont, Viscount de. *Les Liaisons dangereuses.* The handsome seducer of women and partner in crime of the brilliant Marquise de Merteuil when she decides to avenge herself of Gercourt's insult. Valmont is not fully aware of himself and brings about his own destruction by falling in love with his most challenging female victim, the Presidente de Tourvel, thereby incurring the wrath of the Marquise de Merteuil, who has him killed.

Valville. *La Vie de Marianne*. Mme. de Miran's son who falls in love with Marianne but is eventually unfaithful to her, once the obstacles to their marriage have been removed.

Vanda. *A Rebours*. A prostitute who is paid by Des Esseintes to seduce Auguste Langlois.

Vandael, Mlle. *L'Education sentimentale*. An actress who is a guest at an all-night party attended by Frédéric Moreau.

Vandenese. *Le Père Goriot*. A smug man of fashion in Paris society.

Vanderdendur. "Candide." A Dutch skipper who profits from Candide's naïveté by robbing him of two of his Eldorado sheep.

Vanderhaghen, Dr. *Germinal*. An unsympathetic doctor who is hired by the Montsou Mining Company to look after the miners.

Vandeuvres, Count Xavier de. *Nana*. A well-groomed, extremely distinguished man who, along with many others, is destroyed by his passion for Nana. Completely wiped out by losses at the Grand Prix de Paris, he immolates himself with his horse by setting fire to the stable and locking both of them inside.

Vane, Philip. *Le Rouge et le noir*. A famous, imprisoned English philosopher whom Julien Sorel visits in London.

Vaneau, Félix. *Le Rouge et le noir*. The lawyer who unsuccessfully defends Julien Sorel at his trial.

Vanneroy. *L'Education sentimentale*. A man from whom Arnoux has borrowed money.

Varthon, Mlle. *La Vie de Marianne*. A young lady who comes to live in the convent. She and Marianne become good friends, but the friendship ends when Valville falls in love with Mlle. Varthon.

Varthon, Mme. *La Vie de Marianne*. A woman who leaves her daughter at the same convent where the young Marianne is staying, while she goes to England to collect an inheritance.

Vasi. *La Chartreuse de Parme*. A friend of Fabrice who gives him his passport so that Fabrice may go to Waterloo.

Vatnaz, Mlle. Clémence. *L'Education sentimentale*. An elderly spinster who is one of Jacques Arnoux's former mistresses. She is also Rosanette Bron's rival for the affection of Delmar.

Vaubois, Mlle. *Les Misérables*. A friend of Mlle. Gillenormand.

Vaufrilard. *Madame Bovary*. An artist friend of Homais who never ceases to make puns.

Vaumerland, Baroness de. *Le Père Goriot*. A supposed friend of the Countess d'Ambermesnil.

Vauquer, Mme. *Le Père Goriot.* The crafty, middle-aged proprietress of a boardinghouse where Père Goriot and Eugène de Rastignac live for a time.

Vautier. *L'Education sentimentale.* The owner of a restaurant where Frédéric Moreau looks for Regimbart.

Vautrin. *La Cousine Bette.* The head of the detective department at the Prefecture de Police.

Vautrin. *Le Père Goriot.* A bold, cynical resident of the Maison Vauquer who attempts to shape the destiny of young Eugène de Rastignac, to whom he is attracted. He is finally arrested and revealed to be an escaped convict known as "Cheat-Death."

Vauvinet. *La Cousine Bette.* A small moneylender. He has shady dealings with the Baron Hulot, who borrows exorbitant sums from him.

Velasco, doña Anna de. *Gil Blas.* A friend of the Marquise de Chaves.

Velasco, Lope de. *Gil Blas.* An outraged nobleman who kills don Mathias de Silva in a duel.

Velasquez, Baltazar. *Gil Blas.* A cloth merchant who becomes the employer of Scipion.

Velasquez, Gaspard. *Gil Blas.* The libertine son of Baltazar Velasquez.

Velesco, doña Juana de. *Gil Blas.* The daughter of the Duke de Castille. She marries don Henri-Philippe de Guzman.

Venot, Théophile. *Nana.* A little Jesuit of sixty with bad teeth and a subtle smile who is a retired lawyer specializing in church cases. He is suspected of being evil, although he does try to save the soul of Count Muffat de Beuville, Nana's chief victim.

Ventoleria, Carlos Alonso de la. *Gil Blas.* A bombastic braggart who was once an actor.

Ventriloquist (unnamed). *A Rebours.* A woman whom Des Esseintes pays to be with him because he is fascinated, as well as sexually aroused, by her profession.

Verdier, Baron. *Nana.* The owner of a horse racing in the Grand Prix de Paris.

Verdonck. *Germinal.* A grocer in Montsou. He is somewhat sympathetic to the miners.

Verneuil, Baron. *La Cousine Bette.* An official in the government who owes his position and advancement to Baron Hulot. Like the baron, he also enjoys the company of courtesans, such as Josépha.

Vernisset, de. *La Cousine Bette.* A guest at Héloïse Brisetout's housewarming party.

Vetturino. *La Chartreuse de Parme.* The driver of the carriage at the time when Fabrice del Dongo is forced to kill Giletti in self-defense. He is bought by the Marquise Raversi to testify against Fabrice.

Veuvain, Mère. *Les Misérables.* The landlady of Marius's friend, Courfeyrac.

Vezou. *L'Education sentimentale.* The former tutor of Alfred de Césy.

Vicar of Village (unnamed). *Jacques le fataliste.* A libertine who is jealous of sexual favors bestowed upon Jacques.

Victoire. *Les Liaisons dangereuses.* Mme. de Merteuil's faithful servant.

Victorine. *Nana.* The cook at Nana's house on the Avenue de Villiers. She and her husband finally leave Nana, but carry off valuable possessions as they depart.

Victurnien, Mme. *Les Misérables.* A vicious gossip who, upon discovering that Fantine has an illegitimate child, has her dismissed from her job.

Vignon, Claude. *La Cousine Bette.* Secretary to the Prince de Wissembourg and habitué of Valérie Marneffe's apartment. He adores her in secret while pursuing a promising political career.

Vigouroux, Mme. *L'Assommoir.* Gervaise's neighbor, a charcoal dealer.

Villanuno, Julien de. *Gil Blas.* A nobleman who frequents a literary tavern in Madrid.

Villaréal, Marquis de. *Gil Blas.* A Portuguese nobleman who is a friend of don Gaston de Cogollos and because of whom Don Gaston is arrested.

Villa-Viciosa, Sébastien de. *Gil Blas.* A successful playwright whom Gil Blas and Fabrice see in a Madrid tavern.

Villegas, Melchior de. *Gil Blas.* An opinionated man of letters who argues about Euripides's *Iphigénie* and the role of the wind in the tragedy.

Villeroy, Nicholas de Neufville, Seigneur de. *La Princesse de Clèves.* The Secretary of Finance under Henri II who is banished by the Duchess de Valentinois.

Villot. *La Vie de Marianne.* A mediocre young bourgeois who is chosen to be Marianne's husband and whom she refuses to marry.

Villot, M. *La Vie de Marianne.* The former farmer of Tervire's grandfather, he and his wife take her in after the death of her grandparents.

Villot, Mme. *La Vie de Marianne.* The wife of M. Villot. Both she and her husband treat Tervire kindly.

Vinçart. *Madame Bovary.* A Rouen banker who is a friend of Lheureux and who institutes legal proceedings against Emma Bovary for failure to repay her debts to Lheureux.

Vinegrower (unnamed). *La Vie de Marianne.* A worker in Mme. de Tresle's farmyard.

Violaine, Louise. *Nana.* A courtesan who arrives late at Nana's midnight supper party. She later becomes Nana's understudy in *Blonde Venus* and arouses Nana's jealousy when she becomes a success in the role.

Violante. *Gil Blas.* The neglected wife of don Baltazar. Don Raphaël falls in love with her.

Virginie. *L'Assommoir.* A dressmaker and the sister of the woman Lantier runs off with. Later, when she marries the policeman Poisson, she and Gervaise become friends for a time, then become enemies once again.

Virginie. *Paul et Virginie.* The virtuous daughter of Mme. de la Tour. She is deeply in love with her neighbor, Paul, throughout her short life, even though she is separated from him for years.

Viry, M. de. *La Vie de Marianne.* A friend of Mme. Darneuil.

Vlajean, Jean. *Les Misérables.* Jean Valjean's father, who died when very young. His name is probably a sobriquet and a contraction of "*Voilà Jean.*"

Volanges, Cécile. *Les Liaisons dangereuses.* A naïve, innocent young woman, just out of the convent. She falls into the clutches of Mme. de Merteuil and Valmont, and unknowingly becomes their puppet, whom they proceed to deprave.

Volanges, Mme. *Les Liaisons dangereuses.* The mother of Cécile Volanges. This upright woman is totally unaware of what Mme. de Merteuil and Valmont are doing to her daughter until it is too late.

Vourda. *L'Education sentimentale.* A sculptor who frequents Jacques Arnoux's art shop.

Vraulard. *La Cousine Bette.* A friend of the actress, Josépha Mirah.

Vressac. *Les Liaisons dangereuses.* A lover of the Viscountess de M....

Vyder. *La Cousine Bette.* An assumed name of the Baron Hulot when he is in hiding. See Hulot, Baron Hector.

Wallachian (unnamed). *Nana.* A mock count who pays money for Nana's favors at irregular intervals. Nana discards him after her success as *Blonde Venus.*

War Minister (unnamed). *Jacques le fataliste.* An intermediary who separates the Captain and his friend to prevent them from fighting.

Watchman (unnamed). *Madame Bovary.* A guard who spends the night in the Bovary attic, watching over their legally confiscated possessions.

Widow (unnamed). *Jacques le fataliste.* A woman who spends her entire life experiencing alternating feelings of pleasure and remorse. Desglands falls in love with her.

Widow (unnamed). "*Zadig.*" A virtuous and charitable woman whose young nephew is killed by the hermit (the angel Jesrad in disguise).

Wife (unnamed) of Doctor. *Jacques le fataliste.* A loving spouse who asks Jacques to speak favorably to Desglands in her husband's behalf.

Wife (unnamed) of Innkeeper. *La Vie de Marianne.* The assistant of her husband in taking advantage of the young Marianne, after the death of Marianne's foster mother.

Wife (unnamed) of Pastry Cook. *Jacques le fataliste.* An unfaithful woman whose lover is jailed instead of her husband.

Wife (unnamed) of Peasant. *Jacques le fataliste.* Against her husband's will, she treats the badly wounded knee of Jacques.

Wife (unnamed) of Peasant. *La Vie de Marianne.* The infant Tervire's wet nurse.

William of Orange. *La Princesse de Clèves.* The marriage negotiator in behalf of Philip II of Spain.

Wine merchant (unnamed). *L'Education sentimentale.* A guest at a party given by Dussardier in honor of Sénécal, recently released from prison.

Wissembourg, Prince de. *La Cousine Bette.* Baron Hulot's superior in the War Office. Also Hulot's friend, he tries to ward off the Baron's impending disgrace.

Wolmar, Baron de. *La Nouvelle Héloïse.* The rational and magnanimous older man whom Julie d'Etange is forced to marry and with whom she seemingly finds peace and tranquillity.

Wolmar, Mme. de. *La Nouvelle Héloïse.* See Etange, Julie d'.

Woman (unnamed). *Adolphe.* An elderly woman companion of Adolphe whose death he witnesses.

Woman (unnamed). *L'Assommoir.* A little old lady who silently watches Coupeau fall from a rooftop.

Woman (unnamed). *L'Assommoir.* A young woman whom Lantier flirts with when she is about to replace Virginie as proprietress of the shop which once belonged to Gervaise.

Woman (unnamed). *Corinne.* A provincial lady who is more sensitive than her peers. She tells Corinne either to submit to customs or to flee Scotland.

Woman (unnamed). *Corinne.* A disfigured woman who seeks alms from Corinne.

Woman (unnamed). *La Chartreuse de Parme.* A lady at the Court of Parma who predicts to Clélia Conti that Fabrice del Dongo will not leave the Farnese tower alive.

Woman (unnamed). *L'Education sentimentale.* A worker in Arnoux's mill who is severely reprimanded by Sénécal for eating and drinking on the job. She eventually becomes Arnoux's mistress.

Woman (unnamed). *Germinal.* The elderly mother of a striking miner, she faints by the roadside because of hunger.

Woman (unnamed). *Jacques le fataliste.* Desglands's mistress who leaves him because of his penchant for gambling.

Woman (unnamed). *Jacques le fataliste.* A friend of Father Hudson. Her husband refuses to take final rites before he dies.

Woman (unnamed). *Jacques le fataliste*. A friend of Richard and also of Father Hudson.

Woman (unnamed). *Jacques le fataliste*. A young woman who has been abducted and seduced by Father Hudson.

Woman (unnamed). *Madame Bovary*. A lady in attendance at the ball given by the Marquis d'Andervilliers. She chats aimiably with Emma and treats her as an equal.

Woman (unnamed). *Les Misérables*. Known as the "chief lodger," she spies on Jean Valjean when he and Cosette live next to her in the Gorbeau tenement building.

Woman (unnamed). *Salammbô*. An old hag who is forced by Salammbô's guide to provide his mistress with food and lodging.

Woman (unnamed). *La Vie de Marianne*. A companion of M. de Climal.

Woman (unnamed). *La Vie de Marianne*. A young woman in the convent who is jealous of Marianne.

Woman (unnamed). *La Vie de Marianne*. A society chatterbox who pays a social call on Mme. de Miran.

Woman (unnamed). *La Vie de Marianne*. A vain socialite who spends all her time at Mme. de Miran's trying to attract Valville's attention.

Woman (unnamed). *La Vie de Marianne*. An ugly relative of Mme. de Miran who lures Marianne away from the convent where Mme. de Miran placed her.

Xerica, don Manuel de. *Gil Blas*. Lucinde's husband, an impoverished nobleman who dies six years after their marriage.

Yanoda. *Madame Bovary*. Charles Bovary's medical predecessor at Yonville-l'Abbaye.

Yébor. "Zadig." A stupid Chaldean Archmagi who wishes to persecute Zadig.

Yeoubas. *Salammbô*. One of the important men in Hamilcar's party.

Zachi. *Les Lettres persanes*. A member of Usbek's harem. She writes to him of her unhappiness.

Zadig. "Zadig." A sincere, wise, educated young man of Babylon whose fate at the hands of Providence is ultimately a happy one.

Zaïre, Mlle. *La Cousine Bette*. One of Crevel's mistresses. She is bored by the aging roué.

Zapata, Melchior. *Gil Blas*. An actor whom Gil Blas meets.

Zarxas. *Salammbô.* An agitator among the Mercenaries who incessantly reminds all his fellow soldiers of all the atrocities the Carthaginians have committed, up to the moment of his death in battle.

Zaxas. *Salammbô.* A messenger sent by Spendius to Mâtho.

Zélis. *Les Lettres persanes.* A member of Usbek's harem who writes to him about several problems in the seraglio.

Zelphine. *Les Misérables.* A grisette who is the mistress of Fameuil.

Zendono, Pedro. *Gil Blas.* The treasurer and bursar of the house where Laure is imprisoned. He is a terrible hypocrite and thief who escapes with Laure, marries her, and then deserts her.

Zenette, Marquis de. *Gil Blas.* A dissipated young man of the privileged class whom Gil Blas meets.

Zéphis. *Les Lettres persanes.* A member of Usbek's harem who complains to him about the chief eunuch's treatment of her.

Zidore. *L'Assommoir.* Coupeau's assistant on the job when he falls from a roof and is critically injured.

Zingarelli. *Le Rouge et le noir.* Geronimo's voice teacher in Naples.

Zoé. *Nana.* Nana's seemingly faithful maid who keeps all of Nana's lovers separated. She is plotting a long-range scheme and eventually purchases the business of a retiring procuress, Mme. Tricot.

Zuléma. *Les Lettres persanes.* A Persian woman who rivals the most learned dervish in her knowledge of the Alcoran. She tells the story of Ibrahim and Anaïs to illustrate that, in Paradise, women are treated as well as men.

Zuñiga, don Baltazar de. *Gil Blas.* The uncle of Guzman, Count d'Olivarès.

Zuñiga, don Francisco de. *Gil Blas.* A nobleman who reprimands don Rodrigue de Calderone for his haughty behavior.

Zurla-Contarini, Count. *La Chartreuse de Parme.* An incompetent who is the Minister of the Interior at the Court of Parma.